The Institute of British Geographers
Special Publications Series

17 River Channels

The publishers apologize for the error in numbering this
volume of the series. This is volume 18, not 17 as given on
the half-title and copyright pages.

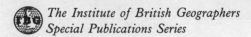 *The Institute of British Geographers*
Special Publications Series

For a complete list see p. 392

River Channels

Environment and Process

Edited by
Keith Richards

Basil Blackwell

First published 1987

Basil Blackwell Ltd
108 Cowley Road, Oxford, OX4 1JF, UK

Basil Blackwell Inc.
432 Park Avenue South, Suite 1503
New York, NY 10016, USA

British Library Cataloguing in Publication Data
River channels: environment and process –
 (Institute of British Geographers special
 publication, ISSN 0073-9006; no. 17).
 1. Rivers
 I. Richards, Keith, *1949-*   II. Institute
 of British Geographers III. Series
 551.48′3   GB1205

ISBN 0-631-14577-X

Library of Congress Cataloging in Publication Data
River channels – environment and process
 Includes bibliographies and index.
 1. River channels. 2. Rivers. 3. Alluvium
4. Sediment transport. I. Richards, K. S. II. Institute
of British Geographers.
GV561.R59 1987   551.48′3   87-5178
ISBN 0-631-14577-X

Phototypeset in 11 on 13 pt Plantin
by Dobbie Typesetting Service, Plymouth
Printed in Great Britain by Page Bros Ltd, Norwich

Contents

1

Rivers: Environment, Process and Form

Keith S. Richards

AN EXPLANATORY CONTEXT

Explanation of process-form relationships in fluvial geomorphology can be viewed in the light of recent discussions of methodology in physical geography. In particular, Haines-Young and Petch (1980; 1986) have emphasized the critical rationalist framework for explanation based on deductive reasoning (Popper, 1959). Its duality, combining universal laws and sets of initial conditions, clearly establishes the contributory roles of (a) physical and (b) contextual (or geographical/spatial and geological/temporal) explanation. The universal 'covering law' is a general physical statement which deals with 'immanent' properties of a phenomenon (Haines-Young and Petch, 1983), and which is therefore space- and time-invariant, and uniformitarian in Gould's (1965) methodological sense. The 'initial conditions' are 'configurational' aspects of the phenomenon, defining spatial and temporal circumstances which, in combination with the general law, explain a particular instance or event. A typical example of a covering law acceptable in fluvial geomorphology would be an empirical statement such as:

(A) unconfined alluvial rivers exhibit a braided pattern if stream power per unit bed area exceeds $50\,Wm^{-2}$ at the mean annual flood, but a meandering pattern if power is less than $50\,Wm^{-2}$ at this discharge.

The initial conditions are time-bound, specific, case-related statements of geographical or historical circumstances, such as:

(B) the South Platte River, which was braided before 1850, has experienced a decrease in flood magnitudes following upstream reservoir impoundment

such that its power per unit bed area at mean annual flood is now only
$c. 2.5\,\mathrm{Wm}^{-2}$.

A conclusion which can be deduced from the initial conditions and the covering
law is that:

(C) the South Platte River has changed its channel pattern from a braided to
a meandering state because of a decline in its stream power following
reservoir impoundment in its headwaters.

The basis for explaining a particular instance of river morphological change
is therefore a combination of physical understanding and knowledge of
geographical and historical environmental conditions: hence the concern of this
collection of essays with environment, process and form.

This model for explanation emphasizes the necessity for two *kinds* of
complementary statement. It is insufficient to state that reservoir impoundment
led to the South Platte becoming a meandering river, since this was not the
direct cause. It is necessary to know *why* impoundment had this consequence.
However, it is equally insufficient to state that channel pattern reflects a critical
stream power, because a *changing* pattern can only be interpreted in the context
of the background, environmental conditions which, through the operation of
particular physical processes, led to the change. The essays in this collection,
individually and in concert, seek to provide a balance between the geographical/
configurational and physical/immanent layers of explanation of river form and
process.

However, there are two issues rendering the covering law model of explanation
less than straightforward in its application to fluvial geomorphology. The first
is its ability to cope with the *kind* of dynamic behaviour occurring in river
systems, and the second arises from the complexity of those systems.

The combination of a covering law and a set of initial conditions should provide
the basis for causal explanation of dynamic system behaviour, but Hey (1979)
has rejected the notion of causality in dynamic systems of interdependent
variables, quoting as an example the gas law relating the volume, pressure and
temperature of a gas. He argues that, in this covering law, '. . . if any variable
. . . is changed the others will react instantaneously . . . [and] . . . any of these
variables may be considered as a "cause" while the others are "effects"' (p. 180).
However, the adjustment predicted by the gas law is a result of dynamic
behaviour imposed and constrained by changing initial conditions. As Haines-
Young and Petch (1981) have responded, '. . . mathematical functions taken
in isolation do not provide causal explanation . . . [but] . . . form the basis
of causal explanation when coupled with statements about the initial conditions

relating to the occurrence of a particular event' (p. 208) This disagreement in part reflects differences of definition and objective. Hey (1979) distinguished between 'static' and 'dynamic' systems, but was actually concerned with 'equilibrium' and 'transient' system states. The gas law is an equilibrium law, and in general the changing initial conditions which trigger adjustments according to the law are slow relative to the molecular-scale processes of adjustment – which are nevertheless not strictly 'instantaneous'. Hey's objective is to focus on the damped, oscillatory non-equilibrium responses of systems which are reacting to circumstances in which the initial conditions change faster than the processes of system adjustment, leading to transient behaviour in which feedback occurs between system state (form) variables and process variables. An example is the upstream and downstream feedback which causes oscillatory response at a river section after a sudden fall in base level, and which arises when the developing morphology (bed slope and cross-section geometry) affects the sediment transport capacity, resulting in temporal fluctuations in the balance between local transport capacity and sediment supply from upstream. This complex, organized behaviour of a non-equilibrium system is characteristic of the irreversible process in which a sequence of configurations known as 'dissipative structures' (Prigogine, 1980) occurs as a system reorganizes itself to accommodate an extreme perturbation (Huggett, 1985, pp. 222–32).

If covering laws are, in general, 'equilibrium' statements, they define the state *to* which a system will change when the initial conditions necessitate an adjustment. Thus, the value of such covering laws in fluvial geomorphology depends on the relaxation times of fluvial systems (Howard, 1965; Brunsden and Thornes, 1979). Where relaxation is (relatively) rapid, equilibrium states will be recognizable and a covering law may be applicable. Relatively slow relaxation results in a preponderance of transient forms, and explanation and prediction of behaviour based on a combination of universal (equilibrium) covering laws and sets of intial conditions will be impossible. This is particularly the case if various elements of a complex system have *different* relaxation times (e.g. channel width and slope), and therefore a state exists of quasi-equilibrium continually disturbed by mutual interdependence (Langbein and Leopold, 1964).

This complexity of environmental systems represents the second problem area in the use of the covering-law model, reflecting as it does 'the logic of scientific discovery' in the experimental physical sciences where controlled conditions are attainable. Complexity arises both because of the numerous controlling environmental variables and because of the multivariate, interdependent nature of environmental 'objects', such as rivers. For example, braided streams have been predicted to occur below critical depth-width ratios (Parker, 1976), but the depth-width ratio of a channel itself depends on the channel pattern. Given the uncertainty surrounding the behaviour of such complex systems, it is unlikely that the criteria of universality, physical necessity, and deductive validity required by the covering-law model can be met.

Statement A, for example, is not universal. The threshold power discriminating braided from meandering patterns is not constant but varies with bed material calibre and bank sedimentology, which together influence energy losses and channel perimeter erodibility. For gravel-bed rivers, the critical power is 150–200 Wm^{-2} (Ferguson, 1984; chapter 6, this volume), but uncertainty remains over the quantitative effect of bank material on the threshold. The statement also lacks physical necessity and therefore cannot claim the status of a scientific law (Guelke, 1971). This is because it relies on consensus definitions of imprecise categories (unconfined alluvial rivers, braided and meandering patterns, mean annual flood), and because although high stream power can be seen to produce intensive sediment transport, in order to explain the creation of bar forms and channel patterns this macroscale consideration has to be disaggregated into its spatial variation (cf. Dietrich, chapter 8). Statement B, which defines the initial conditions, only gives those that appear relevant in the context of the stated covering law. Nadler and Schumm (1981), however, have shown that reservoir impoundment for irrigation water supply in the upstream Platte and Arkansas basins has been associated with a rise in downstream floodplain water tables, because of percolating irrigation water. As a result, increased floodplain vegetation has stabilized sediment and encouraged deposition and floodplain accretion, converting unstable braided channels to stable single-thread rivers. This demonstrates that several independent consequences can arise from a disturbance of the natural environment, and that these *interact* to cause changes in dependent systems.

A deductively valid explanation requires that the covering laws and sets of initial conditions are themselves 'true', exclusive statements, and that the explanation follows logically from them. Statement C is only in part a valid and logical explanation, since it is an incomplete explanation because its premises are weakly defined. One consequence of such a poorly specified explanatory model is that empirical testing of the validity of its 'universal law' is inhibited by inability to identify correctly the initial conditions; for example, deterministic hydrodynamic models of river bend migration predict a narrower range of migration styles than empirical classification of bend migration suggests. This mismatch may either be because model assumptions are invalid, or because environmental heterogeneity distorts the hydrodynamic processes described by the models in an unknown, unmeasurable manner (Richards, 1986). Not only is the formal *structure* of critical rationalism difficult to apply, but also formal *testing* (and therefore falsification) becomes an elusive goal.

To render the explanation of channel change in the South Platte River 'deductively valid' requires considerable effort. The initial conditions could clearly be more specific, identifying for example the calibre of bed material in the South Platte River, and coupling with a covering law in which the threshold power is defined as a function of bed material size. However, there would remain problems: of incorporating the influences of bank sediments and vegetation on bank erodibility; of specifying more rigorously the morphological characteristics of streams with different rates of potential energy dissipation; of dealing with the fundamental physical limitation that macro-scale criteria such as the threshold power fail to *explain* the mechanisms whereby spatially varied bedload transport fields and bank erosion rates trade material to construct bars and evolve channel pattern forms; and of separating the effects of interaction between quite distinct influences brought into simultaneous operation by a change in the initial conditions. Perhaps the kind of causal explanation envisaged by the covering-law model constitutes little more than an idealized limiting condition, applicable directly only in highly simplified cases: a 'science of complexity' may be more appropriate in the study of environmental systems.

The contribution that geographical investigations can make to the resolution of this dilemma is suggested by Pitty (1979), who argues that environmental heterogeneity and complexity should form the basis for a *geographical* method of explanation. He contrasts the methodology of agricultural experimentation formalized by Fisher (1935), which demands that controlling factors are varied one at a time, with the study of natural systems characterized by variables which interact during simultaneous spatial and temporal variation. A geographical method is, for Pitty, one in which '. . . the variability at the earth's surface . . . [is used] . . . as a source of natural selectors . . . and depends on the exploration for and discovery of localities naturally simplified by the marked presence or absence of selectors of particular interest' (Pitty, 1979, p. 279). Exploitation of this strategy in fluvial geomorphology is evident in some of the chapters in this collection. For example, understanding the physical processes of sediment transport, bedform construction, and morphological change is simplified by the identification of spatially discrete zones, within the upstream-downstream continuum of a river course, wherein critical sedimentological controls are uniform. Thus Warner (chapter 2) adopts Pickup's (1984) five-zone classification of river profiles into source, armoured, transition, sand-bed and backwater zones, and is able to identify distinctive patterns of adjustment and degrees of channel stability between these zones. Knighton (chapter 5) further demonstrates that the heterogeneity of downstream hydraulic geometry relationships is rationalized when these are defined for specific categories of channel classified by perimeter sedimentology (cf. Simons and Albertson, 1960). Mosley (chapter 12) also adopts a classificatory approach prior to evaluating river management problems which vary in nature downstream according to the scale, geometry, flow regime, and sedimentology of the river.

Clearly, laws can be more readily derived which explain process-form relations for *specific* channel types; for example, Ferguson (1986) has reviewed physical models of channel form in the 'threshold' (gravel-bed) and 'mobile-bed' (sand-bed) cases. Dietrich (chapter 8) shows how within-reach spatial variation of bed shear stress and sediment transport can be rigorously modelled for single-thread meandering streams of small size, low width-depth ratio and a *sand* bed whose topography is in equilibrium with the flow. In this context, successful testing is required before it is possible to assess the effects of, say, a high width-depth ratio, or disequilibrium flow-bed topography relationships during stage change. Bathurst (chapter 11) identifies the problems of measurement and modelling bedload transport in *gravel*-bed rivers, continuing the general theme that a sedimentological criterion is a critical classificatory variable through which to confine geographical sampling in order to identify, describe, and explain physical processes correctly. Ultimately this procedure improves understanding to the extent that macro-scale theories of wider applicability can be developed. Thus, Howard (1980; chapter 4, this volume) discusses a physical model which applies to *alluvial* channels in general (but not to *bedrock* channels), and which explains why some are *gravel*-bed and some *sand*-bed. It therefore provides a covering law which explains the spatial context which then represents the initial condition of natural variability which must be constrained in order that other covering laws at different scales and of different types can be derived. There appears therefore to be an interaction – a kind of reflexive or reciprocal explanation – between macro-scale, geographical/spatial and micro-scale, physical explanation, which the following chapters collectively demonstrate.

Recognition of this reflexive relationship between environmental and physical elements of explanation is of particular importance in attempts to employ process-form relationships in the reconstruction of past Quaternary environmental conditions, an area of intensive research activity in recent years (e.g. Starkel and Thornes, 1981; Gregory, 1983). As table 1.1 illustrates, both for palaeohydrology and by way of comparison, for the reconstruction of past vegetation, the causal linkages between past environmental conditions and preserved 'forms' (the pollen record, palaeochannels, and fluvial sediments) are tenuous, being mediated by intervening processes whose relationships to *both* environment and product are not clearly understood. In the palaeohydrological case, the reconstruction of hydrological *regime* from local sedimentological evidence cannot readily be undertaken because sediment transport and deposition themselves depend physically on local hydraulic conditions, not on average flow conditions or water discharge. Furthermore, aggradation and incision appear not to relate continuously to environmental conditions, leading to problems in identifying one-to-one relationships between terrace formation and environmental 'causes' (Patton and Schumm, 1981).

Table 1.1 Relationships between environment, process and the preserved 'product' investigated in Quaternary environmental reconstruction

Context	Environment	Process	Product
Vegetation history	Climate (rainfall, temperature) Soils	Plant physiology Population ecology	Pollen assemblage
Palaeo-hydrology	Climate (rainfall, temperature) Hydrology (flood regime) Sediment yield (quantity, calibre)	Hydraulics of flow (velocity, depth, shear stress, power) Sediment transport (capacity *v.* supply)	Palaeochannel forms Sedimentary deposits and structures

Causal linkage

Reconstruction

This, however, does not necessarily imply that fluvial processes are inevitably characterized by discontinuities, non-linearities, and thresholds. It may simply mean that sedimentary processes are controlled by hydraulic conditions that are not themselves uniquely determined by environmental conditions. A central conceptual problem in fluvial geomorphology therefore appears to be the arrangement of a successful marriage between physical and environmental understanding of, respectively, river process and evolution, and Richards *et al.* argue in chapter 14 that a viable and appropriate form of applied fluvial geomorphology should develop from this liaison.

THEMES IN FLUVIAL GEOMORPHOLOGY

The foregoing discussion identifies the *general* context for this collection of essays: that is, a joint concern with the geographical/configurational and physical/immanent properties of fluvial systems. The balance of emphasis varies between the individual chapters, which therefore address more *specific* issues such as those outlined below.

The first two chapters are explicitly concerned with spatial and temporal environmental controls of river morphology. Warner (chapter 2) considers river morphology in an Australian climatic environment characterized by step-functional temporal changes in rainfall regime. Although individual cases of channel adjustment are here difficult to explain because of the interacting effects of climatic and human influence, it is clear that channel stability and sensitivity to change, in response to regime variation between flood- and drought-dominated periods, are themselves spatially varied in relation to discrete zones within river long profiles. These zones are sedimentologically defined, and are therefore in part self-formed by the river through a sediment-sorting process. In chapter 3, Gregory and Schumm use experimental and field evidence to demonstrate the consequences for channel morphology of a localized, external (environmental) influence – neotectonic deformation at rates of $4-10\,\mathrm{mm\,yr^{-1}}$ on axes aligned transverse to a river course. River adjustment upstream and downstream of such an axis involves aggradation or degradation and channel pattern change, the nature of which varies with rates of deformation and with the *initial* channel pattern characteristics. Here, the *environmental* control is the neotectonic deformation; this in turn produces a *physical* control, for example by reducing slope and stream power above an *uplift* axis and increasing them downstream, and this then provides the mechanism for change.

Although an axis of tectonic deformation is locationally fixed, the spatially separated processes of deposition and erosion it induces are similar to those in 'sedimentation zones', which form 'steps' in valley long profiles and are initiated by tributary sediment input or intensive sediment supply localized in time and space (Church and Jones, 1982). In appropriate circumstances these sediment 'slugs' migrate downstream as kinematic waves, the wave translation being determined by the local variation of transport capacity relative to sediment supply through the waves and the intervening transport reaches (hydraulic mining debris migrating down the Sacramento River provides an example; Gilbert, 1917).

The second theme, which permeates chapters 4 to 8, concerns the sedimentological control of channel form and process. Channel perimeter sediments initially reflect the characteristics of material supplied from sediment sources, but sorting, weathering and abrasion processes during transport impose regular patterns on downstream sediment size variation. These patterns are commonly discontinuous, with thresholds between zones characterized by particular bed material sizes (Yatsu, 1955) and associated forms (cf. Warner, chapter 2). In chapter 4, Howard outlines a theoretical explanation for sharp transitions between bedrock, gravel-bed, and sand-bed channel types. This is based on consideration of the gradients required to transport each size fraction of the load supplied from upstream, and the quantities supplied in each size fraction. The relationship between gradients required to transport the coarse and fine fractions of the load determines both the *actual* gradient, and the size fraction which is dominant in the bed. Since the theory assumes independent transport of each size fraction, it may need detailed modification in the light of experiments on transportation of grain size mixtures, designed specifically to investigate Yatsu's (1955) observed slope discontinuity (Ikeda and Iseya, 1987). However, it provides a first attempt at a physical model of the discontinuous spatial variation of bed material size.

Within each long-profile zone, channel forms respond to the local sedimentological conditions in particular ways. Thus, for example, Knighton (1975) has suggested that channel gradient is an adjustable morphological property where bed material grain size is in the gravel-size range, but that channel cross-section forms constitute the more readily adjustable morphological 'dimension' when the bed is dominated by sand. In chapter 5, he also summarizes empirical evidence showing downstream hydraulic geometry relationships to be distinctive between gravel-bed river reaches predominantly at the threshold of motion at bankfull discharge, and sand-bed rivers which experience active transport over a wide range of flows. The same sedimentological distinction between threshold and mobile-bed conditions has been used to classify and review hydraulic theories of channel cross-section form (Ferguson, 1986). The third 'dimension' of channel morphology – channel pattern – is discussed in chapter 6, where Ferguson identifies the multivariate sedimentological control exercised by bed and bank materials over the meandering-braiding threshold, and emphasizes the need for physical models which relate pattern characteristics to the mechanics of sediment transport.

Chapters 7 and 8 then provide separate illustrations of relationships between sediment transport, bedform and bar characteristics and channel morphology in, respectively, gravel-bed and sand-bed rivers. Bluck (chapter 7) argues that selective particle size rejection or retention occurs as a result of turbulence associated with micro-scale pebble bedforms (such as transverse clast dams). This, therefore, results in size sorting over longer reaches and represents a fundamental link between sediment yield in source areas, and the depositional sink locations for particular size fractions. This argument has some parallels in chapter 4, therefore, and is also pivotal in linking larger-scale morphological variation to localized physical processes. In chapter 8, Dietrich is concerned with bar forms in sand-bed, single-thread meandering streams, and presents the kind of physical model demanded by Ferguson: one which explains the mechanics of interaction between bed topography, channel curvature and flow in order to predict the spatial fields of boundary shear stress, bedload transport, and the equilibrium grain-size distribution and bed geometry.

Flow resistance in sand-bed rivers is quantitatively indeterminate because the flow interacts with its mobile bed to cause sediment transport, which occurs in a wave-like motion associated with a sequence of bedforms (ripples, dunes, plane bed, antidunes; Simons and Richardson, 1966). This unpredictable form roughness, which is quantitatively significant relative to the grain roughness, then complicates theoretical estimation of bedload transport from hydraulic data, because the transport is driven by that part of the bed shear stress balanced by the grain drag, and the *total* bed shear stress therefore has to be partitioned. In Dietrich's study of transport in a bend, there is an additional complexity in that bedforms skew across the channel, cause secondary currents close to the bed, and have a strong influence on local transport paths. One theoretical approach used to evaluate the development of bedforms has employed extremal hypotheses, which argue that channel forms are created which minimize rates of potential energy loss, or maximize frictional resistance or bed shear stress; that is, that the morphology of a river dissipates energy efficiently. Braided rivers, for example, are efficient energy dissipators because of the subdivision of the flow and its frequent diversion around bars: these forms are created by, and dissipate, the high rates of potential energy loss per unit length characteristic of reaches that develop a braided pattern. In chapter 9, Davies discusses the extremal hypothesis of maximum bed shear stress, seeking a *physical* explanation for metaphysical concepts which have been shown to have some *predictive* value, but whose generality across a range of morphological scales and bed material contexts detracts from its *explanatory* capability. The two-dimensional geometry of the sand-dune bedforms in Dietrich's study, and the spacing and scale of gravel microforms described by Bluck, may both be explicable as structures which maximize friction and bed shear stress. The Davies chapter therefore links chapters 7 and 8 to those which consider a third theme: structural arrangement of gravel particles and bedload transport in gravel-bed rivers.

Development pressures and river management problems in upland environments have encouraged a recent emphasis on flow resistance, sediment transport and river morphology in gravel-bed rivers (Hey et al., 1982). Generally these rivers are characterized by relatively low transport stages even at bankfull discharge, these being defined as the ratio of prevailing shear velocity to the threshold shear velocity given by the Shields criterion (Abbott and Francis, 1977). This implies that rolling and sliding transport modes predominate, and mutual particle interference during transport creates a variety of structural arrangements of clasts in the gravel-pebble-cobble-boulder size ranges. In chapter 10, Naden and Brayshaw consider both the formation and the destruction of these clast groupings, which constitute micro-forms (Bluck, chapter 7) ranging from pebble clusters to transverse ribs and gravel antidunes. Their formation is modelled using a stochastic queuing model in which bedform size is a function of the probabilities of clast deposition and erosion, which in turn depend on turbulent velocity fluctuations at the river bed. Destruction is then considered in relation to local bed shear stress, and field measurements suggest that interlocking of particles in these bedforms necessitates a higher shear stress for their entrainment than the Shields criterion predicts. Bathurst (chapter 11) continues this theme more generally in the context of modelling and measuring gravel bedload transport. Clustering and armouring produce structures on and within gravel beds which make the definition of threshold hydraulic conditions problematic: Andrews (1983), for example, has shown that the threshold shear stress is largely independent of particle size because of the countering effect of shielding which inhibits entrainment of smaller grains. It is clear that better understanding of the threshold of motion is needed before the effects of supply limitation can be evaluated, and both of these issues are complicated in gravel-bed rivers not only by structural arrangement of the bed, but also by their wide range of bed particle sizes. Furthermore, there is clearly a difference between entrainment and deposition thresholds, defined by bed shear stress, and this has recently been re-emphasized as a factor ignored in most bedload transport equations (Reid and Frostick, 1984).

A fourth theme emerges in the last group of chapters, and this concerns the nature of applied fluvial geomorphology. Environmental management contexts range from conservation of aquatic ecology to engineering control of river processes, and all can benefit from an integrated concern with both the environmental background and the process mechanics of river behaviour. Mosley (chapter 12) discusses approaches to classification of rivers which break down the continuum of downstream, gravity-controlled nutrient transfers into discrete ecological zones characterized by river size, geometry, flow regime and substrate type. This practical concern with ecological management therefore has much in common with the classificatory scheme introduced in chapter 2 and rationalized by the physical theory presented in chapter 4. Modern approaches emphasized by Mosley also focus on within-reach spatial variation of hydraulic conditions across a range of flows (cf. chapter 8). Gravel bedload transport re-emerges, as a critical aspect of aquatic ecological management, in chapter 13 (Carling). This is significant, because it might otherwise seem ironic that research effort is expended on a process which in the engineering context is rarely a major problem; gravel-bed alluvial rivers are near-threshold, and are *relatively* stable (consider the stability of channels in the 'armoured' zone discussed by Warner in chapter 2). Bed scour to between 8 and 30 cm at critical times can, however, have a major impact on invertebrate fauna and the hatching of salmonid fish eggs. It is not the bedload transport *rate* that is of immediate concern, but the depth of distrubance of the bed, and this applied focus therefore demands a somewhat different approach to the transport problem. The final chapter (Richards et al.) emphasizes the combined assessment of environmental and physical controls of river behaviour that the fluvial geomorphologist can bring to engineering project appraisal. Case studies are used to illustrate: the evaluation of fluvial landform sensitivity; the relative contributions of progressive and extreme processes of river adjustment; the magnitude and frequency of hydrological and sediment transport events; and interrelationships between river behaviour and processes of sediment transfer elsewhere in the landscape.

This final chapter therefore explicitly raises conceptual issues which are nevertheless implicit throughout the collection; for example, the balance between equilibrium and transient river behaviour, the relative roles of gradual and catastrophic temporal change, continuous and discrete spatial variation, thresholds in both temporal and spatial variation and in environmental and physical controls. The contributors to this review of alluvial channel morphology in its environmental and process contexts include geomorphologists, geologists, engineers and river managers from Britain, the USA, New Zealand and Australia. The strong connections that are evident between their individual contributions are indicative of general agreement on the critical issues facing students of fluvial geomorphology; of the health of interdisciplinary analysis of river behaviour; and of the value of a geographical or spatial framework for the isolation and analysis of the mechanics of the sediment transport process which is the immediate cause of channel morphology.

REFERENCES

Abbott, J. E. and Francis, J. E. 1977: Saltation and suspension trajectories of solid grains in a water stream. *Phil. Trans. Royal Soc.*, 284A, 225–53.
Andrews, E. D. 1983: Entrainment of gravel from naturally sorted riverbed material. *Geol. Soc. America Bull.*, 94, 1225–31.
Brunsden, D. and Thornes, J. B. 1979: Landscape sensitivity and change. *Trans. Inst. Brit. Geog., New Ser.*, 4, 463–84.
Church, M. and Jones, D. 1982: Channel bars in gravel-bed rivers. In R. D. Hey, J. C. Bathurst and C. R. Thorne (eds), *Gravel-bed Rivers*, Chichester: Wiley, 291–324.
Ferguson, R. I. 1984: The threshold between meandering and braiding. In K. V. H. Smith (ed.), *Channels and Channel Control Structures*, Berlin: Springer-Verlag, 6.15–6.29.
Ferguson R. I. 1986: Hydraulics and hydraulic geometry. *Prog. in Phys. Geog.*, 1, 1–31.
Fisher, R. A. 1935: *The Design of Experiments*. London: Oliver & Boyd, 248.
Gilbert, G. K. 1917: Hydraulic mining debris in the Sierra Nevada. *US Geol. Survey, Prof. Paper*, 105.
Gould, S. J. 1965: Is uniformitarianism necessary? *Am. Journ. Sci.*, 263, 223–8.
Gregory, K. J. (ed.) 1983: *Background to Palaeohydrology*. Chichester: Wiley & Sons, 486.
Guelke, L. 1971: Problems of scientific explanation in Geography. *Can. Geogr.*, 15, 38–53.
Haines-Young, R. and Petch, J. R. 1980: The challenge of critical rationalism for methodology in physical geography. *Prog. in Phys. Geog.*, 4, 63–77.
Haines-Young, R. and Petch, J. R. 1981: Causal and functional relationships in fluvial geomorphology: a reply. *Earth Surf. Proc. & Landforms*, 6, 207–9.
Haines-Young, R. and Petch, J. R. 1983: Multiple working hypotheses: equifinality and the study of landforms. *Trans. Inst. Brit. Geog., New Ser.*, 8, 458–66.
Haines-Young, R. and Petch, J. R. 1986: *Physical Geography: its nature and method*. London: Harper & Row, 230.

Hey, R. D. 1979: Causal and functional relationships in fluvial geomorphology. *Earth Surf. Proc.*, 4, 179–82.

Hey, R. D., Bathurst, J. C. and Thorne, C. R. 1982: *Gravel-bed Rivers*. Chichester: Wiley, 875.

Howard, A. D. 1965: Geomorphological systems – equilibrium and dynamics. *Am. Journ. Sci.*, 263, 302–12.

Howard, A. D. 1980: Thresholds in river regimes. In D. R. Coates and J. D. Vitek (eds), *Thresholds in Geomorphology*, London: George Allen & Unwin, 227–58.

Huggett, R. J. 1985: *Earth Surface Systems*. Berlin: Springer-Verlag, 270.

Ikeda, H. and Iseya, F. 1987: Thresholds in the mobility of sediment mixtures. In V. Gardiner et al. (eds), *International Geomorphology 1986 Vol. 1*, Chichester: Wiley, 561–70.

Knighton, A. D. 1975: Channel gradient in relation to discharge and bed material characteristics. *Catena*, 2, 263–74.

Langbein, W. B. and Leopold, L. B. 1964: Quasi-equilibrium states in channel morphology. *Am. Journ. Sci.*, 262, 782–94.

Nadler, C. T. and Schumm, S. A. 1981: Metamorphosis of South Platte and Arkansas rivers, eastern Colorado. *Phys. Geog.*, 2, 96–115.

Parker, G. 1976: On the cause and characteristic scales of meandering and braiding in rivers. *Journ. Fluid Mechs.*, 76, 457–80.

Patton, P. C. and Schumm, S. A. 1981: Ephemeral-stream processes: implications for studies of Quaternary fills. *Quat. Res.*, 15, 24–43.

Pickup, G. 1984: Geomorphology of tropical rivers. I. Landforms, hydrology and and sedimentation in the Fly and lower Purari, Papua New Guinea. *Catena, Supplement*, 5, 1–17.

Pitty, A. F. 1979: Conclusions. In A. F. Pitty (ed.), *Geographical Approaches to Fluvial Processes*, Norwich: Geo Books, 261–80.

Popper, K. R. 1959: *The Logic of Scientific Discovery*. London: Hutchinson, 480.

Prigogine, I. 1980: *From Being to Becoming: Time and Complexity in the Physical Science* San Francisco: Freeman, 272.

Reid, I. and Frostick, L. E. 1984: Particle interaction and its effect on the thresholds of initial and final bedload motion in coarse alluvial channels. In E. H. Koster and R. J. S. Steel (eds), *Sedimentology of Gravels and Conglomerates*, Can. Soc. Petrol. Geol., Mem. 10, 61–8.

Richards, K. S. 1986: Fluvial geomorphology. *Prog. in Phys. Geog.*, 10, 401–20.

Simons, D. B. and Albertson, M. L. 1960: Uniform water-conveyance channels in alluvial materials. *Journ. Hydraul. Div., Am. Soc. Civ. Eng.*, 86, 33–71.

Simons, D. B. and Richardson, E. V. 1966: Resistance to flow in alluvial channels. *US Geol. Survey, Prof. Paper*, 422J.

Starkel, L. and Thornes, J. B. 1981: Palaeohydrology of river basins. Guide to sub-project A of IGCP project No. 158. *British Geom. Res. Grp, Tech. Bull.*, 28, 107.

Yatsu, E. 1955: On the longitudinal profile of the graded river. *Trans. Am. Geophys. Union*, 36, 655–63.

2

Spatial Adjustments to Temporal Variations in Flood Regime in Some Australian Rivers

Robin F. Warner

INTRODUCTION

In New South Wales, channel changes involving channel size and position are common even in incised reaches of coastal rivers. This was first noticed in the early 1960s when using in the field large-scale air photographs taken by the RAAF towards the end of World War II (1943–1945). Comparison between these and later photographs, as well as field observation, often revealed considerable changes in width and sometimes position in the Bellinger River (Warner, 1968). These were thought to relate to the effects of several major floods, beginning in 1949 and continuing to about 1967, as well as to the impacts of intensive dairy farming in the period 1930–60. Farm sizes were small and it was necessary to clear and graze hill country above the river flats in dry winters and springs, with attendant hydrological consequences.

Later more detailed work on both climatic and discharge records showed that a major change in regime had occurred in many parts of eastern Australia since about the mid-1940s. Increased rainfall occurred mainly in summer storms in New South Wales (NSW) (Cornish, 1977) and this led to higher and more frequent flooding. Morphological impacts of changed regime were investigated by Pickup (1974; 1976a; 1976b) on the Cumberland Plain, west of Sydney. Subsequent work has revealed widespread increases in so-called channel-forming discharges (notably the most probable annual flood $Q_{1.58}$ and mean annual flood $Q_{2.33}$; Dury, 1969).

If there are causative links between these flows and channel size (Wolman and Miller, 1960; Leopold et al. 1964; Baker, 1977; Andrews, 1980; Richards, 1982;

Pickup, 1986, in press) it follows that with such increases there was potential for significant channel adjustments. These have been investigated in studies of channel change, where a major aim has been to explain modifications in terms of both regime variation and human activities in the catchment and channel. Such investigations, some of which are reviewed later, are dependent on earlier investigations of channel dimensions and locations. Where these 'historical windows' are few in number and widely spaced in time, it is difficult to associate net change with either natural or human events. However, archival finds have allowed some appreciation of changes through time.

More recently, with the availability of an extended record of flood stages at Windsor on the Hawkesbury River (figure 2.1), it has been possible to study longer-term variations in flooding (Riley, 1980; 1981). These stage records have been converted to discharge for upstream stations at Penrith and Warragamba and, although of doubtful quality, can be used to give an idea of variation over 180 years seeming to indicate several changes in regime.

It now seems probable that within what is already a very variable regime, there are alternations between what have been called flood-dominated (Hickin, 1983) and drought-dominated regimes (Erskine, personal communication) (FDR and DDR respectively). The former are periods of up to four or more decades when floods are more frequent, larger, and when high stream power within and beyond the channel can effect modifications. The latter are not wholly dry, but are characterized by fewer, lower-magnitude floods, where some sort of recovery can be achieved over several decades. In the Hawkesbury-Nepean, the 1799–1820 period appears to have been flood-dominated. Many big floods have been described which caused great losses to the early settlers. From 1821 to 1864, the lack of major reports of flooding probably indicated a drought-dominated period, but this was followed (1864–1900) by nearly four decades of large and frequent floods. The two biggest floods were experienced during this period (1867 and 1900). By contrast, the period 1901–48 was drought-dominated with considerable recovery evident in the Nepean above Penrith (Warner, 1984b). The present flood-dominated regime began in about 1949. Many gauging records began after this date, but previous regimes are indicated from flood-stage records in coastal towns, and from rainfall observations. Although records are not nearly as long as for the Hawkesbury, similar patterns are being revealed (see figure 2.1 for locations).

This chapter represents an attempt to discuss in broad terms these regime variations and their spatial impacts on predominantly coastal river systems. It commences with a review of ideas of spatial variation in channel character using the ideas of Schumm (1977) and Pickup (1984; 1986). These provide a framework in which to assess the potential adjustment to regime variations. There follows a consideration of the evidence for temporal variations in flood regime and

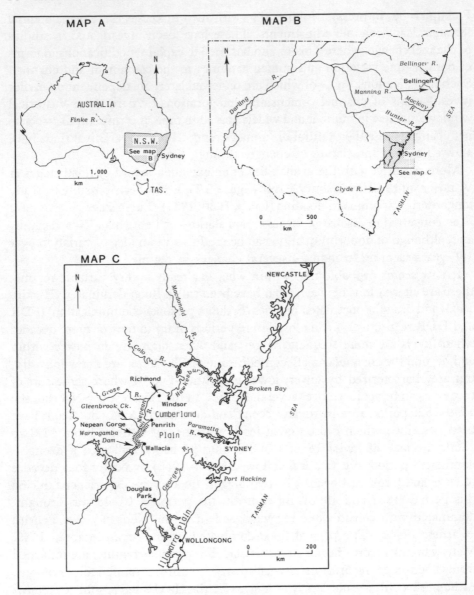

Figure 2.1   General location maps

associated problems. The final two sections are concerned with spatio-temporal interactions and the evidence for stability and change, together with the problems of distinguishing changes due to natural events and human-induced modifications to catchments and channels. The chapter also represents an Australian example of work on flood impacts, to parallel those by Baker (1977) in Texas, Harvey (1984) in Spain and Graf (1983) in Arizona.

SPATIAL CHARACTERISTICS

Spatial controls of channel morphology reflect not only discharge variations related to basin size, but also direct and indirect geological influences on the channel perimeter (Leopold et al., 1964; Schumm, 1977; Richards, 1982). Direct impacts may involve bedrock bluffs in undercut reaches, rock steps affecting long-profile gradients, and gorges where most of the channel is in contact with bedrock. Indirectly geology also influences the perimeter sediments forming the depositional elements of the channel and the alluvium through which the river flows. These may reflect the effects of both past and contemporary processes. The distribution of these controls of the channel and its floodplain varies spatially and interacts with the passing flows.

The annual pattern of events may be considered to be the regime, with regularity characterizing some systems and quite variable conditions affecting others. Thus, for instance, summer dominance of runoff is common in the northern tropics of Australia, while winter runoff predominates in the south. Between these, and particularly in the arid areas, regimes are very irregular. Aquatic and riparian vegetation also form part of the perimeter conditions. The resistance of part of this perimeter has to be overcome by stream power (Bull, 1979) before erosion can occur. Conversely, there must be loss of power to effect deposition of material being transmitted through a section. Where there is an approximate balance between imports to and exports from a reach, equilibrium conditions prevail (Mackin, 1948; Pickup, 1986). The time-frame for equilibrium is thought to be short-term in more humid environments and longer-term in more arid areas (Chorley, Schumm and Sugden, 1984). In the cases described here, there are progressive trends towards an erosional condition in flood-dominated regimes, and a depositional, recovery condition in drought-dominated regimes. These increase both the amplitude of departure from, and time for re-establishment of, equilibrium in what are quite humid environments.

Thus any spatial consideration of variations in channel morphology needs to consider: direct and indirect geological impacts; discharge variations over both short and intermediate time-spans; the varying role of vegetation; and the impacts of human action. This can be done with respect to local reaches and for the whole long-profile.

Concern here is with spatial variability throughout the whole system. Although Australia extends latitudinally from savanna tropics in the north to the cool-temperate, west coast climates of Tasmania in the south, the dominant river

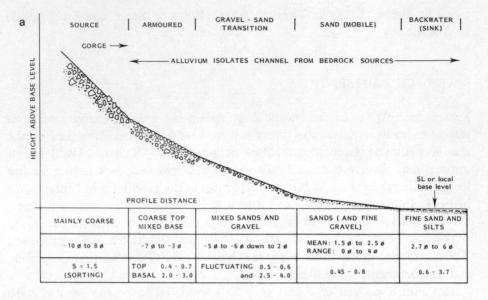

Figure 2.2(a) An idealized profile showing the Pickup (1984) zones
Based on Pickup (1984 and 1986)

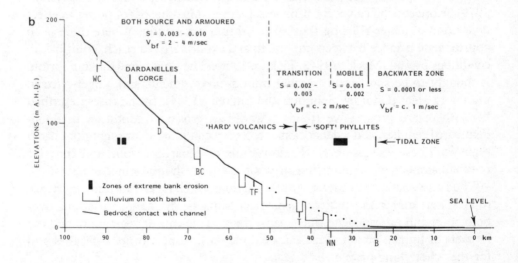

Figure 2.2(b) The long profile of the Bellinger River (an incised coastal stream)
Based on data from Warner (1968): WC, D, BC, etc. are sites in tables 2.1 and 2.2

system is the dry, unco-ordinated, disconnected arid channel which occupies two-thirds of its total area (Warner, 1985a; 1986). These are often inherited from previous climates, and are used only infrequently and for short periods ending in flood-outs. Few of these systems have been studied in the context of this chapter, where the main concern is with small east-coast systems which are adjusted to present regimes however variable they may be. Catchment areas range from less than 1000 km² to over 20 000 km². In their long profiles, bedrock influences are extremely varied, from tableland sources, through gorges, into coastal ranges and downstream to the narrow coastal plains. Incised conditions eventually give way to more continuous floodplains which end in deltas or rias. Such rivers may rise at elevations close to 1000 m and have fairly steep gradients down to near-tidal conditions.

Schumm (1977) envisaged an idealized fluvial system as consisting of three zones: an upper zone of sediment production (source) where the major controls were climate, diastrophism and land use; a middle zone (transfer) essentially in equilibrium; and a lower zone (a sink or depositional area) where controls were base level and diastrophism. In each, the processes of erosion, transmission and deposition of sediment respectively dominated but were not necessarily exclusive. This simple model has now been extended and used by Pickup (1984; 1986) to explain variations in bedload characteristics and movement. The scheme, developed for large tropical rivers in Papua New Guinea, can be extended to most systems. It consists of five zones: source, armoured, transition, sand, and backwater zones (Pickup 1984; 1986).

In the upper source zone, there is a wide range of mainly coarse poorly sorted material (< 10 − > 1000 mm), added directly to the channel from adjacent slopes (figures 2.2a and 2.2b). This may be restricted to gorges where both slopes contribute, or to undercut reaches where only one slope adds material directly to the stream bed. Downstream, there are frequently armoured reaches, where the bed surface consists of well sorted materials (> 10 mm) which mantle and protect a poorly sorted substratum. Surface layers are only mobilized infrequently and such zones may exist in lower gorge-upper valley areas. In the transition zone, the range of bed material is both wide and bimodal, with rapid fluctuations in size and sorting (figure 2.2a). In tropical rivers, these zones are very short (Pickup, 1984) and located at the upper part of the piedmont plains. Elsewhere they may include very long reaches where local tributaries and undercut slopes continually add coarser fractions (Pickup, 1986) (figure 2.2b). The sand or mobile zone contains well sorted finer materials which can include gravels. The main distinction is that material can be moved frequently by low-power events. In the tropics, these are long zones crossing the piedmont plains and there is little change in sorting downstream (Pickup, 1984). Elsewhere, they may be long in sand-bed streams where the bedload is very mobile, or short where mixed load contributions become smaller when detached from further bedrock sources (figure 2.2b). The backwater zone is characterized by a wide range of poorly sorted finer material (sands to clays). This occurs where gradients are very flat, such as above the junction with a major river (for example, 70 km of the Fly River, Papua New Guinea, above the Strickland junction exhibit backwater characteristics) or close to the tidal limit.

These zones reflect variations in the controls of gradient, bed material, stream power potential and the streams' ability to move different-sized material at different frequencies. They do not always occur simply or in order and some may be missing, whilst some zones may be repeated. Stream power in the source zone (Bull, 1979) is high, with steep gradients in gorges and wholly bedrock channels. The deposition of protective surface gravels in the armoured reaches reflects accumulation of uniform coarser material, where lower power means less frequent movement of bedload. Finer materials are transmitted through, although temporary storages of finer gravel are not uncommon. The transition zone marks the break-up of the armoured reaches and increased mobility of finer materials. This material is moved into the sand/mobile zone, where bedload movement frequency is high, as is the potential to adjust. Even less power is available at marked breaks in the long profile above major stream junctions or above tidal limits. Bedload is much finer, and in this backwater zone, movement is again limited, this time by low power and high cohesion of sediments. Most of these zones can be distinguished in coastal rivers in NSW, although source zones may be fragmented and repetitive; armoured zones may be short or absent, particularly in sand-bed rivers; transition zones may be much longer; mobile zones are long in sandy sediments, perhaps short elsewhere; and backwater zones are largely tidal (figure 2.2b).

The zones distinguished not only indicate different bedload characteristics through the long profile but also differences in potential sediment movement frequencies. Therefore the ability of the channel to adjust to new regime conditions varies. In gorges, there are no alluvial morphologies, and adjustments are in terms of stage, and frequency of moving gravity-added materials out of source zones. Bed modification in armoured reaches is usually at a frequency much lower than bankfull discharge. Thus while the potential for movement may be increased in a flood-dominated regime, it may still be low relative to other zones. In such reaches channel-modifying discharges are at low frequencies and therefore adjustments to wetter regimes may be slow, requiring discharges well above the mean annual flood. In the transition zone, movement of the finer load is much more frequent and therefore channel adjustment can potentially occur at a faster rate. Movement frequencies of bedload in Cumberland Plain streams were 3–5 times a year (Pickup and Warner, 1976), but cohesive banks restricted whole-channel adjustments to flows of 4–7 year return period. In the sand or mobile zone, any velocity over about $0.3\,m\,s^{-1}$ may begin to move medium sand. Thus ability to adjust to new conditions may be rapid if banks can be undercut and vegetation destroyed. There is a loss of power in this zone, with lower gradients more than offsetting the effects of much higher discharges. Both are reduced considerably in the backwater reaches, which are characterized by low gradients, low roughness, high bank cohesion and much off-channel storage of high-flow events (extensive floodplains, large capacity flood basins and entry through levee low points or tributary channels). Flood tides can further reduce effective gradients and lower flood velocities. Thus this spatial distinction does allow for differential adjustments to changed discharge conditions (figure 2.2b, table 2.1). It is worth noting that Pickup (1986) sees equilibrium conditions as prevailing only in the central zones; source zones are areas of net loss, and backwater areas are sediment sinks, both of which are progressive, on-going conditions. So with alternating regimes, there is scope for rapid or slow adjustment in both directions (degradation or recovery), mainly in the central zones.

Table 2.1 indicates the downstream changes that occur in the Bellinger at seven sites. The median diameter of material moved under present bankfull conditions is given in table 2.2. These data reveal a decline in grain size downstream, together with loss of power per unit bed area (Bull, 1979). Distinguishing the actual zones is difficult with these limited data, but suggested categories are given below for what is a complex system where, because of incised conditions and tributaries, source inputs are frequent (figure 2.2b).

Stream power per unit length (Ω) is given by γQs (the product of unit weight of water, discharge, and slope). Power per unit bed area (ω) involves dividing Ω by width, w. Gradients were surveyed in the Bellinger (Warner, 1968) and can be used tentatively to assign different reaches to the zones defined above. In incised reaches and gorges (delivery sources) slope (s) $= 0.003 - 0.010$. In reaches that may be armoured but are certainly transitional, slope decreases to 0.002–0.003. The lower floodplain and tidal reaches, constituting a backwater zone, have gradients of 0.001 to 0.002 and 0.00003 to 0.0001 respectively (table 2.1). Given mean bankfull depths of 2–5 m (R or hydraulic radius) and roughness values (n) between 0.035 and 0.055, bankfull velocities fall from about $4\,ms^{-1}$ in upper to $1\,ms^{-1}$ in lower, near-tidal reaches (figure 2.2b).

This pattern would be typical for longer coastal rivers but with lower gradients and longer reaches in zones 4 and 5. However much of the Hawkesbury-Nepean is a sand-bed stream with long mobile reaches well downstream from the Warragamba gravels, and a sediment sink located in the ria of Broken Bay. Inland rivers frequently rise on the tablelands and experience a similar sequence of zones to those of the coastal streams until they reach the slopes and plains. They then have long mobile and backwater zones, with low gradients, velocities and

Table 2.1 Stream power for various discharge levels in the Bellinger River

Site	Basin area (km²)	$Q_{1.58}$ (1) estimated (m³ s⁻¹)	$Q_{2.33}$ (2) estimated (m³ s⁻¹)	Q_{bf}(3) actual (m³ s⁻¹)	Slope (m/m)	Stream power for three levels of Q (W m⁻¹)			Power per unit bed area ($\omega=\Omega/w$) (W m⁻²)		
						1	2	3	1	2	3
Woods Creek	157	160	235	205	0.010	15692	23054	20111	266	384	335
Dardanelles	292	270	400	280	0.004	10595	15696	10987	125	185	129
Bishops Creek	360	325	470	375	0.002	6377	9221	7358	118	171	136
Twin Falls	405	360	535	565	0.002	7063	10497	11085	118	175	185
Thora	450	395	575	850	0.001	3875	5641	8339	37	54	79
Never Never	536	450	660	515	0.001	4415	6475	5052	42	62	48
Bellingen	671	500	800	370	0.0001	491	785	363	7	11	5

$\Omega=\rho g\,Qs$ where Ω is stream power (W m⁻¹), ρ is density, g is acceleration of gravity, Q is discharge and s is channel slope.
$\omega=\Omega/w$ where ω is power per unit bed area (W m⁻²) and w is width.

Table 2.2 Bankfull discharge, channel properties, and threshold size of material moved at bankfull (using equations of Graf, 1983)

Site	Q_{bf} (m^3 s^{-1})	w (m)	n (est.)	s (m/m)	D_{50} (at threshold at Q_{bf}) (mm)	Zone
Woods Creek	205	60	0.05	0.01	259	(single bank/source)
Dardanelles	280	85	0.06	0.004	195	(gorge/source)
Bishops Creek	375	54	0.045	0.002	168	(single bank/source)
Twin Falls	565	60	0.04	0.002	180	(bedrock in bed and lower bank)
Thora	850	105	0.035	0.001	126	(mainly alluvium/armoured/ transition)
Never Never	515	105	0.035	0.001	107	(mainly alluvium/transition)
Bellingen	370	73	0.03	0.0001	45	(mainly alluvium/mobile/ backwater)

Q_{bf} is bankfull discharge, w is width, n is Manning roughness coefficient, s is slope, and D_{50} is median grain size.

channel capacities, and high silt-clay contents in perimeter sediments. Truly arid rivers like the Finke have sand beds, but flow frequencies are low and of limited longitudinal persistence except in super-floods.

TEMPORAL VARIATIONS IN REGIME

Australia is a land of climatic and hydrological extremes (Warner, 1985a; 1986). It is therefore surprising to find some apparent order in hydrological regimes which alternate between flood-and drought-dominated conditions. This section reviews evidence for these temporal variations of regime. Initial research concentrated on precipitation changes through time, but attention has now switched to the impacts of these changes on discharge, and the channel adjustments which have followed. Long-term discharge records are not readily available and have in most cases to be derived from stage records. Flood heights in the past have been recorded in many places but in converting them to discharge, it is necessary to assume no changes in stage-discharge relations. This implies no channel change which is difficult to substantiate except in gorges, in view of all the changes which have been described.

Climatologists have widely recognized evidence of precipitation changes throughout eastern Australia (Pittock, 1975). A more specific contribution on rainfall in NSW was made by Cornish (1977). He found annual increases of between 10 and 30 per cent, the biggest increases being west of Sydney. More importantly, summer increases of 20 to 60 per cent were described for wide areas of the state. These were thought to be associated with an increased frequency and/or intensity of storm events. Such additions could promote gully, sheet and stream-bank erosion (Cornish, 1977), but in fact, the onset of this wetter period coincided with a decline in many farming enterprises, more deliberate conservation measures, the eradication of rabbits and noxious weeds, and the increasing use of fertilizers and exotic grasses. These meant a decrease in hillslope erosion, as noted by Pickup (1976a) and Erskine and Bell (1982), and an increase in channel erosion. The latter authors have carefully documented significant increases of precipitation in the Hunter Valley since 1946, together with increased rainfall intensities and flood magnitudes. They pointed out that floods are more relevant to channel change than rainfall and its intensity. Significant increases in flood magnitude were demonstrated for three major gauging stations in that valley. Milne (1971) found a threefold increase in $Q_{1.58}$ in the Macleay, while Pickup (1976a; 1986) describes a near seven-fold increase at Wallacia on the Nepean. Bellinger figures show a doubling of $Q_{1.58}$, $Q_{2.33}$, and Q_5 and Q_{10} since the late 1940s (Warner, 1985b; Warner and Paterson, 1985). The increase at Penrith, downstream of the Warragamba Dam (1960), is less than twofold, but the impacts of the dam affect nearly 80 per cent of the area. Prior to 1959, $Q_{2.33}$ had more than doubled (Warner, 1983; 1984b) (table 2.3), with other stations on the upper Nepean showing a more confused picture. Four dams were built from 1907–35 and these modified flows in a dry period. Also, gauging was abandoned at several places to reduce available records in the succeeding wet period.

Geomorphologists saw changing precipitation as one means of explaining apparent channel instability (Pickup, 1976a; 1976b; Bell and Erskine, 1981; Erskine and Bell, 1982; Erskine and Melville, 1983; Warner, 1984a; 1984b; 1984c). However, human impacts have confused the pattern of modifications in many valleys. In the tidal Georges River, changes were attributed to urbanization, channel dredging and to increased runoff (Warner and Pickup, 1974; Warner et al., 1977). Runoff variation in urban areas was impossible to assess because there are no gauges. In seeking to explain the changes that have been identified and documented, researchers were forced to assess the impacts of process events. For instance, Henry (1977) detailed changes in the sand-bed Macdonald River north of Sydney. Bank erosion and bed aggradation had been pronounced since 1955, but he nevertheless concluded that recovery was being effected. Later Erskine, working in the same valley, found a 0.3 m aggradation in a large 1978 flood and 0.1 m degradation in a succeeding smaller event the same year. Secular climatic change and associated regime modification explained the variations (Erskine and Melville, 1983).

Channel changes have been investigated in many parts of the Hawkesbury-Nepean system. Scholer (1974) was concerned with the impact of dams, particularly Warragamba, on sediment supply to the downstream channel, and with sand dredging. Long-profile conditions between Douglas Park and the Grose Junction were surveyed in 1911 as part of the creation of a flight of weirs to provide riparian waters for the Nepean about to be dammed on four head-water systems. Parts of this were resurveyed in 1980-1 to reveal scour in sandstone gorges and sediment build-up in the weirponds (Warner, 1983; 1984b). Runoff records were used to assess impacts of both the dams and the changed regime. Cross-section surveys were replicated in 1982 and 1983 to show changes from 1900 for 46 sections in the five km above Penrith railway bridge. In the earlier year, the end of a flood-dominated regime (1864-1900), the channel was very wide and shallow with sand shoals in the throat of the gorge. The later surveys (showing net change 1900-82/3) were undertaken 30-40 years into another flood-dominated regime (FDR) following almost 50 years of drought domination. Consequently width analysis from 1949 air photographs had to be used to establish bank recovery, which was considerable and up to 60-70 m in some reaches (Warner, 1984b). Nepean gorge changes were clarified by Bertazzo (1982), who noted depth increases of up to 5 m, and this in gravels. Almost half the Warragamba catchment is in metamorphics and granites, thus providing this coarser bedload to the Nepean below the junction. The impacts of dams and regime changes on vegetation zonation in the gorges have been studied by Abood (1983). She found that eucalyptus species do not survive in the zone affected by floods up to about the 1 in 20 year frequency. Thus flood attenuation by dams was marked by younger trees at lower levels, while increased runoff has caused a retreat back to higher elevations.

The initial work in this area was on flood strategy planning (Gutteridge, Haskins and Davey, 1980) following release of federal funds, whilst the impacts of individual floods has provided more information (Riley, 1978; NSW Department of Public Works, 1978). Conversion of flood-stage data at Windsor was possible by comparing overlapped data from 1908 when the gauge at Penrith was set up. This has allowed some crude analysis of changing flood magnitudes. For the whole period 1860-1978 (n + 1 = 120 years), $Q_{2.33}$ was just less than 2600 $m^3 s^{-1}$ (figure 2.3a) and $Q_{1.58}$ about 900 $m^3 s^{-1}$. Changing relations between stage and discharge can only be included for the period of gauging, when corrections have been made. High stages in the late nineteenth century may have been associated with lower discharges if they were based on a much-reduced railway bridge cross-section area in 1863.

Table 2.3 shows that in the later part of the nineteenth century, channel-forming discharges were about four times higher than for the subsequent drought-dominated regime (DDR; 1901-48). In the latest FDR they were nearly doubled,

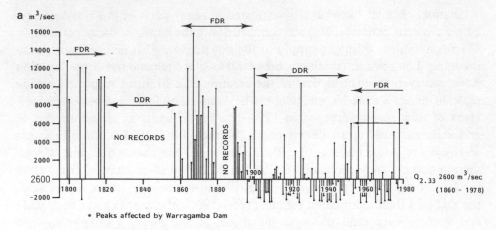

Figure 2.3(a) Annual peak discharges at Penrith above and below $Q_{2.33}$

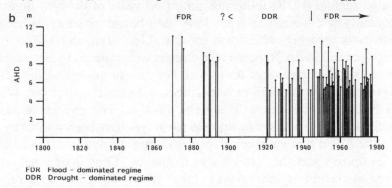

FDR   Flood – dominated regime
DDR   Drought – dominated regime

Figure 2.3(b) Stage heights for floods 1921–1978 plus some earlier floods at Bellingen Town
Source: Cameron McNamara (1980)

prior to attenuation effected by the Warragamba Dam. Very few floods are assumed to have occurred between 1820 and 1863, although estimates of 9700 (1857), 9300 (1860) and 4700 $m^3 s^{-1}$ (1861) exist. These may be part of the following FDR, but in the absence of other data, 1820–1863 is assumed to be a DDR. Earlier, between 1799 and 1819, estimates based on stage are available for 8 of 21 years, and seven of these are for floods greater than 10 000 $m^3 s^{-1}$, indicating high-magnitude events in this earlier period.

From the 1900 survey, it is evident that the channel was wide and shallow, somewhat different from the single bridged cross-section available in 1863. Between 1901 and the 1949 air photography, there was considerable reduction in width, in the form of in-channel, below-bankfull benches (Warner, 1984b). As Wolman and Gerson (1978) showed, repetition of big floods, or what Pickup

Table 2.3 Variations in specific flood magnitudes ($m^3 s^{-1}$) at Penrith for the period 1864–1978 (figure 2.3a)

	1864–1900 *FDR all years*[a]	1864–1900 *FDR available record*	1901–1948 *DDR*	1949–1959[b] *FDR*	1949–1978[c]
$Q_{1.58}$	2400	6500	700	1200	1000
$Q_{2.33}$	6000	9500	1400	3400	2500
Q_5	10400	12400	3200	8600	6600

FDR Flood-dominated regime.
DDR Drought-dominated regime.
[a]gaps assumed to be lower than lowest annual flood.
[b]pre-Warragamba Dam.
[c]pre- and post-dam.

(1976a) has called near-catastrophic events, allows an erosional trend to continue. In the FDR, little recovery is evident even in what is a humid environment. This has been shown in recent surveys where the impacts of the dam and a tributary delta at the junction with Glenbrook Creek (formed in 1943) have encouraged bed erosion (Warner, 1984b). Thus an FDR is unstable, with bank erosion predominating, especially when sediment inputs from the catchment are reduced. It is possible to speculate that the period 1799–1820 was one of channel enlargement, as was that from 1864–1900 when there is more direct evidence of change. The present FDR has also been associated with man-induced changes, mainly caused by dams and sand and gravel extraction. Again it is necessary to speculate that recovery predominated in the first DDR, while in the later DDR (1901–1948), there is evidence of substantial decrease in channel width, but not much on depths. It should be pointed out that the alluvial channel between Penrith and the Nepean gorge is large and that overbank conditions would not occur very often, although some back-up of water would occur in tributaries. This means that most of the power of floodwater in the last 100 years has been confined to the channel with little loss to overbank flow, as might be the case where the channel capacity is limited to floods of $Q_{1.58}$ and $Q_{2.33}$. Perhaps this is a major reason for so much modification. In-channel benches marking DDR recovery (Woodyer, 1968) are progressively removed in a subsequent FDR. Future work on this reach will involve complete analysis and resurvey of all old surveys, together with investigation of bank conditions (which are currently being modified by bank-protection works).

Temporal changes have also been studied in the Bellinger Valley (figure 2.3b) (Warner, 1985b; Warner and Paterson, 1985). Mean annual floods have doubled since 1949 but the downstream channel has not yet adjusted to the new discharges in some parts (table 2.1). Elsewhere it has over-adjusted and the present bankfull capacity may be $> Q_{10}$. These changes are modern, as comparisons with air photographs from the 1940s and later reveal large-scale bank erosion and channel shifts. In the Manning, channels have not adjusted and are relatively small in capacity (Maroulis, 1985). However, high flood overbank activities have involved alluvial stripping, thought to be cyclic by Nanson (1985). Other overbank adjustments are high-level benches recorded in the Macleay (Abrahams and Cull, 1979). Overbank stripping seems to indicate other forms of morphological adjustment in erratic regimes.

Temporal changes in regime can be demonstrated from discharge records. The fact that adjustments may be rapid or slow, in-channel or overbank would seem to offer some explanation for the lack of conformity between many Australian rivers. It certainly reinforces the evidence for widespread channel instability.

INTERACTION OF TEMPORAL VARIATIONS AND SPATIAL PATTERNS

Temporal variation in the magnitude of channel-forming discharge is uniform neither in time nor in space. There seem to have been more pronounced flood-dominated regimes in the past, and rainfall increases in the present regime have varied, being lower on the coast and highest to the west of Sydney (Cornish, 1977). There is also a natural tendency, because rainfall impacts are not uniform over large areas, for discharge to increase less rapidly than basin area (Wolman and Gerson, 1978). In their figure 1b, exponents of a power-law regression of discharge (Q) on catchment area (A) were only 0.5 for ephemeral Californian streams, although a high of 0.98 for others. At flood discharge levels in the Bellinger, the coefficients are about 0.85 (Warner, 1985b). This may vary regionally, depending on lower catchment runoff contributions and 'spottier' rainfall. In coastal NSW, high precipitation generally helps maintain high coefficients, while inland, where rivers pass through more arid environments, discharges eventually decrease with increasing area (figure 2.4).

Thus there are spatial variations in mean annual flood, as well as in bankfull capacities. Responses of channel capacities to temporal changes have only been studied systematically in a few cases (Pickup, 1974; Maroulis, 1985; Warner, 1985b). Much depends on the channel zone, the additional or reduced stream power operating within the channel boundary, and the elements there resisting change. By definition, overbank flows cannot exert much additional erosive impact on the channel, except perhaps where there is wholesale removal of flanking vegetation and bank destruction. They can, however, change the channel shape by increasing the rate of floodplain aggradation relative to the channel bed.

Pickup (1974) was mainly concerned with small incised unstable channels on the Cumberland Plain, but found evidence of relative stability downstream,

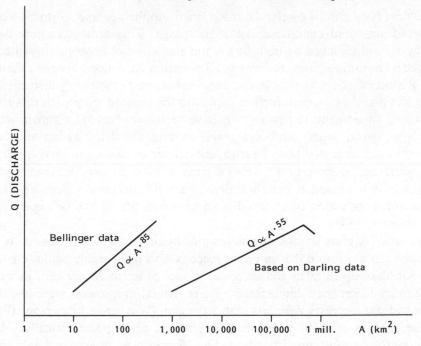

Figure 2.4 Discharge-area relations for coastal and inland systems

and sedimentation in sediment sink zones. In the Manning, Maroulis (1985) discovered little change in pre-FDR capacities. Overbank modifications have already been referred to above (Nanson, 1985). Detailed work at seven sites in the Bellinger indicates that in the upper part of the valley, where floodplains are limited and bedload coarse, the channel flood capacity is less than the contemporary $Q_{2.33}$ (table 2.1). These are in source, armoured and transition zones which are complicated by tributary inputs and undercut source slopes. Towards the middle reaches the flood capacity exceeds $Q_{2.33}$. This has been effected by channel enlargement, mainly by bank-erosion, in the lower transition and upper mobile zones. Then, approaching the sediment sink zone, flood capacities again fall below the mean annual flood level (Warner, 1985b). These variations may indicate under- and over-adjustment to the new regime, part of which can be confirmed when assessing channel changes from air photographs.

Above the Warragamba junction, the Nepean is a sand-bed river which alternates between sandstone gorges (yielding little sediment) and alluvial reaches set in shales (Warner, 1983). Moderate, steep and flat gradients have been modified by weirs which disrupt the movement of sand in what is a long mobile zone. Below the junction is another gorge with coarse load added from the granites and metamorphics of the upper Warragamba catchment. These bedrock sources have now been cut off by the dam, but once supplied coarse sediment which imposed armoured conditions below the gorge. This armour is now being disrupted and removed by high flows, and starvation of appropriate sediment prevents the armour from re-forming. Transition conditions between Penrith and Richmond above the backwater zone have been considerably disrupted by sand and gravel extraction, further depleting the bedload supply. In this river, therefore, adjustments to new regimes have been complicated by human action involving dams, weirs, sand and gravel mining, flood mitigation and bank protection structures. Above Penrith, these have combined to increase depth and width except close to the weir (Warner 1984b). Below Richmond, while widths have increased at bankfull, depths are still decreasing and the effects of sediment starvation transmitted from upstream are still to be experienced (McNamara, 1985).

In a study of bank erosion downstream of Bellingen, which is essentially the sink zone, it was found that in upper reaches with more sandy banks, changes in position of up to 60 m and increases in size of up to 28 per cent in width were much larger than downstream. There, lateral movements were less than 30 m and size increases were less than 5 per cent (Warner and Paterson, 1985). These changes over 40 years were determined photogrammetrically. More importantly, bankfull capacity indicated by 35 cross sections averaged only about 50 per cent of present $Q_{2.33}$. This suggests that in the backwater zone, because of wide, low-lying floodplains, large flood basins for storage, very low gradients and the highly cohesive and vegetated banks, there is very slow adjustment to increased discharges. Consequently, the frequency of flooding has increased, a fact well recognized by residents and flood mitigation engineers. The latter have in part reversed this trend by restricting tributary backup flows with flood gates and by raising levees. The fact that low floods are now kept in the channel has increased available power, leading to increased bed scour and bank erosion (Cameron McNamara, 1980).

A similar reduction in channel capacity in the lower parts of small Illawarra streams has been studied by Nanson and Young (1981a,b). They attributed the reduced capacity to a spatial change in the alluviation process, where the dominant role was played by overbank sedimentation with little if any lateral accretion.

The junction between mobile and backwater zones is in reality fairly sharp with a marked loss in gradient. This was imposed on a pre-existing long profile by the backwater curve of the post-Pleistocene marine transgression about 6000 yrs BP. Systems yielding high sediment supply have built large deltas landward of coastal bars, while the Sydney rivers with low sediment yields like Port Hacking, Georges River, Parramatta River and the Hawkesbury, all have ria estuaries. These have long tidal backwater zones, and above these, because they are sand-bed rivers, long sand or mobile zones.

The downstream loss of power (table 2.1) and the decrease in median diameter material (D_{50}) moved by $Q_{2.33}$ (table 2.2) on the Bellinger reflect changing conditions along a profile which has not been modified by human action. On the basis of these limited observations and other published evidence, a summary can be made of the elements of typical profiles and their characteristic adjustments to temporal changes of regime:

Zone 1 Source: Gorges and undercut slopes contribute directly to the main channel, other additions come indirectly through tributaries. Catchment slopes now yield less sediment with land use recovery and conservation. Even steep bedrock slopes add only limited amounts (the Nepean Gorge is thought to be at least 20 million years old (Bishop et al., 1982).

Zone 2 Armoured: These zones have been found in many valleys (Erskine et al., 1985), but tend to be interrupted by further limited source reaches in incised valleys. Downstream they tend to merge with longer transition zones. These are slow to react to temporal changes in discharge because gravel movement thresholds are high and adjustment (figures 2.5a and 2.5b), other than by bank erosion, can only occur when the armour layers are disturbed. This is more frequent in flood-dominated regimes.

Zone 3 Transition: These zones are longer than in the tropics (Pickup, 1986) but the finer parts of a bimodal load are moved much more frequently (figures 2.5a and 2.5b). Consequently adjustment to changing discharge can occur more readily. The erosion of sandy banks following the breaching of bank vegetation is such that flood capacities may far exceed $Q_{2.33}$.

Zone 4 Sand or Mobile: Where the bedload is fine gravel and/or sand, the bed is mobile and may be modified by most flows (figures 2.5a and 2.5b). Sand-bed rivers have very long mobile zones compared with mixed-load streams. Thus with bank erosion, adjustments may be rapid because of efficient sorting.

Zone 5 Backwater: The great reduction in slope in this zone markedly reduces stream power. Bankfull velocities in the channel become smaller (figures 2.2a and 2.2b). Finer sediments increase cohesion of banks and, as a consequence, adjustment is very slow. Therefore much of the additional discharge is overbank, thereby increasing the frequency and amount of vertical sedimentation. In larger rivers however, there may still be some lateral movement (Nanson and Young, 1981a; 1981b).

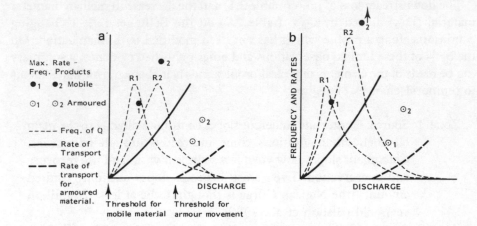

Figure 2.5(a) Hypothetical relations between frequency of flooding and transport rates of both fine and armoured material for DDR (1) and FDR (2)

Based on Wolman and Miller (1960) and Baker (1977)

Figure 2.5(b) Similar relations for increases in both magnitude and frequency in FDR. Dots in both a and b represent maximum rate-frequency products in mobile zones (full circles) and in armoured zones (open circles)

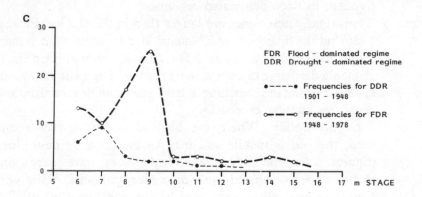

Figure 2.5(c) Flood frequencies at Windsor for DDR and FDR illustrating increases in both magnitude and frequency (in floods over 6 m)

Based on Riley (1981). NB increases in range 8–10 m.

A flood-dominated regime not only imposes higher magnitude floods, but also a greater frequency of flooding. The impact of this on work done (i.e. sediment transport) is shown hypothetically in figure 2.5b. Increases in stage magnitudes and frequences are shown for standardized periods at Windsor in figure 2.5c.

EVIDENCE OF STABILITY AND CHANGE IN AUSTRALIAN RIVERS

In this section it is possible to review more broadly the evidence for stability and change, to consider the problems associated with both available historical data and the complexities imposed by man-induced changes (Warner, 1976; 1984a; 1984c; 1985a), and to evaluate the difficulties in trying to apportion responsibility for changes between human action and natural regime fluctuations. In discussing both spatial and temporal impacts and their interactions, several examples have already been cited. These and other changes can now be summarized, together with evidence of stable conditions.

In the last section, it was shown that areas least prone to change were in the upper reaches, involving source and armoured zones, and in lower backwater zones, where any additional discharge power can be dispersed in overbank flows on wide floodplains, especially if banks are cohesive and protected by vegetation. These then are areas of potential stability in the short term showing least reaction to changing regimes. The greatest changes undoubtedly occur in those reaches where beds and banks are more easily mobilized, and where thresholds of resistance are lower. These coincide with limited floodplain width (little loss of power overbank), where gradients are relatively steep, bed and bank materials are finer and less cohesive, and where vegetation can be disrupted. This is why the Nepean above Penrith reacts so readily. Because most flows pass through the channel, width and depth respond readily to changing flow conditions. Slope cannot change because of the presence of a concrete weir and a 16 km-long weir pond, except temporarily in high flows when it increases.

Woodyer (1968), discussing bankfull frequencies in NSW, used mainly stable sites. His upper alluvial bench was regarded as an incipient floodplain with surcharging frequencies ranging from $Q_{1.24}$ to $Q_{2.69}$. Many of his sites were in backwater zones of the Darling, whilst others were in armoured or source zones of head-water reaches. When a similar kind of exercise was repeated for north and central coast areas, the level of stability was not so apparent (Warner et al., 1975). However, channel stability was also identified in Nanson and Young's work (1981a; 1981b), where there was no evidence of bedload away from the present channel floor in broad floodplains of small south coast rivers. In-channel stability is also implied for the Clyde and Manning in Nanson's (1985) ideas on cyclic alluvial stripping. It seems probable that coarse bed material, fine bank material, resistant bank vegetation, and the presence of parallel chutes all help to stabilize the valley alluvium, except in very extreme events.

It would appear from these studies that the most important factor determining the stability or otherwise of a channel is its location in the zones of the long profile. Sites which by definition (Pickup, 1986) are never in equilibrium (source and sink zones) are relatively stable in the intermediate time frame, because although change is progressive, it is slow. Of the equilibrium zones, where given a stable regime, there is a gentle fluctuation about some mean condition, only the armoured zone is slow to adjust to new regimes. Elsewhere, response in the transition and mobile zones is fairly rapid (Pickup, 1986).

Set against these initial generalizations, which need more rigorous testing, are problems involving data sources and the complexities imposed by human action. Some discussion of these concludes this section.

Historical data include old maps, surveys, descriptions and air photographs. Maps and descriptions are less reliable than surveys and air photographs. However, the timing of these is both infrequent and haphazard relative to specific events. Therefore it is necessary to find what is available, check its reliability and use with caution. In near-metropolitan areas useful data have been found, although archival cataloguing could be improved. They have been located more by accident while much has been lost or is earmarked for destruction. Flow data, particularly derived from stage information elsewhere, must be in doubt, especially in cases quoted for Windsor stages, which are affected by backwater effects of the Colo, tides, and some probable changes in channel configuration. The need to establish the 1 in 100 year floodplain for planning purposes has necessitated extrapolation. In more recent times, it has been NSW Department of Public Works' policy to survey tidal channel cross sections at regular distances along the channel. Resurvey using concrete bench-marks can then establish changes in detail (McNamara, 1985).

The roles of catchment land-use change and deliberate channel modification complicate considerations of the effects of regime changes. The impacts of human activities have been reviewed elsewhere (Warner, 1984a; 1984c). Those associated with land-use are harder to establish than direct impacts on channels, because they are of variable areal intensity. Urbanization and deforestation by clear felling involve greater potential for change (Warner, 1976; Olive and Rieger, 1985). Sheet erosion, rilling and gullying undoubtedly occurred in earlier stages of farming, when there were droughts and overgrazing which depleted vegetation. Such land-based erosion does not imply high sediment delivery ratios, and material reaching the channel probably helped in recovery during the drought-dominated regime in the first half of the twentieth century. Pickup (1976a) showed how land recovery had occurred, in a series of maps. From the 1950s, land and soil conservation has increased with better farming, aerial top-dressing, eradication of rabbits and noxious weeds, and the use of exotic grasses. These coincided with the regime change. Thus additional runoff has led to channel erosion, rather than to catchment degradation.

More formal work addressing the problem of relative impacts of man-induced and natural changes in a varying regime system needs to be attempted. Specific studies like that of Petts and Lewin (1979) are required, where two valleys (one of which was dammed in this case) are compared. Originally, in the Nepean it was thought that the impacts of dams could be assessed, but this was confused not only by the regime change, which produced more runoff than before the dam was there, but also by the removal of sand and gravel from the reach below, where scour had occurred. A channel is hardly likely to get smaller when it is being dredged and when more sediment-deficient water is passing through it. Modification also occurs initially in sandstone gorges below the dams in most cases. Thus scour or erosion cannot occur as readily as in an alluvial valley. Further complications were introduced by weirs which acted as sediment traps below the dams. Scour and increased sediment-free runoff caused erosion, the products of which were then caught in the weirs. These changes together with bigger floods prompted the need for channel-improvement works, which has meant the removal of soil and sand, and a complete modification of the channel morphology (Gutteridge, Haskins and Davey, 1980).

The large Warragamba Dam was completed a decade after the recent FDR began. Its impacts on sediment movement and channel modification have been marked above Penrith Weir (Warner 1983; 1984b). Below Penrith in the 22 km reach to North Richmond, some $40 \times 10^6 \, \text{m}^3$ of sand and gravel have been removed from the channel (mainly large bar systems) and the floodplain. This, together with the FDR, has not allowed channel recovery. Although bank erosion has been a problem downstream of Richmond (Gutteridge, Haskins and Davey, 1980; McNamara, 1985), there has been no increase in bed capacity. In fact there has been net aggradation, indicating that below-dam sources (the Grose River, a tributary) and bank erosion are still providing excess material which is not all passing through the sand zone.

Human impacts have been less severe in the Bellinger but there is no way to compare natural and human-induced changes, most of which involved farming and forestry. The Macdonald and Colo, both left-bank tributaries of the Hawkesbury, are sand-bed streams which have not been greatly modified by farming activities. However, gauging records are shorter, and channel changes are similar to those in the Hawkesbury (increased width and reduced depth). Even though banks are fairly cohesive, they tend to be undercut in basal sands. A great deal of sand has been mobilized in this way, leading to channel-floor aggradation (Erskine and Melville, 1983). There is now some suggestion that this extra sand is slowly moving into the unchanged Hawkesbury (Erskine, personal communication). Dury (1970) found no changes in the 100 years following a naval survey in 1870. These valleys however cannot be compared directly with the dam-affected Hawkesbury-Nepean because there are no shale reaches in these sandstone valleys. Most of the changes in the Nepean are in the alluvium above the shales. Perhaps someone will eventually find a data base to enable a systematic study of the relative impacts of man-induced and natural changes. In the meantime, Erskine and Bell (1982) are in no doubt that the secular climatic change has had more impact than human influence. Undoubtedly the impact of changing regime is apparent in most channels able to adjust. Human impacts are more localized (Gregory, 1977) and probably only involve significant changes of discharge where dams are involved. Erskine (1984) for example found that the floods below Glendawn Dam are so attenuated that the channel has in fact become armoured in the lower power of the new regime.

CONCLUSIONS

In this chapter some attempt has been made to analyse spatial variations in channels and channel adjustments as they relate to the classifications of Schumm (three zones) and Pickup (five zones). Channel reaches may be classified into five zones based on bedload size and frequency of movement, thereby indicating potential for adjustment to new regimes. These are: source (gorge), armoured, transition, sand (mobile) and backwater zones. Their sequence and lengths may vary depending on geology, and some may be absent. Such a classification offers a spatial framework in which to assess the impacts of temporal regime change. In south-eastern Australia, these alternate between flood- and drought-dominated periods over time-spans of several decades. The former are characterized by frequent flooding of high magnitude, where mean annual floods have been shown to increase by a factor of 2 to 7. Such more frequent flows impose great stresses on channels, particularly on the banks, and offer little time for the channel to recover between floods. The latter are associated with fewer and lower magnitude floods, when, given the necessary sediment supply, there is time for the channel to recover. In-channel benches certainly seem to be one form of adjustment which needs further investigation (Woodyer, 1968).

However, because of the difference in channel morphologies in the five zones, responses to changed regimes or human impacts will vary. There is little change in gorge zones and change is only effected with high-magnitude events in armoured reaches. The transition and mobile zones react more rapidly to regime change, particularly those involving increased discharges, while the backwater zones, because of low gradients, low velocities, cohesive banks and large overbank storage areas, react much more slowly. Thus source, near-source and sink zones are more stable on an intermediate time-scale, but in the long-term, they are associated respectively with progressive degradation and aggradation.

Suggested reactions have in part been confirmed using specific examples, but there are problems with early data sources in terms of quality, frequency and relevance to regime channels. Natural variations are complicated by man-induced changes.

Many more studies need to be completed to confirm some of the concepts discussed in this chapter. Ideas on the spatial aspects of the frequency and nature of bankfull conditions need to be clarified. Some of these have received attention (Woodyer, 1968; Pickup and Warner, 1976; Pickup, 1986) but as yet there is not enough conclusive evidence. In such a variable set of regimes, where even year-to-year conditions are very irregular, it is possible to conclude that adjusted river channels have seldom existed. Thus the channel that exists today is merely some inherited condition plus or minus the integrated effects of the most recent set of floods – an idea suggested in the model of Pickup and Rieger (1979).

ACKNOWLEDGEMENTS

Many of the ideas expressed in this paper have benefited from discussions with G. Pickup, S. Riley and W. Erskine. They cannot be blamed for what appears here. The author appreciates the help of almost a generation of students from the University of Sydney who have endured projects in the Georges, Nepean and Bellinger Rivers.

REFERENCES

Abood, M. 1983: *The Geomorphic Implications of Vegetation Zonation in the Sandstone Gorges of the Upper Nepean River System*. Unpublished BSc thesis, University of Sydney.

Abrahams, A. D. and Cull, R. F. 1979: The formation of alluvial landforms along New South Wales coastal streams. *Search*, 10, 187–8.

Andrews, E. D. 1980: Effective and bankfull discharges of streams in the Yampa River basin, Colorado and Wyoming. *Journal of Hydrology*, 46, 311–30.

Baker, V. R. 1977: Stream-channel response to floods, with examples from central Texas. *Geological Society of America Bulletin*, 88, 1057–71.

Bell, F. C. and Erskine, W. D. 1981: Effects of recent increases in rainfall on floods and runoff in the upper Hunter Valley. *Search*, 12, 82–3.

Bertazzo, K. 1982: *An Investigation of Channel Changes in the Nepean River above Penrith, in Response to Change in Regime since 1900*. Unpublished BSc thesis, University of Sydney.

Bishop, P., Hunt, P. and Schmidt, P. W. 1982: Limits to the age of the Lapstone Monocline, N.S.W. - a palaeomagnetic study. *Geological Society of Australia Journal*, 29, 319–26.

Bull, W. D. 1979: Threshold of critical power in streams. *Geological Society of American Bulletin*, 90, 453–64.

Cameron McNamara 1980: *Bellinger Valley, N.S.W. Rivers Floodplain Management Studies*. Consultants' Report for NSW Department of Public Works.

Chorley, R. J., Schumm, S. A. and Sugden, D. E. 1984: *Geomorphology*. London: Methuen.

Cornish, P. M. 1977: Changes in seasonal and annual rainfall in New South Wales. *Search*, 8, 38–40.

Dury, G. H. 1969: Hydraulic geometry. In R. J. Chorley (ed.), *Water, Earth and Man*. London: Methuen, 319–30.

Dury, G. H. 1970: A re-survey of part of the Hawkesbury River, N.S.W. after one hundred years. *Australian Geographical Studies*, 8, 121–32.

Erskine, W. D. 1984: *Downstream impacts of Glenbawn Dam on the Upper Hunter River, N.S.W.*. Unpublished paper presented at the 19th Institute of Australian Geographers Conference, Sydney.

Erskine, W. D. and Bell, F. C. 1982: Rainfall, floods and river channel changes in the upper Hunter. *Australian Geographical Studies*, 20, 183–96.

Erskine, W. D. and Melville, M. D. 1983: Impact of the 1978 flood on the channel and floodplain of the lower Macdonald River, N.S.W. *Australian Geographer*, 15, 284–92.

Erskine, W. D., Geary, P. M. and Outhet, D. N. 1985: Potential impacts of sand and gravel extraction on the Hunter River, New South Wales. *Australian Geographical Studies*, 23, 71–86.

Graf, W. L. 1983: Flood-related channel change in an arid-region river. *Earth Surface Processes and Landforms*, 8, 125–39.

Gregory, K. J. 1977: Channel and network metamorphosis in northern New South Wales. In K. J. Gregory (ed.), *River Channel Changes*. Chichester: Wiley, 389–410.

Gutteridge, Haskins and Davey 1980: *Hawkesbury, N.S.W. Coastal Rivers: Flood Plain Management Studies*. Consultants' Report for NSW Department of Public Works.

Harvey, A. M. 1984: Geomorphological response to an extreme flood: a case from southeast Spain. *Earth Surface Processes and Landforms*, 9, 267–79.

Henry, H. M. 1977: Catastrophic channel changes in the Macdonald Valley, New South Wales. *Journal of the Royal Society of N.S.W.*, 11, 1–16.

Hickin, E. J. 1983: River channel changes: retrospect and prospect. *Special Publication, International Association of Sedimentologists*, 6, 61–83.

Leopold, L. B., Wolman, M. G. and Miller, J. P. 1964: *Fluvial Processes in Geomorphology*. San Francisco: Freeman.

Mackin, J. H. 1948: Concept of the graded river. *Geological Society of America Bulletin*, 59, 463–511.

Maroulis, J. C. 1985: *Downstream Variations in Channel Morphology in the Manning River Valley, New South Wales*. Unpublished BSc thesis, University of Sydney.

McNamara, R. L. 1985: *Channel Changes in the Upper Hawkesbury River, New South Wales, since 1890*. Unpublished BA thesis, University of Sydney.

Milne, A. K. 1971: Underfit analysis of the lower Macleay River basin: problems of the application of a model. *Geographical Education*, 1(3), 329–52.

Nanson, G. C. 1985: Cycles of floodplain stripping and reconstruction along coastal rivers of New South Wales. *Geological Society of Australia Abstracts*, 13, 17–19.

Nanson, G. C. and Young, R. W. 1981a: Downstream reduction of rural channel size with contributing urban effects in small coastal streams of southeastern Australia. *Journal of Hydrology*, 52, 239-55.

Nanson, G. C. and Young, R. W. 1981b: Overbank deposition and floodplain formation on small coastal streams of New South Wales. *Zeitschrift für Geomorphologie*, 25, 332-47.

NSW Department of Public Works 1978: *Hawkesbury River March 1978 Flood Report*. Government Printer.

Olive, L. J. and Rieger, W. A. 1985: Variation in suspended sediment concentration during storms in five small catchments in southeast New South Wales. *Australian Geographical Studies*, 23, 38-51.

Petts, G. E. and Lewin, J. 1979: Physical effects of reservoirs on river systems. In G. E. Hollis (ed.), *Man's Impact on the Hydrological Cycle of the United Kingdom*. Norwich: Geo Abstracts, 79-91.

Pickup, G. 1974: *Channel Adjustment to Changed Hydrologic Regime in the Cumberland Basin, NSW*. Unpublished PhD thesis, University of Sydney.

Pickup, G. 1976a: Geomorphic effects of changes in runoff, Cumberland Basin, NSW. *Australian Geographer*, 13, 188-93.

Pickup, G. 1976b: Adjustment of stream channel shape to hydrologic regime. *Journal of Hydrology*, 30, 365-73.

Pickup, G., 1984: Geomorphology of tropical rivers. I. Landforms, hydrology and sedimentation in the Fly and lower Purari, Papua New Guinea. *Catena, Supplement*, 5, 1-17.

Pickup, G. 1986: Fluvial landforms. In D. N. Jeans (ed.), *Australia - a Geography*, 2nd edition. Sydney: University Press, 148-79.

Pickup, G. and Rieger, W. A. 1979: A conceptual model of the relationship between channel characteristics and discharge. *Earth Surface Processes*, 4, 37-42.

Pickup, G. and Warner, R. F. 1976: Effects of hydrologic regime on magnitude and frequency of dominant discharge. *Journal of Hydrology*, 29, 51-75.

Pittock, A. B. 1975: Climatic change and patterns of variation in Australian rainfall. *Search*, 6, 498-504.

Richards, K. 1982: *Rivers: Form and Process in Alluvial Channels*. London: Methuen.

Riley, S. J. 1978: The March 1978 flood on the Hawkesbury and Nepean Rivers between Penrith and Pitt Town. *Geography Bulletin*, 10, 42-65.

Riley, S. J. 1980: Aspects of the flood record at Windsor. In *Proceedings, 16th Institute of Australian Geographers Conference*, Newcastle, 325-40.

Riley, S. J. 1981: The relative influence of dams and secular climatic change on downstream flooding, Australia. *Water Resources Bulletin*, 17, 361-6.

Scholer, H. A. 1974: Geomorphology of New South Wales rivers. *Water Research Laboratory Report, University of NSW*, 139.

Schumm, S. A. 1977: *The Fluvial System*. New York: Wiley.

Warner, R. F. 1968: *Some Aspects of the Geomorphological Evolution of the Bellinger Valleys, N.S.W.* Unpublished PhD thesis, University of New England.

Warner, R. F. 1976: Water and Man in the city: modifications to hydrologic and geomorphic systems. *Geography Bulletin*, 8, 74–89.

Warner, R. F. 1983: Channel changes in the sandstone and shale reaches of the Nepean River, New South Wales. In R. W. Young and G. C. Nanson (eds), *Aspects of Australian Sandstone Landscapes*. Australia and New Zealand Geomorphology Group, Special Publication, No. 1, 106–19.

Warner, R. F. 1984a: Man's impacts on Australian drainage systems. *Australian Geographer*, 16, 113–41.

Warner, R. F. 1984b: *Impacts of dams, weirs, dredging and climatic changes: an example from the Nepean River, NSW, Australia*. Unpublished paper presented at 25th International Geographical Union Congress, Paris.

Warner, R. F. 1984c: Channel changes in Australian rivers since European settlement. *Engineering Geology Specialist Group Papers*, Series No. 3, 14–21.

Warner, R. F. 1985a: Themes in Australian fluvial geomorphology. In A. F. Pitty (ed.), *Themes in Geomorphology*. London: Croom Helm, 85–101.

Warner, R. F. 1985b: Downstream variations in channel morphology in the Bellinger Valley, New South Wales. *Geological Society of Australia Abstracts*, 13, 22–4.

Warner, R. F. 1986: Hydrology. In D. W. Jeans (ed.), *Australia – a Geography*, 2nd edition. Sydney: University Press, 49–79.

Warner, R. F. and Paterson, K. W. 1985: *Bank erosion in the Bellinger Valley, New South Wales, definition and management*. Unpublished paper presented at 20th Conference of the Institute of Australian Geographers, Brisbane.

Warner, R. F. and Pickup, G. 1974: Estuary sand dredging: a case study of an environmental problem. In *Proceedings, International Geographical Union Regional Conference, Palmerston North*, 325–33.

Warner, R. F., McLean, E. J. and Pickup, G. 1977: Changes in an urban water resource, an example from Sydney, Australia. *Earth Surface Processes*, 2, 29–38.

Warner, R. F., Sinclair, D. and Ewing, J. 1975: A comparative study of relations between bedrock meander wavelengths, benchfull discharges and channel perimeter sediments for the Sydney Basin and the northeast of New South Wales. In I. Douglas, J. E. Hobbs and J. J. Pigram (eds), *Geographical Essays in Honour of Gilbert J. Butland*. Armidale: University of New England, 159–295.

Wolman, M. G. and Gerson, R. 1978: Relative scales of time and effectiveness of climate in watershed geomorphology. *Earth Surface Processes*, 3, 189–208.

Wolman, M. G. and Miller, J. P. 1960: Magnitude and frequency of forces in geomorphic processes. *Journal of Geology*, 68, 543–74.

Woodyer, K. D. 1968: Bankfull frequency in rivers. *Journal of Hydrology*, 6, 114–42.

3

The Effect of Active Tectonics on Alluvial River Morphology

Daniel I. Gregory and Stanley A. Schumm

INTRODUCTION

Alluvial rivers are sensitive to changes in sediment load, water discharge, and variations of valley-floor slope. Therefore, in addition to the dramatic effects when stream channels and terraces are offset along faults (Wallace, 1967; Stevens, 1974), there are other more subtle effects when deformation of the valley floor is vertical, and slow. This modern on-going deformation is termed *active tectonics* (Wallace, 1986), whereas *neotectonics* refers to deformation that has occurred within the last million years, and it includes active tectonics. Trifonov (1978) differentiates three types of tectonics as follows: neotectonics (Neogene-Quaternary), young tectonic motions (the last few tens of thousands of years; that is, the late Pleistocene and the Holocene), and recent tectonic motions (the last few hundred years).

In spite of the practical significance of understanding active tectonics, only a few investigators have considered its effects on alluvial rivers (Tator, 1958; Schumm, 1977; Adams, 1980; Russ, 1982; Burnett and Schumm, 1983). Usually geologists concentrate on the identification of geologic structures that are assumed to be quiescent (Howard, 1967; Ollier, 1981, p. 180) rather than on the effect of on-going deformation. Nevertheless, DeBlieux (1951; 1962), Tator (1958) and Lattman (1959) indicate that fluvial anomalies, such as local development of meanders or a braided pattern, local widening or narrowing of channels, anomalous ponds, marshes or alluvial fills, variations of levee width or discontinuous levees, and any anomalous curve or turn, are possible indicators of active tectonics.

Active tectonics can take several forms. In the vertical dimension, nick-points and convexities or concavities of the longitudinal profile are formed. Deformation can be along faults (shear, normal, or reverse in a downstream sense) or pairs of faults (horst and graben), which should have the same effect as a monocline, dome, or basin. In addition, the entire valley may be tilted upstream, downstream or laterally. The possibilities are great, but in reality, the primary effect of tectonics will be a local steepening or reduction of gradient or a cross-valley tilting.

In addition to these primary influences, there will be secondary effects as the rivers respond to changed gradient (aggradation or degradation), and tertiary effects as decreased or increased sediment loads influence reaches downstream of the deformed reach and as aggradation or degradation in the deformed reach progress upstream.

EFFECTS OF ACTIVE TECTONICS

The most commonly cited evidence for deformation is the warping of alluvial terraces. The oldest terrace is the most deformed by uplift (convex) or subsidence (concave) and it shows the greatest offset by faulting (Machida, 1960; Zuchiewicz, 1979; 1980). The extent of displacement can be determined by comparison with the longitudinal profile of the present river, or by comparison with a negative exponential function in a downstream direction as suggested by Machida (1960). Rates of uplift can be calculated from the elevation difference between terraces of estimated ages based on carbon-14 dating and soil chronology (Rockwell et al., 1984).

Valley-floor deformation is also indicated by depth to bedrock. Alluvium is thickest over grabens or synclines and thinnest over areas of uplift (Kowalski and Radziokowska, 1968).

When uplift is too rapid to be accommodated by a river there will be disruption of the drainage course and even of the entire drainage network (Sparling, 1967; Twidale, 1971, pp. 133–6; Ollier, 1981). The Murray River on the Riverine Plain near Echuca, Victoria, Australia, is an impressive example of channel modification by tectonic activity (Bowler and Harford, 1966). At this location the Cadell Fault block has diverted the Murray River and converted it from a single channel to an anastomosing system of channels that surrounds the obstruction. An abandoned segment of the Murray River is preserved on the dipslope of the fault block.

The preceding examples provide evidence for past deformation but not necessarily for active tectonics; accurate and repeated river and valley-floor surveys can, however, provide geomorphic evidence of on-going deformation. The most reliable indicators of change are longitudinal profiles of valley floors and streams (Bendefy et al., 1967; Zuchiewicz, 1979). In addition, degradation and aggradation can be evidence of active tectonics, and they are accompanied by changes of channel morphology (depth and width) as the channel incises or aggrades.

Stream patterns are also sensitive indicators of valley-slope change (Schumm et al., 1972; Schumm, 1977). Adams (1980) demonstrated a relation between measured tilt rates and downstream changes of sinuosity (ratio of channel length to valley length) for the Mississippi River between St Louis and Cairo and for the lower Missouri River. In order to maintain a constant gradient a river that is being steepened by downstream tilt will increase its sinuosity, whereas a reduction of valley slope will lead to a reduction of sinuosity (Schumm, 1977).

Unfortunately, it is not possible to be dogmatic about pattern and channel change because different types of river respond differently to active tectonics; therefore, the characteristics of alluvial channels must be reviewed before their response can be predicted. This can best be done by discussing a simple classification of alluvial channels based on the type of sediment load (bed load, mixed load, suspended load) and pattern (figure 3.1).

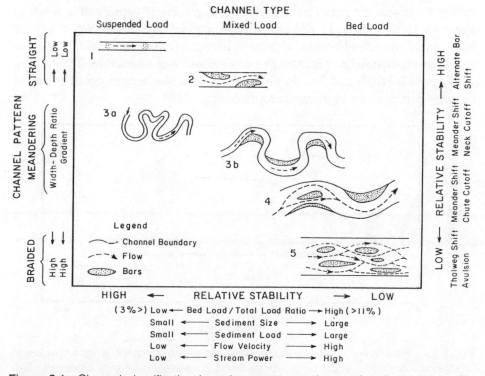

Figure 3.1 Channel classification based on pattern and type of sediment load, with associated variables and relative stability indicated
(from Schumm, 1981)

Five basic channel patterns exist (figure 3.1). These are straight channels either with migrating sand waves (pattern 1) or with a sinuous thalweg and alternate bars (pattern 2). There are two types of meandering channel, a highly sinuous channel of uniform width (pattern 3a) and channels that are wider at bends than in crossings (pattern 3b). The meandering-braided transition (pattern 4) and a typical braided-stream (pattern 5) complete the sequence. The relative stability of these channels in terms of their normal erosional activity and the shape and gradient of the channels are related to relative sediment size, sediment load, velocity of flow and stream power (figure 3.1). It has been possible to develop these patterns experimentally by varying the gradient, sediment load, stream power, and the type of sediment load transported by the channel (Schumm and Khan, 1972).

The range of channels from straight through braided forms a continuum, but experimental work and field studies have indicated that the pattern changes between braided, meandering and straight occur at river-pattern thresholds (figure 3.2). Pattern change takes place at critical ranges of stream power, gradient and sediment load (Schumm and Khan, 1972).

The types of river observed can be placed within the five general categories. However, within the meandering-stream group there is considerable range of sinuosity (1.25 to 3.0). In addition, in the braided-stream category there are bar-braided and island-braided channels. Islands are vegetated bars. There are also multiple-channel patterns termed anastomosing or anastomosed (Schumm, 1977, p. 155; Smith and Smith, 1980). In fact, it has been suggested that 14 channel patterns can be recognized (Schumm, 1981).

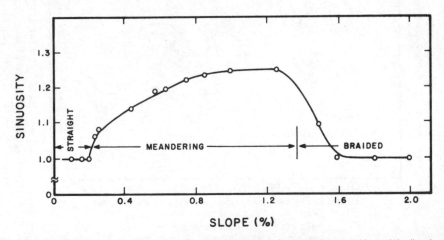

Figure 3.2 Relation between valley (flume) slope and sinuosity (channel length/valley length or valley slope/channel slope) during experiments at constant discharge. Sediment load, stream power, and velocity increase with slope and a similar relation can be developed with these variables
(from Schumm and Khan, 1972)

The experimental studies and field observations confirm that a change of valley-floor slope will cause a change of channel pattern. The change will differ, however, depending on the type of channel (figure 3.1) and depending on the amount and rate of deformation. Slight increases in valley slope will shift river patterns from left to right on figures 3.1 and 3.2, as the river adjusts its gradient by pattern change. With greater changes of valley slope, incision may produce sufficient sediment to cause a change from one type of channel to another with a metamorphosis of a mixed-load channel to a bed-load channel. In addition, significant reductions of slope or greatly increased sediment loads will produce aggradation and very possibly a braided channel.

In addition to the primary valley-floor deformation by active tectonics and the secondary channel response to this deformation, there are third-order effects beyond the area of deformation; for example, deposition upstream from the axis of a dome can progress further upstream by backfilling beyond the area of active deformation. This means that the uplift is acting as a dam, and unless erosion on the steeper downstream side of the uplift produces sufficient sediment to compensate, erosion will occur downstream beyond the limits of deformation. However, it is more likely that reduced load will accelerate erosion on the steeper reach, and when this increased load moves downstream, aggradation will result.

Another aspect of both active tectonics and neotectonics is the appearance of more resistant materials in the channel as the channel degrades. Resistant alluvium or bedrock will confine the channel and retard meander shift and bank erosion. The result should be deformed or compressed meanders upstream and a change of meander character at the contact (Gardner, 1975).

Alluvial channels are sensitive indicators of change, but they also adjust to changes of hydrology and sediment load as well as to active tectonics. Therefore, it may be difficult to determine the cause of channel change when, in fact, man's activities have been changing both discharge and sediment load during historic time. Pattern change alone is not sufficient evidence for active tectonics; rather it is one piece of evidence that must be supported with other morphologic evidence and/or surveys that provide clear evidence of deformation. In many areas the evidence will be circumstantial. Nevertheless, anomalous reaches that are not related to artificial controls or to tributary influences may reasonably be assumed to be the result of active tectonics until proved otherwise.

In some circumstances the evidence is unequivocal. For example, the Shaurn Anticline forms a range of low hills in southeastern Iran. Folding began in late Pliocene, and it still continues (Ambraseys, 1978). In the first or second century AD two canals were cut across the anticline in order to lead water from a canal system on the northeast flank to the more extensive and fertile plains on the south-west. One canal still carries water, but where it crosses the anticline it has cut down about 3.5 m below its original bed. The other canal has been abandoned. The energy of its flow was not sufficient to enable the canal to excavate its bed, and in addition its maintenance may have been neglected. An accurate survey along its alignment shows that at the anticlinal axis, the bed of the canal has risen at an average rate of approximately 1 meter per century (Lees, 1955). In the Tigris and Euphrates valley, canals have also been abandoned. They show reversed gradients, and they have incised where there is active tectonics (Lees, 1955; Adams, 1965; Mirjayer, 1966).

EXPERIMENTAL STUDIES

In an effort to determine the effects of active tectonics on alluvial channels experimental studies were performed by Ouchi (1983; 1985) and Jin (1983) in a large flume (8.5×2.4 m), the centre section of which could be raised or lowered by hydraulic jacks. Figure 3.3 summarizes the results for braided and meandering channels during uplift and downwarping.

The braided channel could not change its sinuosity as a result of uplift, but it incised to form terraces. The sediment produced by the incision caused aggradation downstream, and the reduced gradient upstream of the axis of uplift also caused aggradation (figure 3.3).

During subsidence the channel degraded in the upstream steepened portion of zone B, and it aggraded downstream. Adjustment was much faster during uplift because channel incision is concentrated in a narrow width of valley,

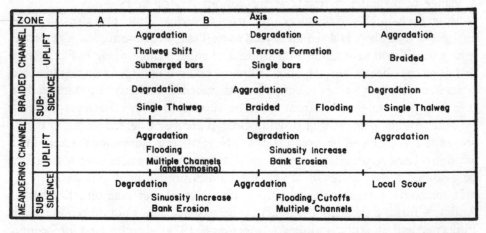

Figure 3.3 Response of experimental channels to uplift and subsidence. Zones B and C are on the flanks of the uplift or subsidence and they are directly affected by deformation. Zone A, upstream of the deformation, and Zone D, downstream, experience third-order effects
(after Ouchi, 1985)

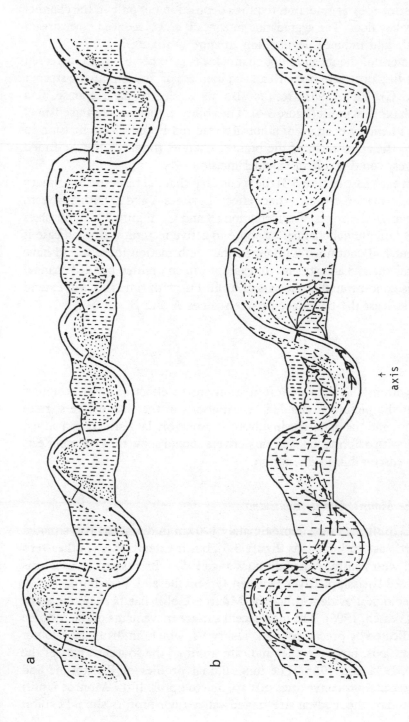

Figure 3.4 Effect of uplift on experimental meandering channel: (a) channel before uplift; (b) channel after uplift. Upstream reach shows evidence of overbank flooding, development of multiple channels and aggradation. Downstream reach shows increase of meander amplitude, wavelength and sinuosity as well as degradation and a cutoff. Flow is from left to right. Stippled pattern represents sand on floodplain. Vertical line pattern represents silt and clay deposits on floodplain (from Jin, 1983)

axis

whereas adjustment by aggradation requires deposition not only in the channel but over the valley floor. The aggradation in zones B and C reduced downstream sediment loads and induced degradation in zone D (figure 3.3).

The adjustment of the meandering channel was as expected, with increased overbank flooding upstream (zone B) and an increase of sinuosity in the steeper reaches (zone C). Jin's (1983) results also show clearly the response of a meandering channel to uplift (figure 3.4). The ability of the meandering channel to alter its gradient by changes of sinuosity resulted in only local incision in comparison to the adjustment of the braided channel (figure 3.3). Continued uplift, however, could result in channel incision.

Note that in each case (figure 3.3) the secondary channel response to primary valley-floor deformation caused tertiary effects in zones A and D both upstream and downstream of the zones of deformation (B and C). Figure 3.3 emphasizes the complexity of alluvial-channel response to active tectonics. In each case if the experiment had continued without further deformation there would have been additional channel adjustment; for example, in an uplifted braided channel degradation is concentrated at the axis of uplift but with time this will extend upstream to at least the boundary between zones A and B.

FIELD STUDIES

Field investigations also provide information on the effect of active tectonics on rivers, but the picture is clouded by variations in the size of rivers, rates of deformation, and the materials involved. Presumably large rivers can adjust and keep pace with deformation, and small rivers should show the greatest effects and be more susceptible to disruption.

Streams of the Monroe Uplift, Louisiana

The Monroe Uplift is a dome approximately 120 km in diameter. It is situated mostly in northeastern Louisiana (figure 3.5), but it extends into southeastern Arkansas and west central Mississippi (Wang, 1952). Its eastern extension is crossed by the Mississippi River between Greenville and Vicksburg.

There is geological evidence that the Monroe Uplift has been active since the Tertiary (Veatch, 1906). The most recent surface movements of the Monroe Uplift are indicated by precise geodetic resurveys, which unfortunately do not cross the uplift axis; however, they indicate uplift of the southern part of the area between 1934 and 1966. The longitudinal profiles of Pleistocene and Holocene terraces show convexities that are due to uplift. If the Monroe Uplift is still active today, the modern stream and valley-floor profiles should exhibit

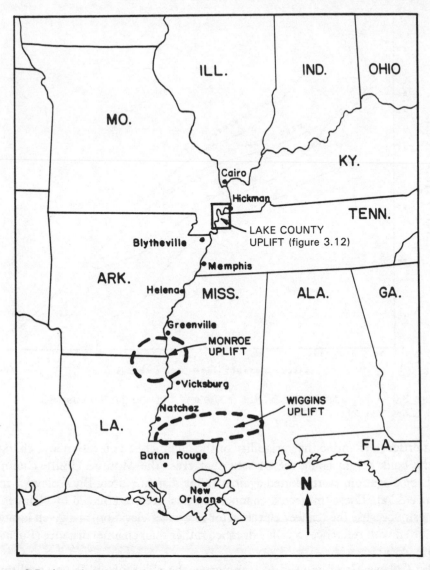

Figure 3.5 Location map of the Lower Mississippi valley showing uplifts which affect the Mississippi River and adjacent stream channels

effects of the uplift similar to those shown by terrace profiles. Several streams (Ouachita River, Bayou Bartholomew, Boeuf River, Big Colewa Creek, Bayou Macon, and Deer Creek) cross the Monroe Uplift in northeastern Louisiana, and they generally parallel the course of the Mississippi River. The valley profiles of these streams show an obvious zone of upward convexity (figure 3.6).

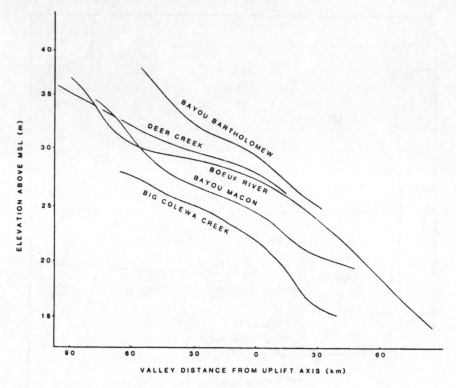

Figure 3.6   Longitudinal valley profiles of streams crossing the Monroe Uplift
(after Burnett and Schumm, 1983)

In order to examine the variability of the channel-bed elevation and changes
in the bank height along the streams that cross the Monroe Uplift, channel-
thalweg elevations were plotted against valley distance along Big Colewa Creek
(figure 3.7a). These 'projected channel profiles' are not affected by changes in
sinuosity because the thalweg elevation (or low-water elevation) at a given location
is plotted with reference to valley distance rather than channel distance (Burnett,
1982).

Big Colewa Creek is used to summarize the effect of uplift on an alluvial
channel. It can be divided into three zones of activity along its valley (figure
3.7b). The lower zone, from the mouth to km 30, has a high average bank height
of about 6 m. The middle zone, from km 30 to 60 shows a clear upstream decrease
in the average bank height from 6 to 2 m. The upper zone, above km 60, has
a constant low average bank height of 2 m. Degradation has occurred in the
lower zone, whereas incision is still in progress in the middle zone, and in the
upper zone adjustment has not yet occurred. Figure 3.7c shows changes in valley
slope and channel thalweg slope with valley distance. The valley slope remains

high from the mouth to km 60 and then it suddenly decreases. The break in slope, at km 60, defines the apparent location of the uplift axis. The channel slope is high from the mouth to km 40 and then, it also suddenly decreases. The fact that the two curves do not coincide suggests that the channel has incised through the axis of uplift.

Sinuosity is approximately 1.2 in the upstream reach of Big Colewa Creek (figure 3.7d) as it approaches the axis of uplift (zone B, figure 3.3). Downstream between km 55 and 40, sinuosity increases to about 1.7 on the steep downvalley side of the uplift (zone C, figure 3.3), and then it gradually decreases to 1.5 at the mouth (zone D, figure 3.3). The sinuosity of other streams decreases markedly as the axis of uplift is approached (Burnett, 1982).

In summary, morphology of the streams and terraces that cross the Monroe Uplift, as well as the limited data from repeat geodetic surveys, indicate that the area is still active tectonically, and the deformation is affecting the streams as previous experimental studies suggest (figures 3.2 and 3.3).

Streams of the Wiggins Uplift, Mississippi

Holdahl and Morrison (1974) summarize evidence from precise relevelling that indicates moderately active uplift of the Wiggins Uplift in southern Mississippi (figure 3.5). Figure 3.8 shows deformation that occurred between 1934 and 1969 along a survey line that crosses the Wiggins Uplift, from Jackson, Mississippi, to New Orleans, Louisiana. The apparent axis of uplift is near McComb, Miss., and the maximum uplift rate is 3.3 mm/year (figure 3.8). The anomalously large value at km 130 is probably caused by localized bench-mark movement not associated with the broad-scale unwarping.

The Pearl River (figure 3.9), Tallahala Creek, and Bogue Homo (figure 3.10), which cross the Wiggins Uplift in central Mississippi, are responding to uplift (Burnett, 1982). The responses include channel entrenchment in the uplifted section, mobilization of bed and bank materials at local nick-points associated with the entrenchment, and increased channel activity and braided-pattern development below the axis of uplift. However, the streams are at different stages of adjustment because the rate of response appears to be related to stream size or stream power (figure 3.11). Being the largest, the Pearl River has entrenched throughout the warp, thereby maintaining a fairly straight projected-channel profile. However, the terraces of the Pearl River show distinct convexities that coincide with vertical surface movement measured by the National Geodetic Survey (figure 3.9). The lower zone of the Pearl River appears to be in an advanced stage of readjustment to the unwarping with new floodplain development taking place (figures 3.9 and 3.11). The smaller streams such as Tallahala Creek and Bogue Homo, on the other hand, have not entrenched

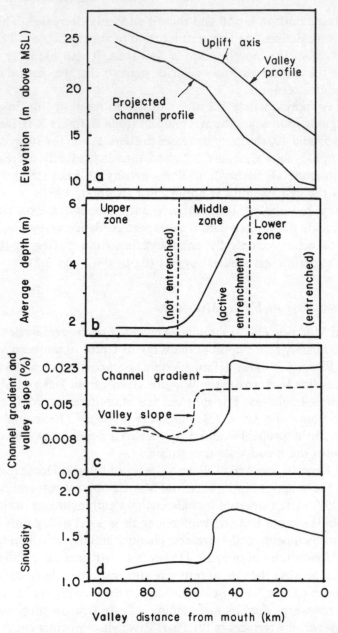

Figure 3.7 Effect of uplift on Big Colewa Creek. (a) Valley and projected-channel longitudinal profiles of Big Colewa Creek on the Monroe uplift. Note the increased gradient of both profiles and the increased depth of the channel, below the axis of the uplift; (b) variation of channel depth. Three reaches show different degrees of response to uplift; (c) variation of channel gradient and slope of the valley floor; (d) variation of sinuosity (after Burnett and Schumm, 1983)

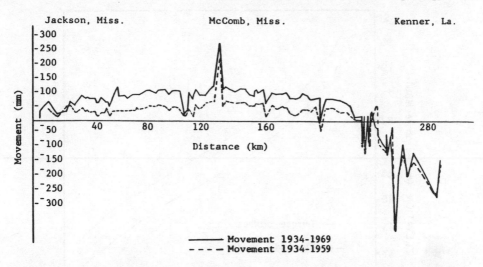

Figure 3.8 Vertical benchmark movement along Jackson, Miss.-New Orleans, La. survey route

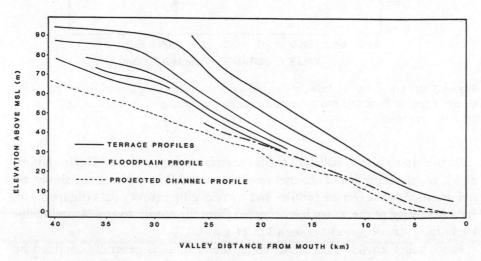

Figure 3.9 Longitudinal profiles of Pearl River valley, terraces, floodplain and projected channel profile. Note that a floodplain exists only below the uplift axis
(from Burnett, 1982)

significantly above the axis, and their upper reaches are dramatically affected by the backtilting, where an anastomosing channel pattern has developed as an initial response (figures 3.10 and 3.11). Subsequent entrenchment will change the anastomosing pattern into a single channel, that is analogous to the upper reach of the Pearl River.

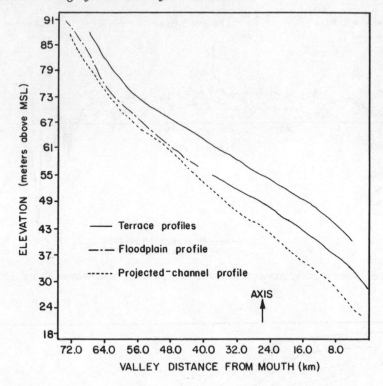

Figure 3.10   Longitudinal profiles of Bogue Homo valley, terraces, floodplain and projected channel profile. Note that the floodplain becomes a terrace in the zone of uplift (from Burnett, 1982)

Bogue Homo is the smallest of the three streams that cross the Wiggins Uplift, and it is representative of channel response to uplift in the area. As shown by deformation of the terrace profiles and by relevelling survey data (figure 3.10), forward tilting of the valley has occurred from the mouth to km 24, and major backtilting has occurred between km 24 and 60.

From valley km 48 to the headwaters, the channel is generally confined by a narrow valley cut into Tertiary sediments, and it has a typical concave up profile. Along the lower 45 km of the valley, however, Bogue Homo is predominantly an alluvial channel, and as based upon channel characteristics, the lower 45 km may be divided into three zones.

The upper zone, between km 32 and 45, is immediately above the uplift axis on the backtilted portion of the valley, and it has a broad floodplain 1.5 to 3 km wide and 2 to 3 m above the low water channel. Numerous interconnecting flood-channel depressions are evident on the floodplain, which are similar to those in the upper zone of Tallahala Creek. Numerous side channels and tree-covered

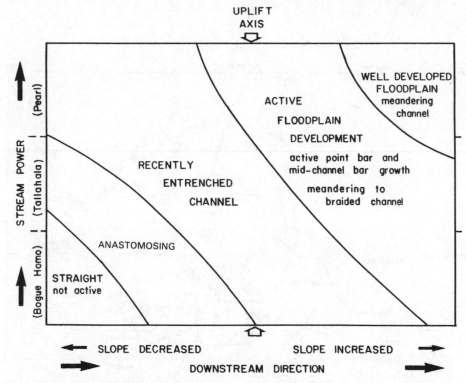

Figure 3.11 Alluvial-river channel characteristics in relation to relative stream power and location relative to the axis of active uplift. Note that as stream power increases the zone of active channel entrenchment moves upstream through the axis of uplift indicating a more complete response to the uplift by larger streams
(from Burnett, 1982)

islands have developed in association with this anastomosing pattern. Apparently reduction of valley gradient has facilitated the development of this anastomosing pattern.

Immediately below the axis (km 25) to valley km 15, a single confined channel has entrenched to between 5 and 6 m below the floodplain surface. This surface now forms a low terrace along this reach, and a lower active floodplain has not yet developed (figure 3.10). Although there has been entrenchment of the meanders into the underlying Tertiary sediments, channel straightening is evident by the high frequency of recent cutoffs. In addition, numerous mid-channel bars have developed causing local braided reaches.

Within the lower 15 km of the Bogue Homo valley the channel is active with lateral migration accompanied by valley widening, recent floodplain development, and active point-bar growth. Also, numerous mid-channel bars and chute cutoffs

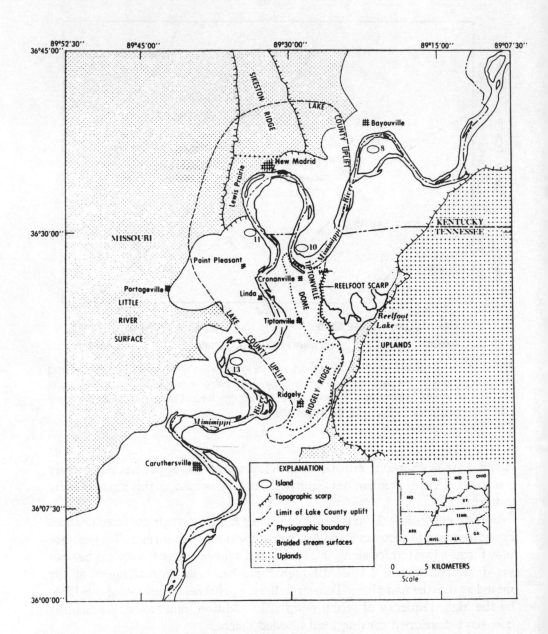

Figure 3.12   Map of New Madrid region showing the Lake County Uplift
(from Russ, 1982)

have developed to form local braided reaches. Bogue Homo appears to be readjusting to recent channel entrenchment and to increased valley slope.

Bogue Homo has responded to uplift, but is smaller than the Pearl and Tallahala Rivers, and should respond more slowly to the valley deformation. This appears to be the case, since channel incision has not progressed beyond the uplift axis, and in the lower zone of Bogue Homo the channel is generally more confined, and an active floodplain is less well developed. Figure 3.11 summarizes the difference in the extent of adjustment of the three Wiggins Uplift channels.

Mississippi River

The Mississippi River crosses both the Monroe Uplift and the Wiggins Uplift between the confluence with the Arkansas River and Baton Rouge, Louisiana, and it crosses the Lake County Uplift south of the Ohio River mouth. As the smaller streams (figure 3.6) are responding, the Mississippi River should also be responding to the deformation caused by active tectonics.

Lake County Uplift   The occurrence of the great 1811–12 earthquakes near New Madrid, Missouri, has created considerable concern about the possibility of a repetition. Therefore, extensive studies have been carried out in this area, and the literature relating to the geophysics and geology of the Mississippi embayment between Memphis and Cairo is abundant (McKeown and Pakiser, 1982).

The area of deformation near New Madrid is referred to as the Lake County Uplift (figure 3.12). The surface of the uplift is as much as 10 m above the general level of the Mississippi River valley, and the deformed area has a maximum length of about 50 km and a maximum width of about 23 km. Its relief is uneven, and the surface is dominated by two elongate bulges.

Russ (1982) cited the following evidence for active deformation of the Lake County Uplift:

1 the structure is significantly higher than the naturally occurring landforms of the modern meander belt (figure 3.13a);
2 the longitudinal profiles of abandoned river channels and natural levees have been significantly warped, some to the extent that the original river-flow direction has been reversed;
3 the modern flood-plain is also warped (figure 3.13b);
4 the Reelfoot scarp vertically offsets abandoned Mississippi River channels, which once flowed across the area.

An examination of figure 3.13 reveals that all of the profiles have a similar shape suggesting that they may be the result of the same events. The profiles

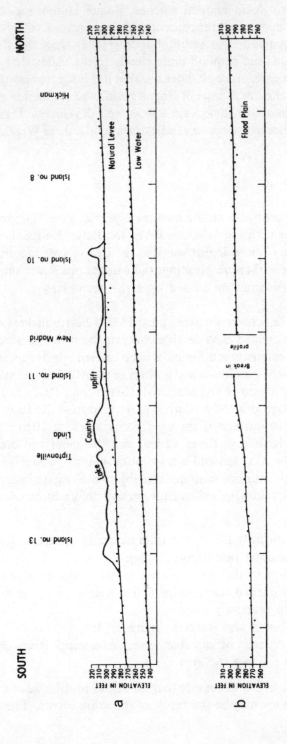

Figure 3.13 Longitudinal profiles in the vicinity of the Lake County Uplift. Locations are shown on figures 3.5 and 3.12. (a) Natural-levee profile and low-water profiles; (b) Floodplain profile (from Russ, 1982)

are convex upward, and Russ (1982) concluded that this shape is due to recent if not active deformation. Russ also stated that several aspects of the meander pattern of the Mississippi River suggest control by tectonic processes. Above the uplift axis, between Cairo, Illinois, and Hickman, Kentucky, the river is presently relatively straight (figure 3.5). From Hickman south to Blytheville, Arkansas, however, it is sinuous (figure 3.5). It is possible that the river course was straightened in order to increase gradient in an area where tilting is reducing valley slope, whereas downstream the high sinuosity reflects valley steepening (figures 3.2 and 3.3).

Monroe and Wiggins Uplifts A profile of valley-floor (backswamp) elevations along the Mississippi River shows convexities at Greenville, Lake Providence, and near Natchez (figure 3.14). The convex reaches at Greenville and Lake Providence correlate with the margins of the Monroe Uplift, and the convexity below Natchez correlates with the Wiggins Uplift. These convexities suggest that there is deformation of the alluvial-valley floor due to these uplifts, but their influence is more than a simple uplifting of alluvial material. The river is, in fact, flowing on Tertiary bedrock on the Monroe Uplift. For instance, the convexities at the margins of the uplift are due to the resistant Yazoo clays, and the concavity in the middle of the Monroe Uplift is related to the less resistant Cockfield sands, which form the centre of the uplift.

Figure 3.14 also shows thalweg profiles of the Mississippi River taken from 1880 and 1915 hydrographic surveys before there was major modification of the river by cutoffs in the 1930s. There is a sharp convexity in both profiles between Natchez and the Atchafalaya River, which correlates with the Wiggins Uplift and a similar convexity in the valley-floor (backswamp) profile. Upstream from this point the thalweg profiles are variable and the only consistent trend is a broad convexity between Vicksburg and Greenville. This convexity roughly corresponds to the Monroe Uplift, but it does not mirror the convexities in the valley-floor profile. It appears from these profiles that the river is capable of adjusting to slow surface deformation before significant deformation of the river bed occurs.

Sinuosity was measured on maps that show ancient courses of the river (Fisk, 1944). Fisk's stage 11 was the oldest course included in the analysis. Older courses flow in a different meander belt and channels older than stage 11 are difficult to reconstruct due to the overlapping of younger channels. Radiocarbon dating of archaeological sites within the present meander-belt system (Saucier, 1974) suggests that stage 11 could be 3600 years old.

A three dimensional plot of time (Fisk stage), valley mile, and sinuosity shows how sinuosity varies in both time and space (figure 3.15). Regions of historically high sinuosity occur just upstream of Greenville, upstream of Lake Providence,

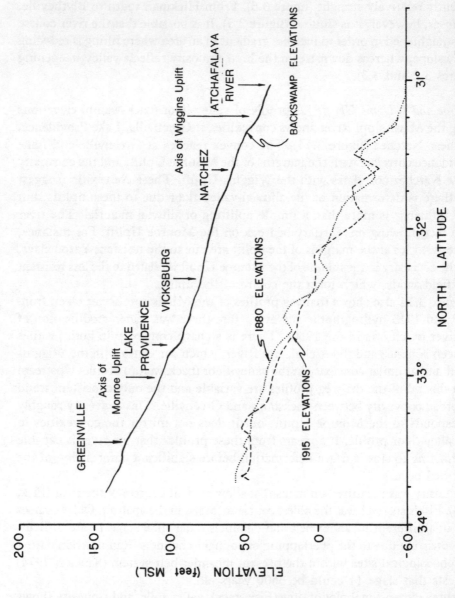

Figure 3.14 Longitudinal profiles of backswamp and thalweg elevations (1880 and 1915) along Mississippi River between latitudes 34°15' and 31°0' (see figure 3.5)

between Vicksburg and St Joseph, and upstream of Natchez. The first two locations correspond to the upstream and downstream edges of the Monroe Uplift where resistant bedrock is controlling meander migration. The Greenville Bends were caused by the compression of meander bends where Tertiary clays restrict meander migration at the upstream edge of the Monroe Uplift. At the downstream edge of the uplift sinuosity is also highly variable due to compression of meander bends by Tertiary outcrops, but an increase in valley slope between Lake Providence and Vicksburg causes an increase in sinuosity through this reach. Variations in sinuosity below Vicksburg are related to the influence of bedrock controls on meander migration.

The variations of sinuosity with time suggest that the influence of the Monroe Uplift is intermittent. The topography of the Tertiary bedrock surface is irregular, and as the river shifts back and forth across the valley, it may occasionally encounter high points on the Tertiary surface which can modify sinuosity as at Greenville. In addition, cutoffs naturally reduce sinuosity.

The New Madrid earthquakes occurred in 1811 and 1812 (see Lake County Uplift, figure 3.5), and large amounts of sediment were introduced into the channel of the Mississippi River as a result of bank caving (Walters, 1975). Stage 18 represents the channel of the river in 1820, which is just after the earthquakes. Note that after 1820 sinuosity continued to increase rapidly at Greenville, and it decreased sharply between Vicksburg and St Joseph and downstream of Natchez. These changes, although in different directions, may be caused by the increase in sediment. In areas of low to moderate sinuosity the increase in sediment load caused deposition on the point bars and thus increased meander growth, as at Greenville. In areas of high sinuosity, as at Yucatan Point and below Natchez, the increase in sediment load may have caused cutoff of meander bends. This is a good example of tertiary effects of active tectonics on river reaches a long distance from the disturbance.

Although it has been demonstrated experimentally (Schumm and Khan, 1972) and in the field (Schumm et al., 1972) that sinuosity is related to valley slope, it appears from this study that the influence of bedrock control is also important in determining the planform geometry of this large river. Tectonic processes have warped the sediments underlying the Mississippi valley, and they have emplaced a variety of resistant rocks close to the bed of the river. The emplacement of resistant sediments (Yazoo Clay) in the bed masks the effects of active tectonics on valley slope. Presumably, the Mississippi River can cope with the slow (3–4 mm/year) deformation associated with Monroe and Wiggins Uplift, but not where the more resistant Tertiary sediments are exposed in its bed and banks.

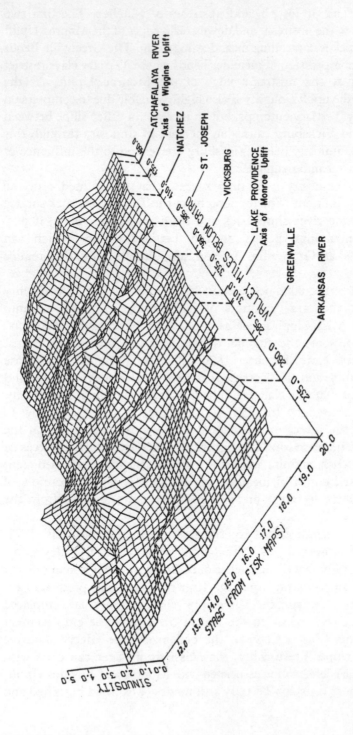

Figure 3.15 Three-dimensional plot of sinuosity for the Mississippi River from Fisk's stage 11 to 1932 betwen Helena, Ark. and the Atchafalaya River. Time (stage) increases along the left axis and stage 20 represents the most recent pre-cutoff channel. Valley miles increase in a downstream direction along the right axis from the bottom corner of the plot

Middle Rio Grande, New Mexico

In the Rio Grande valley, New Mexico, rapid uplift has been reported between Belen and Socorro (Reilinger et al., 1980). The uplift, which was detected by repeated geodetic surveys, is a roughly elliptical domal uplift with its centre about 25 km north of Socorro, New Mexico. The maximum uplift near the centre is about 20 cm relative to the periphery, as measured between 1911 and 1951 (5 mm/year). Reilinger et al. (1980) suggested that the uplift is caused by expansion of the Socorro magma body (Sanford et al., 1977).

The Rio Grande flows across the uplift roughly along its major axis. Late Pliocene alluvium of the ancestral Rio Grande River is displaced 85 m (279 ft) vertically over a distance of about 11 km (6.9 miles) (Bachman and Mehnert, 1978). Assuming the original channel slope to be the same as the modern Rio Grande, the relative uplift occurring here is about 75–80 m since the late Pliocene. The estimated profile of the Quaternary-age Loma Parda terrace indicates about 37 m of incision due to the uplift (Ouchi, 1983). Deformation of these Tertiary deposits and Quaternary terraces indicates that modern uplift is a continuation of long-term deformation.

Six thalweg profiles (1917–72) show a pronounced convexity in the uplifted area (figure 3.16). Happ (1948) has already pointed out that this 'hump' existed at least since the 1918 mapping and probably since 1880, as inferred from the railway construction profile. The fact that this convexity coincides almost perfectly with the uplift suggests that it is related to the uplift rather than excess local sedimentation from Rio Puerco.

The pattern of the Rio Grande should reflect the change caused by uplift, although man's activities, especially channelization, make it difficult to see the natural pattern (Ouchi, 1985). Terraces in the central area of uplift, a strongly braided pattern in the downstream reaches and submerged bars in the upstream reaches, are the pattern adjustment to uplift observed in Ouchi's experiments (figure 3.3). Aerial photographs taken in 1948 by the US Bureau of Reclamation show that there are alternate bars with a braiding tendency in the upstream part of the uplift, whereas a strongly braided pattern is obvious in the reach near Lemitar downstream of the uplift. Old stream patterns on the floodplain, which can be detected from the aerial photographs, also indicate a strongly braided pattern from San Acacia to Socorro. Perhaps of more significance is the wildfowl refuge that has been established upstream where the floodplain is swampy, a condition in considerable contrast to the downstream reach.

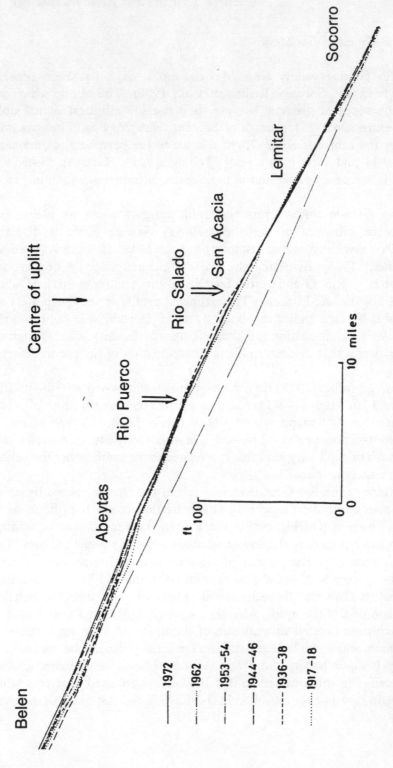

Figure 3.16 Longitudinal profiles of the Rio Grande from Belen to Socorro, NM
(from Ouchi, 1983)

DISCUSSION

The field examples and experiments indicate how sensitive rivers can be to slight changes of valley-floor slope. Channel morphology, therefore, appears to provide a means of detecting active tectonics, as well as subsidence due to groundwater and petroleum withdrawal and differential compaction of sediments over bedrock highs. When the changes of valley-floor slope are continuing as a result of active tectonics, river adjustment must be continuous or episodic. In either case the effects should be clearly displayed by geomorphic evidence of uplift as follows:

1 deformation of the valley-floor longitudinal profile (figures 3.6, 3.9, 3.10, 3.14, 3.15);
2 deformation of the channel projected profile (figures 3.7, 3.10, 3.14, 3.16);
3 change of channel and valley gradient (figures 3.7c, 3.16);
4 change of channel pattern (figures 3.2, 3.3, 3.4, 3.7d, 3.15);
5 change of channel width and depth (figures 3.7a, 3.7b);
6 conversion of the floodplain to a low terrace (figure 3.10);
7 active floodplain development (figure 3.11);
8 variations of channel stability, e.g. reaches of active channel incision, lateral shift, deposition, and nick-points (figures 3.3, 3.4, 3.7b, 3.11);
9 tertiary effects both upstream and downstream of the zone of deformation (degradation, aggradation, flooding, bank erosion, etc.) (figure 3.3).

Some alluvial rivers are presently adjusting to active tectonics, and this must be considered as an additional explanation for river instability. Active tectonics can be responsible for aggradation, degradation, channel avulsion, and pattern change, both downstream and upstream of the deformed reach. Therefore the net result of active tectonics is unstable river reaches that are characterized by incision, deposition, bank erosion, meander cutoffs, or development of meandering, braided or anastomosing patterns.

This has practical significance as river navigation can be affected by aggradation and the development of bars. Bank erosion, incision, and pattern change can have an impact on riparian land use and cause loss of valuable structures (bridges, loading docks) as well as agricultural land and homes. The frequency of overbank flooding will be increased in reaches of aggradation and reduced gradient. Changes in the frequency of over-bank flooding through a zone of active tectonics will change the position of 'ordinary high water', which is usually a legal boundary, and this may lead to confusion and litigation.

If rivers are affected by active tectonics then obviously canals will be also. Canals are usually constructed to carry relatively clear water on gentle slopes.

As in the Middle East, a slight warping can seriously affect the efficiency of the canal (Leary et al., 1981).

Geodetic measurements reveal deformation at rates of 10 mm/year (Rio Grande valley) and of 4 mm/year (Gulf Coast). These rates will have important effects within a few years; for example, valley-floor deformation can lead to major avulsive shifts of a river.

The type of active tectonics discussed herein is primarily related to aseismic deformation rather than faulting, but it is this slower deformation that has generally been ignored when river behaviour is studied.

REFERENCES

Adams, J. 1980: Active tilting of the United States midcontinent: geodetic and geomorphic evidence. *Geology*, 8, 442-6.

Adams, R. M. 1965: *Land Behind Baghdad*. Chicago: University of Chicago Press.

Ambraseys, N. N. 1978: Studies in historical seismicity and tectonics. In W. C. Brice (ed.), *The Environmental History of the Near and Middle East*, New York: Academic Press, 185-210.

Bachman, G. O. and Mehnert, H. H. 1978: New K-Ar dates and the late Pliocene to Holocene geomorphic history of the central Rio Grande region, New Mexico. *Geol. Soc. Am. Bull.*, 89, 283-92.

Bendefy, L., Dohnalik, J. and Mike, K. 1967: Nouvelles methodes de l'etude genetique des cours de eau. *Int. Assoc. Sci. Hydrology, Publ.* (Berne) 75, 64-72.

Bowler, J. M. and Harford, L. B. 1966: Quaternary tectonics and the evolution of the Riverine Plain near Echuca, Victoria. *Geol. Soc. Austral.*, 13, 339-54.

Burnett, A. W. 1982: *Alluvial Stream Response to Neotectonics in the Lower Mississippi Valley*. Unpublished MS thesis, Fort Collins: Colorado State University.

Burnett, A. W. and Schumm, S. A. 1983: Active tectonics and river response in Louisiana and Mississippi. *Science*, 222, 49-50.

DeBlieux, C. 1951: Photogeologic Study in Kent County, Texas. *Oil and Gas Jour.*, 50, 86.

DeBlieux, C. 1962: Photogeology in Louisiana coastal marsh and swamp. *Gulf Coast Assoc. Geol. Soc. Trans.*, 12, 231-41.

Fisk, H. N. 1944: *Geological investigation of the alluvial valley of the lower Mississippi River*. Vicksburg, Miss: US Army Corps of Eng., Mississippi River Commission.

Gardner, T. W. 1975: The history of part of the Colorado River and its tributaries: an experimental study. In *Four Corners Geol. Soc. Guidebook, 9th Field Conf., Canyon Lands*, 87-95.

Happ, S. C. 1948: Sedimentation in the middle Rio Grande Valley, New Mexico. *Geol. Soc. Am. Bull.*, 59, 1191-216.

Holdahl, S. R. and Morrison, N. L. 1974: Regional investigation of vertical crustal movements in the U.S., using precise relevelings and mareograph data. *Tectonophysics*, 23, 373-90.

Howard, A. D. 1967: Drainage analysis in geologic interpretation. *Am. Assoc. Pet. Geol.*, 51, 2246-59.

Jin, De Sheng, 1983: *Unpublished Report on Experimental Studies*. Fort Collins: Colorado State University.

Kowalski, W. C. and Radzikoska, H. 1968: The influence of neotectonic movements on the formation of alluvial deposits and its engineering-geological estimation. In *Proc. 23rd Inter. Geol. Congr.*, Prague Czech: Section 12, 197-203.

Lattman, L. H. 1959: Geomorphology: new tool for finding oil. *Oil and Gas Jour.*, 57, 231-6.

Leary, P. C., Malin, P. E., Strelitz, R. A. and Henyey, T. L. 1981: Possible tilt phenomena observed as water level anomalies along the Los Angeles aqueduct. *Geophys. Res. Letts.*, 8, 225-8.

Lees, G. M. 1955: Recent earth movements in the Middle East. *Geol. Rundschau*, 43, 221-6.

Machida, T. 1960: Geomorphological analysis of terrace plains-fluvial terraces along the River Kuji and the River Ara, Kanto District, Japan. In *Science Reports Section C 7, Tokyo Kyoiku Daigaku* (Tokyo University of Education), 137-94.

McKeown, F. A. and Pakiser, L. C. (eds) 1982: Investigations of the New Madrid, Missouri Earthquake region. *US Geol. Surv. Prof. Paper*, 1236.

Mirjayer, K. M. 1966: Recent tectonic movements and the development of the Euphrates River Valley. *Akad. Nauk. SSSR, Izvestuya Ser. Geograf.*, 5, 80-5.

Ollier, C. C. 1981: *Tectonics and Landforms*. New York; Longman.

Ouchi, S. 1983: *Response of Alluvial Rivers to Active Tectonics*. Unpublished PhD dissertation, Fort Collins: Colorado State University.

Ouchi, S. 1985: Response of alluvial rivers to slow active tectonic movement. *Geol. Soc. Am. Bull.*, 96, 504-15.

Reilinger, R. E., Oliver, J. E., Sanford, Allan and Balazs, Emery 1980: New measurements of crustal doming over the Socorro magma body, New Mexico. *Geology*, 8, 291-5.

Rockwell, T. K., Keller, E. A., Clark, M. N. and Johnson, D. L. 1984: Chronology and rates of faulting of Ventura River terraces. *Geol. Soc. Am. Bull.*, 95, 1466-74.

Russ, D. P. 1982: Style and significance of surface deformation in the vicinity of New Madrid, Missouri. *US Geol. Surv. Prof. Paper*. 1236, 45-114.

Sanford, A. R., Mott, R. P., Jr., Shuleski, P. J., Rinehart, E. J., Caravalle, F. J., Ward, R. M., and Wallace, T. C. 1977: Geophysical evidence for a magma body in the crust in the vicinity of Socorro, New Mexico. *Geophysical Monograph Am. Geophysical Union*. 20, 385-404.

Saucier, R. T. 1974: Quaternary geology of the Lower Mississippi Valley. *Arkansas Archaeological Survey Research Series*, 6.

Schumm, S. A. 1977: *The Fluvial System*. New York: John Wiley.

Schumm, S. A. 1981: Evolution and response of the fluvial system, sedimentologic implications. *Soc. Econ. Paleontol. Mineral. Spec. Pub.*, 31, 19–29.

Schumm, S. A. and Khan, H. R. 1972: Experimental study of channel patterns. *Geol. Soc. Am. Bull.*, 83, 1755–70.

Schumm, S. A., Khan, H. R., Winkley, B. R. and Robbins, L. G. 1972: Variability of river patterns. *Nature*, 237, 75–6.

Smith, D. G. and Smith, N. D. 1980: Sedimentation in anastomosed river systems, examples from alluvial valleys near Banff, Alberta. *J. Sed. Petrol.*, 50, 157–64.

Sparling, D. R. 1967: Anomalous drainage pattern and crustal tilting in Ottowa County, Ohio. *Ohio J. Sci.*, 67, 378–81.

Stevens, G. R. 1974: *Rugged Landscape, the Geology of Central New Zealand.* Wellington: A. H. and A. W. Reed.

Tator, B. A. 1958: The aerial photograph and applied geomorphology. *Photogram. Eng.*, 24, 549–61.

Trifonov, V. G. 1978: Late Quaternary tectonic movements in Western and Central Asia. *Geol. Soc. Am. Bull.*, 89, 1059–72.

Twidale, C. R. 1971: *Structural Landforms.* Canberra: Australian National University Press.

Veatch, A. C. 1906: Geology and underground water resources of northern Louisiana and southern Arkansas. *US Geol. Surv. Prof. Paper.* 46.

Wallace, R. E. 1967: Notes on stream channels offset by the San Andreas Fault, southern coast ranges California. *Stanford University Pub. (Geol. Sciences)*, 11, 6–20.

Wallace, R. E. 1986: Overview and recommendations. In *Active Tectonics*, Washington, D.C: National Academy Press, 3–19.

Walters, W. H. 1975: *Regime Changes of the Lower Mississippi River.* Unpublished Master's thesis, Fort Collins: Colorado State University.

Wang, K. K. 1952: Geology of Ouachita Parish. *Louisiana Geol. Surv. Bull.*, 28.

Zuchiewicz, W. 1979: A possibility of application of the theoretical longitudinal river's profile analysis to investigations of young tectonic movements. *Annal. Soc. Geol. Pologne*, 49, 327–42.

Zuchiewicz, W. 1980: Young tectonic movements and morphology of the Pieniny Mountains (Polish Western Carpathians). *Annal. Soc. Geol. Pologne*, 50, 263–300.

4

Modelling Fluvial Systems: Rock-, Gravel- and Sand-bed Channels

Alan D. Howard

CHANNEL BED TYPES: ROCK, GRAVEL AND SAND

The beds of stream channels can generally be classified as bedrock, sandy alluvium, or gravelly alluvium. Bedrock channels are distinguished by the absence of alluvial sediment, except in isolated scour holes. The sandy, or fine-bed alluvial channels have beds dominated by sand with small percentages of gravel, and the reverse is true for the gravel, or coarse-bed channels. Downstream transitions between these channel types are usually abrupt. Howard and Kerby (1983) document the sudden transitions in badlands between shale-floored rills and gullies and sand-bed channels or pediments downstream. Yatsu (1955) and Shaw and Kellerhals (1977) cite rapid downstream transitions from gravel to sand beds in streams in Japan and Canada, respectively. Empirical data on the grain sizes of bed sediment collected from widespread localities generally show bimodal distributions, with peaks in the sand and gravel sizes and a paucity of granule sizes (2 to 10 mm) (Williams, 1978b). Channel armouring downstream from dams is an example of a temporal change from fine- to coarse-bed channels. Howard (1980) discussed the reasons for such thresholds in natural channels; a summary is provided in this chapter. The implications of these thresholds for modelling and prediction of fluvial landforms are also examined, as are the limitations and uncertainties of the model proposed by Howard (1980). Finally, suggestions are made for future directions of theoretical modelling, field research, and flume experimentation that would help improve our understanding of these thresholds.

Bedrock channels

Bedrock channels are defined as channel segments which lack a coherent bed of active alluvium. In addition to consolidated rocks, 'bedrock' in this context can also include cohesive fluvial deposits now undergoing dissection. Bedrock sections are common along many rivers in mountainous regions, often occurring as short riffles or waterfalls, but most commonly forming the headwater tributaries in otherwise alluvial channel networks.

Bedrock channels remain free of bed sediment because of steep gradients. They generally transport sediment concentrations comparable to alluvial channel segments occurring upstream or downstream, but sediment is not deposited on the bed, even during waning flows. Thus bedrock channels generally carry bed sediment in less than capacity quantities, in contrast to alluvial channels, which have gentler gradients than bedrock channels for a given discharge–sediment load regime and which generally transport a capacity bed material load (figure 4.1). In a bedrock channel segment lying downstream from an alluvial channel, the bed sediment during waning flows is preferentially deposited on the low-gradient alluvial section. For bedrock channels in headwater areas, the lack of low-flow deposition occurs because of high tractive forces and because sediment supply primarily occurs from runoff during rising stages, whereas transport continues during waning stages.

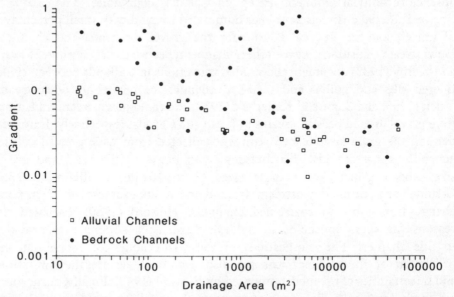

Figure 4.1   Plot of gradient versus drainage area for alluvial and bedrock channels in a badlands in Virginia, USA
(after Howard and Kerby, 1983)

One factor that may contribute to the sharpness of the transition between bedrock and alluvial channels is enhanced rebound of sediment grains on hard bedrock relative to impacts of grains upon a bed composed of grains of similar size, where much of the momentum of the impacting grains is lost to frictional losses and small displacements of bed grains. This phenomenon is best documented in aeolian environments (Bagnold, 1941; Ellwood et al., 1975). Bagnold suggests that the transport capacity of grains over hard surfaces is larger than over loose grains of the same size as those in motion; as a result, downstream transitions from bedrock to alluvial beds should be abrupt due to the sudden loss of mobility.

The gradient of bedrock channels exhibits no necessary correlation with discharge and sediment characteristics, which contrasts with strong correlations in alluvial channels (figure 4.1). Rather, the gradients are determined by the distribution of bedrock resistance to erosion along the channel and the erosional history of the channel network. However, the rate of erosion of bedrock channels is determined jointly by the bedrock resistance and the hydraulic regime (discharge, sediment load, and size distribution of supplied sediment).

Erosion of bedrock channels requires both weathering and detachment, which often go hand in hand. Resistant rocks may be eroded primarily by sediment abrasion. By contrast, limestone beds are primarily attacked by solution. In the case of gully erosion in shales, weathering may be of secondary importance to detachment, so that erosion rates are either related to the erosive capability of the sediment load, or are simply due to hydraulic plucking when the shear stress exceeds a critical value. Therefore no universal model of bed erosion can be formulated for bedrock channels. However, Howard (1980) and Howard and Kerby (1983) suggest a model for detachment-limited rills and gullies in badlands in which erosion rates are proportional to high-flow bed shear stress. If the hydraulic geometry of badland bedrock channels shows consistent downstream relationships, then the rate of channel bed erosion, E, depends upon drainage area, A, local channel gradient, s, and bed erodibility, K. In particular, if the width-depth ratio and hydraulic roughness remain constant downstream, then erosion proportional to shear stress implies:

$$E = K\,A^{0.38}\,s^{0.81} \tag{4.1}$$

Data from rapidly eroding badland channels (Howard and Kerby, 1983) indicate drainage area and gradient exponents of 0.44 and 0.68, respectively, which are reasonably close to the predicted values.

Bedrock channels and alluvial channels with either fine or coarse beds commonly coexist in many drainage basins. Short sections of bedrock channel commonly occur where especially resistant rocks occur; erosion rates lag when resistant rocks are exposed, resulting in steepened gradients and a transition to a bedrock channel. However, resistant bedrock also acts as a local base-level control to channel sections lying upstream, and a zone with a low rate of erosion, and correspondingly low gradients, commonly occurs above resistant outcrops (Howard, 1980); these low gradient sections are generally alluvial, even if the majority of the channel system is bedrock. Alluvial channel segments also commonly occur above other base-level controls, such as oceans, lakes, or reservoirs. Rejuvenation of drainage by relative change of land-ocean levels can also create bedrock channel sections in otherwise alluvial rivers, such as the nearly ubiquitous bedrock rapids at the fall line along Atlantic Coast rivers in the United States. These rivers are generally alluvial above the fall line. Howard (1980) also suggests that downstream transitions from bedrock to alluvial channels may occur even in basins undergoing steady-state erosion, although exclusively bedrock channel networks would occur for very rapid erosion rates (very high relief) and exclusively alluvial channels for very low erosion rates.

Change in the sediment supply and hydraulic regime can convert bedrock channels to alluvial ones, or vice versa. High rates of sediment supply and low discharges during winter in badlands in the eastern United States result in steep channel gradients, and many of the washes are aggraded with sandy alluvium (Howard and Kerby, 1983). However, during the summer smaller sediment yields due to reduced mass wasting and slope surface sealing, coupled with high intensity rainstorms, result in bed degradation and gradient reduction. Some channels with relatively thin winter alluvial mantles are completely stripped of alluvial cover during the summer; thus they are seasonally converted to bedrock channels.

Fine- and coarse-bed alluvial channels

Bed material transport rates increase non-linearly with increases in flow primarily because of the existence of a threshold of motion. Howard (1980) showed that this non-linearity implies the existence of threshold transitions between coarse and fine alluvial beds. Channels with coarse, usually gravel beds experience bed sediment transport only during high-flow stages, with generally slow net rates of gravel transport. On the other hand, channels with fine, primarily sandy alluvial beds exhibit motion at moderate stages and are characterized by high rates of sand transport. Abrupt spatial (downstream) or temporal thresholds can occur between these bed types even where the hydraulic regime varies gradually. Alluvial channels tend towards an equilibrium gradient which is just sufficient, over a period of years, to transport the supplied sediment with the available discharges (Mackin, 1948; Howard, 1982). However, in some channels it is the sparse load of coarse gravel that determines the equilibrium gradient, whereas in others it is the requirement to transport the more abundant sediment near the median size that controls the gradient. Transport continuity is maintained in alluvial channels by mutual adjustment of gradient and cross-section geometry, but the latter also depends on bank material characteristics in a complex way. The adjustment of gradient alone can, however, be assessed by considering the transport of bed material for a particular specific discharge (discharge per unit width).

The reasons for these thresholds can be illustrated by consideration of the channel gradient that would be required to transport each size fraction of bed sediment in a given hydraulic regime under the assumption that transport of each size fraction occurs independently. This is a variation on the normal engineering usage of transport formulae in which gradient is specified and transport rate is calculated. The critical assumption in Howard's (1980) analysis is that the required gradient for a given specific discharge can be calculated independently for each size fraction of supplied sediment, with each size fraction having a characteristic long-term rate of supply. Although interactions obviously occur between different grain sizes in transport (for example, Einstein's (1950) transport relationship uses a 'hiding factor' to account for such interactions for naturally graded alluvial beds), the size composition of bed sediment in natural channels is generally a small portion of the total size range of supplied sediment. The size fractions represented on the bed are presumably those that at that section of the channel are the most difficult to transport, that is, which require the steepest gradient. Supplied sediment which is finer than the bed is transported as wash load in below-capacity concentrations, whereas grains coarser than the dominant bed size are carried in such small quantities that they are dispersed over the bed, or they may be areally sorted into riffles or cobble bars. Thus, of the total range of supplied sediment, a relatively restricted portion dominates the bed and determines the required gradient and is carried in capacity quantity. Howard (1980) therefore assumes that the required gradient for the channel can be determined by finding that size range which, when its characteristic supply rate and size is input into an appropriate sediment transport formula for the dominant discharge, predicts the largest gradient.

Figure 4.2 shows a typical plot of required gradient as a function of grain size. In making the calculations the Einstein-Brown sediment-transport relationship (Henderson, 1966) was used and the quantity of supplied sediment was assumed to follow a lognormal distribution (characterized by the log-mean grain size, D, and the variance, V). For the fine grain sizes an arbitrary value of the Manning resistant coefficient, n, was assumed, but for the coarse sediment grain roughness was assumed to dominate so that n varied as the ⅙th power of grain size. The particular plot shown in figure 4.2 assumes a specific water discharge, q, of $10 \, \mathrm{m^2 \, s^{-1}}$, a sediment concentration, c, of 0.01, D=0.3 mm,

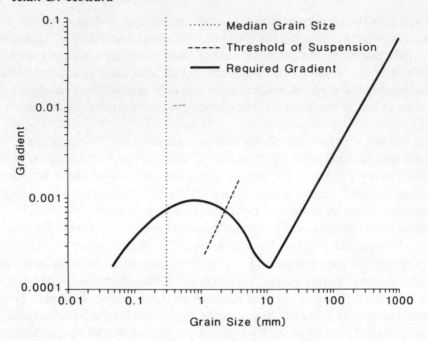

Figure 4.2 Curve of required gradient versus grain size. Median grain size is 0.3 mm. Gradients calculated using Einstein-Brown transport formula (after Howard, 1980)

$V = 0.87$, and $n = 0.02$. Calculations of required gradient using other total-load sediment formulae exhibit the same general form of relationship to that shown in figure 4.2. In particular, for the input conditions noted above, the required gradient has a local maximum for a grain size somewhat larger than the median grain size, a local minimum near 10 mm, and an indefinitely increasing required gradient as grain size increases beyond 10 mm. In the coarse size ranges the required gradient is determined by the threshold of motion and is nearly independent of the quantity of sediment, whereas in the fine size ranges the sediment load is important in addition to the grain size.

Naive interpretation of the indefinitely increasing required gradient in the coarse size range would suggest that alluvial channel gradients are invariably determined by the coarsest grains in transport and the bed is correspondingly dominated by coarse grains. However, as is evident from the occurrence of numerous sand-bed channels, coarse grain sizes do not always dominate the bed. This is because above some *critical* grain size, weathering and slope erosion supply so little sediment of that size and coarser, that they are incapable of forming a coherent alluvial bed. If this critical grain size is coarse enough such that the corresponding required gradient is larger than the peak required gradient in the fine size range, then the bed of the channel can be expected to be composed primarily of grain sizes close to the critical grain size that is, it will be a coarse-bed channel. Because of the steep gradient, fine grain sizes will seldom accumulate on the bed, except possibly as an infilling between the coarse grains. On the other hand, if the supply of coarse grain sizes is so restricted that the critical grain size is small enough that its required gradient is less than that for the maximum in the fine sediment sizes, then the bed will be dominated by fine grain sizes in the range near the peak required gradient. In this case, coarser grain sizes will be present in the alluvial bed, but their concentration will be diluted by the abundant fine bed material. Sediment that is much finer than the size corresponding to the largest required gradient will primarily be carried as wash load and is seldom deposited on the bed.

Implications of the fine- to coarse-bed threshold

Conditions favouring gravel or sand channels.   Figure 4.3 shows the effect on the required gradient curves of varying sediment concentration (a), specific discharge (b), and variance in grain size (c and d). Figure 4.4 shows the effect of variations in the mean grain size. In each of these figures the remaining parameters were held constant. As sediment concentration increases (figure 4.3a) the valley between the fine-grain peak and the threshold curve deepens; for example, at a concentration of 0.0001 a coarse grain-size about six times the size corresponding to the peak in the sub-millimeter sizes gives the same critical gradient; this size ratio increases to about 60 for a concentration of 0.1. This suggests that alluvial streams with high imposed loads are more likely to be fine bed. Following similar reasoning, figure 4.3b shows that narrower streams, when compared to wider streams with higher specific discharges but the same sediment concentrations and total discharges, are more likely to be fine bed. Increase in the mean grain size in transport (figure 4.4) increases the grain size of the peak required gradient in the fine size range as well as the local minimum required gradient. For the Einstein-Brown sediment transport relationship streams with coarser average sediment size are somewhat more likely to be coarse-bed channels. However, other sediment transport formulae are either indifferent to average sediment size or predict the opposite of the Einstein-Brown relationship. Streams with a narrow range of supplied sediment sizes show a strong peak in the required gradient in the fine size range, and thus are more likely to be fine-bed channels. Channels receiving a wide range in sediment sizes have a less pronounced fine-grained peak gradient, or for a very wide range of sizes, essentially no fine-grained peak, so that the channel will probably be coarse-bed (figures 4.3c and 4.3d). In the case of very large variance in supplied sizes, the required gradient is not a strong function of grain

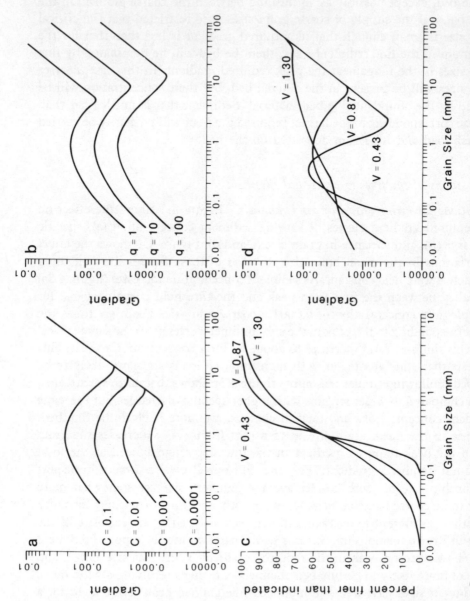

Figure 4.3 Curves of required gradient versus grain size, showing effects of variations in sediment concentration (a); specific discharge in m² s⁻¹ (b); and variance (V) in grain size distribution (c and d). Other parameters held constant in each case (after Howard, 1980)

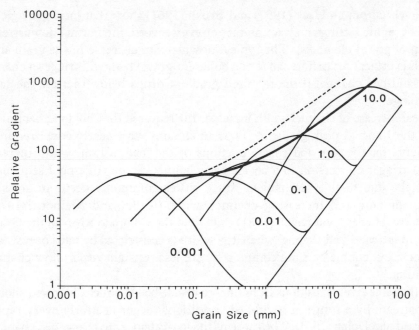

Figure 4.4 Variation of maximum required gradient for fine-bed alluvial channels with average particle size. Dashed line shows relationship between median particle size of supplied sediment and channel gradient, whereas solid line shows relationship between bed material size and gradient
(after Howard, 1980)

size, so that the bed may be characterized by a large range of grain sizes, possibly areally sorted into riffles and pools.

In summary, fine-bed channels would be expected in streams where concentrations are high but the grain size range is narrow, as in many badlands and in the semi-arid Great Plains, where erosion of poorly consolidated sedimentary rocks yields high sediment yields but little coarse detritus. On the other hand, coarse-bed channels are favoured by low sediment loads and relatively large proportions of coarse detritus, such as in mountain areas with resistant bedrock, steep slopes, and a predominant role of physical weathering.

Spatial transitions between bed types   Transitions between coarse and fine beds in a channel system may occur spatially (downstream) or temporally at a given location. In natural channel systems, the most common spatial transition is the threshold change from headwater coarse-bed channels to downstream sand-bed channels (Yatsu, 1955; Shaw and Kellerhals, 1977). This threshold occurs because grain size in gravel channels generally decreases more rapidly downstream than it does in sand channels, due to more effective comminution and sorting of gravels (although Hack (1957) and Brush (1961) show that local geologic or physiographic settings may counteract or even reverse the normal downstream fining of gravel channels). The typical downstream decrease in the grain size, which is critical for maintenance of a coherent gravel bed, will trigger a change to a sand-bed channel if the required gradient drops below that for the sand size range.

Local increase of channel width increases the required threshold gradient more than the fine-bed peak gradient. Thus in streams with nearly equal required gradients for the fine and coarse portions of the load, a local width increase might trigger conversion to a coarse-bed channel. Some riffle-pool sequences might be due to this mechanism, since riffles commonly occur in areas of divergent flow and increasing channel width (Keller and Melhorn, 1973). Similarly, Howard and Dolan (1981) show that the Colorado River in the Grand Canyon is a sand-bed channel where the width is constricted by talus or resistant bedrock, but cobble bars are common where less resistant rocks allow channel widening.

In the same river transitions from fine- to coarse-bed channels, followed shortly downstream by a return to sand-bed conditions, occur at nearly every rapids (Howard and Dolan, 1981). The cause of the local changes to coarse-bed channels is the local injection of boulder-rich sediment where steep sidewall tributaries debouch into the main river. The steep tributaries have high competence during intense thunderstorms, permitting transport of boulders up to several metres in size. Because of the abundant gravel, the critical grain size for forming a coherent gravel bed is increased, resulting in the transition to a threshold-of-motion gravel-bed channel with a gradient several times that of the between-rapids sandy reaches. However, the long-term rate of supply of coarse boulders from these tributaries is insufficient to force throughput of these coarse boulders along the canyon; rather, the boulders are comminuted in place by weathering, abrasion, and fracturing until they are transportable with available discharges at the between-rapids gradients. Because of the high sand loads and the narrow river, the Colorado River remains a sand-bed channel except at the rapids despite the high rate of local supply of coarse debris from the canyon walls (except, as noted above, at local wide channel sections where transitions to a gravel bed occur).

Temporal transitions between bed types   A change of hydraulic regime can trigger conversion of sand-bed channels to gravel, or the reverse. The armouring that occurs below dams in otherwise sand-bed channels is a classic example (Williams and Wolman, 1984). The interception of nearly all the sediment load of the stream by the dam reduces the sediment size/required gradient curve to essentially a threshold relationship, so that the stream would generally convert to a coarse-bed channel. This conversion is aided and accelerated by the bed degradation that accompanies the reduction in sediment load, which rapidly concentrates at the bed surface coarse-grained sediment that was formerly dispersed in small quantities through the alluvium. The general reduction in peak discharges also aids this conversion, because it may render the coarsest bed material no longer transportable.

The reverse case, of conversion of a gravel channel to a sand bed, can occur as a result of increased sediment supply. Timber harvesting, forest fires, and poor agricultural practices can increase sediment yields by up to an order of magnitude relative to geologic norms. In addition, such increases commonly increase the relative proportion of sand to gravel. If the channel is initially gravelly, aggradation and the conversion to a sand bed will occur if the additional load requires a gradient for transport in the sand size range that is greater than the existing gradient. For very coarse gravel channels this is unlikely to occur.

Transport rates of bed sediment in gravel channels are generally very low when compared with rates of sand transport in sand-bed channels (although gravel channels may transport large quantities of sand, largely in suspension). As a result, the time-scale for adjustment of gradients in gravel streams to altered hydrologic conditions will generally be much longer than for sand-bed channels of equivalent size. In fact, some of the coarse cobble pavements of alpine streams may have originated during periods of accentuated physical weathering and mass movement during the late Pleistocene (Miller, 1958; Brush, 1961). Sand-bed channels respond much more rapidly to change in regime, with response times on the order of months to hundreds of years, depending upon the size of the alluvial channel (Howard, 1982).

The difference in characteristic response-times for gravel and sand rivers can result in short-term adjustments to altered hydraulic regime that are distinct from the ultimate response; for example, channelization of a river by elimination of meandering can increase channel gradients by up to twice the natural value. The response of sand channels will be to degrade their beds (Daniels, 1960; Daniels and Jordan, 1966; Emerson, 1971; Piest et al., 1977); if there is a sufficient gravel component in the alluvium, an armoured bed can result due to the slow transport rates of the gravel (Schumm et al., 1984), even though the ultimate response would be a sand-bed channel with approximately the same gradient as existed before channelization (since the hydraulic regime has not been directly altered). Conversely, aggradation due to change in hydraulic regime or a rising base-level may result in temporary conversion of a gravel river to sand; for example, if upstream deforestation or urbanization result in a greater influx of sediment to a gravel channel without change in the grain size distribution, the ultimate equilibrium channel, given the changed regime, may be a steeper gravel channel. However, if the influx of sediment is sufficient to raise the required gradient for the fine sediment above the existing gradient, the immediate response will be a temporary conversion of the channel to a sand bed. In fact, if the increase in sediment supply is short-lived, the steeper gravel channel will never form, and the sand bed will be scoured away.

A rise in local base-level (such as by construction of a dam) requires upstream alluviation, with the ultimate equilibrium channel having approximately the same gradient and bed type as the original channel (since the hydraulic regime is unchanged). However, if the channel is originally gravel, the initial alluviation will occur by deposition of the sand load at a gradient smaller than the original channel gradient, because of the slow transport rates of gravel sizes. For practical purposes, the long-term equilibrium may not be established during the lifetime of the dam.

Downstream hydraulic geometry of coarse- and fine-bed channels. As cited previously, confirmation of these concepts and the existence of the threshold relationship between coarse- and fine-bed channels come partly from observations of sudden downstream transitions from coarse- to fine-bed channels, as well as of the paucity of channels with beds dominated by intermediate grain sizes. In addition, sediment transport relationships indicate that the downstream hydraulic geometry of fine- and coarse-bed channels should differ, particularly in the relationships between gradient and the variables of discharge and size of bed sediment. Howard (1980) shows that coarse-bed channels with beds near the threshold of motion at peak flows will exhibit a dependency of gradient on grain size (D) and specific discharge (q) of the form

$$s = K_1 q^a D^b, \tag{4.2}$$

where, for the Shields threshold-of-motion criterion, the exponent a, has a value of -0.86 and b a value of 1.29. Data from eastern USA coarse-bed streams (Hack, 1957; Brush, 1961) show estimated values of a near -1.0, close to the predicted value, but a value of b near 0.5, lower than predicted.

Transport formulae predict rather different exponents for fine-bed channels for which dominant shear stresses are well above threshold of motion:

$$s = K_2 q_s^e q^f F(D), \tag{4.3}$$

where F(D) can be approximated by D^g for narrow ranges of grain size. Values for e, f and g vary considerably for different transport formulae but cluster near 0.6, -1.0, and 1.1, respectively, for channels of medium sand. Data on downstream hydraulic geometry from fine-bed channels in Virginia badlands (Howard and Kerby, 1983), Utah badlands (Howard, 1980), sandy Great Plains streams (Schumm, 1960), and ephemeral streams in New Mexico (Leopold and Miller, 1956; Renard and Laursen, 1975) are generally consistent with the e and f exponents in equation (4.3) when downstream changes in width and in the relative values of q and q_s are accounted for (Howard, 1980). However, these channels have insufficient ranges in grain size to evaluate g. Furthermore, multicolinearity amongst the independent variables in both equations (4.2) and (4.3) results in bias in the least-squares exponents which obscures the empirical testing of theoretical predictions.

The difference in downstream gradient changes in gravel- and sand-bed rivers underscores the necessity for stratifying hydraulic geometry data on the basis of bed type (see chapter 5). Hydraulic engineers generally recognize this necessity by proposing different relationships for sand and gravel bed rivers (e.g. Parker, 1978a; 1978b; Chang, 1979a; 1980). In a related vein, Carson (1984) suggests that the meandering-to-braiding transition in alluvial streams occurs at higher slopes (for a given discharge) in gravel streams than in sand-bed channels because of the higher threshold of motion (see chapter 6).

Deficiencies of intermediate bed particle sizes. The curves of required gradient versus grain size (figures 4.2–4.4) show a local minimum between the peak in gradient in the fine size range and the monotonically increasing gradients in coarse grain sizes. This minimum is in the range of 1 to 10 mm for reasonable ranges in the median size of sediment supplied from upstream. This size range corresponds to the commonly observed deficiency of these grain sizes in fluvial sediments (Yatsu, 1955; Slatt and Hoskins, 1968; Church and Gilbert, 1975; Emmett, 1976; Williams, 1978b). The usual explanations for this deficiency are either that weathering produces little detritus in this size range or that transport comminution processes are particularly effective in this size range relative to sand, which has lower momentum and is generally monomineralic. However, the deficiency may be due in part to sorting processes related to the minimum in the required gradient curves.

The relative proportion, P_D, of different grain sizes on the bed is proportional to the ratio

$$q_{sD}/(Dv_D), \tag{4.4}$$

where q_{sD} is the specific sediment discharge of grains of size D measured in volume of solids per unit time and channel width, and v_D is the average velocity of grain movement. Grains in the sand size range are strongly represented in the bed due to large q_{sD} and small grain size despite large v_D. Coarse gravel is strongly represented due to low v_D despite low q_{sD} and large D. However, because of the high actual gradient relative to the required gradient for grain sizes near the minimum, P_D is low due to low q_{sD} and high v_D; that is to say, the small quantity of granule-sized bed material moves relatively rapidly along the channel, so that it is poorly represented in fluvial sediments. If the bimodal distribution of fluvial sediments is largely due to this sorting process, then the missing granule sizes should be found in their original proportions in still-water sediment sinks, whereas they will also be missing in such deposits if original scarcity or differential comminution is the main cause of the deficiency. If the sorting process is responsible for the deficiency, then the grain size range of the deficiency will vary among fluvial environments in relation to differences in the mean and variance of sediment sizes supplied to the channel system. This may help to account for the lack of bimodal grain size distributions in aggregate averages of grain size distributions from diverse fluvial environments (Shea, 1974).

Thresholds in sand-bed channels

Chang (1979a, 1979b, 1984, 1985, 1986) has proposed the existence of a threshold in channel morphology and bed type distinct from those discussed above. Flume experiments and some field data have demonstrated the existence of multiple-valued average depths as a function of flow velocity in sand-bed channels of constant gradient (figure 4.5) due to the successive occurrence of different bedform types (dunes, upper-stage flat, bed, and antidunes). As a result, bed material transport rates also exhibit non-linear behaviour. By accounting for variations in flow resistance with bed type, Chang has shown that for a given sediment and water discharge, the channel gradient required for equilibrium generally exhibits a minimum value for a particular channel width (figure 4.6). In some cases two local minima occur in equilibrium gradient associated with upper- and lower-stage flows, respectively. The narrower width is associated with the upper-stage flow. Chang calculates the required gradient for a given channel width, water discharge, and sediment discharge by assuming a flow depth and calculating velocity and gradient from sediment transport relationships, and then calculating discharge using predicted flow resistance. If the calculated and assumed discharge do not agree, the flow depth is adjusted in additional iterations until agreement occurs.

As a second and independent assumption, Chang hypothesizes that channels adjust their width to minimize gradient, thereby also minimizing the rate of energy dissipation. Under conditions where two local minima occur in required gradient (for relatively high sediment transport rates), the one of lower gradient (subcritical flow) would be the more stable. Chang finds, however, that the two minima can become equal if the bank steepness of the narrower upper regime channel is steeper. Chang suggests that these two minima may thus coexist as riffles (wide, shallow, lower-stage flow) and pools (narrow, deep, upper-stage

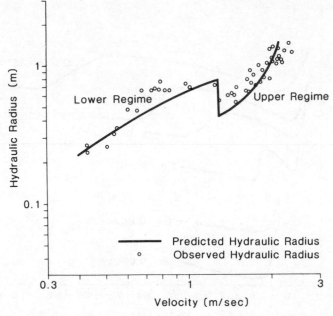

Figure 4.5 Observations of channel depth as a function of flow velocity for the Rio Grande River, with curve showing values predicted by Engelund's (1966) flow resistance model (after Raudkivi, 1976)

flow) in the same channel reach. He therefore implies that riffles and pools in steep gradient sand-bed streams represent threshold transitions between these two minima.

Chang's analysis seems to provide fairly accurate predictions of channel width and depth for a given discharge and observed gradient and bed material size. It also suggests that for channels with low sediment loads, channel width increases with discharge but is relatively independent of sediment load and channel gradient. However, for high sediment loads channel width is an increasing function of both discharge and sediment load (or gradient). Channels of the latter type are likely to be braided due to the high width-depth ratio, whereas the narrower channels associated with lower sediment transport rates are likely to be meandering or straight. Chang's analysis is actually somewhat more involved than suggested here, with greater attention to channel planform pattern and a distinction between four possible regions of regime behaviour.

Although Chang's analysis is innovative and worthy of further empirical testing, the hypothesis that channel width is optimally adjusted to provide minimum channel gradient has less basis in established hydraulic principles than the co-assumption that channel gradients vary with channel width due to changes in flow resistance. Several potential difficulties with the model

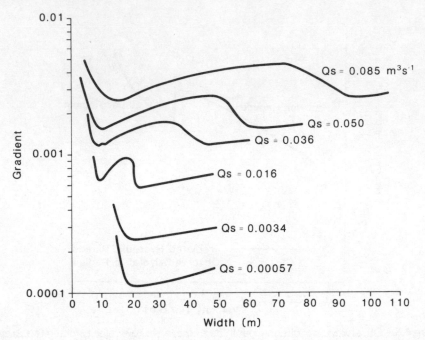

Figure 4.6 Calculation of equilibrium gradient as a function of channel width for fixed sediment grain size, discharge, and bank slope and for various values of sediment discharge (Qs). Curves illustrate minima in equilibrium gradient due to variations in flow resistance (after Chang, 1985)

assumptions can be mentioned. Firstly, the assumption of optimal width adjustment has little direct basis in fluid mechanics and sediment transport. Like other optimal models of channel geometry, such as minimum variance models of hydraulic exponents (Langein, 1964; Williams, 1978a), minimum rate of work models of channel junctions (Howard, 1971; Roy, 1985), and other minimum energy expenditure models (Yang, 1971; 1976; Cherkauer, 1973), the optimal geometry has not been directly linked with causal mechanisms for its attainment (however, see the discussion of extremal hypotheses by Davies, chapter 9). A case can be made for a stabilizing feedback mechanism for a channel that is narrower than the optimum, since the increased gradient and greater flow depth relative to the optimum would increase fluid stresses on the banks, and help to restore the optimum. However, in a channel wider than the optimum it is unclear that decreased flow depth would offset the effects of steeper gradient in decreasing bank shear stresses and encouraging deposition.

Secondly, channel width is subject to multivariate controls, as discussed below, so that width is likely to depart strongly from the hypothesized optimum in many channel networks.

Thirdly, natural streams are subject to widely varying flows. Each discharge is associated with a different optimal width. Although a dominant discharge and associated optimal width may occur, the effect of the varying discharges will probably be to broaden and weaken the gradient minimum associated with the optimal width, correspondingly diminishing the efficiency of any mechanisms tending to adjust the width to an optimal value. In addition, if the stream is subject to rapidly varying discharges, equilibrium bedforms may not fully develop at each flow stage, further blurring the optimum conditions (Allen, 1976a; 1976b).

DISCUSSION

This discussion focuses upon several related issues, including: the limits of applicability of the scenario predicting channel bed types outlined in the preceding sections; the relationship of the bed-type model to other components of fluvial morphology such as cross-sectional shape and river pattern; and the prospects for quantitative modelling of channel evolution.

Model limitations

Several assumptions underlying the calculations of the required gradient versus grain size relationship (figures 4.2–4.4) deserve closer scrutiny. The most crucial assumption is that the required gradient can be calculated independently for different grain-size categories – that is, that these size fractions are hydraulically independent. One justification for this has been suggested that is, the narrow range of bed sediment sizes compared to the total range of supplied sediment. Sediment finer than the range of grain sizes represented on the bed is generally carried as wash load, in below-capacity quantities, so that the assumption seems valid for finer grain sizes. However, all grain sizes in transport that are coarser than the modal bed sediment size are also carried as bedload, so that interaction between size ranges is probable (see p. 8 and p. 73). The basic argument remains valid, however, as long as the method gives reasonable estimates of required gradient for both coarse and fine components. For a sparse population of coarse grains on a fine bed, the effect of the coarse grains on the motion of the fine bedload is probably less important than the enhancing effect of the fine bed on the mobility of the coarse grains (due to greater exposure). The size range of bed sediment in sand channels is generally small, so that the assumption of independence should not be grossly in error.

A related issue is the choice of range of grain sizes included within each grain size category for calculating the required gradient. For the fine grain sizes, it is apparent from equation (4.3) that the required gradient is dependent upon the sediment discharge of the selected grain size range, and that this will tend towards zero as the grain size range narrows, giving a seemingly paradoxical result. On the other hand, inclusion of too wide a grain size range will include grains carried as wash load in calculation of the peak required-gradient and will reduce the resolution of the resulting relationship. Clearly there must be an optimal grain size range dictated by the degree of interaction of related grain sizes. One indicator of this optimum is the range of grain sizes dominating the bed; the range used in the required gradient calculation should probably be neither much larger nor much smaller than this range. Another indication may be the range of grain sizes near the peak in the required-gradient curves, which suggests a dependency of the range width on the variance of supplied grain sizes (figure 4.3); however, the peak varies in width among different assumed transport relationships for the same hydraulic regime.

For the coarse grain sizes near the threshold of motion the model assumes that the Shields relationship governs the threshold of motion, which requires that grains act independently of one another. However, recent research has shown that bed particles ranging from about one-third to four times the median size of the *subsurface* bed material are entrained at nearly the same discharge (Parker, Klingeman and McLean, 1982; Andrews, 1983). Furthermore, this research shows that a surface pavement of grains coarser than both the mean bedload transported and the median subpavement grain size (which are nearly equal) is a stable feature of gravel-bed streams for transport conditions near the threshold of motion (Parker, Dhamotharan and Stefan, 1982; Parker and Klingeman, 1982). At first this near-equality of mobility over a grain size range of about 12 times seems to negate the use of Shields-type threshold equations to calculate required gradients. However, as Carson and Griffiths (1985) point out, one must be careful not to confuse threshold criteria formulated and used for different purposes. Firstly, the median size of the sub-pavement bed material *can* be used with the Shields (entrainment) dimensionless shear stress to predict the onset of motion (although a somewhat smaller constant, 0.033, is suggested than the generally accepted value of about 0.06). Secondly, the equality of mobility does not apply to grains either coarser or finer than the range quoted above. Finer grains move in suspension or wash load, and are only represented in the bed to the degree that they filter down between the coarser bed particles. Particles coarser than 4.2 times the sub-pavement median grain size are not as mobile as smaller grains (otherwise gravel channels would be overwhelmed with house-sized boulders), but have a constant dimensionless shear stress of about 0.02 (Andrews, 1983). Thus, with the exception that a certain range of sizes about the median has nearly constant mobility, these recent findings do not contradict the general pattern proposed in the model. In fact, the range of grains with nearly constant mobility can be viewed as an indication of the range of strongly interacting grain sizes (discussed in the previous paragraph) characteristic of the gravel component.

The assumption of independence of transport for different size ranges clearly will be inapplicable for channels characterized by very high sediment concentrations or mudflows. The sorting processes responsible for the threshold changes in bed type cannot operate in such viscous flows.

The calculations also assume that a dominant discharge can be defined which is equivalent in transporting capability to the wide range of natural discharges. For a narrowly-graded supply of sediment this poses few problems. However, with a well-graded sediment input, the dominant discharge will vary with grain size, becoming larger for coarser sizes. Although the calculations do not account for this effect, its inclusion would not change the basic character of channel behaviour and the threshold behaviour. More problematic is the effect of varying discharges and varying sediment supply in restricting availability of certain size ranges of bed sediment, as a result of either temporary bed armouring during waning and low flows hiding underlying fine sediments, or influx of fine sediment during runoff events burying coarse sediment (summer runoff from desert floods has this effect on the Colorado River in the Grand Canyon; Howard and Dolan, 1981). However, these are probably second-order effects that do not change the essential nature of the thresholds.

The calculations also assume a flow resistance for fine sediment that is independent of grain size and required gradient. In fact, as the discussion of the Chang papers has suggested, the occurrence of bedforms implies that flow resistance, and hence transport capacity and required gradient, will vary with the assumed size of bed sediment and the channel width. More elaborate, iterative calculations of required gradient would be required to account for this effect, or a nomograph approach could be used (Parker and Anderson, 1977). This refinement would be valuable in predictive use of the required gradient for fine-bed channels, but the effect is not in conflict with the occurrence of the coarse to fine threshold transition.

Although the required gradient calculations offer an explanation of the threshold between channel types, the model is not particularly useful in making *a priori* predictions of whether a coarse- or fine-bed alluvial channel or a bedrock channel would occur for those natural streams operating close to a threshold transition. The required gradients depend crucially upon the size-distribution and rate of supply of sediment supplied by slope erosion to the channel system. Since supply and grain size range cannot be easily predicted from morphological characteristics of the drainage basin, intra-stream measurements are required. The fine component of the load, and therefore the peak required gradient in the fine grain size range, can be reasonably estimated from long-term measurements of bed and suspended load. However, the critical grain size for coarse-bed streams and the corresponding required gradient depend upon the relatively small rate of supply of coarse grain sizes and upon the frequency of flood peaks. Sampling of coarse bedload is not routinely undertaken, especially not for long time-periods. The estimation problem is further compounded by the variable fabric of gravel beds; for example, Reid et al. (1985) show that recently reworked gravel beds are more readily entrained, so that there is an ordering effect (Wolman and Gerson, 1978; Brunsden and Thornes, 1979) in entrainment. Also complicating prediction are the actions of sorting (Brierly and Hickin, 1985) and comminution (Schumm and Stevens, 1973), as well as the possibility of disequilibrium between channel bed type and hydraulic regime due to the longer time-scale for adjustment of coarse-bed than fine-bed channels. The occurrence of bedrock channels depends upon past erosional history and resistance of the bedrock to erosion, factors which are difficult to quantify. However, the measurement of channel gradient will indicate whether it is steep enough such that an alluvial bed will not form, although because of the difficulty in estimating the critical grain size, this may not be possible for the bedrock, coarse-bed threshold except for gradients well above the threshold.

Channel cross section and planform

The present model of bed types and channel gradients in alluvial channels is formulated in terms of specific discharges of water and sediment, so that predictions of hydraulic geometry require specification of bank material control of channel width as an additional independent influence. This approach has been taken for several reasons. Firstly, transport relationships are defined in terms of specific discharges, allowing development of the threshold model with fewest additional hypotheses and constraints.

Secondly, channel width is subject to multivariate control, so that in some cases knowledge of the hydraulic regime may not be sufficient to predict width; for example, along most of the Colorado River in the Grand Canyon the channel walls are bedrock or talus although the bed is alluvial (Howard and Dolan, 1981); the channel width is therefore narrower than would be the case for alluvial banks.

Thirdly, even in the more common case of channels with self-formed alluvial banks, the width is determined by different components of the sediment load from the bed (with a greater role exercised by the suspended and wash load), and width responds to different aspects of the flow regime. In particular, channel width is sensitive to the effects of large floods (Schumm and Lichty, 1963; Burkham, 1972). Deterministic predictive models of cross-sectional geometry have so far been limited to cases where the bed and bank sediment are the same. Li et al. (1976) have modelled stable gravel channels where bed and banks are at the threshold of motion. The predicted width-to-depth ratio of about 7 to 8 is close to the average value of about 10 observed by Brush (1961) in eastern United States gravel-bed streams. Parker (1978b; 1979) has extended this analysis to the more frequent case of gravel channels with stable banks but which experience finite sediment transport rates at high discharges; he shows that equilibrium channel widths are greater than for the stable channel case, which in turn requires steeper gradients. Parker (1978a) has also provided a model for sand-bed channels with sand banks in which the bank profile is determined by the balance between the downslope transport of bank sediment and the deposition from suspension. Pizzuto (1984) has applied this model to sand-bed channels. However, only empirical models are available for the more typical case of banks finer than the bed material, particularly when the banks are cohesive and/or vegetated.

'Closure' of predictive models for channel gradients requires determination of channel width; channel width may be estimated by locally-determined width-discharge hydraulic geometry, by multivariate hydraulic geometry relationships that incorporate information on bank sediment characteristics and, possibly, vegetation (Schumm 1960; 1969; Charlton et al., 1978; Osterkamp et al., 1983; Andrews, 1984; Hickin, 1984; Gurnell and Gregory, 1984), or by theoretical models where appropriate.

Comprehensive discussion of channel pattern and its effects upon gradient and bed type is beyond the scope of this chapter. In heavily engineered streams with protected banks the channel pattern is determined. But for natural streams knowledge of the equilibrium channel pattern is important not only to be able to predict valley gradients in addition to channel gradients, but also because the channel pattern has mutual interactions with cross-sectional shape and sediment transport mechanisms: for example, transport efficiency in braided channels should be lower than for a single-thread channel of equivalent hydraulic regime because of increased bank resistance (although differences in bedforms in single-thread and braided channels may complicate the issue). Also, several authors have suggested that a meandering pattern is more efficient in sediment transport than a straight channel (e.g. Langbein and Leopold, 1966; Yang, 1971; Chang, 1979b).

Furthermore, valley slope may be an independent variable during short-term adjustments of channels to change in hydraulic regime. Schumm (1968) for example suggests that the Murrumbidgee River in Australia responded to changes in hydraulic regime by combining changes in channel width and sinuosity which absorbed the change in regime without aggradation or entrenchment. More likely is that the valley gradient constrained the possible short-term responses of channel width and sinuosity to changes in regime. Thus, were the regime to be indefinitely held constant following a change in regime, systematic aggradation or entrenchment would probably eventually change the valley gradient. The short-term decreases in sinuosity in response to widening of channels during floods and the increase in sinuosity as the channel gradually narrows (Schumm and Lichty, 1963; Burkham, 1972) confirm this interpretation.

More complete discussions of the extensive literature on channel patterns are provided in texts by Richards (1982) and Knighton (1984), in recent papers by Carson (1984) and Ferguson (1984), and in the chapter by Ferguson in this volume.

Prospects for simulation modelling

The analysis presented in this chapter is limited in quantitative treatment to equilibrium bed morphology and gradient, although some qualitative conclusions have been made concerning transient response. In view of the dynamic nature of geomorphic processes and landforms, equilibrium models are informative about the structure of the system, although of restricted predictive applicability (Howard, 1982). In recent years more general temporal simulation models have been developed for particular fluvial systems. These include aggradation and degradation models based upon routing of fine-grained sediment e.g. Howard, 1982; Park and Jain, 1986; and references in these papers), models of channel armouring below dams (e.g. Garde et al., 1977, and Lu and Shen, 1986), and simulations of meander pattern development (Howard and Knutson, 1984). Such models oversimplify the natural interactions between processes and morphology, restricting the range of their applicability or rendering them of heuristic value only. However, as knowledge of these interactions improve, simulation models will become more general and useful in examining both short- and long-term fluvial responses to disturbances.

CONCLUSION

The existence of thresholds in bed type between bedrock, gravel, and sand-bed channels seems well-established, and the general factors leading to these thresholds have been examined in this chapter. Thresholds may also occur in bed type within fine-bed channels as a result of transitions between bedform regimes. However, several questions remain to be answered, such as the limits of applicability of the fine- to coarse-bed threshold for high sediment concentrations or for large variance in sizes of supplied sediment. Furthermore, the role of the thresholds, if any, in the formation of riffles and pools is uncertain.

Therefore, further examination of the threshold concept as applied to channel bed types is desirable, either by more refined theoretical modelling, through application of field observations, or by flume experiments. Flume experimentation involving input of sediments with a large variance in grain size and with variable discharges would be particularly valuable.

REFERENCES

Allen, J. R. L. 1976a: Time-lag of dunes in unsteady flows: an analysis of Nasner's data from the R. Weser, Germany. *Sedimentary Geology*, 15, 309–21.

Allen, J. R. L. 1976b: Computational models for dune time lag: population structures and the effects of discharge pattern and coefficient of change. *Sedimentary Geology*, 16, 99–130.

Andrews, E. D. 1983: Entrainment of gravel from naturally sorted riverbed material. *Geological Society of America Bulletin*, 94, 1225–31.

Andrews, E. D. 1984: Bed-material entrainment and hydraulic geometry of gravel bed rivers in Colorado, USA. *Geological Society of America Bulletin*, 95, 371–8.

Bagnold, R. A. 1941: *The Physics of Blown Sand and Desert Dunes*. London: Methuen.

Brierly, G. J. and Hickin, E. J. 1985: The downstream gradation of particle sizes in the Squamish River, British Columbia. *Earth Surface Processes and Landforms*, 10, 597–606.

Brunsden, D. and Thornes, J. B. 1979: Landscape sensitivity and change. *Transactions of the Institute of British Geographers, New Ser.*, 4, 463–84.

Brush, Jr. L. M. 1961: Drainage basins, channels, and flow characteristics of selected streams in central Pennsylvania. *US Geological Survey Professional Paper*, 282-F, 145–81.

Burkham, D. E. 1972: Channel changes of the Gila River in Safford Valley, Arizona, 1846–1970. *US Geological Survey Professional Paper*, 655-G.

Carson, M. A. 1984: The meandering-braided river threshold: a reappraisal. *Journal of Hydrology*, 73, 315–34.

Carson, M. A. and Griffiths, G. A. 1985: Tractive stress and the onset of bed particle movement in gravel stream channels: different equations for different purposes. *Journal of Hydrology*, 79, 375–88.

Chang, H. H. 1979a: Geometry of rivers in regime. *Journal of the Hydraulics Division American Society of Civil Engineers*, 105, 691–706.

Chang, H. H. 1979b: Minimum stream power and river channel patterns. *Journal of Hydrology*, 41, 303–27.

Chang, H. H. 1980: Geometry of gravel streams. *Journal of the Hydraulics Division, American Society of Civil Engineers*, 106, 1443–56.

Chang, H. H. 1984: Modeling of river channel changes. *Journal of Hydraulic Engineering*, 110, 157–72.

Chang, H. H. 1985: River morphology and thresholds. *Journal of Hydraulic Engineering*, 111, 503–19.

Chang, H. H. 1986: River channel changes: adjustments of equilibrium. *Journal of Hydraulic Engineering*, 112, 43–55.

Charlton, F. G., Brown, P. M. and Benson, R. W. 1978: The hydraulic geometry of some gravel rivers in Britain. *Hydraulics Research Station Report*, IT 180.

Cherkauer, D. S. 1973: Minimization of power expenditure in a riffle-pool alluvial channel. *Water Resources Research*, 9, 1613–28.

Church, M. and Gilbert, R. 1975: Postglacial fluvial and lacustrine environments. In *Glaciofluvial and Glaciolacustrine Sedimentation*, Society of Economic Paleontology and Mineralogy, Special Publication, 23, 22–100.

Daniels, R. B. 1960. Entrenchment of the Willow Drainage Ditch, Harrison County, Iowa. *American Journal of Science*, 258, 161–76.

Daniels, R. B. and Jordan, R. H. 1966: Physiographic history and the soils, entrenched stream systems and gullies, Harrison County, Iowa. *US Department of Agriculture, Technical Bulletin*, 1348.

Einstein, H. A. 1950: The bed-load function for sediment transportation in open channel flow. *US Department of Agriculture, Soil Conservation Service, Technical Bulletin*, 1026.

Ellwood, J. M., Evans, P. D. and Wilson, I. G. 1975: Small scale eolian bedforms. *Journal of Sedimentary Petrology*, 45, 554–61.

Emerson, J. W. 1971: Channelization: a case study. *Science*, 172, 325–6.

Emmett, W. W. 1976: Bedload transport in two large, gravel-bed rivers, Idaho and Washington. In *Proceedings of the Third Federal Inter-Agency Sedimentation Conference*, 5-1–5-12.

Engelund, F. 1966: Hydraulic resistance of alluvial streams. *Journal of the Hydraulics Division, American Society of Civil Engineers*, 92, 315–26.

Ferguson, R. I. 1984: The threshold between meandering and braiding. In K. V. H. Smith (ed.), *Channels and Channel Control Structures*, Berlin: Springer Verlag, 6-15–6-29.

Garde, R. J., Ali, K. A. and Diette, S. 1977: Armoring process in degrading streams. *Journal of the Hydraulics Division, American Society of Civil Engineers*, 103, 1091–5.

Gurnell, A. M. and Gregory, K. J. 1984: The influence of vegetation on stream channel processes. In T. P. Burt and D. E. Walling (eds), *Catchment Experiments in Fluvial Geomorphology*, Norwich: Geo Books, 515–35.

Hack, J. T. 1957: Studies of longitudinal stream profiles in Virginia and Maryland. *US Geological Survey Professional Paper*, 294-B, 45–97.

Henderson, F. M. 1966: *Open Channel Flow*. New York: Macmillan.

Hickin, E. J. 1984: Vegetation and river channel dynamics. *Canadian Geographer*, 28, 111–26.

Howard, A. D. 1971: Optimal angles of stream junctions: geometric, stability to capture, and minimum power criteria. *Water Resources Research*, 7, 863–73.

Howard, A. D. 1980: Thresholds in river regimes. In D. R. Coates and J. D. Vitek (eds), *Thresholds in Geomorphology*, London: Allen and Unwin, 227–58.

Howard, A. D. 1982: Equilibrium and time scales in geomorphology: application to sand-bed alluvial streams. *Earth Surface Processes and Landforms*, 7, 303–25.

Howard, A. D. and Dolan, R. 1981: Geomorphology of the Colorado River in the Grand Canyon. *Journal of Geology*, 89, 269–98.

Howard, A. D. and Kerby, G. 1983: Channel changes in badlands. *Geological Society of America Bulletin*, 94, 739–52.

Howard, A. D. and Knutson, T. R. 1984: Sufficient conditions for river meandering: a simulation approach. *Water Resources Research*, 20, 1659–67.

Keller, E. A. and Melhorn, W. N. 1973: Bedforms and fluvial processes in alluvial stream channels: selected observations. In M. Morisawa, (ed.), *Fluvial Geomorphology*, New York: Allen and Unwin, 253–83.

Knighton, D. 1984: *Fluvial Forms and Processes*. London: Edward Arnold.

Langbein, W. B. 1964: Geometry of river channels. *Journal of the Hydraulics Division, American Society of Civil Engineers*, 90, 301–12.

Langbein, W. B. and Leopold, L. B. 1966: River meanders – theory of minimum variance. *US Geological Survey Professional Paper*, 422H.

Leopold, L. B. and Miller, J. P. 1956: Ephemeral streams – hydraulic factors and their relation to the drainage net. *US Geological Survey Professional Paper*, 282-A.

Li, R., Simons, D. B. and Stevens, M. A. 1976: Morphology of cobble streams in small watersheds. *Journal of the Hydraulics Division, American Society of Civil Engineers*, 102, 1101–17.

Lu, J-Y. and Shen, H. W. 1986: Analysis and comparisons of degradation models. *Journal of Hydraulic Engineering*, 112, 281–99.

Mackin, J. H. 1948: Concept of the graded river. *Geological Society of America Bulletin*, 59, 463–512.

Miller, J. P. 1958: High mountain streams – effects of geology on channel characteristics and bed material. *New Mexico Bureau of Mines and Mineral Resources, Memoir*, 4.

Osterkamp, W. R., Lane, L. J. and Foster, G. R. 1983: An analytical treatment of channel-morphology relations. *US Geological Survey Professional Paper*, 1288.

Park, I. and Jain, S. C. 1986: River-bed profiles with imposed sediment load. *Journal of Hydraulic Engineering*, 112, 267–80.

Parker, G. 1978a: Self-formed straight rivers with equilibrium banks and mobile bed. Part 1. The sand-silt river. *Journal of Fluid Mechanics*, 89, 109–25.

Parker, G. 1978b: Self-formed straight rivers with equilibrium banks and mobile bed. Part 2. The gravel river. *Journal of Fluid Mechanics*, 89, 127–46.

Parker, G. 1979: Hydraulic geometry of active gravel rivers. *Journal of the Hydraulics Division, American Society of Civil Engineers*, 105, 1185–1201.

Parker, G. and Anderson, A. G. 1977: Basic principles of river hydraulics. *Journal of the Hydraulics Division, American Society of Civil Engineers*, 103, 1077–87.

Parker, G. and Klingeman, P. C. 1982: On why gravel bed streams are paved. *Water Resources Research*, 18, 1409–23.

Parker, G., Dhamotharan, S. and Stefan, H. 1982: Model experiments on mobile, paved gravel bed streams. *Water Resources Research*, 18, 1395–1408.

Parker, G., Klingeman, P. C. and McLean, D. G. 1982: Bedload and size distribution in paved gravel-bed streams. *Journal of the Hydraulics Division, American Society of Civil Engineers*, 108, 544–71.

Piest, R. F., Elliot, L. S. and Spomer, R. G. 1977: Erosion of the Tarkio Drainage System: 1845–1976. *American Society of Agricultural Engineers Transactions*, 20, 485–8.

Pizzuto, J. E. 1984: Equilibrium bank geometry and the width of shallow sand bed streams. *Earth Surface Processes and Landforms*, 9, 199–207.

Raudkivi, A. J. 1976: *Loose Boundary Hydraulics*. Oxford: Pergamon.

Reid, I., Frostick, L. E. and Layman, J. T. 1985: The incidence and nature of bedload transport during flood flows in coarse-grained alluvial channels. *Earth Surface Processes and Landforms*, 10, 33–44.

Renard, K. G. and Laursen, E. M. 1975: Dynamic behavior model of ephemeral stream. *Journal of the Hydraulics Division, American Society of Civil Engineers*, 101, 511–28.

Richards, K. 1982: *Rivers: Form and Process in Alluvial Channels*. London: Methuen.

Roy, A. G. 1985: Optimal models of river branching angles. In M. J. Woldenberg (ed.), *Models in Geomorphology*, Boston: Allen and Unwin, 269–85.

Schumm, S. A. 1960: The shape of alluvial channels in relation to sediment type. *US Geological Survey Professional Paper*, 352-B.

Schumm, S. A. 1968: River adjustment to altered hydrologic regimen – Murrumbidgee River and paleochannels, Australia. *US Geological Survey Professional Paper*, 598.

Schumm, S. A. 1969: River metamorphosis. *Journal of the Hydraulics Division, American Society of Civil Engineers*, 95, 255–72.

Schumm, S. A. and Lichty, R. W. 1963: Channel widening and flood-plain construction along Cimarron River in southwestern Kansas. *US Geological Survey Professional Paper*, 352-D, 71–88.

Schumm, S. A. and Stevens, M. A. 1973: Abrasion in place: a mechanism for rounding and size reduction of coarse sediments in rivers. *Geology*, 1, 37–40.

Schumm, S. A., Harvey, M. D. and Watson, C. C. 1984: *Incised Channels – Morphology, Dynamics, and Control*. Littleton, Colorado: Water Resources Publications.

Shaw, J. and Kellerhals, R. 1977: Downstream grain size changes in Albertan Rivers (Abstract). In *First International Symposium on Fluvial Sedimentology*, Calgary.

Shea, J. H. 1974: Deficiencies of clastic particles of certain sizes. *Journal of Sedimentary Petrology*, 44, 985–1003.

Slatt, R. M. and Hoskins, C. M. 1968: Water and sediment transport in the Norris Glacier outwash area, upper Taku Inlet, southeastern Alaska. *Journal of Sedimentary Petrology*, 38, 434–56.

Williams, G. P. 1978a: Hydraulic geometry of river cross sections – theory of minimum variance. *US Geological Survey Professional Paper*, 1029.

Williams, G. P. 1978b, Bankfull discharge of rivers. *Water Resources Research*, 14, 1141–54.

Williams, G. P. and Wolman, M. G. 1984: Downstream effects of dams on alluvial rivers. *US Geological Survey Professional Paper*, 1286.

Wolman, M. G. and Gerson, R. 1978: Relative scales of time and effectiveness of climate in watershed geomorphology. *Earth Surface Processes*, 3, 189–208.

Yang, C. T. 1971: Potential energy and stream morphology. *Water Resources Research*, 7, 311–22.

Yang, C. T. 1976: Minimum unit stream power and fluvial hydraulics. *Journal of the Hydraulics Division, American Society of Civil Engineers*, 102, 919–34.

Yatsu, E. 1955: On the longitudinal profile of the graded river. *Transactions of the American Geophysical Union*, 36, 655–63.

5

River Channel Adjustment – the Downstream Dimension

A. D. Knighton

INTRODUCTION

Natural rivers develop a wide range of network and channel forms, the characteristics of which are a function of position within the fluvial system. Channel geometry at any particular location reflects the influence of upstream controls such as climate, geology, land use and basin physiography, which together determine the hydrologic regime and the quantity and type of sediment supplied. Whether position is defined in topologic, geometric or flow-related terms, the most striking element of fluvial change is in the longitudinal direction, and this chapter focuses on the downstream adjustment of width, depth and slope, components which specify in a broad way two of the three dimensions of the geometry of river channels.

Figure 5.1 presents in summary form the main downstream trends in control and response variables, some of which are less certain than others. Even the most commonly cited elements of longitudinal change – increasing discharge, decreasing bed-material size and decreasing slope – are not universally applicable. One problem in assessing downstream trends stems from the general lack of data at sufficient locations along individual rivers, particularly for sediment-related variables. Consequently in testing theory and in empirical analysis, sequent position along a single river is often replaced by relative position within a group of rivers chosen from a given physiographic area, with the attendant risk of increasing heterogeneity in environmental conditions as the sampled region expands to augment the data base. Bearing this limitation in mind, three related issues are considered here: firstly, the overall *consistency* of downstream adjustment, with emphasis on the main control variables and their relationships to width, depth and slope; secondly, the *adjustability* of those form elements,

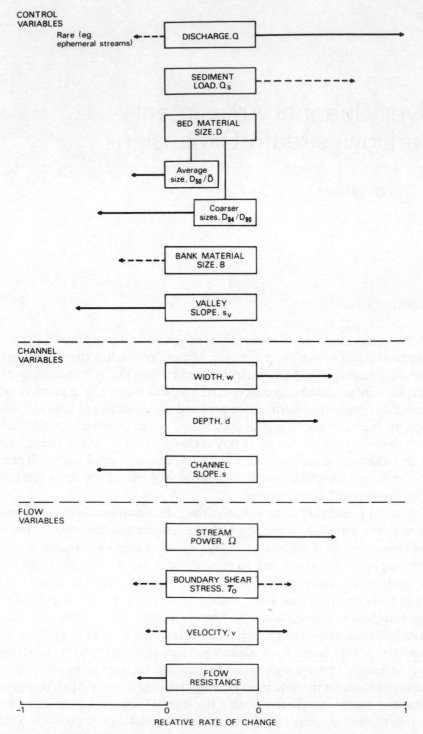

Figure 5.1 Schematic diagram of the relative rates of downstream change. Dashed lines signify greater uncertainty in behaviour

which brings the time factor into account; and thirdly, the *continuity* of adjustment, which focuses more on longitudinal behaviour in single systems and considers the links between networks and channels. All of these issues, but particularly the first two, are related to the question of the ability of a river to develop and maintain an average channel geometry.

DOWNSTREAM CHANGES IN THE CONTROL VARIABLES

The main factors controlling channel form are discharge, sediment load, bed and bank material composition, and valley slope. All can vary considerably along and between rivers. Partly for the practical reason of data availability, discharge has assumed the dominant role in empirical relationships between control and channel-form variables.

Discharge

Downstream change in river discharge is most commonly associated with increasing drainage area. In one of the most comprehensive studies of streamflow variation (Flood Studies Report, 1975), drainage area (A_d) was consistently the dominant catchment characteristic influencing the mean annual flood ($Q_{2.33}$). The overall relationship for the British Isles (table 5.1) was re-analysed on a regional basis and the coefficient a in

$$Q_{2.33} = aA_d^{0.73} \tag{5.1}$$

shown to range between 0.22 and 1.62. Reducing the spatial scale still further and dealing with individual catchments in the Central Region where a = 1.40, sample calculations reveal that coefficient values for the Trent and Tweed basins are 0.57 and 1.78 respectively. Clearly the form of the discharge-area relationship can vary not only between regions but also between basins within the same region, and even within single basins. Nevertheless the relationship serves as a first-order expression for the downstream change in discharge and several results (table 5.1) confirm its general form, with exponent values usually in the range of 0.7 to 0.85. That the exponent is less than unity reflects in part the influence of valley storage on the downstream transmission of higher flows. The way in which flood flows are transmitted can influence channel form, for Burkham (1976) differentiates between low-flow and high-flow systems where the latter are characterized by wider and straighter channels.

As regards channel form adjustment, the quantity of water is less important than its capacity to do erosional and transportational work. Consequently stream

Table 5.1 Discharge-drainage area relations

Source	Location	Drainage area (km²)	Discharge	a	b
Nixon (1959)	England, 28 stations	111-7276	Q_b	0.24	0.85
Brush (1961)	Pennsylvania	20-162 300	$Q_{2.33}$	0.50	0.80
Benson (1962)	New England, 164 stations	4-25 070	$Q_{2.33}$	0.56	0.85
Nash and Shaw (1966)	Great Britain, 57 stations	8-9900	$Q_{2.33}$	0.76	0.74
Thomas and Benson (1970)	Potomac River Basin	15-30 000	Q_2	0.86	0.80
	Sacramento and San Joaquin River basins	19-4380	Q_2	0.64	0.83
	Louisiana	14-4410	Q_2	4.49	0.56
Emmett (1975)	Upper Salmon River, Idaho	0.4-4670	Q_b	0.42	0.69
Flood Studies Report (1975)	British Isles, 533 stations	0.05-9868	$Q_{2.33}$	0.68	0.77

Discharge (Q) defined as the mean annual flood ($Q_{2.33}$), the flood having a recurrence interval of two years (Q_2), and bankfull (Q_b).
Symbols: $Q = a\, A_d^b$.

power (γQs), which expresses the rate of doing work per unit length and figures as a parameter in several bed-load transport equations (e.g. Bagnold, 1980), may be more significant than discharge alone but its spatial characteristics at the regional or network scale are poorly understood (Graf, 1983). Nevertheless, the parameter has been used as a basis for theory development (Yang, 1971; 1976; Chang, 1980) and for defining process zones along ephemeral streams (Bull, 1979). Bearing in mind its relationship to bed-load transport, stream power should increase along most perennial rivers at a moderate rate (figure 5.1), with unit stream power remaining approximately constant.

Discharges vary in their effectiveness to transport sediment and modify channel form. Magnitude-frequency analysis suggests that moderate events with return periods in the approximate range of 1.2-3 years transport most sediment (Wolman and Miller, 1960; Pickup and Warner, 1976; Andrews, 1980), one corollary of which being that channel form is adjusted to a similar range of flows. However, the effective or dominant discharge varies with the type of load transported and the hydrologic regime. Thus, as the flow regime becomes more variable because of increasing aridity or decreasing drainage area, more extreme events may have a greater influence on channel form (Baker, 1977; Wolman and Gerson, 1978). Despite the potential longitudinal variation in flow effectiveness, downstream hydraulic geometry is invariably analysed in terms of a single index of discharge.

Sediment load

Such is the lack of data and intermittency of the transport process that sediment movement patterns at the basin scale are exceedingly difficult to predict. As floodplain width and surface area increase downstream (Bhowmik, 1984), so does the potential for sediment storage. For basins in the southern Piedmont and Wisconsin, Trimble (1975; 1983) has estimated that more than 90 per cent of the sediment eroded from upland slopes since European settlement began is still stored on hillslopes, floodplains and in channels. Thus the sediment delivery ratio which indicates the disparity between supply and transport generally decreases downstream, falling below ten per cent at drainage areas over 100 km^2 (Walling, 1983). Sediment movement patterns are complicated not only by storage but also by the strong contrasts in sediment-streamflow relations both between and within river basins (Andrews, 1980; Meade, 1982).

Sediment transport equations developed for at-a-station conditions translate with unknown efficiency to the downstream case, especially where supply limitations apply. Inasmuch as discharge and stream power increase longitudinally, so should the quantity of sediment load although at a lower rate than that of discharge. Along the upper Salmon River in Idaho (Emmett, 1975), suspended load (in tonnes d^{-1}) increases with bankfull discharge (Q_b in m^3 s^{-1}) according to

$$Q_{susp} = 13.1 \ Q_b^{0.75} \tag{5.2}$$

Bogardi (1974) gives similar results for Hungarian rivers but emphasizes the importance of local supply conditions and the difficulty of obtaining generalized downstream trends, even for a single river system. Sediment transport rates can vary markedly even over river distances of less than one kilometre (Andrews, 1982).

A particular size fraction moving as bed load at one section may be transported entirely as suspended load at another. Along five New Zealand rivers the ratio of bed load to suspended load declines sharply to approximately ten per cent in lowland reaches (Griffiths, 1983). Even lower values have been recorded elsewhere (Bogardi, 1974; Emmett and Thomas, 1978). Thus the type as well as the quantity of sediment load varies downstream, with bed load transport being possibly dominant only in headwater areas.

Despite the uncertainties surrounding the downstream characteristics of sediment transport, attempts have been made to predict equilibrium channel

Table 5.2 Downstream change in bed material size

Source	Location/River	River distance (km)	Parameter	Bed material range (mm)	Type	β
Yatsu (1955)	Japan: Kinu	0–52	D_{50}	20–70	G	−0.0253
		60–100		0.4–0.9	S	−0.0238
	Watarase	0–21		30–80	G	−0.0531
		23–37		0.3–0.9	S	−0.0416
	Tenryu	14		15–50	G	−0.0532
	Kiso	0–15		35–70	G	−0.0348
		15–55		0.4–0.6	S	−0.0104
	Nagara	0–13		25–40	G	−0.0446
		13–49		0.7–1.2	S	−0.0173
	Sho	0–20		20–50	G	−0.0288
	Abe	0–23		15–90	G	−0.0715
	Yahagi	0–35		1–2	S	−0.0247
Hack (1957)	Virginia, Maryland: Calfpasture	0–27	D_{50}	42–75	G	0.0034
	Tye	0–14		230–680	B/G	−0.0837
	Gillis Falls	0–13		7–45	G	0.115
Bradley et al. (1972)	Knik River, Alaska	0–26	$\bar{D}$	44–330	B/G	−0.081
Rana et al. (1973)	Mississippi, Vicksburg district	440	D_{85}	0.3–0.9	S	−0.0010
			D_{50}	0.2–0.55		−0.00055
			D_{15}	0.18–0.33		−0.00045
Simons and Şentürk (1977)	Rhine	200	D_{50}	50–160	G	−0.011
	Mur	140		34–83	G	−0.0195
	Mississippi, from Fort Jackson	1770		0.12–0.72	S	−0.00085
	Rio Grande, from Otowi	240		0.14–0.50	S	−0.0057
Church and Kellerhals (1978)	Peace	140	D_{90} $\bar{D}$	45–280 25–120	G	−0.0048 −0.0034
Knighton (1980)	Bollin-Dean	0–50	$\bar{D}$	0.33–67	G/S	−0.118
	Noe	0–20		29–69	G	−0.042
Nordin et al. (1980)	Amazon, from Iquitos	3300	D_{50}	0.15–0.50	S	slightly negative

Bed material size defined as the median (D_{50}), mean ($\bar{D}$), or that size for which 90 per cent (D_{90}), 85 per cent (D_{85}) or 15 per cent (D_{15}) of the sample is finer.
Symbols: β – rate of change of bed material size downstream in $D = \alpha e^{\beta L}$; B, G, S refer to boulder-bed, gravel-bed and sand-bed streams respectively.

geometry based on transport criteria, in particular the principle of maximum sediment transporting capacity (Kirkby, 1977; White et al., 1981; Ferguson, 1986). As White et al. admit there is no physical justification for such a principle and, given the poverty of the data base, little opportunity for testing it. Nevertheless it is generally agreed that the quantity, type and continuity of sediment transport exert a strong influence on channel form.

Boundary composition

Bed material is derived from slope, tributary and channel boundary sources. Its average size at any location along a river depends on the characteristics of the initial input and on the nature and rate of subsequent modifications to that input, either in place or during transport. With a few exceptions and despite high levels of variability, bed material size generally decreases downstream through the action of such processes as abrasion, weathering and sorting, the rate of decrease tending to be largest in headwater reaches and where gravel sizes dominate the bed (table 5.2). Given this trend a gradual transition from gravel-bed to sand-bed status might be expected along many rivers but the transition, if it exists, is often abrupt once D_{50} approaches 10 mm (Yatsu, 1955; Howard, 1980; Kellerhals, 1982), a discontinuity which has implications for and is related to channel form adjustment (see chapter 4, this volume). In particular particle size and slope are usually strongly related.

Changes in bed material properties also influence the magnitude and type of sediment transport and resistance. Thus, for example, with an idealized downstream sequence of boulder, gravel and sandy beds (see chapter 4, this volume), suspension transport becomes more probable and the dominant type of roughness might alter in the sequence form-grain-form, the first form roughness being associated with the drag exerted by large individual particles (Bathurst, 1978) and the second with the bed forms commonly developed in sand-bed streams. As regards energy degradation by grain roughness, it is reasonable to expect that the larger bed-material sizes (e.g. D_{84}, D_{90}) have a greater effect, and from the limited evidence available (table 5.2) they appear to decrease more rapidly downstream than do average ones.

Whereas an abundant literature exists on downstream changes in bed material properties, the same is not true of bank material despite its acknowledged influence on channel form, especially width. Given relatively uniform supply conditions and a tendency for transported sediment to become finer downstream, channel banks should become more cohesive and have a higher silt-clay content, which is one measure of their erosional resistance. To a certain extent this trend applies to rivers in the mid-west United States (figure 5.2), but it is unlikely to be well defined everywhere and even there, bank material composition is

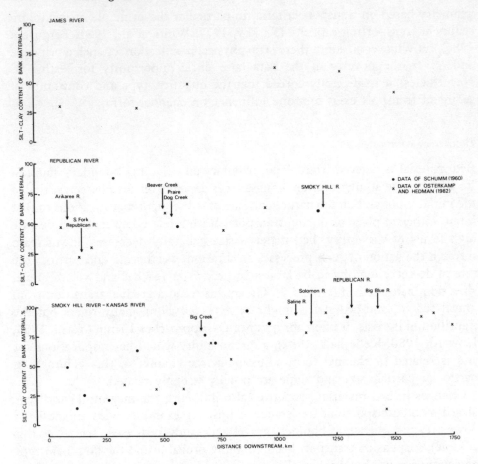

Figure 5.2   Downstream variation in bank silt-clay content along three rivers in the mid-west United States

highly variable. In addition, channel banks are often vertically stratified with a basal gravel layer overlain by fine alluvium (Klimek, 1974; Andrews, 1982; Pizzuto, 1984). In such conditions, bank resistance, and therefore the maintenance of channel width, are strongly related to the strength of the less cohesive basal layer, erosion of which induces block failure in the undercut cohesive material (Thorne and Tovey, 1981).

Regional, longitudinal and local variation exists in the composition of channel boundaries, the level of which is partly dependent on geomorphic history. Nevertheless, one of the more practical classifications of river channels is based on boundary composition (Knighton, 1984), the primary subdivision being into cohesive and non-cohesive channels (table 5.3). Most natural channels are type B, with B1 and B2 dominant. Frequently the bed and banks are composed of

Table 5.3   Channel classification based on boundary composition

Primary type	Secondary type	Characteristics
A Cohesive	A1 Bedrock channels	No coherent cover of unconsolidated material; generally short reaches
	A2 Silt-clay channels	Boundaries have a high silt-clay content, giving varying degrees of cohesion
B Non-cohesive	B1 Sand-bed channels	'Live-bed' channels composed largely of sandy material (0.063–2 mm) which is transported at a wide range of discharges
	B2 Gravel-bed channels	Channels of gravel (2–64 mm) or cobbles (64–256 mm) which are transported only at higher discharges
	B3 Boulder-bed channels	Composed of very large particles (>256 mm) which are moved infrequently; grades into A1.

different material, a common contrast being between cohesive banks and a non-cohesive bed. Given the influence of boundary composition on channel form, empirical results obtained for one type of channel may not apply to another.

Valley slope

This variable is defined as the longitudinal slope of the valley measured along the main valley axis. It is largely an inherited characteristic related to past flow and sediment transport conditions. Despite an overall tendency to decrease longitudinally, the slope of the valley floor can vary significantly as a result of non-alluvial effects such as tectonic activity (Burnett and Schumm, 1983; chapter 2, this volume), or intra-basin contrasts in fluvial history. Thus, below the confluence of the Arkansas and Mississippi rivers, valley slope steepens markedly in response to the relatively high sediment loads carried into the main valley by the Arkansas River during the Pleistocene (Schumm, 1977). Such variations influence the adjustment of channel form, particularly channel slope.

DOWNSTREAM CHANGES IN RIVER CHANNEL FORM

Alluvial rivers with erodible boundaries flow in self-formed channels which, when subject to relatively uniform governing conditions, are expected to show a consistency of form, or average geometry, adjusted to transmit the imposed water and sediment discharges. The problem is to determine the nature of the adjustment process and establish relationships which link control and response variables.

Various approaches have been used to achieve those ends (Ferguson, 1986). *Theoretical* ones fall into two main categories:

> 1 those which are deterministically based and rely on equations descriptive of the dominant processes, e.g. threshold theory, or Parker's (1978; 1979) model of lateral diffusion, which attempts to resolve the paradox that stable banks are incompatible with a mobile bed;
> 2 those which postulate additional conditions regarding the behaviour of stable rivers, e.g. minimum variance theory (Langbein, 1964), minimum stream power concepts (Yang, 1976; Chang, 1979), the principle of maximum sediment transporting capacity (White et al., 1981).

While symptomatic of a healthy concern for defining a stable channel geometry, the proliferation of theoretical treatments does underline the fundamental problem of providing sufficient good quality data for effective testing.

Empirical approaches include the regime 'theory' of the Anglo-Indian school of engineers (Lacey, 1930) and its extensions (Blench, 1969), and the hydraulic geometry methodology pioneered by Leopold and Maddock (1953). The two are not strictly equivalent but they become approximately so when downstream hydraulic geometry is applied to rivers with relatively homogeneous conditions of the independent variables.

Relationships have been formulated in a variety of ways, with those based on discharge as the single independent variable dominating analysis. The hydraulic geometry approach expresses the dependent variables, width (w), mean depth (d), mean velocity (v) and slope (s), as simple power functions of discharge-

$$w = aQ^b \qquad (5.3)$$
$$d = cQ^f \qquad (5.4)$$
$$v = kQ^m \qquad (5.5)$$
$$s = gQ^z \qquad (5.6)$$

Since not all discharges have the same capacity to perform work, a critical issue is the choice of an appropriate discharge with assumed channel-forming significance. Bankfull discharge is an obvious candidate but it cannot always be defined and is not necessarily of constant frequency (Williams, 1978a). Flows with a specified return period (e.g. the median (Q_2) or mean annual ($Q_{2.33}$) flood) or duration circumvent the latter problem but their accurate definition requires a long period of records. In addition hydraulic geometry relationships refer specifically to the channel only when related to a geomorphic reference level, such as the bankfull state, rather than a particular stage. If discharges with return periods in the range of 1.2–3 years do transport most sediment, then the appropriate choice would seem to lie in that range. Bankfull discharge, which Hey (1978) advocates for design purposes, usually fulfils that condition.

Several extensions of this approach have been proposed; for example, Parker (1978; 1979) introduced dimensionless hydraulic relations based on $w^* = w/D_{50}$, $d^* = d/D_{50}$ and $\tilde{Q} = Q/\{(s_g - 1)gD_{50}{}^5\}^{1/2}$, arguing that they convey more physical information than their dimensional counterparts. This last point leads naturally to multivariate approaches which include the effects of factors additional to water discharge. However, many of them are not easily quantified. With the paucity of sediment load data, bed and bank material composition have been the main factors involved, largely through the application of multiple regression methods.

Comparison of results is inhibited by the variety of approaches and the use of different discharge indices. Also, many investigations, and particularly those covering a large geographic area, include data from different river types. Distinctions can be drawn between three types of channel:

1 threshold channels in which bed material is entrained only at the highest discharges;
2 channels in which bed material is frequently entrained but transport rates are generally small; and
3 'live-bed' channels where entrainment occurs at discharges well below bankfull and sediment loads are usually high.

Relative to the previous classification (table 5.3), 1 and 2 belong largely to type B2 and 3 to type B1. Maddock (1969) has argued that these different types will not have the same channel characteristics.

Width and depth relationships

Table 5.4 gives the main results obtained at or close to bankfull discharge, grouped according to channel type. Despite the range of conditions covered, the data support the oft-quoted opinion that width varies approximately as the square root of discharge. However, it has been suggested that the rate of change of width is dependent on basin size (Klein, 1981) and climate through its influence on flow regime (Wolman and Gerson, 1978). Wolman and Gerson show that whereas width changes consistently in humid areas, it increases more rapidly in arid ones up to a drainage area of $100\,\text{km}^2$ but remains almost constant thereafter, a distinction not only between perennial and ephemeral streams but also in the relative effectiveness of extreme flows to produce channel widening. However, most of the evidence points to $b \sim 0.5$ where flow is perennially maintained.

The depth exponent (f) has a similar variability to that of b and again there is no clear difference between channel types. Church (1980) suggested the

Table 5.4 Downstream hydraulic geometry relations

Source	Location/Applicable conditions	Discharge	Coefficients		Exponents		
			a	c	b	f	z
i Threshold channels							
Kellerhals (1967)	Western Canada (1)	$\sim Q_3$	3.26	(0.42)	0.50	(0.40)	
Li et al. (1976)	Threshold theory	Q_b			0.46	0.46	−0.46
ii Gravel-bed rivers and canals							
Nixon (1959)	Britain (2)	Q_b	3.15		0.49		
Brush (1961)	Appalachians (3)	$Q_{2.33}$	1.85	0.28	0.55	0.36	
Simons and Albertson (1963)	Indian and USA canals, non-cohesive banks (4)	$\sim Q_b$	2.61	0.31	0.50	0.36	−0.24
Emmett (1975)	Upper Salmon River, Idaho (5)	Q_b	2.77	0.27	0.56	0.34	−0.24
Charlton et al. (1978)	Britain (6)	Q_b	3.74	0.31	0.45	0.40	−0.34
Bray (1982)	Alberta (7)	Q_2	4.79	0.26	0.53	0.33	−0.44
*Andrews (1984)	Colorado: thick bank vegetation	Q_b	3.91	0.49	0.48	0.37	−0.44
	thin bank vegetation	Q_b	4.94	0.48	0.48	0.38	−0.41
*Parker (1979)	Theoretical-momentum diffusion	Q_b	4.40	0.25	0.50	0.42	−0.41
Chang (1980)	Theoretical-minimum stream power	Q_b			0.47	0.42	
iii Sand-bed rivers and canals							
Lacey (1930)	Canals - Punjab (8)	$\sim Q_b$	4.83	(0.39)	0.50	(0.33)	
Simons and Albertson (1963)	Indian and US canals: sandy banks (9a)	$\sim Q_b$	5.23	0.69	0.50	0.36	−0.30
	cohesive banks, small load (9b)	$\sim Q_b$	3.93	0.58	0.50	0.36	−0.30
	cohesive banks, large load	$\sim Q_b$	2.55	0.45	0.50	0.36	−0.24
Mahmood et al. (1979)	Canals - Pakistan (10)	$\sim Q_b$	4.93	0.53	0.51	0.31	−0.09
iv Undifferentiated							
Rundquist (1975)	Rivers and canals with gravel and sand beds	Q_b	4.39	0.38	0.52	0.32	−0.30
Langbein (1965)	Minimum variance theory	$\sim Q_b$			0.50	0.38	−0.55

Discharge (Q) defined as bankfull (Q_b) or the one with a recurrence interval of 2 (Q_2), 2.33 ($Q_{2.33}$) or 3 (Q_3) years.
Symbols: $w = aQ^b$, $d = cQ^f$, $s = gQ^z$
*Analysis in terms of dimensionless variables. Bracketed coefficient and exponent values come from multivariate relations.

possibility of two regime types, $f = 0.33$ and $f = 0.40$, associated with relatively large and small sediment transport rates respectively. If they are tentatively equated with sand-bed channels on the one hand and threshold/gravel-bed channels on the other, the data in table 5.4 provide only limited support for the distinction, although extended results for British gravel rivers do appear to conform (Charlton et al., 1978).

Hydraulic geometry exponents are conservative quantities constrained by $b + f + m = 1$ and may therefore be rather insensitive. Although also subject to a continuity requirement (a. c. $k = 1$), the corresponding coefficient values tend to vary more widely and in so doing reflect more sharply the multivariate character of channel form control. Just a cursory examination of table 5.4 suggests that depths at unit discharge are higher in sand-bed than in gravel-bed rivers.

Discharge, the control whose downstream pattern of variation is best established, acts as a scale variable in determining the gross dimensions of the channel through its largely unknown relationship to the distribution of effective stresses at the channel boundary. That action is constrained by boundary composition. Data from the Missouri basin indicate that, as the bed material changes from a high silt-clay content to sand, there is a systematic increase in the coefficient value (and, to a lesser extent, the exponent) in the width-discharge relation (Osterkamp, 1980). Further increases in bed material size up to a boulder bed reverse the trend. These results suggest that rivers which transport relatively large amounts of sand as bed-material load require a large channel width to maintain sediment movement. Certainly a larger bed load is generally associated with wider, shallower channels, and with respect to gravel-bed streams, Parker (1979) has predicted that a 30 per cent increase in load requires a 40 per cent increase in width. Pickup (1976) has argued that a river adjusts its bed width to optimize bed-load transport, echoing the principle of maximum sediment transport capacity used by White et al. (1981) to predict stable widths and depths. However, sediment load is rarely incorporated in downstream relations and even then only as a derived rather than directly measured quantity (Hey, 1982).

The influence of bed material size on depth is usually contained in multivariate relations, the associated exponent typically lying in the range -0.10 to -0.17 (Lacey, 1930; Kellerhals, 1967; Hey, 1982). Translated into a downstream context, a decreasing bed material size would therefore tend to reinforce the effect of discharge on depth. Comparing Simons and Albertson's (1963) results for gravel and sand-bed canals with non-cohesive banks (4 and 9a in table 5.4, figure 5.3), the latter have width and depth coefficients more than twice those of the former.

Bank material characteristics are an important sedimentological control on the strength and stability of channel banks, and therefore on the adjustment of channel width. Simons and Albertson's (1963) results for sand-bed canals

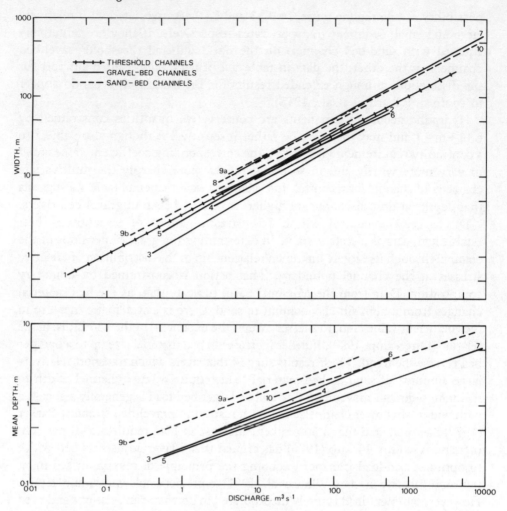

Figure 5.3   Width- and depth-discharge relations plotted over the measured discharge ranges for three types of channel. Numbers refer to table 5.4

illustrate the effect in that the width coefficient for sandy banks is 33 per cent larger than that for cohesive banks (table 5.4, figure 5.3). Although bank strength is not simply correlated with any one material property, it does depend on the degree of cohesion which can be expressed by the silt-clay content of the banks (B) or channel perimeter (M). For sand-bed rivers in the Great Plains, relations have been obtained by Ferguson (1973)

$$w = 33.1 \; Q_{2.33}^{0.58} \; B^{-0.66} \tag{5.7}$$

and Schumm (1971)

$$w = 5.54 \, Q_{2.33}{}^{0.58} \, M^{-0.37} \tag{5.8}$$
$$d = 0.12 \, Q_{2.33}{}^{0.42} \, M^{0.35} \tag{5.9}$$

which imply that uniform bank material should give rise to well-defined width- and depth-discharge relations. If banks become more cohesive downstream (B or M increases), which could be associated with an increasing dominance of suspended over bed-load transport, width will increase more slowly and depth more rapidly than expected from the effect of discharge alone.

The resistance of channel banks to erosion is also influenced by the type of vegetation. Charlton et al. (1978) found that channels with grassed banks were on average 30 per cent wider and those with tree-lined banks up to 30 per cent narrower than the overall width-discharge relation would suggest. Results from Colorado (Andrews, 1984; table 5.4) support this conclusion and, in addition, show that the width-discharge relations for British and Colorado gravel-bed rivers are not significantly different, implying some degree of consistency in adjustment within a given class of river.

Bank stability is thus a critical factor in determining channel form. Parker (1978) has formulated a quantitative model for bank stability based on a principle of lateral diffusion. In order to maintain equilibrium in sand-silt rivers, the depletion of material from the banks is countered by the lateral diffusion of suspended sediment which over-loads the flow near the banks and causes deposition, a mechanism for which there is empirical support (Andrews, 1982; Pizzuto, 1984). In gravel rivers the appropriate mechanism is the lateral transfer of downstream momentum which induces a stress distribution allowing a mobile bed but immobile banks at bankfull or dominant discharge. Although not meeting all of the physical requirements of the theoretical model, Colorado gravel-bed rivers have hydraulic characteristics in broad agreement with prediction, particularly as regards the width relation (table 5.4). Those rivers have cohesive banks able to withstand higher stresses than the non-cohesive material considered in Parker's analysis, and in view of this constraint on width, it is perhaps significant that the depth coefficients are about twice that predicted. It is possible that only rivers with sufficient fine sediment to form stable, cohesive banks can approach a fully adjusted channel condition (Osterkamp et al., 1983).

The width and depth of a channel are not adjusted independently. In applying a multiple-equation model to the question of their mutual adjustment, Miller (1984) concludes that whereas discharge has the dominant direct effect on channel development, sediment variables have the dominant indirect effect. Given that the adjustment mechanism integrates indirect effects, Miller maintains that the mutual adjustment of width and depth is primarily dependent on sediment characteristics. To some extent this is borne out by a re-analysis of Schumm's data set (Richards, 1982),

$$w/d = 800 \ Q_{2.33}{}^{0.15} \ B^{-1.20} \tag{5.10}$$

where the sediment variable has the larger influence on the form ratio. Where the ratio is expressed solely as a function of discharge, the coefficient is seen to depend on the type of bank material (Bray, 1982).

Given the multivariate character of channel-form controls, it is perhaps too much to expect consistency in relations where discharge is the only independent variable. However, the effects of factors other than discharge are not easily incorporated, especially in a downstream context, and this applies particularly to sediment transport whose influence can only be assessed in an indirect way. Dimensionless analysis of the kind proposed by Parker (1978; 1979) may produce some improvement by reducing the differences related to absolute scale and allowing any differences due to dynamics to be more clearly seen, but it cannot alter the data problem.

Subdivision of the dimensional relations into the three types, threshold, gravel-bed and sand-bed channels, produces no unequivocal distinctions, except possibly for depth at discharges less than $100 \ m^3 \ s^{-1}$ (figure 5.3). It should be noted, however, that of all the results considered, only Emmett's (1975) apply to a single river system. In addition, many of the plotted relations cover different types of bank material, and as various results have shown, this factor can have a large influence on coefficient values. If downstream change in channel form is capable of determinate solution, the provision of a physically-based width equation which takes account of bank material composition is a primary requirement.

Slope relationships

Whether slope is regarded as a dependent or independent variable depends partly on the time-scale and physiographic setting in which one is working (Schumm, 1977). If slope is treated as part of the dependent downstream geometry, then threshold and regime theory require respectively that either ds or $d^{1/2}s$ is approximately constant along a channel with the same bed material and sediment concentration (Henderson, 1961). Assuming $d \propto Q^{0.4}$, these conditions imply $s \propto Q^{-0.4}$ or $s \propto Q^{-0.2}$ which, given the tenets of the two theories, might apply to coarse material on the one hand and sandy material on the other. This distinction is only partly borne out by the results in table 5.5.

Slope-discharge correlations for natural rivers tend to be rather poor. Coefficient and exponent values have wide ranges and both have been shown to vary with a diverse collection of factors, including physiography (Bray, 1982), bed material characteristics (Osterkamp, 1978) and Froude number (Barr et al., 1980). Such is the scale of variation that it could be argued that any slope-discharge relation is principally a function of the physiographic province in which measurements are made and that no overall tendency exists. Even a good correlation does not necessarily mean that discharge is a major determinant of slope (Prestegaard, 1983). However, downstream changes in discharge influence the ability to transport sediment on which the adjustment of slope ultimately depends. Application of the principle of maximum transport capacity suggests that slope is strongly dependent on sediment transport rate, especially in sand-bed channels (White et al., 1980).

Correlations can be greatly improved by using dimensionless rather than dimensional discharge (Parker, 1982) which, since the dimensionless form contains two parameters, Q and D_{50}, hints at the joint control of discharge and bed material size on channel slope. Bed material size has implications for both particle mobility and channel roughness. In the multivariate relationships of table 5.5 the bed material exponent always exceeds the discharge exponent in absolute value, suggesting that bed material size has the greater effect. Prestegaard's (1983) results for gravel-bed streams confirm that point but Penning-Rowsell and Townshend (1978) found that only at the local rather than reach scale was bed material the more important factor. There is little consistency of coefficient or exponent values in the relationships except possibly for the discharge exponent (~ -0.40) in types (i) and (ii).

The question arises as to the relative significance of different grain-size parameters. For British gravel rivers Charlton et al. (1978) suggested that slope is better related to D_{65} (the threshold grain diameter at bankfull flow) than to D_{90} (the diameter used to represent the size of roughness elements), which emphasizes the transport rather than resistance significance of bed material. To a certain extent the differences between Coloradan channels with thick and thin bank vegetation underline this point in that the relative narrowness of the former, implying a reduced transport capacity, is counteracted by their larger slope (tables 5.4 and 5.5). However, the resistance effect on slope through bed material size has also been emphasized (Leopold and Bull, 1979; Prestegaard, 1983) and in that respect the larger diameters play the dominant role, at least in coarse bed streams. Along the River Hodder Wilcock (1967) found that slope correlated poorly with the median diameter of all bed material but significantly with the median diameter of the 'residual' bed material (defined as that fraction which is immobile at present bankfull flow), implying that slope is more closely related not only to large sizes but also to previous conditions when that material was more mobile.

The downstream rates of change of channel slope and bed material size are closely related, with profiles being more concave where bed material size decreases

Table 5.5 Slope relationships

Source	Location/Applicable conditions	Type of equation Bivariate	Type of equation Multivariate
i Threshold channels			
Henderson (1961)	Limiting slope for Type B channel		$s = 0.338\, Q_b^{-0.46}\, D_{90}^{1.15}$
Kellerhals (1967)	Western Canada		$s = 0.086\, Q_3^{-0.40}\, D_{90}^{0.92}$
Li et al. (1976)	Threshold theory	$s = g\, Q_b^{-0.46}$	
ii Gravel-bed rivers and canals			
Charlton et al. (1978)	Britain		$s = 0.40\, Q_b^{-0.42}\, D_{65}^{1.38}\, D_{90}^{-0.24}$
Bray (1982)	Alberta	$s = 0.0105\, Q_2^{-0.34}$	$s = 0.060\, Q_2^{-0.33}\, D_{50}^{0.59}$
Hey (1982)	Britain		$s = 0.679\, Q_b^{-0.53}\, Q_s^{0.13}\, D_{50}^{0.97}$
Andrews (1984)	Colorado: thick bank vegetation		$s = 0.318\, \tilde{Q}_b^{-0.44}\ (\sim 0.587\, Q_b^{-0.44}\, D_{50}^{1.10})$
	thin bank vegetation		$s = 0.162\, \tilde{Q}_b^{-0.41}\ (\sim 0.285\, Q_b^{-0.41}\, D_{50}^{1.02})$
Parker (1979)	Theoretical-momentum diffusion		$s = 0.223\, \tilde{Q}_b^{-0.41}\ (\sim 0.395\, Q_b^{-0.41}\, D_{50}^{1.02})$
iii Sand-bed rivers and canals			
Lacey (1930)	Canals - Punjab		$s = 0.211\, Q^{-0.17}\, D_{50}^{0.83}$
Simons and Albertson (1963)	Indian and US canals: sandy banks	$s = 0.00007\, Q^{-0.30}$	
	cohesive banks, small load	$s = 0.0026\, Q^{-0.30}$	
Mahmood et al. (1979)	Canals - Pakistan	$s = 0.0019\, Q^{-0.09}$	
iv Undifferentiated			
Rundquist (1975)	Rivers and canals with gravel and sand beds	$s = 0.0032\, Q_b^{-0.30}$	$s = 0.002\, Q_b^{-0.25}\, D_{50}^{0.36}$

Symbols: Discharge (Q, in m³ s⁻¹): bankfull (Q_b); discharge with a recurrence interval of 2 (Q_2) or 3 (Q_3) years; $\tilde{Q}$ $(= Q/[(s_g - 1)gD_{50}^5]^{1/2})$. Bed material size ($D$, in m): median ($D_{50}$): that size at which 65 per cent (D_{65}) or 90 per cent (D_{90}) is finer. Bed-load discharge (Q_s, in m³ s⁻¹).

more rapidly (Hack, 1957; Ikeda, 1970). In addition, where a rapid transition from gravel-bed to sand-bed conditions occurs, there can be a distinct break of slope (Yatsu, 1955). Indeed Howard (1980; this volume, chapter 4) draws a sharp distinction between the two types of channel and shows that more rapid decreases in slope occur in the former. Along the River Bollin-Dean, slope decreases markedly as bed material is reduced in size from 64 to 4 mm but changes only slowly once the bed becomes sandy (Knighton, 1975). The variability and possibly the adjustability of channel slope seem to be greater where bed material exceeds about 10 mm in average size.

To maintain a constant bed-load discharge (Q_{sb}) where w and d increase and D decreases downstream, a simplified version of the Einstein-Brown bed-load function

$$Q_{sb} = K \frac{w(d. \ s)^3}{D^{1/2}} \tag{5.11}$$

implies that slope must decrease longitudinally at a rate dependent on the rates at which w, d and D change (Knighton, 1984). Based on an assumed equation for shear-stress distribution expressed in terms of the width-depth ratio, Osterkamp *et al.* (1983) demonstrate the co-variation of b, f and z with z normally in the range of -0.25 to -0.40 for w/d < 50. These types of analysis emphasize that in addition to or as an alternative to slope, the cross-sectional (and plan) form of a channel can be adjusted to maintain the continuity of sediment transport. The concept of minimum stream power (Chang, 1979) and its equivalent, the principle of maximum transporting capacity (White *et al.*, 1981), imply that for a given discharge a river will minimize its slope in order to attain equilibrium. However, slope minimization is constrained in part by inherited conditions reflected in the gradient of the valley floor. Thus the time-scales of adjustment for the various elements of channel form become relevant.

ADJUSTABILITY OF CHANNEL FORM

Various causes produce change in river channels. Recent floods and man-induced modifications of the fluvial environment are the best documented of those causes but the response they produce may be different in character from that associated with more gradual, secular changes in control conditions, especially as regards temporal lag. Rates of response depend on many factors, including the magnitude and direction of the change, the size and type of channel, and the climatic regime, so that they can be highly variable even within a small area. Consequently representative rates are difficult to define.

Table 5.6 Width adjustment to large floods

River	Drainage area (km²)	Frequency of event (years)	Maximum widening (%)	Relaxation time (years)	Source
Patuxent	90	200	64	15	Gupta and Fox (1974)
Baisman Run	4	200	160 (average of 10–20)	1–10	Costa (1974)
Appalachian rivers	0.25–25	100	300–400	10	Hack and Goodlett (1960)
Gila	20 000–25 000	200	600	45–50	Burkham (1972)

Cross-sectional form, at least in the width dimension, appears to be one of the most adjustable components of channel geometry and data for extreme floods indicate relatively short relaxation times (table 5.6). Along the Gila River between 1905 and 1917 (possibly the wettest period since 1650), a series of large winter floods carrying low sediment loads destroyed the floodplain and widened the channel from 90 m to 610 m (Burkham, 1972). From 1918 onwards the floodplain was reconstructed by smaller floods carrying large loads so that by the 1960s the channel had almost regained its former width (figure 5.4a). The ability of a river to recover from such extreme events depends upon the supply of sufficient fine material for channel reconstruction and the rate of vegetative regeneration. Channels in more arid areas where vegetation is sparser tend to have not only longer recovery times but also greater susceptibility to such events. Changes in bed elevation and therefore channel depth over time periods ranging from days to decades can also be produced by large floods, especially in sand-bed rivers. Bed height may increase initially due to the influx of eroded material from upstream and then decrease during a period of degradation when outflow exceeds supply (figure 5.4b).

Rivers adjust their cross-sections in response not only to isolated events but also to more sustained changes having longer-term significance. Downstream of reservoirs where flood peaks and sediment load are much reduced, decreases in bankfull cross-sectional area of over 50 per cent are not uncommon (Petts, 1979). In the Platte River system where peak and mean annual discharges have declined to 10–30 per cent of their pre-dam values, channel widths have been decreased by equivalent amounts over 40–60 years (Williams, 1978b), the narrowing process tending to lag behind the reduction in flow by up to 15 years (figure 5.4c). There also, large fluctuations in depth have accompanied the complex regulation of water and sediment delivery to the rivers. Evidence exists of change in the opposite direction. Following flow diversion which increased mean annual discharge fifty-fold, the Cheslatta River widened its channel from 5 m to 75–100 m and entrenched itself 10–15 m below the former floodplain within a period of 20 years (Kellerhals et al., 1979). The larger flood flows which typically accompany urbanization can enlarge cross-sectional area by more than six times over periods measured in years rather than decades (Hammer, 1972).

Width and depth can clearly adjust rapidly to altered conditions, the scale and rate of adjustment depending on environmental factors. There will obviously be a time-lag between cause and effect, particularly when control conditions change abruptly. This is especially evident where channel narrowing is the anticipated change, since it requires the import and redistribution of material to form lateral berms and bars. The sensitivity of cross-sectional form raises the question of a river's ability to attain and maintain a stable width and depth, especially where a few large events can produce substantial change. In environments where vegetation and material properties give stability to channel banks, extreme floods appear to have less effect (Costa, 1974; Gupta and Fox, 1974) so that a mean channel geometry can more readily be maintained. Osterkamp et al. (1983) argue that only streams with sufficient suspended sediment approach a fully adjusted condition, and that the flashier the regime the larger the suspended-sediment concentrations need to be if approximate equilibrium is to be achieved.

In regime 'theory' slope is regarded as a dependent variable which can be adjusted when designing a stable channel. Slope adjustment in natural rivers is brought about by aggradation, degradation and changing channel pattern acting singly or in combination. Major floods which supply and redistribute large amounts of sediment can cause large changes in slope at both the reach (Chang, 1982) and profile (Patrick et al., 1982) scales. The Eel River, which in 1964 experienced a flood having a return period greater than 100 years, subsequently degraded its bed in the middle and upper basin and aggraded in downstream reaches to give a significantly modified profile (figure 5.5a). Along a 35 km diversion channel in Manitoba flood flows initiated a period of degradation (up to 4 m) shortly after construction (Kellerhals et al., 1979). Although relatively gentle (0.0005–0.0011), the original design slopes seem to have been the main cause of the problem, being too steep by a factor of almost ten.

Changes to bed elevation and slope can also accompany artificial modifications which disturb the continuity of sediment transport. Channelization both in and downstream of the Tillotoba Creek basin triggered a period of upstream progressive degradation which lowered the stream bed by up to 4.6 m over 20 years (Patrick et al., 1982). The release of sediment-free water below dams tends to entrain material on the bed, resulting in downstream progressive degradation

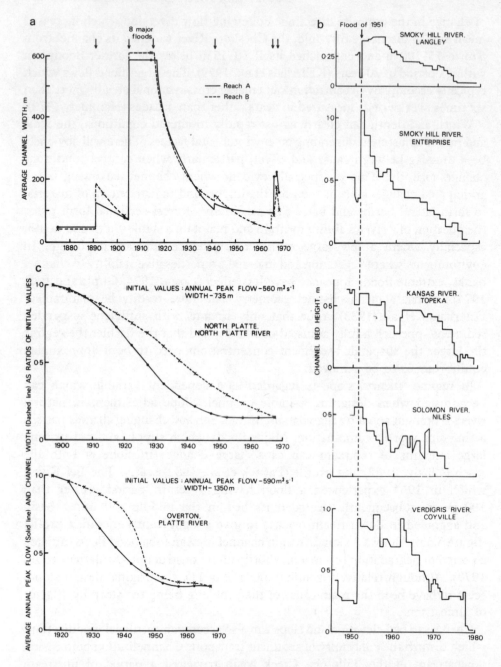

Figure 5.4 Changes in: (a) Channel width, Gila River, Arizona. Arrows indicate major floods (after Burkham, 1972) (b) Channel bed height, Kansas rivers (after Osterkamp and Harrold, 1982) (c) Annual peak discharge and channel width averaged over 5-year periods, Platte and North Platte Rivers, Nebraska (after Williams, 1978b)

and a flatter slope (figure 5.5b). Although initially localized, the effect can be transmitted rapidly over long river distances. Below the Hoover Dam degradation extended 130 km in nine years, reaching a maximum of 7.1 m at a downstream distance of 12.4 km (Galay, 1983).

These and other examples illustrate a potentially rapid rate of slope adjustment where input conditions are substantially modified. However, that adjustment may be constrained by bedrock controls and the effects of bed armouring, notably where degradation is the dominant process for it is slower than aggradation (Gessler, 1971). Also, the attainment of a new stable slope may take many years. In analysing the effects of a flow diversion which trebled mean annual discharge in the Lower Kemano River (Kellerhals et al., 1979), Bettess and White (1983) predict an increase in width and a decrease in slope by a factor of 1.4. Within 20 years width had increased by 1.3 but changes in slope were more modest and they estimate that a complete adjustment of slope could take several hundred years.

This example raises the issue of alternative forms of adjustment. In response to an increased sediment load, the East Fork River has over a period of 40 years changed its depth and roughness without significantly modifying its slope (Andrews, 1979). In Walker Creek, California, which has over 5000 years experienced one episode of infilling and two of incision, the most recent beginning about 100 years ago, gradient adjustments of 2 to 4 per cent have been made but are insignificant when compared with cross-sectional changes (Haible, 1980). Leopold and Bull (1979) conclude from work in semi-arid areas that changes in slope account for only a small part of the adjustment required to achieve a balance between the input and output of sediment load, most of the adjustment being accomplished by changes to other aspects of flow and channel geometry which respond more rapidly.

Because successive channel segments are interdependent, slope adjustment requires the redistribution of very large quantities of material. To that extent alone slope in natural rivers can be regarded either as an imposed parameter, or with valley slope imposed, as a parameter adjustable only over a limited range in the short to medium term. At least part of that limited adjustment can be accommodated by changes to channel pattern, notably sinuosity. Indeed a sinuous river may be better able than a straight one to balance the movement of sediments through the inter-relationship of path length, slope and transport capacity (Winkley, 1982). Schumm's (1968) study of the Murrumbidgee River system illustrates that in response to variations in discharge and load over 10^4 years, the required slope adjustments were almost entirely accommodated by changes to channel sinuosity.

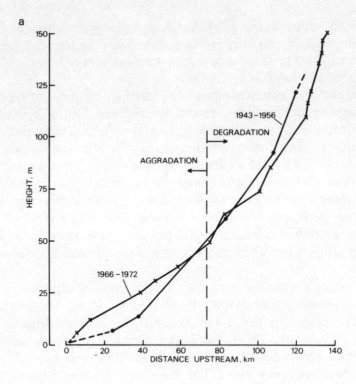

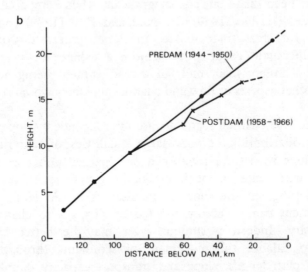

Figure 5.5 Changes in longitudinal profiles
(a) Eel River, California; (b) Downstream of Garrison Dam, Missouri River
(after Patrick et al. 1982)

DISCONTINUITIES IN DOWNSTREAM ADJUSTMENT

The equations which describe downstream change in channel form are invariably presented as continuous functions. However, downstream change along individual rivers is discontinuous, principally because of tributary inflow. Other conditions of a random or systematic nature can also produce more or less abrupt transitions in control and response variables, so that orderly change in natural rivers may be limited in spatial extent.

Variations in bedrock structure and lithology create irregularities in fluvial transport and channel form. In the Grand Canyon where the overall channel gradient is dominated by the fall in rapids, channel width is structurally controlled (Howard and Dolan, 1981). In narrower reaches (largely crystalline rocks) transport competence is enhanced and cobble bars are rare, being preferentially deposited in wider sections.

Discontinuities occur in the supply and transport of material, especially where localized mass movements are a major source. A mass of debris containing size fractions which cannot quickly be dispersed will introduce a perturbation into the channel and affect channel gradient in the neighbourhood of the deposit. Repetition of the process downstream could give rise to a stepped river profile in which zones of sedimentation and transport alternate (Church and Jones, 1982). The Bella Coola River in Canada possesses such a sequence. That river seems to have become more stable within the last century, at least in its lower course, possibly because the large volumes of sediment introduced upstream by the erosion of neoglacial moraines are now being exhausted with downstream progression of the sediment wave (Church, 1983). Thus the effects of an initially localized source can be transmitted over long river distances.

Major structural or physiographic boundaries disrupt orderly downstream trends. Uplift along an axis crossing a river causes decreases in slope and depth upstream and the opposite effects downstream, although in the latter the channel may increase in sinuosity to compensate for the steeper valley slope (Burnett and Schumm, 1983; Gregory and Schumm, this volume, chapter 3). In New South Wales where streams descend from an escarpment onto a coastal lowland there is a sharp decrease in width and channel capacity at the transition despite a continuing increase in discharge (Nanson and Young, 1981). Hydraulic relations may be improved if data are stratified according to physiographic criteria (e.g. Bray, 1982).

Of more general significance are the transitions in channel type associated in particular with downstream changes in bed material size. Along gravel-bed sections average grain size tends to decline irregularly until it approaches 10 mm when there is often a sharp transition to a predominantly sandy bed (Yatsu,

1955; Kellerhals, 1982; table 5.2). Such an abrupt decline can produce a discontinuity in profile form and a change in the behaviour of channel slope (Bennett, 1976). Clearly such a transition has implications not only for sediment transport dynamics but also for general stream behaviour. Howard (1980) argues convincingly that gravel- and sand-bed rivers are distinct types with different adjustment characteristics and that downstream transitions should be common. Interestingly Rana et al. (1973) have developed a sediment sorting model which predicts a related grain size-slope transition when bed material is entirely in the sand fraction.

Of all the causes of discontinuity tributary inflow is the most important. Tributary-main stream interaction is a two-way process, but because tributaries are the primary source of discharge addition and major suppliers of sediment, their influence is dominant, inducing both localized and more persistent response. This is evident in the Guanipa basin of Venezuela where a tributary having a lower mean annual but much larger peak discharge causes a ten-fold widening of the main channel below the confluence (Stevens et al., 1975). Major tributaries which carry a lower discharge can nevertheless input a higher load. Relative to the main stream, the Little Snake River in the Yampa basin supplies 27 per cent of the annual runoff but 69 per cent of the sediment load (Andrews, 1980). Aggradation is a frequent response to a large tributary load, especially if the input contains size fractions which the main stream is locally incompetent to transport, requiring gradient and possibly channel pattern adjustments to be made.

Tributaries can alter bed and bank material composition below junctions. The tendency for tributaries to input coarser debris increases average grain size and worsens bed material sorting in the main channel (Knighton, 1980; Troutman, 1980). With a sequence of tributaries, grain size may vary discontinuously in such a way that an exponential decrease below each junction is followed by a stepped increase at the next junction, the magnitude of which could be related to the relative material and channel sizes of the main stream and tributary at each confluence. Occasionally the opposite occurs. Muddy Creek inputs a relatively large load of finer material into the East Fork River, causing a discontinuous change in median grain size from 35–70 mm to 1.25 mm in a distance of 5 km (Andrews, 1979). The Saline and Solomon Rivers introduce large amounts of silt-clay into the Smoky Hill River, increasing M sharply (Schumm, 1960). In line with equations (5.8) and (5.9) there is an abrupt increase in channel depth, but despite the large addition of flow, only a small increase in width.

These few examples show that the effects of individual tributaries can be large and highly variable. Consequently they are difficult to incorporate in a general model of downstream channel adjustment. Attempts have been made to relate hydrological response to network structure (Gupta and Waymire, 1983), and Richards (1980) reasons that channel width can be treated as a link-associated variable with

$$w_\mu = w_1 \mu^k \tag{5.12}$$

where w_μ is the average width of a link having magnitude μ. Thus step changes at junctions are combined with stochastic variation within links. Flint (1974; 1976) has adopted a similar line with respect to link slope (s_μ):

$$s_\mu = s_1 (2_\mu - 1)^r \tag{5.13}$$

The sequence of tributary sizes down a main stream is not random because of the spatial requirements of tributary development (Jarvis and Sham, 1981). Equally tributary influence on mainstream behaviour may vary longitudinally with changing relative size. In the upper parts of a basin where the incidence of junctions is high and tributaries of similar size to the main stream are relatively common, frequent adjustments to channel form are probably required (e.g. Rendell and Alexander, 1979). Further downstream only the widely-separated larger tributaries are likely to have a marked effect if relative discharge or magnitude is taken as the criterion for comparison (nevertheless, small steep tributaries can still introduce large sediment loads). In assessing patterns of variation according to stream order, Onesti and Miller (1974) suggest that hydraulic relationships should be better defined with distance downstream as flow and channel variables become increasingly interdependent and natural constraints decline in importance. A network-channel model which accommodates variable tributary influence could provide a basis not only for a more realistic assessment of downstream channel adjustment but also for predicting tributary-mainstream interactions in basins subject to disturbance.

CONCLUSION

Assuming that an average geometry can be defined, the results in table 5.4 suggest

$$w = aQ^{0.5} \qquad d = cQ^{0.36} \tag{5.14}$$

at discharges in the neighbourhood of bankfull, with a ϵ (2.5, 4.8) and c ϵ (0.26, 0.56) as one standard deviation limits for the coefficients. Considering the bias toward humid area rivers, these limits remain quite broad. Some improvement can be effected by using dimensionless variables which include a bed material factor (Parker, 1982) or by stratifying relations according to practical criteria such as physiography or boundary composition but the initial sample needs to be large enough to avoid dangerously small subsets. Classification into three channel types suggests that a, and in particular c, are larger in sand-bed rivers than in the other two types with respective averages of 4.3, 0.56 and 3.2, 0.28 but distinctions are not always sharp (figure 5.3). Although the variability of coefficient, and to a lesser extent exponent values, is increasingly recognized, being dependent at least in part on sediment properties, downstream change in channel form cannot be readily generalized from simple power functions. Multivariate relationships provide only a partial answer because many factors are difficult to quantify. Consistency in downstream adjustment is probably limited to river lengths having relatively orderly change in control conditions and may be better defined in those variables which are more dependent on discharge than sediment characteristics. Thus could the less predictable behaviour of channel slope be explained. In addition, with slope adjustment constrained, width and depth should be better related to prevailing conditions. Definition of an average geometry is even more problematic where the various outputs have different time-scales of response as yet unspecified in an acceptable way.

Given the inherent variability of river systems and the poverty of the data base in key areas, theoretical postulates about downstream behaviour are extremely difficult to test effectively. Different elements of channel form may be determinate to different extents (Mosley, 1981), depending on their relative sensitivity to the quasi-random and discontinuous variations in influential factors which are typical of many natural rivers. Tributaries are the major source of discontinuity and their variable influence both as individuals and in sequence needs to be more formally established within a framework which combines network and channel attributes. Such a development would represent a break from the traditional use of continuous functions and introduce greater flexibility in the assessment of downstream channel adjustment.

REFERENCES

Andrews, E. D. 1979: Hydraulic adjustment of the East Fork River, Wyoming to the supply of sediment. In D. D. Rhodes and G. P. Williams (eds). *Adjustments of the Fluvial System*, London: George Allen and Unwin, 69–94.
Andrews, E. D. 1980: Effective and bankfull discharges of streams in the Yampa River basin, Colorado and Wyoming. *Journal of Hydrology*, 46, 311–30.
Andrews, E. D. 1982: Bank stability and channel width adjustment, East Fork River, Wyoming. *Water Resources Research*, 18, 1184–92.
Andrews, E. D. 1984: Bed-material entrainment and hydraulic geometry of gravel-bed rivers in Colorado. *Geological Society of America Bulletin*, 95, 371–8.

Bagnold, R. A. 1980: An empirical correlation of bedload transport rates in flumes and natural rivers. *Proceedings of the Royal Society*, 372A, 453–73.

Baker, V. R. 1977: Stream-channel response to floods, with examples from central Texas. *Geological Society of America Bulletin*, 88, 1057–71.

Barr, D. I. H., Alan, M. K. and Nishat, A. 1980: A contribution to regime theory relating principally to channel geometry. *Institution of Civil Engineers Proceedings*, 69, 651–70.

Bathurst, J. C. 1978: Flow resistance of large-scale roughness. *Journal of the Hydraulics Division, American Society of Civil Engineers*, 1587–604.

Bennett, R. J. 1976: Adaptive adjustment of channel geometry. *Earth Surface Processes*, 1, 131–50.

Benson, M. A. 1962: Factors influencing the occurrence of floods in a humid region of diverse terrain. *US Geological Survey Water-Supply Paper* 1580-B.

Bettess, R. and White, W. R. 1983: Meandering and braiding of alluvial channels. *Institution of Civil Engineers Proceedings*, 75, 525–38.

Bhowmik, N. G. 1984: Hydraulic geometry of floodplains. *Journal of Hydrology*, 68, 369–401.

Blench, T. 1969: *Mobile-bed Fluviology*. Edmonton, Alberta: University of Alberta Press.

Bogardi, J. 1974: *Sediment Transport in Alluvial Streams*. Budapest: Akademiai Kiado.

Bradley, W. C., Fahnestock, R. K. and Rowekamp, E. T. 1972: Coarse sediment transport by flood flows on Knik River, Alaska. *Geological Society of America Bulletin*, 83, 1261–84.

Bray, D. I. 1982: Regime equations for gravel-bed rivers. In R. D. Hey, J. C. Bathurst and C. R. Thorne (eds). *Gravel-bed Rivers*, Chichester: John Wiley, 517–42.

Brush, L. M. 1961: Drainage basins, channels, and flow characteristics of selected streams in central Pennsylvania. *US Geological Survey Professional Paper* 282F, 145–81.

Bull, W. B. 1979: Threshold of critical power in streams. *Geological Society of America Bulletin*, 90, 453–64.

Burkham, D. E. 1972: Channel changes of the Gila River in Safford valley, Arizona, 1846–1970. *US Geological Survey Professional Paper* 655G.

Burkham, D. E. 1976: Effects of changes in an alluvial channel on the timing, magnitude, and transformation of flood waves, southeastern Arizona. *US Geological Survey Professional Paper* 655K.

Burnett, A. W. and Schumm, S. A. 1983: Alluvial-river response to neotectonic deformation in Louisiana and Mississippi. *Science*, 222, 49–50.

Chang, H. H. 1979: Geometry of rivers in regime. *Journal of the Hydraulics Division, American Society of Civil Engineers*, 691–706.

Chang, H. H. 1980: Geometry of gravel streams. *Journal of the Hydraulics Division, American Society of Civil Engineers*, 106, 1443–56.

Chang, H. H. 1982: Mathematical model for erodible channels. *Journal of the Hydraulics Division, American Society of Civil Engineers*, 678–89.

Charlton, F. G., Brown, P. M. and Benson, R. W. 1978: The hydraulic geometry of some gravel rivers in Britain. *Hydraulics Research Station Report*, IT 180.

Church, M. 1980: *On the Equations of Hydraulic Geometry*. Vancouver: Department of Geography, University of British Columbia.

Church, M. 1983: Pattern of instability in a wandering gravel bed channel. In J. D. Collinson and J. Lewin (eds), *Modern and Ancient Fluvial Systems*, Oxford: Blackwell Scientific Publications, 169–80.

Church, M. and Jones, D. 1982: Channel bars in gravel-bed rivers. In R. D. Hey, J. C. Bathurst and C. R. Thorne (eds), *Gravel-bed Rivers*, Chichester: John Wiley, 291–324.

Church, M. and Kellerhals, R. 1978: On the statistics of grain size variation along a gravel river. *Canadian Journal of Earth Sciences*, 15, 1151–60.

Costa, J. E. 1974: Response and recovery of a Piedmont watershed from tropical storm Agnes, June 1972. *Water Resources Research*, 10, 106–12.

Emmett, W. W. 1975: The channels and waters of the Upper Salmon River area, Idaho. *US Geological Survey Professional Paper* 870A.

Emmett, W. W. and Thomas, W. A. 1978: Scour and deposition in Lower Granite Reservoir, Snake and Clearwater Rivers near Lewiston, Idaho. *Journal of Hydraulic Research*, 16, 327–45.

Ferguson, R. I. 1973: Channel pattern and sediment type. *Area*, 5, 38–41.

Ferguson, R. I. 1986: Hydraulics and hydraulic geometry. *Progress in Physical Geography*, 10, 1–31.

Flint, J. J. 1974: Stream gradient as a function of order, magnitude and discharge. *Water Resources Research*, 10, 969–73.

Flint, J. J. 1976: Link slope distribution in channel networks. *Water Resources Research*, 12, 645–54.

Flood Studies Report 1975: London: Natural Environment Research Council.

Galay, V. J. 1983: Causes of river bed degradation. *Water Resources Research*, 19, 1057–90.

Gessler, J. 1971: Aggradation and degradation. In H. W. Shen (ed.), *River Mechanics, Vol. 1*. Fort Collins, Colorado: H. W. Shen, 8.1–8.23.

Graf, W. L. 1983: Downstream changes in stream power in the Henry Mountains, Utah. *Annals of the Association of American Geographers*, 73, 373–87.

Griffiths, G. A. 1983: Stable-channel design in alluvial rivers. *Journal of Hydrology*, 65, 259–70.

Gupta, A. and Fox, H. 1974: Effects of high-magnitude floods on channel form: a case study in Maryland Piedmont. *Water Resources Research*, 10, 499–509.

Gupta, V. J. and Waymire, E. 1983: On the formulation of an analytical approach to hydrologic response and similarity at the basin scale. *Journal of Hydrology*, 65, 95–123.

Hack, J. T. 1957: Studies of longitudinal stream profiles in Virginia and Maryland. *US Geological Survey Professional Paper* 294B.

Hack, J. T. and Goodlett, J. C. 1960: Geomorphology and forest ecology of a mountain region in the Central Appalachians. *US Geological Survey Professional Paper* 347.

Haible, W. W. 1980: Holocene profile changes along a California coastal stream. *Earth Surface Processes*, 5, 249–64.

Hammer, T. R. 1972: Stream channel enlargement due to urbanization. *Water Resources Research*, 8, 1530–40.

Henderson, F. M. 1961: Stability of alluvial channels. *Journal of the Hydraulics Division, American Society of Civil Engineers*, 87, 109–38.

Hey, R. D. 1978: Determinate hydraulic geometry of river channels. *Journal of the Hydraulics Division, American Society of Civil Engineers*, 104, 869–85.

Hey, R. D. 1982: Design equations for mobile gravel-bed rivers. In R. D. Hey, J. C. Bathurst and C. R. Thorne (eds), *Gravel-bed Rivers*, Chichester: John Wiley, 553–74.

Howard, A. D. 1980. Thresholds in river regimes. In D. R. Coates and J. D. Vitek (eds), *Thresholds in Geomorphology*, Boston: George Allen and Unwin, 227–58.

Howard, A. D. and Dolan, R. 1981: Geomorphology of the Colorado River in the Grand Canyon. *Journal of Geology*, 89, 269–98.

Ikeda, H. 1970: On the longitudinal profiles of the Asake, Mitaki and Utsube Rivers, Mie Prefecture. *Geographical Review of Japan*, 43, 148–59.

Jarvis, R. S. and Sham, C. H. 1981: Drainage network structure and the diameter-magnitude relation. *Water Resources Research*, 17, 1019–27.

Kellerhals, R. 1967: Stable channels with gravel-paved beds. *Journal of the Waterways and Harbors Division, American Society of Civil Engineers*, 63–84.

Kellerhals, R. 1982: Effect of river regulation on channel stability. In R. D. Hey, J. C. Bathurst and C. R. Thorne (eds), *Gravel-bed Rivers*, Chichester: John Wiley, 685–705.

Kellerhals, R., Church, M. and Davies, L. B. 1979: Morphological effects of interbasin river diversions. *Canadian Journal of Civil Engineering*, 6, 18–31.

Kirkby, M. J. 1977: Maximum sediment efficiency as a criterion for alluvial channels. In K. J. Gregory (ed.), *River Channel Changes*, Chichester: Wiley-Interscience, 429–42.

Klein, M. 1981: Drainage area and the variation of channel geometry downstream. *Earth Surface Processes and Landforms*, 6, 589–94.

Klimek, K. 1974: The retreat of alluvial river banks in the Wisloka valley (south Poland). *Geographia Polonica*, 28, 59–75.

Knighton, A. D. 1975: Channel gradient in relation to discharge and bed material characteristics. *Catena*, 2, 263–74.

Knighton, A. D. 1980: Longitudinal changes in size and sorting of stream-bed material in four English rivers. *Geological Society of America Bulletin*, 91, 55–62.

Knighton, A. D. 1984: *Fluvial Forms and Processes*. London: Edward Arnold.

Lacey, G. 1930: Stable channels in alluvium. *Institution of Civil Engineers Proceedings*, 229, 259–384.

Langbein, W. B. 1964: Geometry of river channels. *Journal of the Hydraulics Division, American Society of Civil Engineers*, 90, 301–12.

Langbein, W. B. 1965: Geometry of river channels: closure of discussion. *Journal of the Hydraulics Division, American Society of Civil Engineers*, 91, 297–313.

Leopold, L. B. and Bull, W. B. 1979: Base level, aggradation and grade. *Proceedings of the American Philosophical Society*, 123, 168–202.

Leopold, L. B. and Maddock, T. 1953: The hydraulic geometry of stream channels and some physiographic implications. *US Geological Survey Professional Paper* 252.

Li, R.-M., Simons, D. B. and Stevens, M. A. 1976: Morphology of cobble streams in small watersheds. *Journal of the Hydraulics Division, American Society of Civil Engineers*, 102, 1101–17.

Maddock, T. 1969: The behavior of straight open channels with movable beds. *US Geological Survey Professional Paper* 622A.

Mahmood, K., Tarar, R. N. and Masood, T. 1979: *Hydraulic Geometry Relations for ACOP Channels*. Washington, DC: Civil, Mechanical and Environmental Engineering Department, George Washington University.

Meade, R. H. 1982: Sources, sinks, and storage of river sediment in the Atlantic drainage of the United States. *Journal of Geology*, 90, 235–52.

Miller, T. K. 1984: A system model of stream-channel shape and size. *Geological Society of American Bulletin*, 95, 237–41.

Mosley, M. P. 1981: Semi-determinate hydraulic geometry of river channels, South Island, New Zealand. *Earth Surface Processes and Landforms*, 6, 127–38.

Nanson, G. C. and Young, R. W. 1981: Downstream reduction of rural channel size with contrasting urban effects in small coastal streams of southeastern Australia. *Journal of Hydrology*, 52, 239–55.

Nash, J. E. and Shaw, B. L. 1966: Flood frequency as a function of catchment characteristics. In *Institution of Civil Engineers, Symposium on River Flood Hydrology*, 115–36.

Nixon, M. 1959: A study of the bankfull discharges of rivers in England and Wales. *Institution of Civil Engineers Proceedings*, 12, 157–75.

Nordin, C. F., Meade, R. H., Curtis, W. F., Bosio, N. J. and Landim, P. M. B. 1980: Size distribution of Amazon River bed sediment. *Nature*, 286, 52–3.

Onesti, L. J. and Miller, T. K. 1974: Patterns of variation in a fluvial system. *Water Resources Research*, 10, 1178–86.

Osterkamp, W. R. 1978: Gradient, discharge, and particle-size relations of alluvial channels in Kansas, with observations on braiding. *American Journal of Science*, 278, 1253–68.

Osterkamp, W. R. 1980: Sediment-morphology relations of alluvial channels. In *Proceedings of the Symposium on Watershed Management, American Society of Civil Engineers, Boise 1980*, 188–99.

Osterkamp, W. R. and Harrold, P. E. 1982: Dynamics of alluvial channels – a process model. In *Proceedings of the International Symposium on Rainfall-Runoff Modeling, Littleton*, 283–96.

Osterkamp, W. R. and Hedman, E. R. 1982: Perennial-streamflow characteristics related to channel geometry and sediment in Missouri River basin. *US Geological Survey Professional Paper* 1242.

Osterkamp, W. R., Lane, L. J. and Foster, G. R. 1983: An analytical treatment of channel-morphology relations. *US Geological Survey Professional Paper* 1288.

Parker, G. 1978: Self-formed straight rivers with equilibrium banks and mobile bed: Part 1 – The sand-silt river; Part 2 – The gravel river. *Journal of Fluid Mechanics*, 89, 109–46.

Parker, G. 1979: Hydraulic geometry of active gravel rivers. *Journal of the Hydraulics Division, American Society of Civil Engineers*, 105, 1185–201.

Parker, G. 1982: Discussion of Bray, D. I. (1982). In R. D. Hey, J. C. Bathurst and C. R. Thorne (eds), *Gravel-bed Rivers*, Chichester: John Wiley, 542–51.

Patrick, D. M., Smith, L. M. and Whitten, C. B. 1982: Methods for studying accelerated fluvial change. In R. D. Hey, J. C. Bathurst and C. R. Thorne (eds), *Gravel-bed Rivers*, Chichester: John Wiley, 783–812.

Penning-Rowsell, E. G. and Townshend, J. R. G. 1978: The influence of scale on the factors affecting stream channel slope. *Transactions of the Institute of British Geographers, New Ser.*, 3, 395–415.

Petts, G. E. 1979: Complex response of river channel morphology to reservoir construction. *Progress in Physical Geography*, 3, 329–62.

Pickup, G. 1976: Adjustment of stream-channel shape to hydrologic regime. *Journal of Hydrology*, 30, 365–73.

Pickup, G. and Warner, R. F. 1976: Effects of hydrologic regime on magnitude and frequency of dominant discharge. *Journal of Hydrology*, 29, 51–75.

Pizzuto, J. E. 1984: Equilibrium bank geometry and the width of shallow sandbed streams. *Earth Surface Processes and Landforms*, 9, 199–207.

Prestegaard, K. L. 1983: Variables influencing water-surface slopes in gravel-bed streams at bankfull stage. *Geological Society of America Bulletin*, 94, 673–8.

Rana, S. A., Simons, D. B. and Mahmood, K. 1973: Analysis of sediment sorting in alluvial channels. *Journal of the Hydraulics Division, American Society of Civil Engineers*, 99, 1967–80.

Rendell, H. and Alexander, D. 1979: Note on some spatial and temporal variations in ephemeral channel form. *Geological Society of America Bulletin*, 90, 761–72.

Richards, K. S. 1980: A note on changes in channel geometry at tributary junctions. *Water Resources Research*, 16, 241–4.

Richards, K. S. 1982: *Rivers: Form and Process in Alluvial Channels*. London: Methuen.

Rundquist, L. A. 1975: *A classification and analysis of natural rivers*. Unpublished PhD thesis, Fort Collins: Colorado State University.

Schumm, S. A. 1960: The shape of alluvial channels in relation to sediment type. *US Geological Survey Professional Paper* 352B, 17–30.

Schumm, S. A. 1968: River adjustment to altered hydrologic regimen – Murrumbidgee River and paleochannels Australia. *US Geological Survey Professional Paper* 598.

Schumm, S. A. 1971: Fluvial geomorphology: the historical perspective. In H. W. Shen (ed.), *River Mechanics, Volume 1*, Fort Collins, Colorado: H. W. Shen, 4-1–4.30.

Schumm, S. A. 1977: *The Fluvial System*. New York: Wiley-Interscience.

Simons, D. B. and Albertson, M. L. 1963: Uniform water conveyance channels in alluvial material. *American Society of Civil Engineers Transactions*, 128, 65–107.

Simons, D. B. and Şentürk, F. 1977: *Sediment Transport Technology*. Fort Collins, Colorado: Water Resources Publications.

Stevens, M. A., Simons, D. B. and Richardson, E. V. 1975: Non-equilibrium river form. *Journal of the Hydraulics Division, American Society of Civil Engineers* 101, 557–66.

Thomas, D. M. and Benson, M. A. 1970: Generalization of stream-flow characteristics from drainage-basin characteristics. *US Geological Survey Water-Supply Paper* 1975.

Thorne, C. R. and Tovey, M. K. 1981: Stability of composite river banks. *Earth Surface Processes and Landforms*, 6, 469–84.

Trimble, S. W. 1975: Denudation studies: can we assume stream steady state? *Science*, 188, 1207–8.

Trimble, S. W. 1983: A sediment budget for Coon Creek basin in the driftless area, Wisconsin, 1853–1977. *American Journal of Science*, 283, 454–74.

Troutman, B. M. 1980: A stochastic model for particle sorting and related phenomena. *Water Resources Research*, 16, 65–76.

Walling, D. E. 1983: The sediment delivery problem. *Journal of Hydrology*, 65, 209–37.

White, W. R., Paris, E. and Bettess, R. 1981: River regime based on sediment transport concepts. *Hydraulics Research Station Report*, IT 201.

Wilcock, D. N. 1967: Coarse bedload as a factor determining bed slope. *Publication of the International Association of Scientific Hydrology*, 75, 143–50.

Williams, G. P. 1978a: Bankfull discharge of rivers. *Water Resources Research*, 14, 1141–58.

Williams, G. P. 1978b: The case of the shrinking channels – the North Platte and Platte Rivers in Nebraska. *US Geological Survey Circular* 781.

Winkley, B. R. 1982: Response of the lower Mississippi to river training and realignment. In R. D. Hey, J. C. Bathurst and C. R. Thorne (eds), *Gravel-bed Rivers*, Chichester: John Wiley, 659–80.

Wolman, M. G. and Gerson, R. 1978: Relative scales of time and effectiveness of climate in watershed geomorphology. *Earth Surface Processes*, 3, 189–208.

Wolman, M. G. and Miller, J. P. 1960: Magnitude and frequency of forces in geomorphic processes. *Journal of Geology*, 68, 54–74.

Yang, C. T. 1971: Potential energy and stream morphology. *Water Resources Research*, 7, 311–22.

Yang, C. T. 1976: Minimum unit stream power and fluvial hydraulics. *Journal of the Hydraulics Division, American Society of Civil Engineers*, 102, 919–34.

Yatsu, E. 1955: On the longitudinal profile of the graded river. *Transactions of the American Geophysical Union*, 36, 655–63.

6

Hydraulic and Sedimentary Controls of Channel Pattern

Rob Ferguson

INTRODUCTION

The classic paper by Leopold and Wolman (1957) on 'River channel patterns – braided, meandering, and straight' has had a profound influence on fluvial geomorphology, sedimentology, and engineering. Despite its authors' emphasis that natural channel patterns form a continuum, and are influenced by a great variety of environmental controls, the paper is remembered mainly for its graphical discrimination between braided and meandering channels in terms of just two controlling variables, discharge and slope. This threshold rapidly became part of the conventional wisdom on rivers, spawning similar approaches to other phenomena and a philosophical emphasis on geomorphic thresholds in general (e.g. Schumm, 1979), as well as specific applications to palaeo-environmental reconstruction (e.g. Cheetham, 1980) and the forecasting of channel metamorphosis following human intervention (e.g. Schumm and Beathard, 1976).

Surprisingly few fluvial scientists have paused to ask whether Leopold and Wolman's threshold between meandering and braiding is quantitatively, conceptually, or even morphologically correct. Yet it has been clear for many years that not all rivers have the patterns predicted by Leopold and Wolman's diagram, while some combine elements of both meandering and braiding; that changes in channel pattern downstream or over time are often gradual transitions rather than abrupt crossings of a threshold; and that downstream transitions sometimes occur without major changes in discharge or slope. A common factor in many of these anomalies is variation in type or size of bed material, type of bank material and vegetation, or type and amount of sediment load supplied from upstream. The various roles of sediment as controls of channel pattern have been stressed by many authors (e.g. Laboureur, 1951; Mackin, 1956; Schumm, 1963; Tricart and Vogt, 1967) but only in the last decade have serious attempts been made to reconcile this emphasis on sedimentary factors with Leopold and Wolman's emphasis on the hydraulic factors of discharge and slope as determinants of channel pattern.

The qualitative geomorphological arguments, quantitative empirical findings, and physically-based predictive models relevant to this issue are brought together below in an attempt to modify the conventional wisdom on channel pattern and to point to specific implications for engineering impact assessment, palaeoenvironmental interpretation, and geomorphological research.

THE CONVENTIONAL WISDOM

The main theme in textbook accounts of river channel pattern is that pattern is controlled by slope and discharge, with thresholds between different types of pattern at particular critical levels of flow strength. An important second theme is that channel pattern depends additionally or more fundamentally on amount and type of sediment load.

Channel pattern, discharge and slope

The evidence most commonly cited as showing that channel pattern depends mainly on discharge and slope consists of three papers, those of Lane (1957), Leopold and Wolman (1957), and Schumm and Khan (1972).

Lane (1957) in a report for the US Army Corps of Engineers plotted channel slope (s) against mean discharge (Q, m^3s^{-1}) for 36 sand-bed rivers and nine laboratory models and found separate but parallel trends

$$s = 0.0007 \ Q^{-0.25} \qquad\qquad (6.1)$$

for meandering channels, and

$$s = 0.0041 \ Q^{-0.25} \qquad\qquad (6.2)$$

for braided channels. His equations have been handed down in the literature but the original paper is not widely available.

Leopold and Wolman (1957) also plotted slope against discharge for channels of different pattern, some sand-bed but mostly gravel-bed, in the US and India. They used bankfull rather than mean discharge on the grounds that this is the dominant discharge for channel morphology, but in most cases it was estimated by the slope-area method rather than directly measured. As in Lane's investigation braided rivers tended to plot higher than meandering ones, and Leopold and Wolman proposed the threshold relationship

$$s = 0.013 \ Q^{-0.44} \tag{6.3}$$

to separate braided channels, which mostly have steeper slopes than this, from meandering channels which are less steep. Channels classed as straight by Leopold and Wolman plotted on both sides of this line.

Schumm and Khan (1972) reported experimental studies of the equilibrium channel patterns attained by small flume channels, initially straight, with fixed discharge ($0.0042 \ m^3s^{-1}$) and grain size (0.7 mm), but different flume slopes. Channels with slopes less than 0.002 remained straight, steeper ones developed meanders, and those steeper than 0.016 became braided.

Taken together, these papers are generally agreed to show, firstly, that for any given discharge and bed material there is one threshold slope above which channels will meander and another, higher one above which they will braid; and secondly, that the critical slope decreases with increasing discharge.

This conclusion is supported by many other investigations some of which are based on data that are at least as wide-ranging and carefully compiled. Lane's approach was followed up by Osterkamp (1978), again for sand-bed rivers in the US using mean discharge. Slope-discharge trends fitted by log-log regression to subsamples of rivers with different ranges of sinuosity all had exponents not significantly different from Lane's value of -0.25, but least squares fits with this standard exponent imposed had intercepts that increased progressively with decreasing sinuosity. The steepest channels for any given discharge were those classed as braided. These results confirmed those of Lane, and the same tendency can be seen in figure 5 of Schumm (1963), whose data partly overlap Osterkamp's. Leopold and Wolman's graphical threshold between meandering and braiding was followed up in the USSR by Antropovskiy (1972), using gauging-station data on mean annual flood rather than estimated bankfull discharge, for a large sample of rivers covering a very wide range of size and character. Free meandering was found to give way to 'incomplete meandering' (i.e. meanders with many chute cutoffs) at $sQ > 0.35 \ m^3s^{-1}$ and braiding at $sQ > 1.4$. More recently Bray (1982) plotted slope against median annual flood for rivers in Alberta, stratified by sinuosity class and degree of braiding, and found no evidence to contradict Leopold and Wolman's threshold exponent of -0.44, though the critical slope for braiding at any given discharge was about four times higher.

The laboratory experiments of Schumm and Khan (1972) were repeated at different discharges soon afterwards but the results were not published until recently (Edgar, 1984). The extra experiments confirmed that the critical slopes for the straight-meandering and meandering-braided thresholds decrease with increasing discharge in otherwise identical conditions. This had previously been demonstrated for the straight-meandering threshold by Nagabhushanaiah (1967) in the same laboratory at Colorado State University, and by Ackers and Charlton (1970) in outdoor experiments with quite large channels at the UK Hydraulics Research Station. Ackers and Charlton proposed the threshold

$$s = 0.0014 \ Q^{-0.12} \tag{6.4}$$

but Ackers (1982) noted that the data are compatible with

$$s = 0.0008 \ Q^{-0.21} \tag{6.5}$$

which extrapolates better to sand-bed rivers and canals.

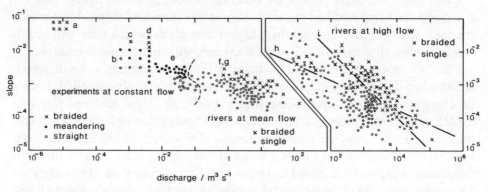

Figure 6.1 Laboratory and river data on channel pattern in relation to slope and discharge. Definitions of variables differ as discussed in text. Key to data sets: a Hong and Davies, 1979; b Nagabhushanaiah, 1967; c Ashmore, 1982; d Schumm and Khan, 1972; e Ackers and Charlton, 1970; f Schumm, 1963; g Osterkamp, 1978; h Leopold and Wolman, 1957; i Antropovskiy, 1972

   The field and laboratory data of these various authors are collected together in figure 6.1 along with the laboratory braided channels of Le Ba Hong and Davies (1979) and Ashmore (1982). The various laboratory thresholds for meandering match well, and a parallel but higher threshold for braiding would be consistent with both the laboratory results and the data for sand-bed rivers at mean discharge.

Channel pattern and stream power

The concept of a critical slope for braiding, lower at higher discharges, is therefore well established and there is substantial laboratory evidence for a similar but lower threshold slope for meandering. These inverse slope-discharge thresholds have been interpreted by Ferguson (1972, 1981, 1984), Richards (1982), and Carson (1984a) as thresholds of specific stream power. Specific power, the rate at which the potential energy of water flowing downhill is supplied to a unit area of the bed, is given by

$$\omega = \varrho g Q s / w \tag{6.6}$$

where w is river width, ϱ water density, and g the acceleration due to gravity. If the traditional downstream hydraulic geometry relationship

$$w = a Q^{0.5} \tag{6.7}$$

applies, it follows that

$$s = (a\omega/\varrho g) Q^{-0.5} \tag{6.8}$$

The exponent -0.5 is not statistically distinguishable from the -0.44 in Leopold and Wolman's threshold between meandering and braiding, which can therefore be interpreted as a constant threshold power of the order of 30-50 W m^{-2} (Ferguson, 1981; Carson, 1984a) according to the value assumed for the hydraulic geometry intercept, a (see chapter 5, this volume).

Ferguson (1981) plotted slope against bankfull Q/w for British rivers using hydraulic geometry data from previous workers and channel pattern classification from maps. Diagonals in such plots are lines of constant power. Inactive straight or sinuous channels tended to have low specific power, actively-shifting low sinuosity channels had high power, and actively meandering channels were intermediate, as can be seen from table 6.1 which summarizes the data.

Table 6.1 Bankfull stream power (W m^{-2}) of British rivers

Channel pattern	No. of rivers	Range of power	Median
Inactive unconfined	25	1-60	15
Confined	24	20-350	100
Active meandering	40	5-350	30
Active low sinuosity	6	120-300	160

See Ferguson, 1981 for data sources

An alternative interpretation of the slope-discharge threshold for braiding was suggested by Begin (1981), who proposed that it represents a critical level of the mean bed shear stress

$$\tau = \varrho gds \tag{6.9}$$

in which d denotes mean water depth. Begin's compilation of previously published data for rivers at mean discharge showed an overall trend

$$s = 0.0051 \, Q^{-0.33} \tag{6.10}$$

Since traditional regime theory maintains that

$$d \propto Q^{0.33} \tag{6.11}$$

the implication is that shear stress, depending as it does on the ds product, is constant along the general slope-discharge trend line. Braided channels therefore have higher than average shear stresses. This argument has much in common with the specific power interpretation, and the two measures of flow strength are of course interrelated by

$$\omega = \tau v \tag{6.12}$$

where v is mean flow velocity.

Other investigators have combined Q and s more simply still as the product Qs, which is proportional to the total stream power per unit length

$$\Omega = \varrho gQs \tag{6.13}$$

Constant thresholds of this are implied by Antropovskiy's (1972) results but not by any other study. Schumm (1977; 1981) discussed the experimental results of Schumm and Khan (1972) in terms of stream power but did not make clear whether he meant total or specific power. Edgar (1984) plotted sinuosity against total power but found the threshold power for braiding was lower at higher discharges; his diagrams suggest a more nearly constant threshold of specific power. The simple Qs index has nevertheless given statistically significant, though weak, correlations with degree of braiding (Howard et al., 1970; Mosley, 1981) and, inversely, with channel sinuosity (Mosley, 1981).

Channel pattern and sediment supply

The above discussion has emphasized the first theme of the conventional wisdom, that channel pattern depends on hydraulic factors. The second theme, emphasizing sedimentary controls of channel pattern, stems from Schumm's (1963) finding that the sinuosity (P) of sand-bed channels in the US Great Plains increases with the percentage (M) of silt and clay in the channel perimeter (bed as well as banks), according to the graphical trend

$$P = 0.94 \ M^{0.25} \tag{6.14}$$

Variations in M were thought to be related partly to bank cohesion but more fundamentally to differences in sediment supply, with high percentages of perimeter mud associated with a low ratio of bed-material load to wash load, although few data were available to support this idea. Schumm subsequently (e.g. 1977) classified alluvial channels into three categories: 'bedload channels' characterized by high width/depth ratio, low sinuosity, and a braided pattern; intermediate 'mixed load channels'; and 'suspended load channels' with low w/d ratio and a high-sinuosity meandering pattern. Discharge was seen as controlling only the scale of the channel (including meander wavelength) with cross-section shape and channel pattern dependent on the relative proportions of coarse and fine load.

This emphasis on sediment load is not totally at variance with other workers' emphasis on hydraulic controls of channel pattern, for Schumm and Khan's (1972) experiments showed, as might be expected, that bedload transport increased with slope at constant discharge; the transition from straight to meandering to braided was therefore associated with increasing bedload as well as increasing slope and stream power. In the fullest recent statement of his views on channel pattern, Schumm (1981) proposed that the experimental results show the effect on channel pattern of increasing slope, power, and bed load in 'bedload' channels only, and that different pattern sequences and thresholds apply to the 'mixed' and 'suspended load' classes of channel. There are thus different types of meandering river, different types of braiding, and also intermediate transitional patterns, and the threshold slope or power for braiding increases from bedload to mixed to suspended-load channels. A total of 14 pattern types were recognized. The main ones are shown in figure 6.2, which attempts to combine Schumm's definition sketches of the pattern sequences with his non-quantitative representation of their environmental controls.

Schumm's original data were for stable sand-bed channels only, but several case studies of temporal or downstream change in channel pattern in both sand- and gravel-bed rivers agree at least qualitatively with his conceptual scheme. Church (personal communication) has identified examples of gravel-bed rivers that have become more braided following the disposal of mine waste; Grant (1950) described similar pattern changes in New Zealand following deforestation; and Bradley (1984) reported how rivers near Mount St Helens became braided following huge inputs of sediment after its 1980 eruption. Downstream transitions from meandering to braiding that can be explained by inputs of coarse sediment

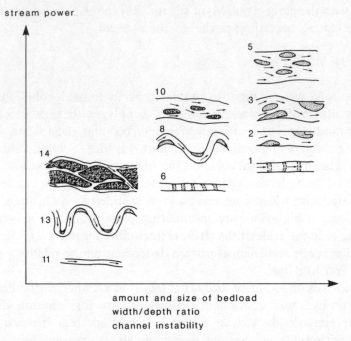

Figure 6.2 An interpretation of Schumm's (1981) classification of channel pattern in relation to bedload and associated variables (horizontal scale) and also stream power (vertical scale). Numbers are pattern types in Schumm's figure 6, which is merged here with his figures 4 and 7

occur at tributary junctions on the Great Plains (Schumm, 1963); where the Rangitata River in New Zealand emerges from a rock gorge to incise into outwash gravels (Schumm, 1979); and where the William River in Saskatchewan crosses an aeolian dunefield (Smith and Smith, 1984).

Limitations of the conventional wisdom

The patchwork of quantitative empirical studies and qualitative observations summarized above is limited in three respects. Firstly, there are quantitative inconsistencies between different studies even though their qualitative results are in agreement. In particular, the various slope-discharge thresholds in figure 6.1 have different numerical exponents and intercepts. Secondly, there is a lack of quantitative integration of those results suggesting that channel pattern depends on discharge and slope, and those suggesting that it depends on sedimentary factors. Finally, there is not yet a generally accepted physical explanation for channel pattern thresholds. The second and third problems are at the root of the first, but there is another reason for quantitative discrepancies that must be tackled first.

Problems of operational definition

Discharge, slope, sediment, and channel pattern have all been defined differently by different researchers. Until standardized data sets are compiled and analysed it will remain unclear whether quantitative differences in results indicate that relevant factors have been omitted or merely that the variables have been defined differently.

In laboratory experiments discharge is normally held constant but in rivers it varies over time. It is widely agreed that river channel morphology is adjusted to flood flows rather than to mean discharge, but floods may be variously indexed by bankfull discharge (Ferguson, 1981; Ackers, 1982), mean annual flood (Antropovskiy, 1972), or median annual flood (Bray, 1982). Bankfull discharge is not independent of channel morphology, and can be hard to define in braided rivers and misleading in incised channels, so a frequency-based definition such as the 2 or 2.33 year flood seems most appropriate. Channel pattern development undoubtedly occurs at a range of discharges, so that it does not matter in principle which index is chosen, but the alternatives can differ by a factor of ten in some rivers so that differences of definition in different studies do substantially alter the intercepts of graphical or statistical thresholds. The mean discharge will of course be much lower than any flood flow index, which explains the lower position of the mean-flow braid thresholds in figure 6.1. More subtly, the ratio of flood flow to mean flow tends to diminish in larger rivers because of flood attenuation, so that the braid threshold becomes steeper with increasing return period as pointed out by Osterkamp (1978), Ferguson (1984), and Carson (1984a).

Slope has generally been measured in a straight line in laboratory studies, but along the channel in field investigations; the ratio of the two is of course the sinuosity of the channel. The choice therefore matters little for straight or braided rivers, but more for meanders. Conversion from channel slope to valley slope, which is the more logical independent variable, reduces the difference between meandering and braided channels in the s-Q plots of Lane (1957), Leopold and Wolman (1957), and others, and almost eliminates the differences Osterkamp (1978) and Bray (1982) found between different sinuosity classes.

Problems of operational definition are more serious still when it comes to possible sedimentary controls of channel pattern. Schumm's (1963) use of silt-clay percentage was marred by a built-in correlation with width/depth ratio; re-analysis using bed mud and bank mud separately, rather than their weighted average, gives weaker correlations with sinuosity which would therefore seem to be linked as much to channel shape as sediment type. Mud percentage is also an uninformative index of boundary materials in gravel-bed rivers (excluded from Schumm's data) where median grain size is more commonly used. This however is a notoriously difficult variable to measure accurately because in most rivers it varies over short distances. It may also fail to index adequately the channel bank erodibility, which is often controlled by cohesive upper horizons and vegetation rather than the grain size in the lower bank. The amount of bed-material load is even harder to measure accurately and even rough estimates of this are seldom available.

There are also significant discrepancies in operational definitions of channel pattern. Leopold and Wolman (1957) termed 'braided' all channels divided either locally or more continuously by unvegetated bars or vegetated islands, and called single channels meandering if of sinuosity 1.5 or greater, otherwise straight. Subsequent authors have recognized different degrees not only of sinuosity (e.g. Schumm, 1963) but also of channel division, quantified variously as twice the total length of bars divided by the reach length (Brice, 1964), one less than the average number of channels per cross section (Howard et al., 1970), the percentage of channel length that is divided (Brice, 1984), or the number of braid bars per meander wavelength (Rust, 1978). Rust proposed that the continuum of channel patterns can be plotted in a diagram with sinuosity and degree of channel division as its two axes (figure 6.3). This gives four end members instead of Leopold and Wolman's three characteristic patterns, since divided channels may be of low or high sinuosity. The former are classic braids with near-straight channels dividing and recombining around what are typically small and unvegetated sand or gravel bars, whereas high-sinuosity divided channels are typically separated by larger, vegetated islands and are described as anastomosing (Miall, 1977; Smith and Smith, 1980). This distinction was

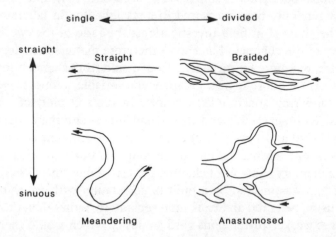

Figure 6.3 End members of the continuum of channel patterns with differing degrees of sinuosity and channel division. Rust's (1978) classification divides each axis arbitrarily to create four pattern types

foreshadowed by Lane (1957), who found that the second type had slopes as low as or lower than meandering channels of similar discharge.

Ferguson (1972) and Richards (1982) have experimented with a different channel pattern index, the 'total sinuosity' defined as total channel length divided by reach length; for example, a braided stream with an average of three channels per cross section would have a total sinuosity in excess of 3. This index tends to increase from straight to meandering to braided patterns, but with a substantial overlap between strongly meandering and mildly braided channels. Richards (1982, figure 7.1) demonstrated a weak but significant positive correlation between total sinuosity and total power for a small sample of rivers from the literature.

In terms of the two-way quantification of figure 6.3, Leopold and Wolman's (1957) 'braided' class is very large since it comprises all channels with even a slight degree of channel division, including those considered anastomosing by Lane (1957) and Rust (1978) and the transitional 'split' and 'wandering' patterns recognized by Canadian workers (e.g. Bray, 1982; Kellerhals, 1982). Careful reading of Leopold and Wolman (1957), and inspection of some of their field sites, shows that many of their 'braided' reaches are essentially single channels divided by short vegetated islands, and would not be classed as braided by some subsequent workers. Their 'meandering' class, on the other hand, is unusually restrictive since it excludes all channels of sinuosity less than 1.5 (e.g. all laboratory meanders), and any more sinuous channels that are counted as braided by virtue of point-bar chutes. It would however include at least some of the sinuous but laterally-inactive channels in lowland Britain that Ferguson (1981) distinguished from actively migrating, and usually more powerful, meandering streams.

EXPLANATIONS FOR THE INFLUENCE OF
SEDIMENT ON CHANNEL PATTERN

It is obviously possible to use sedimentary variables to supplement or even replace discharge and slope in predictions of channel pattern by purely graphical or statistical means. These could include the offsetting of slope-discharge trends or thresholds according to sediment type, the inclusion of sediment size in multivariate threshold equations (e.g. Henderson, 1961; Richards, 1982 (figure 7.12d); Ferguson, 1984), and the inclusion of sedimentary variables in simple (e.g. Schumm, 1963) or multiple regressions for quantitative pattern properties such as sinuosity. Thus, for example, Robertson-Rintoul and Richards (in preparation) have measured *total* sinuosity for 40 gravel-bed rivers from the literature and found

$$\Sigma P = 1 + 5.5 \, D_{84}^{-0.14} \, (Qs)^{0.40} \tag{6.15}$$

where ΣP is total sinuosity and s is valley slope.

The addition of further predictor variables will always improve levels of statistical explanation, but there are two serious limitations to purely empirical regression equations or discriminant functions. The first is that they cannot safely be extrapolated beyond the range of the data to which they are fitted; for example, Baker (1978) found that Schumm's (1963) P-M regression for the mid-western US did not work in South America. The second limitation is that statistical explanation is not the same as physical explanation. Channel patterns develop by non-uniform bedload transport and bank erosion, so mechanistic explanations have therefore concentrated on three ways in which sediment properties interact with flow properties: the influence of bank materials on bank erosion; the influence of bed materials on bedload competence and capacity; and the extent to which meandering or braiding tendencies in stream flow will amplify through non-uniform bedload transport.

Bank erodibility

As explained above, the slope-discharge threshold for braiding is increasingly being interpreted as a threshold of flow strength, whether indexed by specific power, total power, or shear stress. Braiding, which involves a greater amount and rate of channel modification than meandering, is seen to require greater stream power and therefore a steeper slope for any given discharge (figure 6.4a).

The increase in amount and rate of channel modification from straight channels to meandering, then to braiding, is more particularly an increase in the proportion of bank length experiencing erosion. Channels remain straight only if no bank erosion occurs. Meander development requires localized bank erosion on the

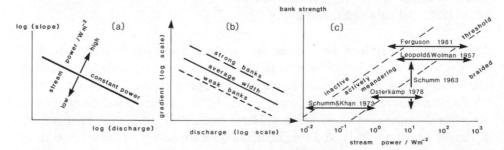

Figure 6.4 Three aspects of the flow strength/bank strength theory of channel pattern: (a) the traditional slope-discharge threshold as a critical stream power; (b) the expected shift in the threshold according to bank strength; (c) the empirical relationship of channel pattern to stream power and bank strength in some published studies (see text for details)

outsides of bends where flow strength is higher, balanced by deposition over a similar fraction of bank length at the insides of bends; braiding involves more extensive bank erosion, widening the channel and destroying bends rather than enlarging them. Progressively stronger flows are required at each stage, but the thresholds must also depend on bank strength (figure 6.4b).

This argument accounts for the observation by Kellerhals (1982), Ferguson (1984) and Carson (1984a) that sand-bed rivers braid at lower slopes than gravel-bed rivers of similar discharge: sand-bed channels also tend to have sandy banks, which can be eroded by currents too weak to affect coarser non-cohesive sediment. The combined influence of flow strength and bank erodibility had previously been noted in a general way by Lane (1957), Tricart and Vogt (1967), and others. More specific evidence was presented by Savat (1975) from the Zaire River basin, where the most braided tributaries drain the sandiest basins, but channels cut in the same Kalahari-derived sand have different patterns according to shear stress and stream power.

A further implication of the flow strength/bank strength theory is that bank vegetation can affect channel pattern by restricting lateral erosion. This too is confirmed by several case studies including Savat's (1975) observation that braiding in Zaire tributaries is least where banks are clayey and vegetated; Mackin's (1956) description of a channel in Idaho that braids on emerging from forest to grassland and then reverts to meandering on re-entering the forest; Grant's (1950) evidence that deforestation in New Zealand caused meandering rivers to braid; and New Zealand engineers' success in stabilizing some of these rivers by planting willows along the banks (S. Thompson, personal communication, 1985).

Figure 6.4c shows how published studies of channel pattern fit into this flow strength/bank strength framework. Ranges of power were calculated from Q and s using actual channel widths (Schumm and Khan, 1972; Ferguson, 1981) or hydraulic geometry curves. The laboratory channels of Schumm and Khan, with particularly weak unvegetated sandy banks, braided at lower specific powers than Osterkamp's (1978) sand-bed rivers, which have somewhat higher bank strength because of silt-clay content and vegetation. Whereas Osterkamp considered differences in slope and discharge in these rivers, Schumm (1963), in looking at an overlapping data set, emphasized the sediment dimension. His Q-s plot nevertheless reveals the usual tendency for braids to plot higher than meanders, and his plot of sinuosity against *bank* mud percentage (thus eliminating the spurious correlation between M and w/d ratio) shows a limit rather than a trend, with sinuosity always low when banks are non-cohesive but highly variable in cohesive-bank channels; this suggests that another factor, presumably flow strength, is relevant. In much the same way Baker (1978) speculated that the departure of South American rivers from Schumm's P-M relationship is because channel pattern depends on discharge characteristics as well as bank stability. Returning to figure 6.4c, Leopold and Wolman's (1957) data related to a mixture of sand- and gravel-bed channels with presumably intermediate bank strength on average, while the British data collated by Ferguson (1981) are for rivers with generally well-vegetated banks of gravel and/or cohesive material.

The obvious limitation of this argument that channel pattern depends on the balance between flow strength and bank strength is that the latter is hard to quantify to any greater extent than the ranking in figure 6.4c. One possible statistical approach focuses on the long neglected intercept of the familiar width-discharge equation of hydraulic geometry, and its possible dependence on bank materials. Ferguson (1973), for example, fitted a regression

$$W = aQ^b B^{-x} \tag{6.16}$$

(in which B denotes bank mud percentage) to Schumm's Great Plains data. The immediate effect of this trend is that rivers with cohesive banks are narrower, and therefore have higher specific power, than others of the same discharge and slope. This is offset by an increase in the critical power for braiding in the more cohesive materials. If the critical power varies as B^y, the critical slope for braiding should vary as

$$s \propto Q^{-(1-b)} B^{y-x} \tag{6.17}$$

Graphically this means the threshold is offset for different materials; if $y > x$, the threshold shifts upwards for more cohesive banks as sketched in figure 6.4b.

A similar argument can be developed for gravel bed rivers. The semi-theoretical hydraulic geometry of Parker (1979) suggests

$$w \propto Q^{0.5} D^{-0.25} \tag{6.18}$$

(where D denotes median bed-material diameter). Since the banks of a gravel channel are at the threshold of motion it is reasonable to assume that the critical flow strength for bank erosion increases linearly with D. The threshold slope for braiding is then

$$s \propto Q^{-0.5} D^{0.75} \tag{6.19}$$

A discharge-slope-grain size discriminant analysis by Church and Ferguson (reported in Ferguson, 1984) showed an insignificantly small positive dependence on median grain-size, but re-analysis using D_{90} showed a dependence which although smaller than just predicted, was at least significant and in the expected direction.

Local and upstream sediment supply

The development of meandering or braiding in an initially straight channel requires not only localized or widespread bank erosion but also the redistribution of eroded bank material as bedload. Brotherton (1979) argued that the relative ease of eroding and transporting bank particles is the key to differences in channel pattern. If erosion is harder than onward transport, for example because of the cohesion of fine-grained banks, the channel will remain straight; if erosion is easier than transport, shoaling will lead to a braided pattern. An approximate balance was assumed to give meandering. Braiding may therefore result either from lack of capacity to remove the amount of sediment eroded from sandy banks, or lack of competence to remove the size of sediment eroded from gravelly banks. Either way channel pattern depends on sediment size as well as hydraulic variables.

Carson (1984a) extended this argument by considering also the sediment load supplied from upstream. If the combined load from upstream and from bank erosion exceeds transport capacity, shoaling will cause braiding. In a related paper (Carson, 1984b), he presented a pattern classification in which meandering occurs where both bank erosion and the load from upstream are low relative to flow strength, braiding occurs where both are high, and transitional patterns occur in between.

Other authors have attempted to explain channel pattern solely in terms of sediment supply from upstream. Braiding has traditionally been regarded as a disequilibrium, aggradational response to increased load or load/capacity ratio. Many rivers have been suggested as examples of this, most recently by Carson (1984b). Others (e.g. Lane, 1957; Leopold and Wolman, 1957; Miall, 1977; Kellerhals, 1982) consider that braiding, like meandering, can be an equilibrium state given the right combination of discharge and slope, but accept that basin sediment yields may control channel slope (and thus channel pattern) through aggradation or incision.

Whether this can happen quickly enough to be relevant at the time-scale of channel pattern adjustment is more doubtful, and it may be that basin yield is important more through the *size* of bed material with its influence on roughness and competence. In the short term, differences in slope *cause* differences in bedload capacity, as Schumm and Khan's (1972) laboratory experiments showed, though as Bridge (1985) pointed out, this was under the special circumstance of fixed sediment size: in nature, at a given discharge, steeper slopes are likely to mean coarser bed material with a moderating effect on transport capacity.

As to *how* a high bed-material load encourages a channel to become braided, two mechanisms have been proposed: local mid-channel incompetence leading to the progressive growth of medial bars (Leopold and Wolman, 1957); and the development of big low-angle point bars which are prone to chute dissection and avulsive channel switching over low channel-banks (Schumm and Khan, 1972; Ferguson and Werritty, 1983; Carson, 1984a; 1984b; Smith and Smith, 1984). Both mechanisms are encouraged by the wide shallow cross-section that is characteristic of streams conveying a large bed-material load.

By concentrating on either competence or capacity, and neglecting either bedload throughput or bank erosion, some authors have obtained quantitative results on (or at least relevant to) the influence of sediment on channel pattern. We look first at approaches based on competence.

Bedload competence

A long-established physical model for hydraulic geometry assumes that all points on the channel perimeter are at the threshold of motion. By combining the narrowest cross-section geometry that achieves this, the Shields competence criterion, and the Manning-Strickler roughness equation, Henderson (1961) derived a regime slope equation of the form

$$s \propto Q^{-0.46} D^{1.15} \qquad (6.20)$$

Channels steeper than this must be wider, and therefore shallower, if they are not to exceed the threshold of motion. On re-analysing the data of Leopold and Wolman (1957), Henderson found that their straight and meandering channels clustered around the regime slope whereas the braided channels tended to be steeper. Braiding could therefore be explained as the result of channel widening due to excessive slope.

The threshold approach was revived in a slightly different form by Carson (1984a) who noted that the Shields criterion $s \propto D/d$ together with the traditional hydraulic geometry relationship $d \propto Q^{1/3}$ imply a threshold of the form

$$s \propto Q^{-1/3} D \qquad (6.21)$$

for bedload movement. Since D tends to be inversely correlated with Q along and between rivers, an undifferentiated scatter plot of s against Q for rivers at the threshold of transport ought to have an exponent bigger than $-1/3$ but with gravel-bed rivers plotting relatively high and sandy channels relatively low. This is essentially what the channel pattern plots of Begin (1981), Kellerhals (1982), and others show, and Carson therefore concluded that Leopold and

Wolman's classic threshold is not so much a discriminator between meandering and braiding as a best-fit trend for channels close to the threshold of motion for 8–32 mm bed material.

Carson's argument, and Begin's (1981) interpretation of plotting position relative to the overall s-Q trend as an index of shear stress, ignore the scatter that exists about the d-Q hydraulic geometry trend. Channel depth is not uniquely determined by discharge but varies also with bed and bank materials, channel pattern itself, and possibly slope (Ferguson, 1986). If braided channels are wider and shallower than meandering ones of similar discharge and grain size, they need to be steeper than meanders simply to have the same depth-slope product, shear stress, and competence. Also, the development of meandering or braiding *requires* bedload transport, therefore shear stress must be above, not at, the competence threshold. Recent research on the entrainment of mixed gravels does however suggest a lower critical dimensionless shear stress than Shields's value of 0.06, so channels at the traditional threshold may in fact be active.

Bedload capacity

Quantitative relationships between channel slope, width, discharge, and bedload have also been proposed by authors whose emphasis is on transport capacity in relation to imposed load rather than competence in relation to imposed grain size. Kirkby (1972; 1980), Chang (1979; 1985) and Bettess and White (1983) have all discussed the implications for channel pattern of an approach to hydraulic geometry that combines roughness and sediment transport equations with the assumption that channel slope is minimized, or equivalently that the efficiency of sediment transport is maximized. The basic idea, introduced by G. K. Gilbert a century ago, is that the channel cross-section adjusts to maximize the product of width and transport per unit width. The greater the imposed load, the wider the channel must be, and it must also be steeper in order to maintain the same shear stress at lesser depth.

Kirkby (1972), using process equations appropriate to gravel, noted that the optimum slope for a given discharge resembles Leopold and Wolman's (1957) braiding threshold with the addition of a slight dependence on grain size. He sketched an argument that channels above the threshold are unstable with respect to local shallowing and will therefore shoal and braid, whereas channels below the optimum slope are stable. In a later paper (Kirkby, 1980), he also considered discrepancies between the maximum transport capacity and the imposed load. If load exceeds capacity the river must aggrade and braid, whereas if capacity exceeds load the river can afford to reduce its slope by meandering.

Chang (1979; 1985) applied a similar approach to sand-bed rivers. For any given discharge and sand size, an increase in slope beyond the threshold for bed movement is associated with an increase in load, width/depth ratio, and (according to Chang) channel pattern in the sequence 'straight-braided', meandering, meandering-braided transition, and 'steep braided'. The threshold for 'steep' braiding is similar to Leopold and Wolman's (though in fact sandy braids occur at lower slopes than this), whereas 'straight' braiding occurs at slopes similar to Lane's (1957) low-gradient braids (which would nowadays be termed anastomosing). In his 1985 paper Chang merged the two middle classes under the title 'braided point bar or wide-bend point bar', using terminology from Brice (1984), and split the 'straight' class into stable canals, equi-width meanders, and low-gradient braids. No clear explanation was given as to why this series of pattern thresholds follows from what is essentially a continuum of hydraulic geometry.

A more attractive capacity-based explanation of why some equilibrium channels meander while others braid was proposed by Bettess and White (1983). Again the starting-point is a computation of the minimum slope for specified discharge, grain size and load followed by comparison of this 'regime' slope with the available valley slope. As in Kirkby's (1980) argument an inadequate valley slope is presumed to cause aggradation whereas one greater than the required regime slope allows meandering to develop. If however the regime slope is much less than the available valley slope, rather than the river developing extremely sinuous meanders, Bettess and White suggested that it will braid so that the total discharge and sediment load are shared between n smaller channels with the higher regime slope appropriate to the discharge Q/n. For illustrative purposes they assumed braiding would occur on valley slopes steeper than the regime slope for discharge Q/3. With any fixed ratio of load to discharge this turns out to allow a wider range of meander sinuosity at low discharges than at high discharges. The meandering domain also narrows with increasing grain size, so that at high discharges the maximum sinuosity is about 1.6 for fine sand but only 1.1 for gravel. This they claim agrees with observation. Quantitative predictions of equilibrium slope for the authors' own experiments, and those of Leopold and Wolman (1957), were satisfactory, but less so for Schumm and Khan's (1972) data. Convincing predictions were also given for a Canadian case study of flow diversion into a gravel river.

The assumption in this approach that valley slope is imposed is welcome. The width, sinuosity and degree of braiding of both small and large rivers can adjust considerably in a few decades, whereas significant alteration in channel slope by aggradation or degradation takes far longer, of the order of 10^3 to 10^5 years in large sand-bed rivers according to numerical simulations by Howard (1982); by this time climatic fluctuations are liable to alter the discharge regime and sediment yield to which the long profile has been adapting. In some environments valley slope may also be inherited from former glacial or marine conditions, or be affected by past or present tectonic activity. In most circumstances valley slope is clearly an independent variable at the time-scale within which distinctive channel patterns are developed.

The problem with predicting sinuosity and braiding by comparing valley slope with regime slope is, instead, that the predicted regime slope is unlikely to be perfectly accurate. The imposed sediment load is hardly ever known at all reliably, and the curves of slope or transport capacity against width or depth from which the regime slope is derived tend to have ill-defined extrema. Some of the hydraulic implications of the approach are also worrying: the dimensionless shear stress of all rivers should be the same, which is unrealistic (Griffiths, 1984), and should be many times higher than the competence threshold, which is not true in gravel rivers (Ferguson, 1986). However, Bettess (personal communication, 1985) suggests that these may be problems with particular quantifications of the approach rather than the concept itself. A more fundamental objection is that minimization of channel slope is a metaphysical assumption that does not explain *how* meanders or braids develop. This still seems to require more or less extensive lateral migration and bedload redistribution, permitted by the excess power available when the valley slope is more than enough to transport the imposed load. But these processes are surely still influenced by bank erodibility, which is ignored in this approach, even though as Schumm (1963) recognized, there is a clear tendency for rivers with a large, coarse load to have non-cohesive banks, whereas 'washload' rivers have cohesive banks.

Stability of bed macroforms

A quite different approach to the prediction of channel pattern considers the stability of flow and bedload transport in channels with incipient meandering or braiding. The geometry, flow, and sediment transport are represented by mathematical equations containing three-dimensional sinusoidal perturbations corresponding to incipient meandering (mode $m = 1$), incipient braiding with $m = 2$ thalwegs that alternately diverge and converge, or a higher mode of braiding. Despite different degrees of simplification of the full Navier-Stokes flow equations, and different choices for the equation linking transport capacity to flow, almost all such analyses show that perturbations of all modes and scales are unstable. Whether they will develop into meandering or braiding depends on which mode grows faster. The analysis of Engelund and Skovgaard (1973) predicted meandering below, and braiding above, a critical width/depth ratio. Other analyses confirm the importance of w/d as a control but predict that the critical ratio varies with slope or a slope-related factor. Parker (1976), for example, deduced that braiding will develop if

$$sw/d > Fr \qquad (6.22)$$

where $Fr = v/(gd)^{1/2}$ is the Froude number of the flow. This criterion compared well with a variety of laboratory, canal and river data and implies that braiding is encouraged by steep slopes and wide shallow channels. The slightly more elaborate models of Hayashi and Ozaki (1980) and Blondeaux and Seminara (1984) also indicate that sw/d is the major control, but now in relation to Fr raised to a power.

In principle these criteria allow prediction of channel pattern from channel slope, width, depth, and velocity but for purposes of environmental impact assessment we may know only the future discharge of the river and not how it will be apportioned between w, d, and v. For this type of application, and for comparison with empirical pattern thresholds such as Leopold and Wolman's, it is useful to re-express stability criteria in terms of discharge and slope. Ferguson (1984) showed that this can be done by substituting hydraulic geometry equations for w, d, v. Traditional hydraulic geometries with fixed intercepts give a simple s-Q threshold for braiding with an exponent of around $-1/6$. More realistic hydraulic geometries with intercepts that vary according to bed or bank materials give families of thresholds offset according to sediment.

Two specific examples will demonstrate the approach, both using the stability criterion of Parker (1976). If Parker's own (1979) semi-theoretical gravel-bed hydraulic geometry is used, the braid threshold is predicted to be

$$s = 0.0049 \ Q^{-0.21} D^{0.52} \tag{6.23}$$

where D is median grain size in mm. A generalized version of the hydraulic geometry allows the exponents to vary in value while remaining in the same $-2:5$ ratio. Alternatively, for channels with cohesive banks and sandy beds, the regression equation of w on Q and bank mud percentage B that Ferguson (1973) fitted to Schumm's US data can be used along with the corresponding depth equation. This gives a braid threshold

$$s = 0.0013 \ Q^{-0.24} B^{1.00} \tag{6.24}$$

In both cases the threshold slope for braiding at a given discharge increases for more resistant sediment (coarser gravel, muddier banks) in accordance with the flow strength/bank strength argument.

Figure 6.5 compares the first of these theoretical thresholds with others and with quality-checked data on braided and near-braided sand- and gravel-bed rivers. Leopold and Wolman's (1957) threshold is clearly too low for braiding in gravel but too high for braiding in sand. The higher gravel-braiding threshold of Bray (1982), not shown in figure 6.5, performs better but both this and Henderson's (1961) threshold incorporating D mis-classify many of the braided gravel

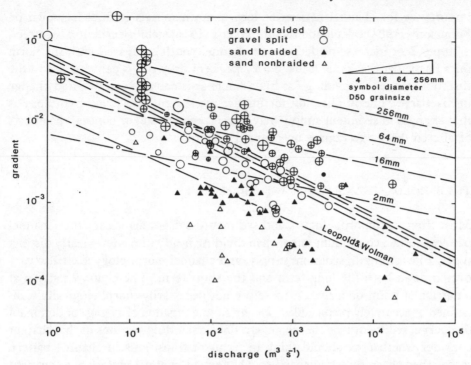

Figure 6.5 Channel pattern in relation to slope, bankfull or 2-year discharge, and grain size showing tendency for fine-grained channels to braid at lower slopes. Data assembled by M. Church and previously published in Kellerhals (1982) and Ferguson (1984); see text for explanation of alternative threshold lines.

channels. The purely deductive threshold based on Parker's stability criterion and hydraulic geometry is represented in figure 6.5 by the family of curves labelled by grain sizes. It fits no worse than the published empirical thresholds but overestimates the sensitivity of the threshold slope to sediment size, at least in comparison with the unconstrained statistical discriminant analysis represented in figure 6.5 by the unlabelled parallel lines just above the Leopold and Wolman threshold. The generalized form of the deductive threshold, with one fitted parameter related to the hydraulic geometry exponents for w and d, plots in between the purely deductive and purely empirical families of thresholds in figure 6.5 and has a high classification success rate especially when grain size is indexed by D_{90} rather than D_{50}.

It is clear from figure 6.5 that the threshold slope for braiding *is* dependent on sediment size as well as type, and that the combined influence of hydraulic and sedimentary controls is modelled quite well by a stability criterion together with hydraulic geometry equations incorporating sedimentary influences. The importance for channel pattern of local bank materials is further shown by Ferguson's (1984) calculation that if Parker's (1976) stability criterion is correct, a 20 per cent increase or decrease in channel width compared with the norm for a particular discharge leads to a 27 per cent drop or 46 per cent rise in the threshold slope for braiding – as big a range as is caused by a five-fold change in discharge. The implication for impact assessment and palaeohydrology is that changes in sediment supply may mimic, exaggerate, or conceal the effects of altered discharge regime on channel pattern.

THRESHOLDS, TRANSITIONS, AND TRANSIENTS

Most fluvial geomorphologists and sedimentologists now accept that channel patterns form a continuum rather than dividing neatly into a few clearly distinct types. Flow strength, sediment supply, and channel morphology itself also vary over time in both the long term and the short term. The channel pattern at a particular point on a river is therefore not necessarily morphologically well-defined or accurately predictable from any simple function of average or dominant discharge, sediment load, or whatever. The concluding sections of this chapter consider whether we should think in terms of transitions in channel pattern rather than sharp thresholds, and to what extent channel pattern is a transient (or sometimes historically inherited) property rather than an equilibrium state as commonly assumed. In both cases there are practical implications for palaeoenvironmental interpretation and environmental impact assessment.

Thresholds or transitions?

Almost every writer on the subject of channel pattern acknowledges the existence of a morphological continuum, even though most go on to discuss one or more distinct types of channel. If a properly designed sampling investigation were made of the natural frequency of different pattern types, or the frequency distributions of sinuosity and degree of division, it is likely that relatively few rivers would have archetypal meandering, braided, or straight patterns, and intermediate or transitional patterns would be the norm, not the exception.

Consideration of the sedimentology and morphology of bars in what are traditionally distinct types of channel pattern also points to a series of transitions rather than sharp thresholds. Figure 6.6 sketches some of the morphological transitions (see also chapter 8, this volume). The common building block is the couplet of chute and bar, usually passively occupied during low-flow conditions by a pool and riffle but actively modified during high flows when bar fronts prograde. Very wide shallow channels have parallel rows of chutes

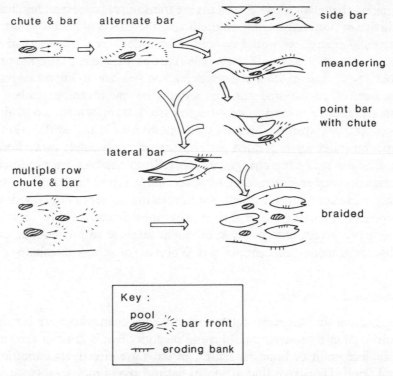

chute & bar   alternate bar   side bar

                                                       meandering

                                                       point bar
                                                       with chute

            lateral bar

multiple row
chute & bar

                                                       braided

Key :

pool
        bar front

        eroding bank

Figure 6.6 Some morphological transitions in bar-pool-riffle arrangement in channels of different patterns, based on gravel-bed rivers (observations by author; Bluck, 1976; Church and Jones, 1982) and sand-bed laboratory channels (e.g. Ackers and Charlton, 1970; Schumm and Khan, 1972; Ashmore, 1982)

and bars, usually developing into a braided pattern, but most rivers have a single series of bars which typically become skewed in alternate directions to give a meandering thalweg. Further evolution can take several forms according to the extent of bank erosion and of the formation of new chutes across the heads of point or lateral bars. Low, intermediate, and high rates of these modifying processes favour the development of straight, meandering, and braided patterns respectively but there are no sharp thresholds in morphology, nor in the developmental mechanisms which in all cases involves non-uniform bedload transport.

Bridge (1985), in an excellent critical review, has emphasized that there are no sharp sedimentological thresholds either, except those between the different types of bedform that may be superimposed upon point and braid bars alike in sandy channels. There are more similarities than differences between the deposits of rivers with different patterns, and supposedly distinctive features such as lateral-accretion bedding and fining upwards are not restricted to meandering channels.

Recognition that many channel patterns are transitional has several implications for predictive or postdictive work. In predicting the effects of natural or artificial environmental change we would do well to consider stochastic alternatives to deterministic thresholds, as in Tung's (1985) use of logistic regression to predict the probability of channel scour at given depth and velocity. In impact assessment the existence of transitional patterns should be an advantage rather than disadvantage: the rivers most susceptible to pattern transformation will already have recognizably transitional patterns with point bar chutes, while rivers with archetypal meandering or braided patterns are probably safely away from the threshold unless really big changes in controlling variables are proposed. In palaeoenvironmental reconstruction, however, the lesson of modern river studies is that great caution is needed both in interpreting ancient alluvial sediments as the product of a particular type of river pattern, particularly if only fragmentary evidence is preserved, and in any subsequent attempt to put bounds on the palaeodischarge using the Leopold and Wolman (or other) threshold.

Transitions and transients

Even in constant-discharge laboratory experiments, channel pattern is a matter of dynamic rather than static equilibrium: meander bends grow or are cut off, and individual point or braid bars alter, in what are effectively conditions of perpetual flood. Discharge fluctuation in natural rivers may merely interpose passive interludes between spells of channel change within dynamic equilibrium, but year-to-year variation in the magnitude of competent floods can complicate matters. In rivers of transitional pattern major floods often cause increased division and reduced sinuosity, minor floods the opposite (e.g Werritty and Ferguson, 1980; Burkham, 1981). If the year-to-year variation in peak discharge is great the channel may be almost perpetually in a transient state of recovery from the last major flood (Stevens et al., 1975), rather than in dynamic equilibrium, and the channel pattern will depend on the time elapsed since this flood. In extreme cases recovery from flood-induced braiding may take decades (e.g. Schumm and Lichty, 1963). There is an obvious danger in palaeohydrological research of mistaking transient fluctuations of this kind for longer-term changes in runoff regime.

Changes in the flood magnitude-frequency regime of a river will in general cause smaller or larger changes in channel pattern according to the magnitude of the hydrologic change, but the situation may again be more complicated than in most laboratory experiments. Doubling the dominant discharge of a river will cause a predominantly erosional change in pattern from state A to state B but halving the discharge again will cause a mainly depositional change which may lead to some state C rather than reversion to pattern A. A possible example of this is 'Osage underfitness' in which a sinuous channel has many pools and riffles per meander bend (e.g. Dury et al., 1972). Richards (1972) and Ferguson (1973; 1981) have attributed this to postglacial reduction in dominant discharge in a stream that initially was just powerful enough to meander actively. If the stream were starting afresh, as in a laboratory experiment, it would stay straight but since it starts with a sinuous channel (and thus an even lower slope) it is unable to erode its banks and can only alter its pattern by depositional narrowing and reduction in pool-riffle spacing.

Transient fluctuations and longer-term regime changes in discharge are not the only causes of channel change. Channel slope tends to be thought of as constant but it decreases as sinuosity increases during meander bend growth, and increases wherever and whenever bends are cut off or braided channels switch into floodplain depressions. The ensuing local and transient channel changes are generally within dynamic equilibrium, but natural or artificial base-level change may cause a transition in channel pattern, and so may neotectonic variation in valley slope as discussed by Gregory and Schumm in this volume (chapter 3).

Moreover if channel pattern depends in one or more ways on sediment type or supply, it is liable to adjust if these alter. A change in the amount of sediment supplied from upstream has direct implications for channel pattern in some views (e.g. capacity arguments) and indirect implications in other views. Increased bedload may also increase the median size of bed material, whereas increased washload may lead to fine deposition on channel banks and a reduction in their erodibility. Changes in sediment supply may be the result of climatic change but they may also be the transient result of major floods, other natural processes (e.g. landslides and volcanic eruptions), or landuse changes such as urban construction, deforestation, or mining activity. If transient, they cause sediment slugs to propagate downstream as diffusing waves marked by 'sedimentation zones' (Church, 1983) in which channel pattern transitions are commonly observed, perhaps with reverse transitions upstream after the wave has passed.

CONCLUSIONS

The question of the controls of channel pattern is complicated. The approaches reviewed in this chapter look at the problem from different angles and stress different controlling variables, but few of them directly contradict each other. This is as it should be, for arguably *all* of the factors separately considered – flow strength, bank strength, competence, capacity, secondary flow – are *simultaneously* involved in the development of non-straight channel patterns. It is legitimate to ask which theoretical approach, or which empirical combination of controls, gives the best quantitative prediction of pattern, but each has some conceptual justification and the main approaches all imply the same qualitative conclusions.

Firstly, since there are no sharp process thresholds, it is not surprising that the classic straight, meandering, and braided patterns are not sharply distinct and possibly not especially common. Patterns instead form a continuum with at least two dimensions (sinuosity and division), and there is a corresponding variety in the type and location of sand or gravel bars. Rivers show gradual transitions in pattern, not sudden changes, in the downstream direction, and patterns also vary over time, mainly because of the variable magnitude and frequency of floods.

Secondly, the commonest part of the continuum is a spectrum from no lateral migration or switching (straight channels and inactive sinuous ones) through localized lateral activity (actively meandering channels) to widespread lateral activity (braided channels). This sequence is associated with increasing discharge and slope (corresponding in broad terms to greater flow strength, shear stress, specific power, and bedload transport capacity), increasing width/depth ratio, and progressive replacement of the traditional secondary circulation in bends by other forms of flow convergence/divergence.

Thirdly, the critical slope for braiding at a given discharge is higher for gravel- than sand-bed channels and there is some empirical and theoretical justification for thinking that it also increases with gravel diameter. It may also decrease with increasing bank erodibility (which affects width/depth ratio, secondary flow, and local bedload supply alike) and increasing bedload supply from upstream. The traditional threshold of Leopold and Wolman (1957) is too low for gravel channels but too high for sandy ones, being based on a mixture of the two.

Fourthly, the relevant slope in most explanations of channel pattern is not the modern channel slope but the available valley slope. This may reflect past rather than present alluvial sedimentation, non-alluvial sedimentation, or neotectonics. Channel slope, rather than adjusted through aggradation or degradation to modern sediment supply from upstream, is commonly determined by the ratio of imposed valley slope to the sinuosity developed on that slope; more occasionally, channel slope is itself relict.

It is clear that channel pattern is influenced by sediment characteristics as well as hydraulic variables. Bed material size, bedload supply, and bank erodibility have each been included, though only separately, in quantitative models for channel pattern based respectively on hydraulic criteria for competence, bedload capacity, and mode of secondary circulation. Each approach is open to criticism on its detailed assumptions as well as its neglect of the other two aspects of the 'sediment factor', and it is not yet clear that any one of them is empirically superior to the others. In appropriate circumstances each gives better predictions than the purely empirical criteria of Leopold and Wolman (1957) and Schumm

(1963). Conceptually, the approach via stability analysis of non-uniform flow is the most attractive since flow strength and bedload transport do vary from point to point in non-straight channels, a fact ignored in approaches *via* mean shear stress, competence, or capacity. Since width/depth ratio is a major controlling variable in most stability analyses the effects of discharge, sediment supply, and local bank erodibility can readily be analysed using hydraulic geometry equations.

Conceptually based, or even purely empirical, pattern discrimination using sedimentary as well as hydraulic variables offers improved predictions of the impact of environmental change, natural or artificial, on rivers. Impact assessment should also be eased by awareness of transitional river types, since recognition of one of these indicates vulnerability to even small changes in controlling variables. Palaeoenvironmental reconstruction from supposed evidence of former channel patterns is, however, fraught with difficulties. Traditional sedimentary indicators of meandering or braiding are now known to be ambiguous, and palaeohydraulic or hydrologic inferences are dubious in view of the transient, flood-dependent nature of many channel patterns and the continuing doubt over quantitative criteria for competence, hydraulic geometry, and channel pattern, even in modern rivers.

REFERENCES

Ackers, P. 1982: Meandering channels and the influence of bed material. In R. D. Hey, J. C. Bathurst and C. R. Thorne (eds), *Gravel-bed Rivers*, Chichester: Wiley, 389-414.

Ackers, P. and Charlton, F. G. 1970: The geometry of small meandering streams. *Proc. Inst. Civ. Engrs. Suppl.*, 12, 289-317.

Antropovskiy, V. I. 1972: Quantitative criteria of channel macroforms. *Soviet Hydrology*, 1972, 477-84.

Ashmore, P. E. 1982: Laboratory modelling of gravel braided stream morphology. *Earth Surface Procs. & Landforms*, 7, 201-25.

Baker, V. R. 1978: Adjustment of fluvial systems to climate and source terrain in tropical and subtropical environments. In A. D. Miall (ed.), *Fluvial Sedimentology*, Can. Soc. Petr. Geol. Mem. 5, 211-30.

Begin, Z. B. 1981: The relationship between flow-shear stress and stream pattern. *J. Hydrol.*, 52, 307-19.

Bettess, R. and White, W. R. 1983: Meandering and braiding of alluvial channels. *Proc. Inst. Civ. Engrs. Part 2*, 75, 525-38.

Blondeaux, P. and Seminara, G. 1984: Bed topography and instability in sinuous channels. In *Rivers '83*, Amer. Soc. Civ. Engrs., 747-58.

Bluck, B. J. 1976: Sedimentation in some Scottish rivers of low sinuosity. *Trans. Roy. Soc. Edinburgh*, 69, 425-56.

Bradley, J. B. 1984: Transition of a meandering river to a braided system due to high sediment concentration flows. In *Rivers '83*, Amer. Soc. Civ. Engrs., 89–100.

Bray, D. I. 1982: Regime equations for gravel-bed rivers. In R. D. Hey, J. C. Bathurst and C. R. Thorne (eds) *Gravel-bed Rivers*, Chichester: Wiley, 517–52.

Brice, J. C. 1964: Channel patterns and terraces of the Loup rivers, Nebraska. *US Geol. Survey Prof. Paper*, 422-D.

Brice, J. C. 1984: Planform properties of meandering rivers. In *Rivers '83*, Amer. Soc. Civ. Engrs., 1–15.

Bridge, J. S. 1985: Palaeochannel patterns inferred from alluvial deposits: a critical evaluation. *J. Sedim. Petrology*, 55, 579–89.

Brotherton, D. I. 1979: On the origin and characteristics of river channel patterns. *J. Hydrol.*, 44, 211–30.

Burkham, D. E. 1981: Uncertainty resulting from changes in river form. *J. Hydr. Engg.*, 107, 593–610.

Carson, M. A. 1984a: The meandering-braided river threshold: a reappraisal. *J. Hydrol.*, 73, 315–34.

Carson, M. A. 1984b: Observations on the meandering-braided river transition, Canterbury Plains, New Zealand. *N.Z. Geogr.*, 40, 12–17 and 89–99.

Chang, H. H. 1979: Minimum stream power and river channel patterns. *J. Hydrol.*, 41, 303–27.

Chang, H. H. 1985: River morphology and thresholds. *J. Hydr. Engg.*, 111, 503–19.

Cheetham, G. H. 1980: Late Quaternary palaeohydrology: the Kennet valley case study. In D. K. C. Jones (eds), *The Shaping of Southern England*, Inst. Brit. Geogrs. Sp. Publ. 11, 203–23.

Church, M. 1983: Patterns of instability in a wandering gravel bed channel. *Int. Assoc. Sedim. Sp. Publ.*, 6, 169–80.

Church, M. and Jones, D. 1982: Channel bars in gravel-bed rivers. In R. D. Hey, J. C. Bathurst and C. R. Thorne (eds), *Gravel-bed rivers*, Chichester: Wiley, 291–338.

Dury, G. H., Sinker, G. A., and Pannett, D. J. 1972: Climatic change and arrested meander development on the River Severn. *Area*, 4, 81–5.

Edgar, D. E. 1984: The role of geomorphic thresholds in determining alluvial channel morphology. In *Rivers '83*, Amer. Soc. Civ. Engrs., 44–54.

Engelund, F. and Skovgaard, O. 1973: On the origin of meandering and braiding in alluvial streams. *J. Fluid Mech.*, 57, 289–302.

Ferguson, R. I. 1972: *Theoretical models of river channel pattern*. Unpubl. PhD thesis, Cambridge University.

Ferguson, R. I. 1973: Channel pattern and sediment type. *Area*, 5, 38–41.

Ferguson, R. I. 1981: Channel form and channel changes. In J. Lewin (ed.), *British rivers*, London: Allen & Unwin, 90–125.

Ferguson, R. I. 1984: The threshold between meandering and braiding. In K. V. H. Smith (ed.), *Proc. 1st Int. Conf. on Hydr. design*, Springer, 615–29.

Ferguson, R. I. 1986: Hydraulics and hydraulic geometry. *Prog. Phys. Geog.*, 10, 1–31.

Ferguson, R. I. and Werritty, A. 1983: Bar development and channel changes in the gravelly River Feshie, Scotland. *Int. Assoc. Sedim. Sp. Publ.*, 6, 181–93.

Grant, H. P. 1950: Soil conservation in New Zealand. *Proc. NZ Inst. Engrs.*, 36, 269-301.

Griffiths, G. A. 1984: Extremal hypotheses for river regime: an illusion of progress. *Water Resources Res.*, 20, 113-18.

Hayashi, T. and Ozaki, S. 1980: Alluvial bedform analysis I: formation of alternating bars and braids. In H. W. Shen and H. Kikkawa (eds), *Application of Stochastic Processes in Sediment Transport*, Colorado: Water Resources Pubs., 7-1 to 7-40.

Henderson, F. M. 1961: Stability of alluvial channels. *J. Hydr. Div., Amer. Soc. Civ. Engrs.* 87, 109-38.

Howard, A. D. 1982: Equilibrium and time scales in geomorphology: application to sand-bed alluvial streams. *Earth Surface Procs. & Landforms*, 7, 303-25.

Howard, A. D., Keetch, M. E. and Vincent, C. L. 1970: Topological and geomorphic properties of braided streams. *Water Resources Res.*, 6, 1674-88.

Kellerhals, R. 1982: Effect of river regulation on channel stability. In R. D. Hey, J. C. Bathurst and C. R. Thorne (eds), *Gravel-bed Rivers* Chichester: Wiley, 685-705.

Kirkby, M. J. 1972: Alluvial and nonalluvial meanders. *Area*, 4, 284-8.

Kirkby, M. J. 1980: The streamhead as a significant geomorphic threshold. In D. R. Coates and J. Vitek (eds), *Thresholds in Geomorphology*, London: Allen and Unwin, 53-73.

Laboureur, S. 1951: La localisation des meandres dans le reseau hydrographique de la plaine du Po. *Bull. Assoc. Geogr. Francais*, 218/219, 100-5.

Lane, E. W. 1957: A study of the shape of channels formed by natural streams flowing in erodible material. *US Army Corps. of Engrs., Missouri River Div., Sediment Series*, 9.

Le Ba Hong and Davies, T. R. H. 1979: A study of stream braiding. *Geol. Soc. Amer. Bull., part II*, 90, 1839-59.

Leopold, L. B. and Wolman, M. G. 1957: River channel patterns: braided, meandering and straight. *US Geol. Survey. Prof. Paper*, 282-B.

Mackin, J. H. 1956: Cause of braiding by a graded river (abstract). *Geol. Soc. Amer. Bull.*, 67, 1717-8.

Miall, A. D. 1977: A review of the braided-river depositional environment. *Earth-Science Reviews*, 13, 1-62.

Mosley, M. P. 1981: Semi-determinate hydraulic geometry of river channels, South Island, New Zealand. *Earth Surf. Proc. & Landforms*, 6, 127-37.

Nagabhushanaiah, H. S. 1967: Meandering of rivers. *Bull. Int. Assoc. Sci. Hydrol.*, 12, 28-43.

Osterkamp, W. R. 1978: Gradient, discharge, and particle-size relations of alluvial channels in Kansas, with observations on braiding. *Amer. J. Sci.*, 278, 1253-68.

Parker, G. 1976: On the cause and characteristic scales of meandering and braiding in rivers. *J. Fluid Mech.*, 76, 457-80.

Parker, G. 1979: Hydraulic geometry of active gravel rivers. *J. Hydr., Div. Amer. Soc. Civ. Engrs.*, 105, 1185-201.

Richards, K. S. 1972: Meanders and valley slope. *Area*, 4, 288-300.

Richards, K. S. 1982: *Rivers: Form and Process in Alluvial Channels*. London: Methuen.

Rust, B. R. 1978: A classification of alluvial channel systems. In A. D. Miall (ed.) *Fluvial Sedimentology*, Can. Soc. Petr. Geol. Mem. 5, 187-98.

Savat, J. 1975: Some morphologic and hydrologic characteristics of river patterns in the Zaire basin. *Catena*, 2, 161-80.

Schumm, S. A. 1963: Sinuosity of alluvial rivers in the Great Plains. *Geol. Soc. Amer. Bull.*, 74, 1089-100.

Schumm, S. A. 1977: *The Fluvial System*. New York: Wiley.

Schumm, S. A. 1979: Geomorphic threshold: the concept and its applications. *Trans. Inst. Brit. Geogrs., New Ser.*, 4, 485-515.

Schumm, S. A. 1981: Evolution and response of the fluvial system, sedimentologic implications. *Soc. Econ. Paleont. Min. Sp. Publ.*, 31, 31, 19-29.

Schumm, S. A. and Beathard, R. M. 1976: Geomorphic thresholds: an approach to river management. In *Rivers '76*, Amer. Soc. Civ. Engrs., 707-24.

Schumm, S. A. and Khan, H. R. 1972: Experimental study of channel patterns. *Geol. Soc. Amer. Bull.*, 83, 1755-70.

Schumm, S. A. and Lichty, R. W. 1963: Channel widening and floodplain construction along Cimarron River in South Western Kansas. *US Geol. Survey Prof. Paper*, 352-D, 71-8.

Smith, D. G. and Smith, N. D. 1980: Sedimentation in anastomosed river systems: examples from alluvial valleys near Banff, Alberta. *J. Sedim. Pedology*, 50, 157-64.

Smith, N. D. and Smith, D. G. 1984: William River: an outstanding example of channel widening and braiding caused by bed-load addition. *Geology*, 12, 78-82.

Stevens, M. A., Simons, D. G. and Richardson, E. V. 1975: Nonequilibrium river form. *J. Hydr. Div. Amer. Soc. Civ. Engrs.*, 101, 557-66.

Tricart, J. and Vogt, H. 1967: Quelques aspects du transport des alluvions grossieres et du faconnement des lits fluviaux. *Geogr. Annaler*, 49A, 351-66.

Tung, Y-K. 1985: Channel scouring potential using logistic analysis. *J. Hydr. Engg.*, 111, 194-201.

Werritty, A. and Ferguson, R. I. 1980: Pattern changes in a Scottish braided river over 1, 30 and 200 years. In R. A. Cullingford, D. A. Davidson and J. Lewin (eds), *Timescales in Geomorphology*, Chichester: Wiley, 53-68.

7

Bed Forms and Clast Size Changes in Gravel-bed Rivers

B. J. Bluck

INTRODUCTION

A wide variety of bed forms characterize gravel-bed rivers (figure 7.1), and those occurring in channels of comparatively low slope have been widely discussed (Church, 1972; Rust, 1972; Smith, 1974; Bluck, 1979; Lewin, 1981; Ferguson and Werritty, 1983). However, bed forms which typify channels on steep (>2 per cent) slopes are not well documented, and require more extensive and detailed description. This chapter examines the gravel bed forms which occur in channels ranging from high (>2 per cent), moderate (2 per cent–0.5 per cent) to low (<0.5 per cent) slopes, using data obtained mainly from Scotland but also from pro-glacial streams in Iceland. It also evaluates the role of these bed forms in controlling the grain size changes along stream channels.

A bed form, as discussed here, comprises one or more types of gravel fabric which are repeatedly combined into a distinctive sediment form. Six commonly occurring gravel bed forms are: longitudinal clast ridges; transverse clast dams; transverse ribs; unit bars; deltas; and undifferentiated gravel sheets. The latter group includes a range of poorly known gravel bed forms and will be discussed later. Bed forms are combined into bars (macroforms), which include fingered riffle bars, lateral (diagonal) bars and point bars (figure 7.1). The distributions of bed forms and the macroforms into which they combine are slope dependent, with transverse clast dams, longitudinal clast ridges and the fingered riffle bars into which they combine being typical of high slopes (>2 per cent), and unit bars and the lateral and medial braid bars into which they combine being typical of moderate and low slopes (<2 per cent). Bed forms typical of sand dominated rivers are not discussed in this chapter.

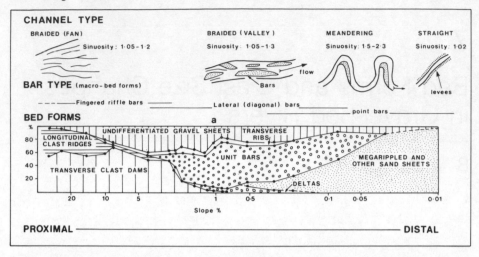

Figure 7.1 Channel type, bar type and bed forms related to channel slope. Based on data obtained mainly from the following Scottish rivers and their tributaries: Bran, Chonoghlais, Clyde, Coire Chailein, Douglas, Dubhaig, Etive, Fillan, Moffat, Portail, Tulla, and a number of small alluvial fans in the Southern Uplands and Southern Highlands. The data are collected for rivers with a wide range of sediment sizes. Transverse clast dams overlap greatly in particle size range with unit bars, and all bed forms occur in a variety of clast sizes (e.g. transverse bars in gravels >4 cm and unit bars in sediments of up to boulder size)

These bed forms act as, and are the result of, a type of sediment trapping phenomenon which has its fundamental control in turbulence at the bar surface. Clasts are transported downstream until they reach a sufficient concentration to become established in the bed as the dominant coarse-grained fabric. When established they control the size of clasts which may then accumulate near them: clasts of their own size are selected and others are rejected. Large river systems with more abundant clasts can sustain a greater number of bars of a given grain size range than smaller systems. This chapter shows that the rate of change of grain size along a channel is partly related (inversely) to sediment yield, and that both channel and source are characterized by logarithmic grain size distributions. There are many variables controlling the downstream rate of grain size decline, but by selecting alluvial fans most of these are avoided and a highly significant relationship between rate of size decline and scale of fan emerges.

The data presented here have been collected from Scottish and Icelandic river valleys all of which have strong glacial influences. Most Scottish rivers occupy glaciated valleys and have sediment sources in glacial deposits. They are typically single or rarely multi-channelled gravel bed-load streams with channel types ranging from braided, to straight and meandering. Icelandic rivers range from meltwater to clearwater streams, and are all braided and usually multi-channelled. In some of the over-steepened valleys both in Scotland and Iceland alluvial fans build laterally onto the floodplains of streams which flow longitudinally down the valley. Taken together these lateral and longitudinal rivers have a variety of channel slopes, and with most rivers occurring within or near mountainous areas, they are also subject to fairly rapid fluctuations in discharge.

DESCRIPTION OF BED FORMS

Transverse clast dams

These forms comprise ridges (fronts) of gravel which are elongated normal to the flow (figures 7.2 and 7.3). They may be over 1.5 m high with clasts > 1.8 m in length, and are arranged in steps along the channel bed (figures 7.2b and 7.2c). Sediments finer than those in the fronts accumulate upstream of them, suggesting that they behave like dams, retaining fine sediments behind them (figures 7.2b, 7.2c and 7.2d). Relationships between various measurable parameters of these structures, together with definitions of the parameters, are given in figure 7.3 and table 7.1. Similar structures have been described by Krumbein (1940; 1942, figure 6, pp. 1364–9), Wertz (1966, p. 206), Eckis (1928, p. 235), Bowman (1977), and Church and Jones (1982, figure 11.5). In many ways they resemble the transverse ribs of McDonald and Banerjee (1971) and Boothroyd and Ashley (1975, figure 16), but these rib structures are smaller and do not have the same fine sediment filling the spaces between the fronts (backfill, figures 7.2 and 7.3).

The backfill is dominantly a low-flow accumulation in which clast size often increases gradually to the next front (figure 7.2d). However, as discussed below, counter-flow is sometimes very much in evidence downstream from high dam fronts. The coarsest of these bed forms are produced during flood peaks, when the flow is directed downstream, but boulder-sized transverse clast dams are also produced during the flow deflections typically generated on bars during the falling stage (figure 7.4).

The length of transverse clast dams is a function of their height (table 7.1), suggesting that bed relief, through its control on turbulence scale, determines the site of the next downstream transverse clast dam front (see chapter 10, this volume, for a more extended process model). An estimate of the turbulence scale and intensity can be obtained by examination of the backfill sediment. Backfills are normally dominated by fine sediments of the low-flow stage. Some however have escaped a low-stage fill or have only a thin or partial veneer of low-stage sediments in them. From examples where low-stage fill is easily removed or non-existent, it is possible to reconstruct the flow path downstream from a front.

Figure 7.2 (a) Transverse clast dam, Markarfljot valley, Iceland, showing a fairly typical horse-shoe shaped front (A) and a backfill (B) filled with fine sediment overlying coarse. Scale: 50 mm

(b) Transverse clast dam, Markarfljot valley showing steps of fronts (A) and also slope of backfill (B). Scale: 50 mm

(c) Transverse clast dam, Markarfljot valley, showing thickened front (A) and low-stage fill (B) together with new dam (I) building out over older dam (II). Scale: 50 mm

(d) Vertical photograph of backfill of transverse clast dam (A_2). Note downstream coarsening to clast dam A_1. Scale: 25 cm

(e) Longitudinal clast ridge, Coire Chailein, showing well sorted clasts and imbrication. Flow towards bottom left corner. Lense cap = 40 mm diameter

(f) Fingered riffle bar and associated channel deposits, Coire Chailein. A = fingered riffle bar; B = area of longitudinal clast ridges

Sediments of the fill often show an increase in clast size downstream (figure 7.2d) but the fill may sometimes fine upstream towards the front (figure 7.5a), and this, taken in conjunction with the imbrication dip directions, shows a strong counter-flow. Downstream from this zone of counter-flow there may be a progressive fining and change in imbrication dip direction (beyond b in figure 7.5a and as shown in figure 7.5b, line 1). This zone where the bed load 'diverges' is taken as the zone of re-attached flow in a turbulence bubble (figure 7.5a). The distance between the front and the 'line' of bed-load divergence is seen to be a function of the height and grain size of the front. An estimate of the intensity of the turbulence is given by the grain size of the sediment at the zone of bed-load divergence. This size also decreases in smaller and finer transverse clast dams.

Some channel reaches do not contain clear sequences of transverse dams, but random distributions of clasts and partly destroyed dam structures. In these instances the transverse clast dams have some years later been seen to become re-established in the channel. They were probably destroyed by an extreme flood event, by the downstream migration of a local sediment slug, or by the downstream movement of a clast larger than the normal bed-load size which created its own turbulence sufficient to destroy the bed fabric.

The fronts of the clast-dams comprise frameworks of sometimes loosely-fitted, well sorted gravels (figure 7.2). Clasts larger than these either get buried in the back-fill (figure 7.5b) or, if they roll onto the front, cause its destruction. Clasts of roughly the same size are sometimes trapped behind the front and increase its thickness (figure 7.2c,I).

It is likely that transverse clast dams behave as bed-load traps which contribute to the downstream decrease of bed-load size. In this sense they are thought to perform the same role as unit bars in channels of lower slope – that is, they control the downstream changes in grain size by local turbulence effects (Bluck, 1982).

The logarithmic topographic profile which characterizes most alluvial fans, and which has been a point of discussion for some time, also typifies the 'wet' fans studied here. Most of the fans upon which the present study is based are undergoing, or have in the recent past undergone, active aggradation so that the topographic profile is an expression of depositional processes operating on the fan. Since transverse clast dams are often the dominant bed-form in the river channels on these 'wet' fans, and show a step-wise profile (figure 7.2b), then it seems probable that they control most if not all of the topographic profile characteristics of the fan. The strength of this suggestion can be supported by the following points:

1 since the height of transverse clast dams is a function of grain size (table 7.1) and grain size declines downstream, then the height of clast dams also decreases downstream (see figure 7.6);

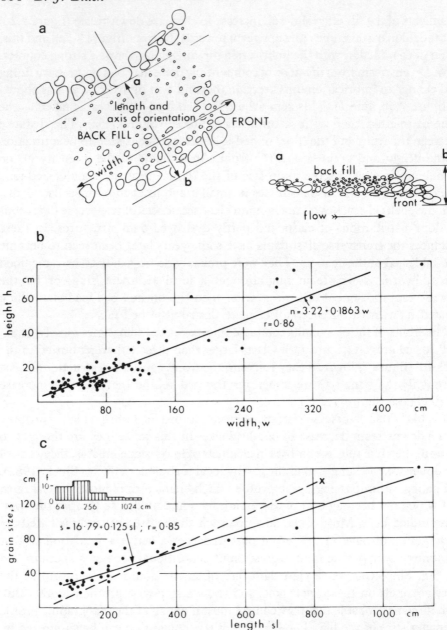

Figure 7.3   Transverse clast dams - (a) A definition of parameters. Axis of orientation refers to direction taken as flow path (see figure 7.4); h is height from base to top of dam front; (b) and (c); Some relationships between parameters; line x in (c) is the relationship between spacing and grain size taken from Boothroyd and Ashley (1975, figure 16). The inset diagram in (c) shows the frequency distribution of lengths of dams. Grain size s = average of ten largest clasts from 1 m^2 on dam front. Data from Iceland and Scotland

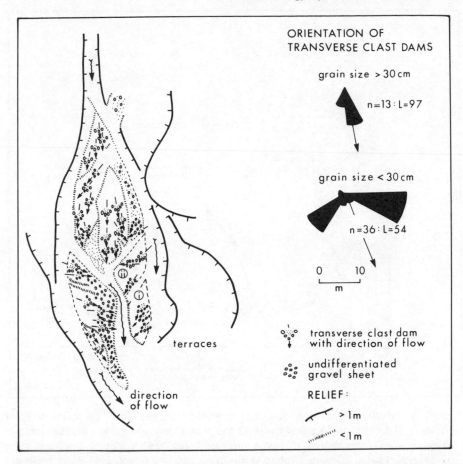

ORIENTATION OF
TRANSVERSE CLAST DAMS

grain size > 30 cm

n = 13 : L = 97

grain size < 30 cm

n = 36 : L = 54

0   10
        m

○ ○ ○
      transverse clast dam
▼   with direction of flow

○ ○ ○
 ○   undifferentiated
      gravel sheet

RELIEF:

      > 1 m

      < 1 m

terraces

direction
of flow

Figure 7.4 Plane table map of bar complex in lower fan, Markarfljot valley. The bar is transitional from a fingered riffle bar to a medial bar occurring in a region of relatively low channel slope. The effects of falling stage flow can be seen in the orientation of the 'axes of orientation' of transverse clast dams with maximum clast sizes > and < 30 cm

Table 7.1 Some relationships between parameters of transverse clast dams

	Equation	r	n
l =	−22.10 + 1.171 w	0.938	31
l =	14.939 + 4.925 h	0.815	31
s =	9.23 + 0.757 h	0.771	72

s = Maximum clast size, w = width of transverse clast dam, l = length (spacing) between fronts of transverse clast dams, h = height of front of transverse clast dam, r = coefficient of correlation, n = number of observations.

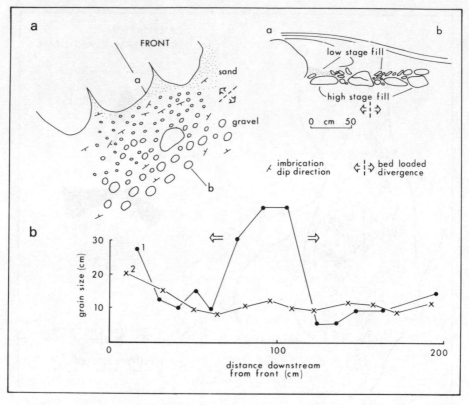

Figure 7.5 (a) plan of sediments downstream from a front showing divergence in dip of imbrication. This plan and section show positions of bed-load divergence, and section a–b is an explanation of this feature; (b) some measurements taken from part of a large-scale transverse dam backfill. Curve 1 refers to the grain size of the high flow stage sediment and the coarse clasts here are isolated (i.e. do not form a dam). Curve 2 is for the low-flow stage fill, measured before its removal to reveal the clasts measured for curve 1

2 the rate of decrease in clast dam height is logarithmic, as is the topographic profile of the fan;
3 on the basis of the meagre data presented in figure 7.6, the rate of decrease in dam height is greater on steeper fans.

Longitudinal clast ridges

These structures comprise ridges of coarse, often imbricated gravels which can be up to seven metres long and one metre high (although most are very much smaller than this). There is generally a lack of size gradation along the ridges, and the clasts in openwork contact are often very well sorted (figure 7.2e). Longitudinal clast ridges are found on the steeper portions of fans (figure 7.1)

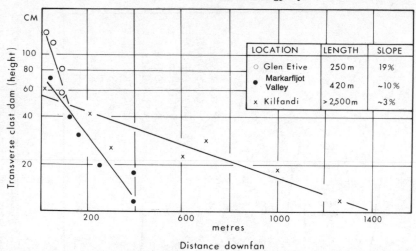

Figure 7.6 Relationship between transverse clast dam height and distance down-fan, showing the influence of slope on the rate of change of height. Kilfandi is an Icelandic fan

where they appear to form sediment splays onto the steep ground adjoining fingered riffle-bars (figures 7.2f and 7.7,b). They are evidently produced during high flow stages when the flow is no longer confined to the channel in the riffle section (figure 7.7,c): they do not occur in association with the broader areas between fingered riffle bars (figure 7.7, a_2).

In some instances these ridges are composed of a downstream sequence of transverse clast dams, in which case they show grain-size discontinuities along their length.

Transverse ribs

These structures have been described in detail by McDonald and Banerjee (1971) and Boothroyd and Ashley (1975). They are repeated ridges of coarse clasts elongated normal to the flow, and resemble in this sense transverse clast dams. They differ from clast dams in, firstly, not having a prominent backfill; secondly, persisting in stream channels with a wider range of slopes; and thirdly, occurring locally on steep accretionary surfaces (e.g. riffles) in streams where the bed-slope is less than 1 per cent (figure 7.1). They do, however, have a spacing length to clast size relationship which is similar to that of transverse clast dams (figure 7.3), and both may share a similar origin.

Unit bars

Unit bars are topographically distinctive sediment forms which:

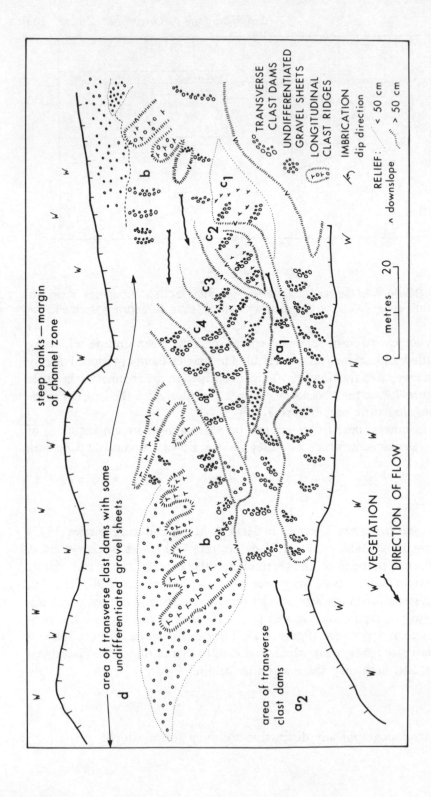

Figure 7.7 Plane table map of fingered riffle bar in Coire Chailein (Nat. Grid Ref NN 3244 3385): (a) channel areas; (b) areas of longitudinal clast ridges which splay out from the finger riffle bar complex; (c) $c_1 - c_4$ are fingers of clast dams, and represent the lateral migration of the channel towards (b); (d) is a low area with transverse clast dams, undifferentiated gravel sheets and in some cases megarippled sands

1 often decline in grain size in a downstream direction;
2 sometimes show clast segregation; and
3 quite often terminate downstream in a distinctive lee face.

They characterize channels with slopes less than 5 per cent and are normally found in combinations on lateral, medial and point bars (figure 7.1).

Unit bars may remain as discrete entities after being attached to, or migrating onto bigger bar forms, but more commonly partly or completely lose their identity by:
1 merging with other unit bars (c and d of 1977, figure 7.8 merge into b of 1981 and 1983) to form a larger unit bar complex;
2 in rare instances, being eroded and truncated to such an extent that they have none of the characteristics of unit bars – in which case they are regarded as undifferentiated gravel sheets;
3 being either totally or partially replaced by coarser sediment, generally involving the first process (1) noted above and taking place over a period of years.

Replacement of fine unit bars by coarse sediment is illustrated in figure 7.8 where coarse clasts are seen to extend gradually downstream from the head (b of figure 7.8) and along the channel (see d and channel margin of c 1981–3). Repeated plane-table mapping and sampling of bars for grain size confirms that the processes of initial growth of a bar by addition of fine unit bars followed by the *in situ* coarsening of the fine accretions as illustrated here in figure 7.8 are common, and that there is usually an upper size limit to the sediment coarsening achieved by any bar (Bluck, 1982). This results in a fairly constant rate of change of grain size along reaches for at least several years despite high mobility in bedload and rapid growth and destruction of gravel bars. There are, however, short-term fluctuations in clast size at sampling sites as bars grow coarser and are then destroyed only to re-assemble again (see figure 7.12a). Migration of coarse gravel sheets for short distances downsteam has, however, been recorded. In figure 7.8 gravels of more than 15 cm MCS have migrated from a (1977) to b (1983), a distance of 30 m in 5 years – the fastest movement recorded by the author in a relatively short monitoring period of 15 years. If all gravel bars were to migrate in such a way, then a downstream increase in grain size would occur throught time, and since all sediment migrations of this kind are downstream, then most gravel rivers should coarsen with time if they comprise tough (e.g. quartzitic) lithologies. Possibly because of the short period of observation, such a coarsening is not recorded in figure 7.12a.

Monitoring of painted clasts and vertical accretion on bars shows that replacement of unit bar surfaces by coarser clasts is achieved by partial or (rarely) complete replacement of the pre-existing unit bar sediment. Partial replacement of fine gravel of the old bar with coarse generates upward coarsening vertical sequences within the bar sediments.

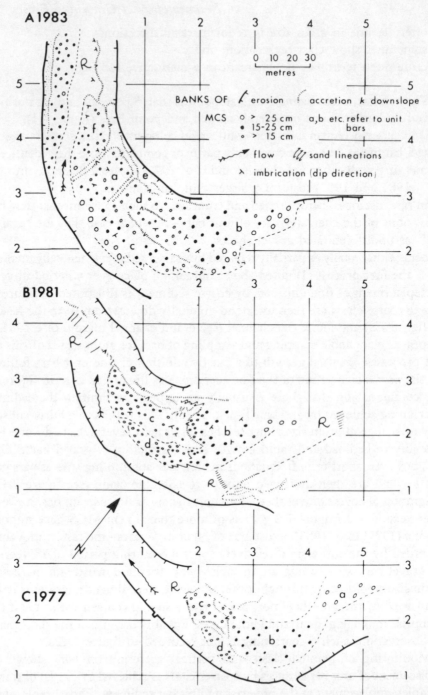

Figure 7.8 Repeated plane table maps of a bar on the Tulla [NN 3262 4498]. MCS refers to maximum clast size recorded from 2 × 2 m square area and represent averages of 20 clasts. R = riffle; a, b, etc. are discussed in text

This coarsening of unit bars through time and the general coarsening of the macro-bar form to which they are attached is thought to be achieved by the local turbulence on the bar surface. The difference in bed height created by different clast sizes on the unit bar surface generates a turbulence intensity and scale which in turn controls the sizes of clasts which can exist on the surface, particularly downstream of an assemblage of large clasts. In this way fine sediments are swept out and only sediment coarse enough to resist movement can remain in these downstream regions.

Turbulence scale and intensity is reduced when clasts of roughly the same size are assembled together, or when an irregular surface of differing clast sizes is covered by finer gravel so as to reduce bed relief. In these ways, and particularly in the former case, stable gravel sheets are produced which resist erosion for long periods of time because not only do they have low bed relief, but they also comprise clasts which are bound in their own interlocking fabric. Some coarse-grained bar heads have not had the coarser elements of their framework replaced in at least 15 years.

Since clast abundance is inversely related to clast size, and stability in gravel sheets is partly dependent on homogeneity of grain size, then fairly extensive sheets of gravel, finer than the bar heads, tend to dominate the downstream areas of bars (figure 7.8).

The development of a stable coarse fabric (as in the bar head) can only be achieved if there is a sufficient concentration of coarse clasts in the bed load – that is, if there are enough clasts in a given size range to cluster initially and build a stable surface. Surface extension of an initial gravel cluster in a given size grade can only take place if there are sufficient clasts in the passing bed load to allow selection and retention of the sizes required in the growing surface (see figure 7.8,b). Figure 7.9 records estimates of the percentage of clasts of given size classes from a sequence of bars in a reach which includes the bar illustrated in figure 7.8. The relative abundance of clasts gradually increases to a peak proportion at which point there are sufficient clasts of a given grain-size class to form extensive sheets of stable gravel and bars of that size range appear in the channel (cf. figure 7.9a and 7.9b). Clasts of the given grain-size class suddenly become less abundant downstream, so that the curve of abundances of grain size is asymmetrical and this may reflect the efficacy of large sheets in trapping clasts, or the fact that larger sheets, in having greater perimeters (and therefore a greater area of active sediment growth), require relatively more clasts to grow at the same rate as a smaller sheet. Replacement of the finer downstream tails of unit bars by coarser sediment during the normal *in situ* coarsening of bars releases clasts which concentrate downstream to form the heads of bars there.

A small number of substantially oversized clasts ($>2\times$ maximum clast size of local gravels) may enter a reach. Being of small concentration they are seen

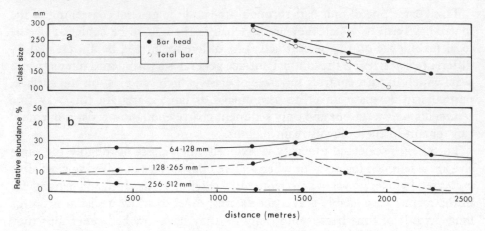

Figure 7.9 (a) The decline in clast size (maximum clast size as for figure 7.8) along a reach of the Tulla. (b) Relative abundance of clasts for the size range 512–32 mm on bars along same reach as in A (64–32 mm clast variation is not recorded here). Percentages were obtained by averaging counts of grain sizes obtained from a grid of 1 m² sampling sites on the bar surface. X marks the site of the bar illustrated in figure 7.8

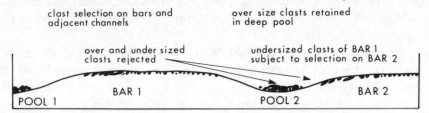

Figure 7.10 Explanation of the size selection and rejection process on bars

to break up only small areas of stable fabric by the increased scale of turbulence they generate and since they are often much greater in size than the open pore size of the bed-gravels, are rejected by the fabric and roll swiftly into pools where they remain trapped (figure 7.10). Clasts of a size which could fit into an existing fabric on a bar surface may fail to be trapped there. These move onto bar heads downstream where they form minor gravel sheets. This partly explains the increasing difference between bar head clast size and total clast size as one moves downstream (figure 7.9a).

Other gravel bed forms

These include deltas and unidentified gravel sheets. Deltas are usually generated during low flow-stages and often build almost normal to the flood flow direction (Bluck, 1979). They consist of cross stratification, build out when the bar is covered by water, but often show progressive dissection as the flow-stage falls.

Undifferentiated gravel sheets are known to have a wide variety of origins some of which can only be identified during monitoring of bed movements. Some are known to be truncated and/or re-worked unit bars; some the result of fabric destruction either by a sudden release of bedload or by migrations of large clasts; and some have clearly grown as individual sheets with an as yet unrecognized typical morphology.

MACRO BED-FORMS (BARS)

Whilst there is a wide variety of macro bed-forms present in braided rivers (Church and Jones, 1982), only those typically found in reaches of various bed slope are given in figure 7.1. Of those macro forms cited, only the fingered riffle bar (figures 7.2f and 7.7) will be discussed, since this appears to be a previously unrecorded form.

Fingered riffle bars are found in channels where the bed slope is >1 per cent and are particularly common where the slope is >10 per cent. They are located at sudden changes in bed slope and comprise two main elements: firstly, a riffle type complex in which there are ridges of transverse clast dams (figure $7.7, c_1$ to c_4) between which there are narrow steep channels possibly representing either the low-stage dissection of a once continuous sheet of transverse clast dams or the sequential lateral migration of a channel (from figure 7.7, c_1 to c_4); and secondly, an area of longitudinal clast ridges usually developed on one side of the fingered riffles. Considering the initial (upstream) height above the channel these longitudinal ridges must have formed at flood (see figure 7.7, area b). Downstream of the riffle area (c) there is a channel (figure $7.7, a_1$) which expands into a wide channel zone of transverse clast dams (figure $7.7, a_2$).

CHANGES IN GRAIN SIZE ALONG THE CHANNEL

Changes in clast size have been studied along the channels of many river systems (Pettijohn, 1975). Factors commonly cited as important in controlling the rate of size decline are selective sorting and abrasion, and the effects of either are particularly difficult to assess when there is a mixed population of clast lithologies in which abrasion and weathering reduce the size of labile clasts faster than others (Church and Kellerhals, 1978). *In situ* weathering whilst sediment is stored in bars or flood plains is also another important factor yielding on erosion a modified grain population to the local channel (Bluck, 1964). Additional problems arise when tributaries bring new sediment of different grain size into the channel (Knighton, 1980), or when local gravels belonging to a totally different sedimentary event (e.g. glacial gravels) occur in the channel bank and contribute to the sediment load. Where rivers enter gorges, then the rate of change of grain size is also modified.

Many of these sources of variability are avoided by examining the rates of clast-size decline on small alluvial fans with drainage areas in a single lithology. Some of the small alluvial fans bordering steep valleys in Iceland and Scotland are of such type (although there is here a lithological variation in some instances). The clasts show no perceptible change in roundness over their surface; there is a single, relatively unconfined channel actively dispersing the sediment, and local clast variation on the fans is usually at the scale of metres so that biased sampling from larger-scale variations is avoided. Where recycling of former sediments is taking place on these fans, tephrochronological studies suggest older deposits are not greatly older than the present river system and have therefore suffered no prolonged weathering and size reduction.

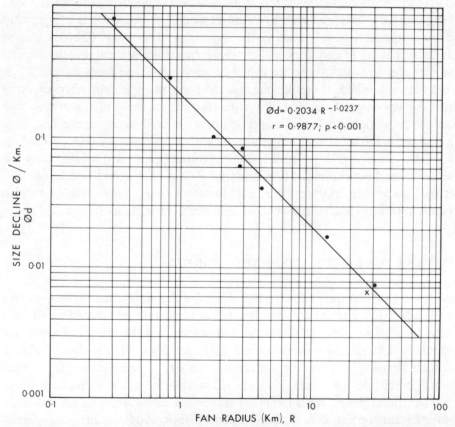

$$\emptyset d = 0.2034\ R^{-1.0237}$$

$$r = 0.9877;\ p < 0.001$$

Figure 7.11   Rate of size decline (expressed as phi units per kilometre) as a function of radial length of fan from fan head to fan toe. The data point x is taken from the Markarfljot sandur for which the full stream length is not calculable, since it flows into the sea still with a fairly coarse bed load. The size decline is calculated from maximum clast size, determined as for figure 7.8

Each small fan shows a logarithmic change in grain size along its channel with the relationship between clast size and distance typified by high correlation co-efficients (normally > 0.85). Moreover, the rate of change of grain size is a function of the scale of the fan (figure 7.11). Since fan slope is also related to the rate of clast size decline (Blissenbach, 1952; Bluck, 1964, figure 3; and Boothroyd and Ashley, 1975, figure 9), and since fan slope is inversely related to fan scale (Cooke and Warren, 1973, p. 180), then an inverse relationship between fan length and rate of change of clast size is to be expected. It also confirms the astute observations of Eckis (1928, p. 233) that the rate of particle size decline is less on large than on small fans. Data from larger braided stream systems are also included in figure 7.11 and a very high degree of correlation is maintained. This suggests that factors other than the stream length (and the immediate controls on it) are not significantly controlling the data collected. An extensive sampling of Scottish braided and meandering rivers which are characterized by numerous tributaries, lithologically variable source rocks, and prolonged floodplain weathering has produced, as expected, a far more variable set of data (not recorded here).

The relationship between fan length and rate of particle-size decline is a fundamental one linking sediment yield in the source to the nature of its distribution in channel systems in the area of deposition. A case has already been made for the effects on grain selection on bars of both relative grain abundance on bars and bed-induced turbulence. In this sense bars are templates using turbulence to select and reject clasts and so produce a downstream change in clast size. However the number of bars of a given size range in a river is a function of the volume of sediment available, the number of channels which distribute it, and the size of the gravel bars. These points are well illustrated for the Tulla River (figure 7.9), particularly when the Tulla River (channel width of about 60 m) is compared with the Markarfljot (channel zone width over 2 km and a dominantly glacial source). Sediments with a maximum clast size range of 180–200 mm are distributed on bars which occupy about 100 m of channel length in the Tulla and over 800 m of channel length in Markarfljot (figure 7.12). In the Markarfljot this can only be achieved by a substantially greater volume of sediment entering the river so that the sediment of any given grain size class is distributed over a greater number of bars (or a greater channel length). The Markarfljot distributes its greater sediment load not only by depositing sediment of a given size class along a greater channel length, but by, firstly, having an average active bar area for the grain size range illustrated in figure 7.12 which is over three times greater than the Tulla ($5.6 \times 10^2 \mathrm{m}^2$ for Tulla, and 18×10^2 m^2 for the Markarfljot); and secondly, being a multi-channel stream with many actively aggrading channels. The relative grain-size abundance curves produced for the Tulla (figure 7.9) are spread over a greater channel length in the Markarfljot, since for each grain-size class there is a greater volume of sediment.

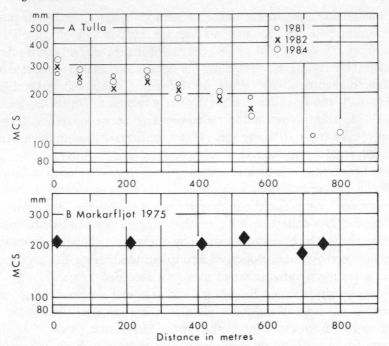

Figure 7.12 Maximum clast size reductions downstream along two river channels which differ widely in scale. In each case the data were taken from bar heads, which in the case of the Markarfljot overlapped considerably in the multi-channelled stream

The volume of sediment supplied to a river system exerts a major, if not dominant, influence on the rate of change of grain size along its channel. For alluvial fans, as recorded in figure 7.11, where their outline is truly fan-like (rather than elongated due to valley restriction) then the fan radius (=length) is directly related to fan area. Since fan area is directly related to fan drainage area (Hooke, 1968), the relationship expressed in figure 7.11 is thought to have sediment yield as its fundamental control. With these points in mind, it also follows that the logarithmic rate of change of grain size with distance is related to a downstream increase in the relative abundance of clasts in progressively smaller sizes (see figure 7.9b). This greater volume of sediment has to be spread over a greater channel length so there are more bars of a given grain-size grouping as one travels further downstream. In the fans studied here this must be an almost direct reflection of the nature of the original size-distributions yielded from the source (i.e. it is, in effect, a log-normal type of grain size distribution strung out along a river channel!). The log-normal distribution is almost certainly the result of breakdown in gravels (Pettijohn, 1975, p. 40). The logarithmic change in grain size along the channel may therefore simply reflect the nature of the size distribution generated at a source and modified during transportation.

SUMMARY

1 Gravel bed rivers have a wide range of grain sizes – from boulders to small pebbles – which construct a wide range of bedforms. A significant difference occurs in bedforms and bars at a channel slope of about two per cent. Coarse grained alluvial deposits accreting on slopes greater than this are normally alluvial fans; are typified by fingered riffle bars or bars transitional to them (figure 7.7); and are dominated by transverse clast dams. All these features can occur in gravels down to four cm or less. Gravels accreting on surfaces less than two per cent are characterized by medial and lateral bars and numerous unit bars. These bars and bedforms can appear in gravels ranging from boulder to small-pebble sizes. This great overlap in the size range of clasts in the beds of these two types of gravel channel precludes grain size as a prominent factor in controlling bedforms and bars and leaves bed slope as the major influence.

2 Longitudinal size decline in stream channels is achieved by selective clast retention and rejection in at least some bedforms – which are, in a sense, the forms taken up by sediment during its textural evolution. There are many known factors influencing the rate of particle-size decline, but the volume of sediment delivered to the dispersal system is a primary one. If the fluvial system is seen simply as a means of dispersing sediment, then the more sediment available the further it goes. This is certainly the case in alluvial fans where many of the other possible controls on rates of sediment dispersal are avoided or minimized: there are no tributaries beyond the fan head; breakdown of clasts during transportation is minimal, there is no prolonged weathering cycle affecting the materials of the bank; and there are no confined or multi-channel reaches. The result is an extremely high degree of correlation between the radial extent of the fan and the rate of particle-size decline.

The nature of the relationship between distance and rate of size decline is related to the availability of grain sizes along the channel. Since there is a logarithmic increase in abundance of clasts as size grades get finer, then the rate of clast decline with distance is less as grain size declines.

REFERENCES

Blissenbach, E. 1952: Relation of surface angle distribution to particle size distribution on alluvial fans. *J. Sediment. Petrol.*, 24, 100–16.

Bluck, B. J. 1964: Sedimentation of an alluvial fan in southern Nevada. *J. Sediment. Petrol.* 34, 395–400.

Bluck, B. J. 1979: Structure of coarse grained braided stream alluvium. *Trans. R. Soc. Edinb.*, 70, 181–221.

Bluck, B. J. 1982: Texture of gravel bars in Braided Streams. In R. D. Hey, J. C. Bathurst and C. R. Thorne (eds), *Gravel-bed Rivers*, Chichester: Wiley, 339–55.

Boothroyd, J. C. and Ashley, G. M. 1975: Process, bar morphology and sedimentary structures on braided outwash fans, northwestern Gulf of Alaska. In A. V. Jopling and B. McDonald (eds), *Glaciofluvial and Glaciolacustrine Sedimentation*, SEPM Spec. Publ. 23, 193–222.

Bowmann, D. 1977: Stepped bed morphology in arid gravelly channels. *Bull. Geol. Soc. America*, 88, 291–8.

Church, M. 1972: Baffin Island sandurs: a study of Arctic fluvial processes. *Geol. Surv. Canada Bull.*, 216.

Church, M. and Jones, D. 1982: Channel bars in gravel bed rivers. In R. D. Hey, J. C. Bathurst and C. R. Thorne (eds), *Gravel-bed Rivers*, Chichester: Wiley, 291–324.

Church, M. and Kellerhals, R. 1978: On statistics of grain size variation along a gravel river. *Can. J. Earth Sci.*, 15, 1151–60.

Cooke, R. U. and Warren, A. 1973: *Geomorphology in Deserts*. London: Batsford.

Eckis, R. 1928: Alluvial fans in the Cucamonga District, southern California. *J. Geol.*, 36, 224–7.

Ferguson, R. I. and Werritty, A. 1983: Bar development and channel changes in the gravelly River Feshie, Scotland. In J. D. Collinson and J. Lewin (eds), *Modern and Ancient Fluvial Systems*, Int. Assoc. Sedimentologists, Spec. Publ. 6, 181–93.

Hooke, R. Le B. 1968: Steady-state relationships on arid-region alluvial fans in closed basins. *Am. J. Sci.*, 266, 609–29.

Knighton, A. D. 1980: Longitudinal changes in size and sorting of stream-bed material in four English rivers. *Bull. Geol. Soc. America*, 91, 55–62.

Krumbein, W. C. 1940: Flood gravels of San Gabriel Canyon, California. *Bull. Geol. Soc. America*, 51, 639–76.

Krumbein, W. C. 1942: Flood deposits of Arroyo Seco, Los Angeles County, California. *Bull. Geol. Soc. America*, 53, 1355–402.

Lewin, J. 1981: Contemporary erosion and sedimentation. In J. Lewin (ed.), *British Rivers*, London: Allen and Unwin, 34–58.

McDonald, B. C. and Banerjee, I. 1971: Sediments and bedforms on a braided outwash plain. *Can. J. Earth Sci.*, 8, 1282–301.

Pettijohn, F. J. 1975: *Sedimentary Rocks*. London: Harper Row.

Rust, B. R. 1972: Structure and process in a braided river. *Sedimentology*, 18, 221–45.

Smith, N. D. 1974: Sedimentology and bar formation in the Upper Kicking Horse River, a braided outwash stream. *J. Geol.*, 82, 205–24.

Wertz, J. B. 1966: The flood cycle of ephemeral streams in south-western United States. *Ann. Assoc. Am. Geogr.*, 56, 598–633.

8

Mechanics of Flow and Sediment Transport in River Bends

William E. Dietrich

INTRODUCTION

In recent years, important progress has been made in the development of a general theory for flow, bed topography and planform evolution of river meanders. This has occurred despite a profound lack of detailed field observations with which to test not only the accuracy of predictions, but also and importantly, the assumptions upon which theory is constructed. The meander problem that has received the most advanced theoretical and experimental work is the analysis of the processes controlling equilibrium bed topography in a channel of a given planform. In this case, bed morphology remains essentially constant despite large fluxes of sediment and substantial shift of the flow through the bend. At every point on the bed, some overall balance of forces and sediment flux rates must obtain.

In river bends with heterogeneous mixtures of sediment sizes, a distinct sorting pattern often develops in which the coarser and finer bed particles trade position through the bend. The coarse particles shift from near the inside bank in the upstream part of the bend to near the outside bank downstream of the axis of the bend. The sorting process and its relationship to equilibrium bed morphology development has attracted sedimentologists concerned with reconstructing ancient rivers from depositional sequences, as well as geomorphologists and engineers seeking to explain observations of present-day rivers. This highly specified problem, then, has attracted researchers from many fields and has served as a common problem on which to hone observational and theoretical skills. These skills are in turn useful for the analysis of many different problems in river mechanics.

This chapter raises questions for both field-oriented scientists and theoreticians regarding what is known about the mechanics of flow and sediment transport controlling bed morphology in river bends. Theory and observation have focused on channels with relatively small width–depth ratios. The first section of this chapter suggests that bed morphology varies with this aspect ratio and that more field and theoretical studies are needed on rivers with large width–depth ratios. The mechanics controlling flow fields in bends can perhaps be more clearly understood by examining separately the forces due to curvature change and bed topography variation through a bend. A simplified theory, containing elements of most flow models, can be employed to predict the velocity field through a bend and to illustrate effects of channel morphology on flow. An answer that is *close* to the correct answer is obtained with this simplest of approaches. For this reason, many theorists have made reasonably successful predictions. It is argued, however, that a complete but more complicated theory, without the use of adjustable parameters, is necessary to predict the form and behaviour of river bed morphology during stage change.

The chapter concludes with a discussion of the sediment transport processes controlling sorting and bed morphology in bends. Clearly the cross-stream bed slope and near-bed inward velocity in bends provide an ideal setting for strong segregation by size of bed materials, with the largest particles rolling downslope toward the pool and the fine particles being carried to the top of the bar by the inward flow. Also the outward shifting zone of maximum boundary shear stress through a bend must be balanced by cross-stream sediment fluxes. What is less clear is the relative importance to bed-morphology equilibrium of sediment suspension, bedform modification of flow and sediment transport direction, and grain size versus sediment flux adjustments to changing boundary shear stress fields. One case study is discussed where all these effects are evaluated and it is argued that some generality can be found through comparison with other less complete studies. More field studies are needed however, particularly in gravel-bedded and fine sand-bedded rivers.

PLANFORM AND BED TOPOGRAPHY

The beds of rivers are usually deformed into deep and shallow areas, often referred to as pools and riffles, respectively. Considerable research has been done to define the relationship between pool to pool or riffle–riffle spacing and channel width (e.g. Keller and Melhorn, 1973), or to investigate resistance and scour and fill tendencies with stage change (e.g. Lisle, 1979). Largely as a consequence of careful experimentation and observation in Japan (e.g. Kinoshita, 1961; Ikeda, 1984), there is a growing appreciation that the pool and riffle are part of a single bed-form, the bar unit (figure 8.1). In straight laboratory channels this bedform can develop into surprising regularity. As indicated in figure 8.1,

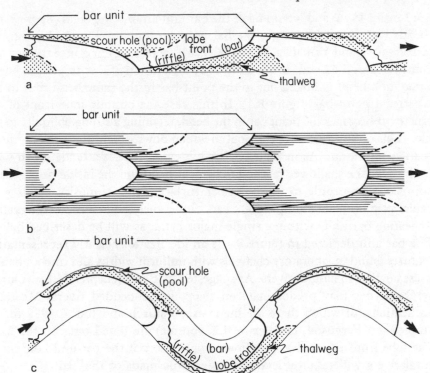

Figure 8.1 Bar unit morphology in straight (a), braided (b) and meandering channels (c). Bar unit consists of a narrow, deep scour hole (pool) that widens and shoals to an oblique lobe front (riffle and bar). The scour hole is shaded in a and c whereas the shading in b represents the low flow water level. Morphologic classification of bars based purely on their exposed portions fails to recognize the inherently three-dimensional nature of these large-scale features

the bedform consists of a downstream widening and shoaling scour hole (pool) terminating in an oblique shallow lobe front, the deepest portion of which is equivalent to the riffle. The shallowest portion of the bar is neither at the most downstream edge of the bar unit, nor along the closest bank; instead it is usually somewhat upstream of the bar front and toward the centre of the channel. When the bar pattern is repeated along opposite banks it is termed an alternate bar pattern; repeating as a mirror image across the channel is described as a row bar. It is argued by many (e.g. Kinoshita, 1961; Ikeda, 1984) that the row bar is the fundamental bed unit of braided channels, the shallowest portion of which in river sections may become stabilized by vegetation. In both the straight alternate-bar case and the braided channel, the bars migrate downstream.

In flume experiments or channelized reaches of rivers, alternate bar formation in channels with erodible banks typically leads to meandering (e.g. Friedkin,

1945; Lewin, 1976) and wrapping of the bar unit around the bend (figure 8.1c). In bends with small curvature, the bar will continue to migrate downstream (e.g. Hasegawa and Yamaoka, 1984), but with increasing curvature the bar will become fixed in the bend. Importantly, in a succession of low amplitude bends the pool of a bend is linked not to the point bar in the same bend, but to the downstream point bar (figure 8.1). In this case the oblique lobe front of the alternate bar becomes the point bar in the bend, retaining a strong obliquity to the banks. This obliquity causes the pool to widen downstream from the radius of curvature minimum. As in the alternate-bar case, there is a tendency in wide point bars for the shallowest portion to be detached from the inside bank, giving a humped cross-profile to the point-bar surface. High sinuosity bends with irregular planform and multiple point bars can be analysed in terms of alternating or repeating bar units within a single major bend, as will be described below.

The bar unit depicted in figure 8.1 is an idealization, clearly representative of features found in laboratory channels with uniform widths and smooth banks, but less obvious in natural rivers. As suggested by Bluck (chapter 7, this volume) other bar types may predominate on steep, gravel-bedded rivers. Most bar classifications (of which there are many – see Church and Jones, 1982 for an example, and Ferguson, chapter 6, this volume) are based only on the form of the lobe front exposed at low flow. Application of the bar-unit concept to natural rivers will require detailed topographic maps of the bed.

Point-bar morphology is greatly influenced by the width–depth ratio (w/d) in the bend. Extensive flume studies in straight channels have demonstrated that in narrow, deep channels alternate bar formation is suppressed. Although slope, Froude number and grain size influence this result somewhat, bars tend not to form below values of w/d of about ten. Brice (1984) labelled meandering rivers lacking point bars 'sinuous canaliforms'. Narrow, deep, curved channels nonetheless may form pools and bars with similar gross morphology to that depicted in figure 8.1 as a result of the curvature-induced secondary circulation, and spatial variations in the boundary shear stress field. Such bars have been called 'forced bars' by H. Ikeda (personal communication, 1985). For a bend of a given planform and radius of curvature to width ratio, however, the cross-channel profile varies significantly with the w/d. Figure 8.2a illustrates the cross-sectional form with varying w/d in the flume studied by Hooke (1974). Note that with increasing w/d, a broad, nearly flat surface formed out to the channel centreline. A similar result was obtained by Onishi (1972) in a flume in which he reduced the channel width by a factor of two by placing a wall along the centreline. Figure 8.2b shows the cross-channel profile change observed by Friedkin at the apex of an initial curved channel with w/d of seven as it widened to form a point bar and increase w/d to 53. Again, a broad, nearly flat bar surface formed over a significant portion of the profile.

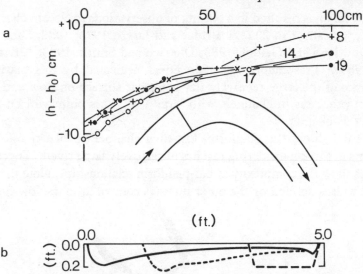

Figure 8.2 Variation in cross-channel profile in the meandering laboratory channel investigated by Hooke (1975) (a) and Friedkin (1945) (b). Vertical axis in a gives the difference between local and mean depth, h and h_0 respectively. Numbers to the right refer to the width to depth ratio of the experiment. In (b), successive lines represent progressive bar development through time along a cross-section. In both cases horizontal axis is the distance across the channel from the left bank.

The importance of w/d as a primary variable in channel form is demonstrated by the frequent use of this ratio as a principal parameter in distinguishing channel patterns (e.g. Parker, 1976; Fujita, 1982). In a channel with relatively erodible banks, alternate bar development will cause bank erosion, and the bar will widen, producing a strongly meandering thalweg in a channel whose banks show relatively low sinuosity. As Friedkin (1945) demonstrated there will be a tendency for the flow to cut off the widened bar along a chute channel once the bar has reached a certain width. Once cut off, a new bar will start to form again. The description provided by Friedkin is very similar to that given by Ferguson and Werritty (1983) for what they called a 'wandering gravel-bedded river'. In a sense this morphology and process represent the extreme bar response to high w/d without making the transition to row bars and braiding. It has also been proposed by Schumm (1963) that meander sinuosity is inversely proportional to w/d, but independent attempts to define a quantitative relationship suggest that it is an important but not dominant factor and that sinuosity depends on many variables (i.e. Chitale, 1970).

The width–depth ratio has received relatively little consideration in recent detailed studies of flow and sediment transport fields in river meanders. The necessity of working on relatively small rivers in order to collect accurate and thorough data has resulted in a biasing of observations to stream channels with low w/d, typically 7 to 20 (e.g. Bridge and Jarvis, 1976; 1982; Dietrich et al., 1979; DeVriend and Geldof, 1983; Dietrich and Smith, 1983; 1984a; Thorne et al. 1985a). Presumably the main effect neglected by this biasing is the importance of the large relatively flat point-bar surface on flow and sediment transport processes in channels with large w/d. This point will be addressed later in this chapter.

Figure 8.3 shows the planform, low-flow channel (in black) and emergent point bars of three meandering reaches of relatively large rivers. Together these examples show the complexity of bar-planform relationships. Note that bankfull channel widths defined by the outer lines (as compared to the low-flow case in

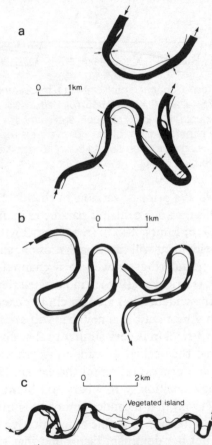

Figure 8.3 Planform, low-flow channel (in black) and emergent point bars (in white) on three meandering reaches of relatively large rivers. (a) Lower Wabash River studied by Jackson (1976); (b) Beatton River investigated by Nanson and Hickin (1983); (c) Lower Babbage River studied by Forbes (1983). Rivers in (a) and (b) are sand-bedded, whereas (c) is gravel-bedded

black) are systematically narrower in the crossings than in the bends (note arrows at crossings in figure 8.3a). Few of the meanders have smoothly varying curvature and parallel banks; instead curvature increases abruptly downstream of the crossing, and then tends to diminish downstream. Large amplitude bends tend to have a second curvature maximum in the downstream ends before the next crossing. Several authors have argued that asymmetry is typical of large bends (see review in Hooke, 1984). Hasegawa (1983), for example, found that a modified 'sine-generated' curve equation which produced an asymmetric meander pathline with two radii of curvature minima (like figure 8.3b) best fits planforms of several rivers in Japan (see summary in Yamaoka and Hasegawa, 1984).

In figure 8.3, the white zones recording the shallow point-bar top (at bankfull stage) distinctly wrap around the convex bank and are elongated in the downstream direction. In the most sinuous meanders (figure 8.3b) multiple bars

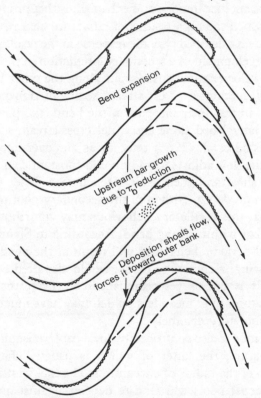

Figure 8.4 Development of compound looping due to bend growth relative to upstream bend. The sequence of channel paths illustrates the hypothesis that as the bend expands, there should be a tendency for boundary shear-stress reduction near the bend entrance due to lengthening of the channel path from apex to apex in successive bends. Reduced boundary shear stress would lead to deposition, bar growth, shoaling induced outward deflection of the flow towards the outer bank and compound looping.

have formed within a single complex bend. Approximately three complete asymmetric bends are represented in each of the two reaches. Within these reaches the average bar spacing in channel widths is eight (left channel) and five (right channel), and a near-alternate bar sequence is present in the downstream convex portion of the left channel. Keller (1972) and Hooke and Harvey (1983) suggest that a path-length dependent bar instability, like that responsible for alternate bar formation, leads to multiple bars in the limbs (Keller) or compound looping (Hooke and Harvey), although the fluid mechanics responsible for this instability in a curved flow are not described. One mechanism is illustrated in figure 8.4, whereby growth of the downstream bend results in a systematic reduction in the boundary shear stress responsible for sediment transport along the inside bank of the bend. This shear stress reduction leads to bar growth, deflection of flow toward the outer bank and compound looping (*sensu* Brice, 1984) of the bend. Perhaps another important mechanism is that proposed by Struiksma et al. (1985) in which the rapid radius of curvature change from the crossing into the bend induces a damped periodic response in the resulting bed topography in a bend. The development of a secondary circulation in the pool and outward shift of the high-velocity core causes scour along the outer bank; in response, the pool deepens, forcing net cross-stream sediment transport across the bar into it. In effect, in the upstream part of the bend, the pool over-deepens to produce a steep lateral bed slope and a net cross-stream sediment transport, a process Struiksma et al. (1985) refer to as an 'overshoot effect'. Further downstream, as the flow adjusts to an imposed constant channel curvature, the pool depth will shoal and then again deepen to a lesser extent, forming a secondary maximum depth. Although the secondary pool maximum is much less than the first, this oscillatory behaviour may contribute to development of an additional bar within a long bend. According to Struiksma et al. (1985) a similar damped periodic behaviour will result at the bend exit and into the downstream crossing. Hence their model would also predict bar instability in long crossings. It is not as yet established, however, that this theory has applications to natural river meanders, which may have much greater frictional damping than laboratory channels.

Point-bar formation is also controlled by local bank resistance and the strength of channel curvature, the latter of which is usually characterized by the diminishing ratio of the radius of curvature to channel width (r_c/w). Along the same channel, deeper pools will tend to develop against more resistant bank material (Friedkin, 1945) and in bends with smaller r_c/w. Sufficiently large bank obstruction relative to the channel size will turn the flow, producing a forced bar with an oblique bar face similar to that in the freely meandering case (Lisle, 1986). Bank obstructions may also 'stall' a meandering loop (Reid, 1984) by preventing bank erosion, such that the upstream bend can overtake it. This causes the upstream inside bank to erode faster than the outside one, resulting in bank migration away from the concave outside bank and deposition of a bar where once the pool lay.

In summary, point bars in meandering rivers are equivalent to the lobe fronts in alternate bars. In wide, shallow channels the bar top is relatively flat in the zone of curvature maximum and may extend well across the channel. In narrow, deep channels the point-bar development is suppressed, the flat bar top may be absent and in rivers that otherwise would not produce alternate bars in straight reaches, channel curvature will produce a 'forced bar'. The break in slope from the bar top to the face into the pool tends to cut obliquely across the channel, extending from close to the outside bank in the radius of curvature minimum to the inside bank further downstream. River meanders typically have distinct curvature maxima, often having more than one in large amplitude bends. These maxima may be a consequence of bar development, or may be responsible for bar formation, depending on their origins. Bend asymmetry is common in some rivers, perhaps more often skewed with an elongated downstream limb, and in such bends multiple bars and downstream-elongated bars are common. This description provides a morphologic framework for investigation of flow through meanders.

FLOW AND BOUNDARY SHEAR STRESS IN RIVER BENDS

Flow fields in rivers are controlled in large part by the resultant of forces arising from channel curvature, changes in curvature and gradients in bed topography. The flow response to channel planform and topography in turn dictates the boundary shear-stress field which controls the transport of sediment – hence for sediment transport studies of bars, an understanding of the flow fields in bends is essential. Here I briefly review observations and theory for flow in meandering streams in order to discuss sediment transport processes. Detailed discussions and other references can be found in Dietrich and Smith (1984a), Elliott (1984), Hasegawa and Yamaoka (1984) and Smith and McLean (1984).

Curvature effects

Channel curvature forces major adjustments in flow patterns. It is well understood that curvature results in a centrifugal force acting in the cross-channel direction. This force is counter-balanced primarily by the cross-stream tilt of the free surface, which causes a cross-stream pressure gradient force. This balance holds only in the vertically-averaged flow because the surface velocity is much faster than the near-bed velocity due to boundary resistance. The slow near-bed flow

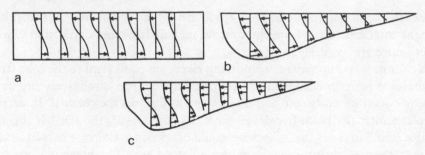

Figure 8.5 (a) secondary circulation in a rectangular channel of constant curvature; (b) the assumed pattern of secondary circulation in bends which may only develop in regions well downstream of radius of curvature minima; (c) the observed pattern in the upstream end of a bend with well developed bar and pool topography. Lines not continued to streambed because of inadequate space to show that they must curve back to zero on the vertical

is turned inward whereas the high centrifugal force of the near surface flow carries it outward against the opposing pressure-gradient force; the net effect is a spiral-like motion, sometimes described as helicoidal flow (figure 8.5).

This rotational motion, a secondary circulation relative to the main flow direction, is usually described as the main effect of curvature on flow, but there is another, very important consequence of curvature: the tilting of the water surface alters the downstream slope of the water surface, generating large cross-stream variation in the downstream boundary shear stress and velocity fields. Figure 8.6 illustrates channel curvature and bed topography effects on flow. Across the top of figure 8.6 three equations are written that in turn express the principal cross-stream and downstream force components on the flow and the dependence of the local downstream slope on water surface elevation change and varying travel distances due to curvature. The equations are written using a co-ordinate system that follows the channel centreline (e.g. Dietrich and Smith, 1983; Smith and McLean, 1984) in which s points downstream parallel to the centreline, z points nearly vertical and n, the cross-stream axis, is positive toward the left bank. The scale factors (metric coefficients) for derivatives with respect to the cross-stream and vertical co-ordinates are unity, but the one associated with the downstream coordinate is $1-n/R=1-N$, *where R is the local radius* of curvature of the centreline. This scale factor compares an arc length measured along the channel centreline to that measured along any other line of constant n.

The first equation is derived from the force balance between the cross-stream centrifugal force term and the cross-stream pressure gradient term

$$\frac{\varrho <u_s^2>h}{(1-N)R} = -\varrho gh\frac{\partial E}{\partial n} \qquad (8.1)$$

$$\Delta E_n \cong \frac{\bar{U}_s^2}{g}\frac{w}{R} \qquad T_b \cong \rho g h S \qquad S = \frac{-1}{1-N}\frac{\Delta E_s}{\Delta s}$$

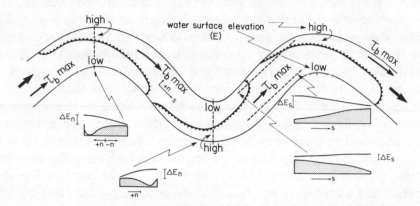

Figure 8.6 Channel curvature and bed topography effects on the boundary shear stress field. Break in bar slopes indicated by serrated edge. Curvature induces centrifugal forces and changes in water-surface elevation that in a meandering reach forces skewing of the downstream boundary shear stress fields. Bar-pool topography causes the maximum boundary shear-stress zone to shift outward further upstream than would occur due to curvature alone. Equations across the top are explained in the text

where $<u_s>$ is the vertically averaged downstream component of velocity, h is the depth of flow, g is the gravitational acceleration, ϱ is the fluid density, and E is the elevation of the water surface. Approximate integration of (8.1) across the channel yields the first equation in figure 8.6, in which $\bar{U}_s$ is the cross-sectionally averaged downstream mean velocity, w is the flow width and ΔE_n is the total water surface elevation change from the inside to the outside of the channel. Although incomplete (e.g. Yen and Yen, 1971; Dietrich and Smith, 1983; Smith and McLean, 1984), equation 8.1 includes the most important terms.

In a channel with smoothly varying curvature and uniform width, as depicted in figure 8.6, ΔE_n will increase into the area of radius of curvature minimum, decrease to zero in the crossing and increase again, but in an opposite direction, into the next bend downstream. Consequently the water surface will rise and become relatively high along the concave outer bank, and drop along the convex ones (figure 8.6). This has an important effect on the boundary shear stress and velocity fields.

In steady uniform flow the local downstream boundary shear stress, τ_b, can be approximated as

$$\tau_b = -\frac{\varrho g h}{(1-N)}\frac{\partial E}{\partial s} \qquad (8.2)$$

Strictly this equation is accurate only for channels with constant curvature and bed topography (e.g. Dietrich and Smith, 1983). For the case depicted in figure 8.6, if the bars were absent and instead the cross-sections were the same throughout, equation (8.2) should be reasonably accurate except in areas of rapid curvature change. In this case, then, variations in flow depth would not contribute to the changes in the boundary shear-stress field. Nonetheless, large changes would develop due to the effect of centrifugal forces on water-surface topography. As shown in figure 8.6, the rising of the water surface near the concave bank of the upstream bend and the dropping downstream along the convex one will generate a locally steep downstream water-surface slope, hence a zone of maximum boundary shear stress. On the opposite side of the channel, the water surface will either drop very little to the downstream high along the outer bank or it may (as shown in figure 8.6) rise, in which case the water-surface slope is reversed and according to equation (8.2) the boundary shear stress would be negative. Hence just the effect of centrifugal forces on the flow through a meander should tend to produce a zone of maximum boundary shear stress (and maximum average velocity) that shifts from near the inside upstream bank to near the outside downstream one through the zone of radius of curvature minimum (figure 8.6). In the special case of uniform bed topography, such as the rectangular or trapezoidal shapes often used in experiments, and a curved section of constant curvature joined by straight reaches, the boundary shear-stress maximum will develop along the inner convex bank and will not shift toward the outer one until the downstream end of the bend where the radius of curvature changes from a small constant value to infinite (Dietrich and Smith, 1983; Smith and McLean, 1984).

To summarize, channel curvature results in centrifugal forces which lead to a secondary circulation. Water surface slope changes due to curvature result in the development of a zone of maximum boundary shear stress near the convex inside bank. Curvature change, from a large value in the bend to zero at the crossing to a large value of opposite sign downstream, results in cross-stream shifting of the zone of maximum boundary shear stress. Bar and pool topography, which will be discussed next, alters the orientation of the near-bed velocity, increases the cross-stream variation in boundary shear stress field and causes rapid shifting of the maximum across the channel.

Bed topography effects in straight and curved channels

Laboratory (Hasegawa, 1983; Ikeda, 1984) and field (Leopold, 1982) measurements, in addition to theoretical investigations (Smith and McLean, 1984), show that alternate bars in straight channels strongly influence the cross-stream distribution of the mean velocity and the near-bed velocity orientation.

Figure 8.7 illustrates the vertically-averaged velocity field in a laboratory channel with self-formed alternate bars. As shown previously in figure 8.1, the bar unit will be deepest at its upstream end and shoal progressively downstream. Note that a complete bar unit is not shown in figure 8.7, only the downstream half of one and the upstream portion of the next unit. A minimum depth downstream typically occurs somewhat upstream of the lobe front (indicated by serrated edges in figure 8.7) and towards the centre of the channel. The flow field depicted in figure 8.7 graphically demonstrates that shoaling of the flow in the downstream direction from pool to lobe front generates a net cross-stream discharge toward the adjacent pool. The vectors representing vertically-averaged velocity are oriented strongly across the channel over much of the downstream outer portion of the bar unit. In addition, the position of the maximum velocity (as indicated by arrows) shifts abruptly across the channel. In effect, the flow finds it 'easier' to go around the bar rather than directly over it. This is due in part to the change in the downstream pressure gradient (right side of equation (8.2)) with depth variation, and in part to convective accelerations due to the downstream gradients in flow depth (see Dietrich and Smith, 1983, p. 1174 and their figure 3 for further discussion).

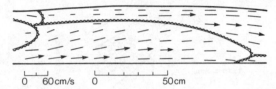

0   60 cm/s   0   50 cm

Figure 8.7 Vertically averaged velocity field over self-formed alternate bars in a laboratory flume (modified from Ikeda, 1984). Only downstream end of one bar and upstream end of next bar unit shown. Arrows indicate position of maximum velocity. Triangular edging points toward deep water. Minimum depth probably occurred at third to last section over central bar

In curved channels with well developed bars, topographically induced forces arise that strongly influence the boundary shear stress and velocity fields. As in the alternate-bar case, shoaling of the flow will tend to turn the flow toward the pool, causing significant net cross-stream discharge. Consequently, where shoaling is strong, the vertically averaged velocity vector over the bar will point toward the pool, and although secondary circulation must still occur, the near-bed velocity and resulting boundary shear stress will be oriented towards the outer bank as well. Hence, bar growth into the flow will radically alter the near-bed cross-stream velocity pattern. This conclusion is supported by numerous flume studies analysed by Dietrich and Smith (1983), by a recent extensive laboratory investigation by Hasegawa (1983) (see Hasegawa and Yamaoka, 1984,

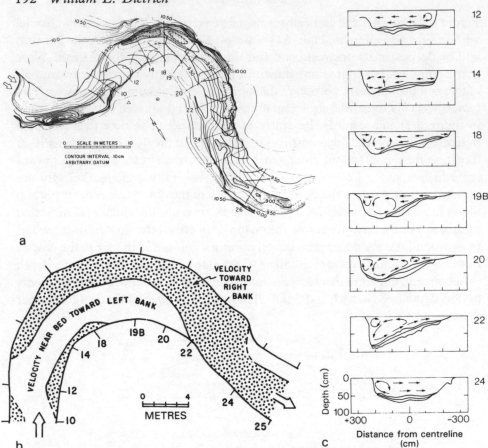

Figure 8.8 (a) bed topography; (b) near-bed velocity orientation; (c) cross-stream velocity field in Muddy Creek, a small sand-bedded stream. Note the evolution of the cross-stream velocity from outward through water column (12), to progressive development of helical motion with inward near-bed velocity over the pool (14–22), to outward at the entrance of next bend downstream. Arrows are qualitative interpretations of the cross-stream velocity field reported in Dietrich and Smith (1983, figure 11)

and Yamaoka and Hasegawa, 1984), by detailed field studies and re-analysis of previously published field data (Dietrich and Smith, 1983) and by new field studies (Thorne et al., 1985a; 1985b).

Figure 8.8 shows the pattern of bed topography, cross-stream velocity field and near-bed velocity orientation in a small, sand-bedded river meander. The site and field methods are described in previous publications (Dietrich et al., 1979; 1984; Dietrich and Smith, 1983, 1984a, 1984b). In brief, Muddy Creek receives nearly constant irrigation outflow each spring which, in combination with an adequate supply of sediment from erodible banks of sandy alluvial deposits, results in the formation of a bed topography in equilibrium with flow. Importantly, direct measurement of bed topography during field experiments and in successive years at the same discharge clearly demonstrates a well-defined equilibrium bed topography. Hence observations could be made under flume-like conditions that defined a mutual adjustment between flow and bed topography to an equilibrium condition. This analysis is important because the effect of bed topography on flow varies strongly as the stage deviates from that in equilibrium with the bed.

In the Muddy Creek bend (figure 8.8), width–depth ratio increases from 10 in the crossings (just upstream of sections 12 and 24) to 17 in the centre of the bend (section 19) and the radius of curvature–width ratio is about 1.5 for the central part of the bend. The central bend had an approximately constant radius of curvature from section 14 to section 20 (Dietrich and Smith, 1983, figure 9) and most of the curvature change occurred at the entrance and exit of the bend over a distance of about one channel width.

The cross-stream velocity field depicted in figure 8.8 shows that strong outward velocity (and net discharge) develops in the crossing (sections 12 and 24) downstream of a bend. Through the crossing and into the centre of the bend, the discharge vector between successive sections is oriented 4° to 7° toward the outer bank relative to the channel centreline path. The spiral motion in the cross-stream plane forms as the pool develops and expands across the channel progressively (section 14 to 22). Shoaling over the bar along the inside bank forces the flow into the pool and the cross-stream velocity is oriented toward the pool throughout the water column. The near-bed velocity direction is towards the pool in the upstream part of the bend where the flow is shoaling; downstream of section 19B the bar deepens and the helical motion expands across the channel. Shoaling, bank effects (which lead to an opposite spiral near the surface and over the upsloping bank), and possibly lee effects of the point bar along the inside bank, cause the zone of spiral motion with outward flow near the surface and inward flow near the bed to be confined to the deepest 20 to 30 per cent of the channel cross-section. Downstream of section 20, weak net cross-stream discharge towards the downstream end of the pool develops as the pool width increases.

Based on available field and laboratory measurements in the references cited above, a sketch of the flow pattern in equilibrium with the bed topography in bends with well developed bars can be constructed (figure 8.9). Two cases are shown, a low amplitude bend with strong curvature and a similar bend with a long downstream 'tail' of nearly constant curvature. Of course many other combinations occur, but these figures illustrate several important aspects of flow in bends. The lobe front is indicated with a serrated edge and the thalweg with a dashed line. The bar top at low flow is shaded in order to relate this pattern

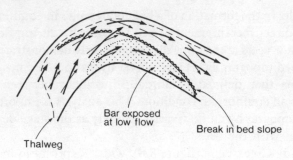

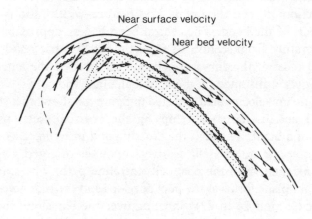

Figure 8.9 Flow field in equilibrium with bed topography in bends with well developed bars. Note shoaling-induced outward flow upstream of radius of curvature minimum, and downstream-growing region of spiral motion with inward near-bed velocity vector. Stippled area represents exposed portion of bar unit during low flow

to the low-stage appearance more commonly seen in rivers. Two arrows, a heavy larger one over a shorter one, represent the surface and near-bed velocity, respectively. The representation is not meant to be quantitative and compromises are made in order to depict important effects. Nonetheless the length and orientation of the arrow crudely represent the corresponding velocity vector.

There are several important features of the illustration. Firstly, in the upstream part of the bend as the flow is adjusting to the sudden reduction in radius of curvature, the shoaling over the bar and deepening over the pool lead to outward deflection of the flow toward the pool. The curvature and consequent centrifugal force and counteracting cross-stream pressure gradient still result in a secondary circulation, but the plane of the circulation is curved and not oriented normal to the channel path. Hence surface velocity vectors are oriented more toward the outer bank than near-bed vectors, but these bottom vectors are also pointed slightly outward toward the pool. Secondly, this pattern differs substantially over the pool (toward the concave bank from the lobe front) and over the bar downstream of its maximum height (which is typically in the zone of radius of curvature minimum). In the pool the near-bed velocity is oriented strongly inward, either parallel to or slightly up the point-bar face of the lobe front. A secondary circulation, the axis of which is oriented approximately parallel to the channel path, develops. The pool width expands downstream and correspondingly, the zone of spiral motion generating inward near-bed velocities increases. Figure 8.5c shows a typical cross-stream velocity pattern in the upstream part of the bend. In addition, the velocity increases downstream through the pool. Downstream of the maximum bar height and the radius of curvature minimum, the velocity rapidly decreases near the inside bank, and weak inward near-bed velocities may develop. Thirdly, if a long reach of constant curvature develops, then the flow adjustments to channel path and topographic changes may be nearly complete and a zone of nearly uniform flow with a high velocity region near the outer bank and a constant spiral motion (figure 8.5b) may develop.

Figure 8.9 is in contrast to the surface flow pattern proposed by Hey and Thorne (1975), and illustrated in several texts (Richards, 1982; Knighton, 1984). At flow stages in equilibrium with the bed, the surface flow is not as strongly oriented across the channel as depicted in their drawing. The cross-stream velocity field must include a shoaling-induced outward flow over the bar if the bar is extended well up into the flow. Dual secondary cells are not clearly present in the crossings of natural channels; apparently one cell does not grow over another one. Finally the cell of opposite motion to the main one in the bend, which they correctly point out as developing along the outer bank, appears to be confined to a region very close to the bank.

It is commonly assumed in modelling of flow and sediment transport processes in bends that over a significant portion of the bend the flow becomes 'fully developed' (e.g. Yen, 1965; Jackson, 1976), meaning that the flow field and bed topography remain constant downstream through the bend. As Jackson (1976) correctly noted, most natural river channels vary too much in form and their bends are too short, in terms of response to imposed changes, for fully developed conditions to obtain. Even in long laboratory channels of constant curvature as mentioned above, it has been observed that a uniform downstream pool depth does not develop (i.e. Odgaard, 1981; Struiksma et al., 1985). Once the high velocity core has crossed to the outer bank, however, a secondary downstream curvature minimum and local bar emergence may have a smaller but not insignificant influence on the flow, as is suggested by the laboratory experiments of Hasegawa (Hasegawa and Yamaoka, 1984; Yamaoka and Hasegawa, 1984).

The pattern of flow in bends is strongly stage dependent. Without topographic adjustments due to sediment transport, an increase in stage away from the equilibrium condition shown in figure 8.9 will reduce the shoaling effect, and increase the near-bed inward component of velocity, allowing an inward component of flow to develop over the bar top. This is perhaps most clearly demonstrated in the theoretical calculations of Smith and McLean (1984, figure 5) in which the effect of increasing bar height relative to flow depth was investigated. A stage drop without topographic adjustment will greatly increase the shoaling effect and the flow downstream in the bend will be confined to the pool exposing the downstream bar top. If the bed remains mobile during a stage drop, as it can in sand-bedded channels, topographic adjustments will occur that reduce the erosive effect of strongly diverging boundary shear stress caused by shoaling. Equilibrium bed morphology can develop at any stage as long as the discharge remains sufficiently constant and the bed remains mobile.

The dependence of flow patterns on stage, as a result of bed immobility or delayed topographic response of a mobile bed, emphasizes the great need to establish whether the flow is in equilibrium with the bed topography when studying flow patterns in channels. Regrettably, most studies have not considered this problem carefully. Imbrication studies on exposed gravel bars during low flow will not give a reliable indication of high-flow patterns and sediment transport directions (Aristov, unpublished data). Although the gravel becomes relatively immobile as the stage drops below that capable of shaping the bed, the individual particles can still be rotated in their resting pockets and imbricated by the flow. Imbrication should therefore express strong shoaling effects with inferred directions oriented toward the outer bank, as is commonly seen on exposed bars.

Three other sand-bedded rivers (besides Muddy Creek) where flow patterns have been reported are the South Esk River (Bridge and Jarvis, 1982), the Fall River (Thorne et al., 1985a; 1985b) and the River Dommel (Van Alphen et al., 1984). In all three cases, bed topography was not clearly shown to be in equilibrium with the imposed flow. The most extensive data, those of Bridge and Jarvis (1982), are reported for several stages. Comparison of cross-sections, particularly in the upstream part of the bend, shows no change in bed topography over a broad range of stages. The highest stage data were collected, apparently immediately after a period of about a month of low flow. It is suggested that the data of Bridge and Jarvis record a high flow over a low-flow bed topography. As Dietrich and Smith (1983) demonstrated, the secondary flow observations of Bridge and Jarvis also do not conform to conservation of mass requirements.

Field measurements of velocity vectors must be done with reference to some cross-section orientation. Two choices for cross-section orientation are: perpendicular to the channel walls if the channel width and curvature are constant (as in the flume case), and parallel to the orientation required by continuity (Dietrich and Smith, 1983). In essence this latter requirement states that velocity or topographic changes between successive sections that alter the local discharge per unit width must be compensated by a cross-stream discharge of water. Thus, for example, at the entrance to the bend the flow often rapidly shoals downstream over the bar, but the average velocity varies little, hence net discharge between successive sections towards the pool must occur. Cross-sections must be oriented such that the measured cross-stream discharge matches that required by this continuity constraint. As virtually no stream has constant width and curvature, the continuity requirement must be employed. Smith and McLean (1984) showed that the vertically averaged continuity equation for steady flow is (in the orthogonal curvilinear co-ordinate system in figure 8.6).

$$\frac{1}{1-N} \frac{\partial <u_s>h}{\partial s} - \frac{<u_n>h}{(1-N)R} + \frac{\partial <u_n>h}{\partial n} = 0 \tag{8.3}$$

and they solved it for $<u_n>h$, the local cross-stream discharge per unit width, to get

$$<u_n>h = -\frac{1}{1-N} \int_{-w/2}^{n} \frac{\partial <u_s>h}{\partial s} \, dn \tag{8.4}$$

Here $<u_n>$ and $<u_s>$ are the cross-stream and downstream vertically averaged velocity, respectively; $-w/2$ is the right-bank position of a channel with a width w. Equation (8.4) can be used in a simple procedure to determine the correct cross-sectional orientation for calculation of the cross-stream velocity field. Field selection of section orientation is used to compute the down-stream and cross-stream components of the vertically averaged velocity. The total cross-stream discharge of water, Q_{nw}, required by continuity can be computed from equation (8.4) by integration from bank to bank:

$$Q_{nw} = \int_{-w/2}^{w/2} <u_n>h \, dn = \int_{-w/2}^{w/2} \left[\frac{-1}{1-N} \int_{-w/2}^{n} \frac{\partial <u_s>h}{\partial s} \, dn \right] dn \tag{8.5}$$

The average direction of flow, θ_w between successive sections with an average downstream discharge Q_{sw} is

$$\theta_w = tan^{-1} Q_{nw}/Q_{sw} \tag{8.6}$$

This angle can be compared with the angle computed from the observed cross-stream velocity components defined relative to the field-selected orientation of the section. The observed angle can then be corrected to give the computed value. This correction is typically small if the field orientation is carefully selected and iteration, correcting the downstream velocity and repeating the procedure, appears to be unnecessary.

The only other river besides Muddy Creek in which the orientation of the cross-sections were apparently correctly oriented following the above procedure is the Fall River (Thorne and Rais, 1984; Thorne et al., 1985a; 1985b). The results for this river are not easily interpreted, however, because, as mentioned above, the bed topography was not demonstrated to be in equilibrium at the stages studied. Furthermore, and more confusing, the results reported in Thorne et al. (1985a), in which they conclude that one bend shows the shoaling effects of outward flow over the bar and an adjacent one does not, do not appear to agree with the basic data shown in a separate report (Thorne et al., 1985b).

As a final comment, looking back at figure 8.6, it can be seen that an additional effect of well developed bar-pool topography in a bend is to cause a rapid shifting of the zone of maximum boundary shear stress into the downstream end of the pool (where hS in equation (8.2) is large) and to reduce the magnitude of the boundary shear stress over the bar downstream of the radius of curvature minimum (where hS in equation (8.2) is small). Similarly, the zone of high velocity would shift rapidly across the channel. The crossing into the pool may be shifted downstream by inertia of the fluid as it crosses over the steeply sloping boundary and locally reduces the vertical velocity gradient (Dietrich et al., 1979, p. 310). In the following, inertial forces will be discussed more quantitatively.

THEORY FOR FLOW IN BENDS

The number of mathematical theories for predicting flow in bends greatly exceeds the number of careful field studies with which to test the theories. There is little sign that the production of new theories will slow down, but unfortunately few detailed investigations of field sites are being conducted and only a small range of channel shapes have been examined. Hence, with the present paucity of detailed field data it is difficult to test the generality of available theories. On the other hand, due to the relatively simple nature of the gross features of flow through a bend, models that include the major forces acting on the flow are going to appear to be fairly successful. However, accurate portrayal of such details of the flow pattern as the outward flow over the bar, though rarely tested for in flow models, strongly affects the usefulness of the model in geomorphic and sedimentologic studies of river bends.

In general, flow models have tended to become increasingly more complex as simplifying assumptions have been shown to be invalid. All models must start with the equation of motion for a general fluid flow:

$$\varrho \, \frac{d\mathbf{u}}{dt} = - \nabla p + \nabla \cdot \tilde{\tau} - \varrho \mathbf{g} \tag{8.7}$$

where u is the velocity vector; t and ϱ represent time and density respectively; p is pressure; $\tilde{\tau}$ is the deviatoric (non-isotropic stress); and g is gravitational acceleration. Equation (8.7) has usually been written in cylindrical co-ordinates and through various assumptions simplified to a series of force balances in each of the three dimensions (i.e. Rozovskii, 1957; Yen, 1965). Natural rivers have continuously varying curvature and a more useful co-ordinate system is that proposed by Smith and McLean (1984) and depicted in figure 8.6. Smith and McLean show in an appendix to their paper the complete derivation of the full equations in the n, s and z co-ordinates. By vertically integrating these equations and employing reasonable arguments for the relative size of terms and discarding the much smaller ones, Smith and McLean arrived at the following important force balance equations:

$$(\tau_{zs})_b = \frac{-\varrho gh}{1-N} \frac{\partial E}{\partial s} - \varrho \frac{1}{1-N} \frac{\partial}{\partial s} <u_s^2>h$$

$$-\varrho \frac{\partial}{\partial n} <u_s u_n>h + \frac{2\varrho <u_s u_n>h}{(1-N)R} \tag{8.8}$$

$$(\tau_{zn})_b = -\varrho gh \frac{\partial E}{\partial n} - \varrho \frac{<u_s^2>h}{(1-N)R} - \varrho \frac{1}{1-N} \frac{\partial}{\partial s} <u_s u_n>h$$

$$-\varrho \frac{\partial}{\partial n} <u_n^2>h + \frac{\varrho <u_n^2>h}{(1-N)R} \tag{8.9}$$

All the terms are the same as defined above and $(\tau_{zs})_b$ and $(\tau_{zn})_b$ are the downstream and cross-stream components of boundary shear stress. Comparisons of equations (8.8) with (8.2) shows that in addition to the pressure gradient force, two momentum-change terms, associated with downstream $\left[\dfrac{\partial h}{\partial s} \right]$ and cross-stream $\left[\dfrac{\partial h}{\partial n} \right]$ bed slopes, and a force due to channel curvature are included in the balance with the downstream component of the boundary shear stress. Comparison of equations (8.9) with (8.1) reveals that the simple force balance represented by equation (8.1) neglects the effects of boundary friction (in generating a cross-stream component of the boundary shear stress), change in momentum terms associated with bed topography and an additional centrifugal acceleration term associated with the cross-stream component of flow. In equations (8.8) and (8.9) the momentum change terms are largely a consequence of the downstream and cross-stream bed slopes, hence are referred to as topographically induced convective accelerations. As suggested in the discussion of figure 8.6 and as will be shown below, equations (8.1) and (8.2) can be used to explain the basic vertically averaged flow pattern in bends. Although only limited data are available from laboratory flumes (Yen and Yen, 1971) and from field studies (Dietrich and Smith, 1983) which are sufficient to calculate the terms in equations (8.8) and (8.9), both quoted experiments demonstrate that the convective acceleration terms, i.e. those forces arising from change in momentum downstream and across the stream, are large and must be included in an accurate determination of the force-balance and resulting boundary shear-stress fields. Dietrich and Smith, however, point out that very close spacing of cross-sections and highly accurate measurement of flow fields and water topography are required to evaluate correctly the terms in equations (8.8) and (8.9); this is very difficult to achieve in natural rivers (see also comments by Sigenthaler and Shen, 1984). They also note that in both their data and those of Yen and Yen, there appears to be a tendency for the momentum change terms to be of opposite sign. This explains why equations (8.1) and (8.2) yield approximately correct results. Nonetheless, theoretical investigations (Kalkwijk and DeVriend, 1980; Smith and McLean, 1984) have shown it essential to include all the terms in equations (8.8) and (8.9) in order to predict with reasonable accuracy the flow and boundary shear-stress field in bends with bar and pool topography. Analysis of these and other theories is beyond the scope of this chapter, but in order to appreciate the mechanics of flow in bends and to understand why many less complete models give approximately correct solutions, a simple analysis is performed below.

Approximation of flow in a bend

The simplest downstream force balance for channel flow is the steady, uniform flow approximation, equation 8.2, rewritten here by noting that τ_b equals $(\tau_{zs})_b$ in equation 8:

$$(\tau_{zs})_b = - \frac{1}{1-N} \varrho g h \frac{\partial E}{\partial s} \tag{8.10}$$

The water surface elevation at any point in the channel can be related to the centreline elevation, E_o, through the cross-stream gradient of the surface,

$$E = E_o + n \frac{\partial E}{\partial n} \tag{8.11}$$

hence,

$$\frac{\partial E}{\partial s} = \frac{\partial E_o}{\partial s} + n\frac{\partial}{\partial s}\left[\frac{\partial E}{\partial n}\right] \tag{8.12}$$

Rearrangement of the dominant cross-stream force balance, equation (8.1), to

$$\frac{\partial E}{\partial n} = -\frac{<u_s>^2}{g(1-N)R} \tag{8.13}$$

and substitution of equations (8.12) and (8.13) into (8.10) yields

$$(\tau_{zs})_b = -\frac{\varrho gh}{(1-N)}\frac{\partial E_o}{\partial s} + \frac{\varrho nh}{(1-N)^2}\frac{\partial}{\partial s}\left[\frac{<u_s>^2}{R}\right] \tag{8.14}$$

Equation (8.14) shows how the boundary shear-stress field will vary with the downstream component of the horizontal pressure gradient as defined by the centreline slope and with the centrifugal force-induced tilting of the water surface. Recall that in this co-ordinate system, n is negative toward the right bank. In the case in which the right bank is the convex inside of the bend, R is also negative. Hence near the inside bank as R decreases into the bend, $\frac{\partial}{\partial s}\frac{1}{R}$ will be negative, n will be negative and the second term will be positive, increasing the local boundary shear stress relative to that of the centreline. Over the pool near the outside bank where n is positive the second term will reduce the local boundary shear stress. Downstream of the curvature minimum, where $\frac{\partial}{\partial s}\frac{1}{R}$ is positive the opposite effect will occur and consequently the boundary shear stress should be high in the pool and low over the point bar. The depth term, h, should tend to make the boundary shear stress greatest in deepest water, but this is counteracted by the $(1-N)$ term, the metric coefficient that accounts for the shorter distance along the inside bank than along the outside one, and by the curvature changes described above. The contribution from $\frac{\partial<u_s>^2}{\partial s}$ cannot be inferred as easily as the geometric and topographic influences on the flow. The following analysis suggests that a reasonable first approximation is to assume it is everywhere small.

In order to test the usefulness of the theoretical analysis leading to equation (8.14), a sequence of calculations was performed with data from the Muddy Creek bend depicted in figure 8.8. In brief, the centreline slope, $\frac{\partial E_o}{\partial s}$ was assumed constant through the bend, with a value assigned from the field data (.001404). The cross-stream variation in elevation was then calculated as

$$E = E_0 - \frac{\varrho n <u_s>^2}{g(1-N)R}$$ (8.15)

The cross-stream variation in boundary shear stress was then computed from equation (8.10). In order to compare these calculated values with observations, the total average boundary shear stress for the bend (55 dynes/cm^2) was related to the bend averaged mean velocity (55 cm/sec) employing a drag coefficient, C_D, i.e.

$$<u_s> = \left[\frac{2\tau_b}{C_D\varrho} \right]^{1/2}$$ (8.16)

in which C_D was found to equal 3.61×10^{-2}, and each calculated boundary shear stress was corrected to a vertically averaged downstream velocity.

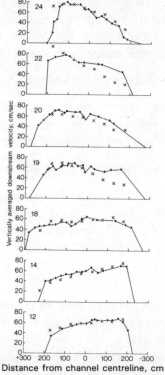

Figure 8.10 Predicted (crosses) and observed vertically averaged downstream velocity in Muddy Creek study bend. Flow section locations are shown in figure 8.8. Flow fields for this stage are graphed in figure 11 of Dietrich and Smith (1983)

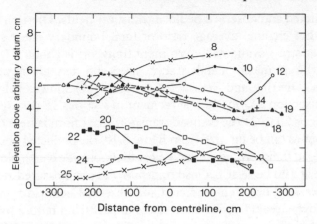

Figure 8.11 Water surface topography for ten cross-sections on Muddy Creek study site. Section locations shown in figure 8.8a. Section 8 is about 5 m upstream of 10 (figure 17 of Dietrich and Smith, 1983). Arbitrary datum. Water surface is tilted upslope in upstream near concave bank area over pool. In axis of bend where channel widens local surface slope is very flat or reversed. Similarity in average cross-channel slope is due to nearly constant radius of curvature from 14 to 20

Despite the approximate nature of the calculated vertically averaged velocity, the comparison between predicted and observed velocity fields in most sections appears to be quite good (figure 8.10). Careful inspection of each section reveals, however, that the cross-stream structure of the predicted velocity disagrees systematically with the observed: at sections 14, 19, 22 the velocity varies too much across the channel, and at sections 12 and 24 it varies too little. Improvements could perhaps be made by repeating the above calculations after adjusting the local centreline slope to satisfy continuity requirements such that the discharge is the same at each cross-section. This may improve predictions at 20 and 24, but such an adjustment was performed and found to be quite small despite the field observation that the centreline slope varies considerably through the bend.

Figure 8.11 shows the successive cross-stream water surface profiles through the meander. From sections 12 to 19 the cross-stream slope is greater than the downstream one, the downstream centreline slope is close to zero and over the upstream part of the pool and middle part of the bar (18–19) the local downstream water surface slope is reversed, an observation not predicted by the above equations and demonstrating the importance of momentum forces which will carry the flow through local reaches with water-slope reversal.

A more critical test of this model involves converting the calculated boundary shear stress to a local boundary shear stress responsible for sediment transport (by removing resistance effects due to the point bar and dunes) in order to compare predicted and observed bedload transport fields. Dietrich et al. (1984) have shown that channel average ratio of total boundary shear stress to the boundary shear stress available for sediment transport is about 3.7. Division of this ratio into the calculated boundary shear stress and comparison with observed bedload fields (Dietrich and Smith, 1984a figure 17) showed relatively close agreement for section 14, but poor agreement in sections 18 through 24 (figure 8.12). In sections 20 to 24 the bedload transport maximum is near the centre of the channel (but as can be inferred from figure 8.10, the predicted boundary shear stress and bedload transport maximum is close to the outside bank). No comparison could be made at 19B because bedload transport was not measured at this section. The poor agreement between predicted and observed bedload transport fields towards the downstream outside bank arises in part from failure to include the topographically-induced convective acceleration in equations (8.8) and (8.9).

The simple calculations performed above suggest that theories that include forms of equations (8.1) and (8.2) will be fairly successful in predicting flow, but much less successful in predicting boundary shear stress and bedload transport fields in curved channels. In part due to the lack of laboratory or field observations on sediment transport, theories that have been employed to predict

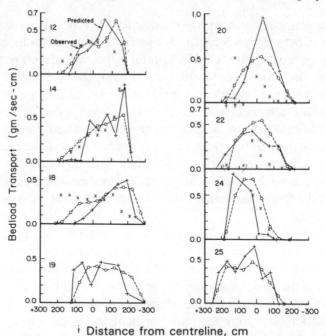

Figure 8.12   Observed bedload transport fields (circles), transport predicted from local velocity measurements (plusses), and that predicted from the simple theory for boundary shear presented in the text. Arrows in section 22 indicate substantial over-prediction of (from left to right) 2.2 and 1.2 gm/cm-sec

bed morphology are rarely tested for their accuracy in predicting sediment transport fields. Nonetheless this simple approach sheds light on the dominant processes controlling bends and may be useful in obtaining quick approximate solutions for practical purposes.

SEDIMENT TRANSPORT PROCESSES IN BENDS

Flow over bar-pool topography and through a sequence of alternate curves generates forces that result in a cross-stream skewed boundary shear-stress field with a distinct zone of maximum boundary shear stress that in the downstream direction shifts back and forth across the channel in response to local channel morphology. In the mobile-bed case, downstream increases or decreases in the local boundary shear stress will either cause erosion or deposition, or at equilibrium, be balanced by corresponding convergent or divergent sediment transport. Transport directions of bedload are controlled by near-bed fluid vectors and cross-channel and downstream bed slope. Transport direction of suspended load will be influenced by flow direction throughout the water column. In strongly heterogeneous grain-size mixtures of sediment, another response to systematic boundary shear-stress change may be a coarsening or fining of the bedload which in turn adjusts the sediment flux rate, as bedload transport rate is strongly grain-size dependent. In partially mobile beds or ones that rarely experience shear stresses significantly above critical, such as is the case in many gravel-bedded streams, response to spatial variations in the boundary shear-stress field may be largely through bed grain-size adjustment. Hence, prediction of channel-bed morphology requires that a quantitative linkage be established between topographically controlled boundary shear-stress fields and the grain-size, bed-slope and flow direction-influenced sediment transport fields. This linkage is currently being explored both theoretically and through field studies.

Forces on a bed particle and channel morphology

Figure 8.13 illustrates the forces acting to move bed particles in a curved channel. Fluid forces are lift and drag, F_L and F_D respectively. When the particle rests or rolls on an inclined bed, the body forces, F_g, have a cross-stream component, F_{gx}, and a component normal to the bed (not shown here). Generally, the downstream component is small when the grain contacts the bed; either at its initial motion, or as it rolls, or when it bounces during saltation, an opposing frictional force is exerted on the grain by the bed. For simplicity, this opposing force is not shown in figure 8.13. The direction in which a particle moves in the cross-stream plane is determined by the magnitude and direction of near-bed

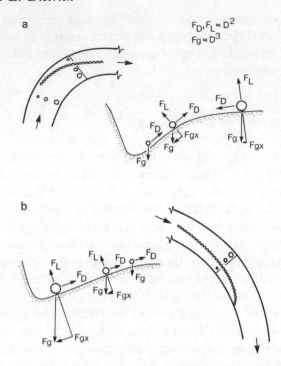

Figure 8.13 Forces acting on particles on or near the bed that contribute to motion. Opposing frictional resistance of the bed not shown. Forces are lift (F_L), drag (F_D), and gravity (F_g) with the cross-stream component of gravity also shown (F_{gx}). Saltating particles once off the bed no longer experience F_{gx} and F_L is negligible. Sorting in bends results from grain size dependent response to fluid and gravitational forces on sediments moving on a cross-stream sloping point-bar surface against an inward component of the curvature-induced secondary circulation. The gravitational acceleration is proportional to the cube of the particle diameter, D, and the fluid forces are proportional to the square of the diameter. The resultant of these forces is further inward for small grains than for large grains. Also, the finest bedload grains will saltate one to three grain diameters off the bed or be intermittently suspended, in which case the particles move primarily in the near-bed flow direction

flow and bed slope. In figure 8.13a the case of shoaling-induced outward flow over the bar top is shown. Typically, at the entrance to the bend in a meander train where shoaling will be most significant, the largest particles in transit are near the inside bank and the smallest ones are near the outside one. All three forces on the particle will tend to give it an outward transport component; in order to move, it must also overcome the frictional resistance of the bed. In contrast, on the bar slope and into the pool, the inward component of drag on resting and rolling particles is opposed by a component of lift, acting perpendicularly to the bed and by the outward component of the particle weight,

F_{gx}. Note that once grains leave the bed they are no longer acted upon by a cross-stream component of particle weight or by a significant fluid lift. Consequently, particles that mostly saltate or are intermittently suspended will tend to travel in the direction of the local fluid motion. Wiberg and Smith (described in Dietrich and Smith, 1984a, pp. 1375–6) have found that flow deflection inward of only a few degrees will compensate for the lateral component of lift on sand on an out-sloping bar.

In figure 8.13b, which represents the downstream end of laboratory flumes with constant curvature, or the zone well downstream of the curvature maximum in natural channels, the same set of forces are shown but the inward component of drag acts over much of the bar (as described in a previous section) and the largest particles are in the pool. The shift in cross-stream grain size distribution from a to b, which could be the downstream end of a, is a consequence of submerged weight and drag-force differences on large and small particles. As Dietrich et al. (1979, p. 313) described, and Parker and Andrews (1985) subsequently modelled, the outward gravitational component is proportional to the cube of the grain diameter, whereas the fluid drag is proportional to the diameter squared. Hence for the same near-bed velocity, large particles will tend to roll outward against the inward flow and smaller ones will be carried inward toward the shallow water. This is the essence of the sorting process in bends. It may also apply to bar units in general in either straight or braided channels.

Many different quantitative formulations of the force balance dictating particle motion have been proposed for both static (e.g. Odgaard, 1981; Ikeda, 1982) and moving particles (e.g. Engelund, 1974; Nelson and Smith, 1985; Parker and Andrews, 1985 (and references therein); Odgaard, 1986). They differ primarily in how lift and bed frictional forces are determined. Linking a particle equation with equation (8.7) to calculate local boundary shear stress and with conservation of mass equations for sediment transport allows prediction of both grain sorting and channel topography. Theories vary greatly as to how this linkage is obtained but have focused on predicting equilibrium bed topography in bends.

The two basic hypotheses for what controls equilibrium morphology in curved channels are:

1 equilibrium is achieved when the cross-stream component of the particle weight (and fluid lift) is exactly balanced by the inward component of the fluid drag due to secondary circulation: particles therefore travel along lines of equal depth (e.g. Allen, 1970; Kikkawa et al., 1976; Bridge, 1977);
2 equilibrium is achieved when the outward shifting zone of maximum boundary shear stress is balanced by convergent sediment transport caused by net outward bedload flux toward the pool (Dietrich and Smith, 1984b; Struiksma et al., 1985).

The difference in these two hypotheses is similar to the distinction between fully developed flow and flow which changes downstream as a consequence of bed topography and planform curvature effects. Unless significant grain-size adjustments can occur in response to shifting boundary shear-stress fields (as suggested by Bridge and Jarvis, 1982), the hypothesis of net outward bedload transport would seem necessary. Once shifting of the boundary shear-stress field through the bend has occurred, and the downstream boundary shear stress remains constant (if this occurs), net cross-stream bedload transport is no longer necessary. During stage change in a channel in which the bed remains mobile, the shoaling hypothesis leads to specific predictions which are supported by field observations (Dietrich and Smith, 1984a). Stage rise will reduce the shoaling effect, but the high boundary shear stress will still shift outward, and without outward flow over the bar, deposition will occur. In the pool, the lack of cross-stream sediment transport will cause erosion. Conversely, during stage decline the bar top and bar slope will be eroded and the pool aggraded. In the following, a brief review is given of quantitative approaches to predicting bed topography in bends.

Bridge (1977) employed the Engelund (1974) theory for flow and boundary shear stress in bends following a sine-generated curved path. He assumed that at equilibrium there is no net cross-stream discharge of sediment, and that instead grain size tracks the boundary shear-stress distribution. Through a bend, as the zone of maximum boundary shear stress shifts outward, the coarsest particles follow it and suppress a tendency for sediment transport to increase. Fine particles move inward to the low shear-stress zone, and the maximum bedload transport zone tends to stay toward the centre of the channel. The Engelund model upon which Bridge's theory is based has several deficiencies (see comments in Dietrich and Smith, 1984a; Parker and Andrews, 1985), both in its basic flow equations and particle force balance. For channels that are approximately sine-generated, Bridge (1984) has shown that his theory stimulates observations reasonably well. As shown above, however, it is fairly simple to get the correct basic average velocity field, which in turn gives the approximate boundary shear stress, and because bedload particle size is proportional to the imposed boundary shear stress, the correct grain size distribution. The bedload transport field is not predicted with this model, and the estimates of bed topography at Muddy Creek (figures 3 and 6 in Bridge, 1984) are fairly crude. Nonetheless, the analytical expression is very simple and it performs impressively well. Dietrich and Smith (1984a, figure 18) show quantitative evidence that the bedload maximum is offset toward the centreline due to grain-size effects in a short section of their bend, but they also demonstrate that this effect in their study site is of secondary importance: net cross-stream transport of most of the bed particles still occurs and the bedload maximum crosses the channel. Bridge and Jarvis (1982) have proposed that their field data support the assumptions of the model, but this is debatable (see review in Dietrich and Smith, 1983; 1984a). They argue that there is field evidence for a downslope-upslope force balance on individual bed particles (their figure 23). However, they do not use observed cross-stream near-bed flow orientations, but rather compute it from an equation they show to be very approximate. In addition, the proposed cross-stream force balance equation (equation 13 of Bridge and Jarvis, 1982) has a large number of redundant terms which, when eliminated, reduce their force balance to the statement (see their equation 15) that the dimensionless Shields number ($\tau_b/(\varrho_s - \varrho)gD$; ϱ_s is grain density) is about 0.3, which must be within an order of magnitude of the correct value. Hence a logarithmic plot of the cross-stream forces on a particle must yield approximately a good comparison, but such an analysis cannot be used to test the cross-stream force balance hypothesis.

The sorting model of Parker and Andrews (1985) is based on an even simpler representation of the flow processes in a bend. They assume that the boundary shear stress is everywhere the same and that sorting arises purely due to cross-stream bed tipping and the relative action of inward (everywhere) boundary shear stress and outward gravitational acceleration on the particle. Bed topography is calculated from the theory. They obtain an analytical solution which allows estimation of the path of 'coarse' sediment through a succession of bends. One result of their theory is the prediction that channels with high width to depth ratios will have less cross-stream shifting of coarse sediment. Although not tested with field data, nor explained physically, this conclusion may be correct. As discussed above, bends of large width–depth ratio have broad, nearly flat point-bar tops. Both the cross-stream gravitational force and the near-bed inward flow will be weak on this surface. Consequently, sediment will not be quickly segregated by size across the channel.

Bridge (1977; 1984), Parker and Andrews (1985) and many others use the approximation that the angular deviation (δ) of the boundary shear-stress vector from the downstream direction is proportional to the flow depth, h, and inversely proportional to the radius of curvature, r:

$$\tan\delta = C\ h/r \tag{8.17}$$

Dietrich and Smith (1983) showed, however, that the assumptions used to derive equation (8.17) from the equation of motion require that the flow be steady and uniform; hence it is strictly applicable only to fully developed flow in parts of bends. Odgaard (1986) has developed a modification of equation (8.17) that allows inclusion of shoaling effects.

The models of Hasegawa and Yamaoka (1984), Nelson and Smith (1985) (which is built upon the Smith and McLean (1984) flow theory) and Odgaard (1986)

have included the shoaling effect (figure 8.13a). The flow theory of Hasegawa
and Yamaoka appears to predict quite well the vertically averaged velocity vectors
in their laboratory meanders. Their particle equation leads to a cross-stream
sediment transport equation (their equation (9)) similar to that of Engelund's
equation (68) (Engelund, 1974), but they did not report a comparison between
observed and predicted bed topography in their channels. Dietrich and Smith
(1984a), however, employed Engelund's equation to predict the net cross-stream
discharge of bedload through their study bend (figure 8.14). In the co-ordinate
system of figure 8.6, the equation can be written as

$$
\frac{Q_n}{Q_s} = \left[\; \nu - \frac{7h}{r} + \frac{1}{\tan\phi} \frac{\partial h}{\partial n} \; \right] \tag{8.18}
$$

in which Q_n and Q_s are the downstream and cross-stream sediment transport,
ν is the ratio of vertically averaged cross-stream velocity to vertically averaged
downstream velocity, 7 is the constant in equation (8.17) and ϕ is the dynamic
friction angle. The first term was interpreted to represent the shoaling effect;
the second term, the secondary circulation effect; and the third, the cross-stream
gravitational effect. Using equation (8.18) very crudely, Dietrich and Smith
(1984a) found it gave approximately correct results (figure 8.14).

Odgaard's model differs significantly from that of Nelson and Smith or Hasegawa
and Yamaoka in that it includes several empirical approximations that permit an
analytical solution. The Nelson and Smith model was not published at the time
of writing, but preliminary applications to the field observations in Muddy Creek

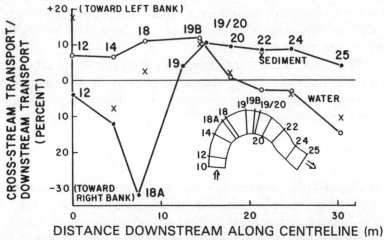

Figure 8.14   Ratio of cross-stream to downstream transport of bedload and water as a
function of distance downstream from section 12. Predicted ratio for bedload from Engelund
(1974) equation also shown as crosses. Geometric crossing to downstream bend is below
22. Negative values are toward right, which in the upstream bend is the inner bank.

Figure 8.15 Well developed oblique dunes with spurs in a sharp bend in Muddy Creek, Wyoming. Spurs migrated inward along trough. Obliquity due to skewed boundary shear stress field with maximum near inside bank

(data of Dietrich and Smith, 1983; 1984a), appear to be very promising. However, there are very few other data with which to test a thorough, physically based model for flow and channel morphology, a point discussed further below

There is one other effect not illustrated in figure 8.13 that may be important in controlling the sorting and morphology in sand-bedded rivers. Figure 8.15 shows a sharp bend upstream from the Muddy Creek study site. At least eight sinuous, oblique dune crests are clearly visible stretching from the point-bar top to the deep pool. Parallel ridges run between dune crests (called 'spurs' by H. Ikeda, personal communication, 1985), and in the deeper water towards the left bank, relatively deep local scour holes have formed. Any oblique step to a mean flow direction will generate a downstream current along the step (figure 8.16). Because crest migration speed is proportional to boundary shear stress in bends, the cross-stream variation in boundary shear stress should produce strong skewing of the dune crests, so that their downstream ends are near the convex bank in the upstream part of the bend (figure 8.17) and shift towards the concave bank in the downstream part (Dietrich et al., 1979; Dietrich and Smith, 1984a). In the upstream part of the bend the troughs of dunes provide low-velocity zones that allow the cross-stream pressure gradient force to overcome

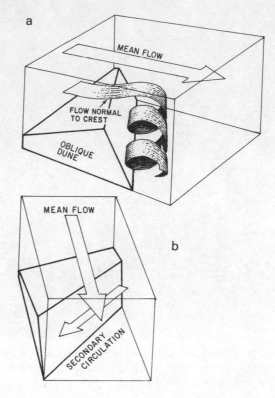

Figure 8.16 Deflection of flow near crest, formation of separation cell and generation of cross-stream current due to bedform obliquity to the near flow (a). Direction of mean flow and secondary circulation (and near-bed troughwise current) induced by bedform obliquity in the trough (b).
Illustration by Leslie Reid

the shoaling-induced outward flow that would otherwise occur, and the obliquity of the dunes adds an additional cross-stream pressure gradient that results in strong troughwise current towards the convex, inside bank. The spurs here and in other bends were observed migrating upslope towards the inside bank. During net deposition the combined migration of the dunes and spurs will generate trough cross-stratification. In the upstream part of the bend the troughwise current may be strong enough to prevent net cross-stream rolling of the coarsest particles toward the pool and to cause net inward transport of sediment even though near-bed flow near the crests is directed outwards due to shoaling effects. This hypothesis was proposed by Dietrich and Smith (1984a) to explain the observed net cross-stream sediment transport near the crossings where the cross-stream bed slope is negligible (sections 12 and 24) and further into the bend (sections 14, 18A) in a direction opposite to that expected from shoaling effects

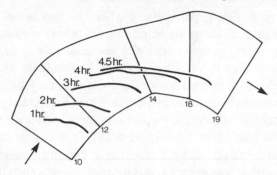

Figure 8.17 Predicted dune crest migration through the Muddy Creek study bend. Lines represent crest location at various hours after entering the reach at section 10 with crest parallel to section line. Prediction used a map of observed downstream dune-crest velocities to compute displacement distance of the crestline increments after one hour and, for the last calculation, one half-hour. Progressive skewing of crest line results from cross-stream decreasing boundary shear stress from inside bank to the outer and corresponding declining crest speed. Note the nearly uniform crest speed along the inside bank. Prediction was not carried further because dunes did not propagate across channel; instead new dunes formed in deeper water and grew with the addition of sediment rolling down the point-bar slope to become the predominant bedforms in the downstream part of the bend.

(figure 8.14). They documented strong troughwise transport along oblique dunes in these sections (Dietrich and Smith, 1984a, figure 21; Dietrich, 1982, figure 5–32). They also noted that where the dunes were nearly perpendicular to the flow, low-velocity zones were created in which large particles could roll across the channel into the deeper water. Where the downstream boundary shear-stress maximum had crossed into the pool downstream of the apex of the bend, the dunes rotated and generated troughwise currents capable of transporting sediment towards the pool in a region where the average near-bed flow orientation is inward.

These observations suggest that dunes, by their effect on local boundary shear-stress directions, may modify the pattern of sorting and equilibrium bed morphology otherwise dictated by shoaling effects, curvature secondary circulation, and differential movement due to relative grain size dependent response to gravity and drag. Near-bed influence of dunes on flow is probably ubiquitous in sand-bedded river bends. In order to appreciate this effect more fully, a summary of Muddy Creek observations follows, with illustrations that complement those presented by Dietrich and Smith (1984a). I will first comment on problems of sediment transport measurement.

Mapping sediment transport fields in river bends

Unlike flow-field observations, where during steady flow fairly sparse data fields and short sampling periods may still give roughly correct results, under-sampling of sediment transport fields, particularly when the bed is not clearly visible, is probably worse than no sampling at all. Poor data may appear to give support to incorrect hypotheses, or more typically are used to suit one's hypotheses. Sediment flux rates, both in suspension and as bedload, are highly variable in space and time, even when on average the local flux may be nearly constant. In sand-bedded streams, bedload and suspended load vary greatly due to bedform migration and periodic suspension of particles associated with unsteady wakes of major bedforms (see below and figure 8.19). In order to map the bedload transport field, repeated sampling is essential at carefully selected locations (if the bed is clearly visible), or at numerous locations across the channel. A single or few measurements at many positions across the channel cannot (except by chance) accurately portray the transport fields (see comments in Dietrich and Smith, 1984a). This is true both for bedload and suspended load. Bedload sampling methods required to map transport vectors are discussed by Dietrich and Smith.

No data on the bedload transport fields of gravel-bedded rivers are, to the author's knowledge, published. This deficiency will be overcome, but it will also require repeated sampling at several positions across the channel. Researchers working on gravel bedload transport have found it highly variable (e.g. Hubble et al., 1985) due, at least in part, to pulses of sediment, or bedload sheets (Whiting et al., 1985), that can dominate transport rates at low excess boundary shear stress. In this case as well as the dune-covered sand-bed case, transport measurements should be repeated enough to average over at least one wavelength of the migrating bed feature causing bedload fluctuations. In any sediment transport study, mass conservation equations of the flow (if data are available), as defined by equation (8.5), or of the sediment transport (equation 4 of Dietrich and Smith, 1984a) must be employed to define correctly the downstream and

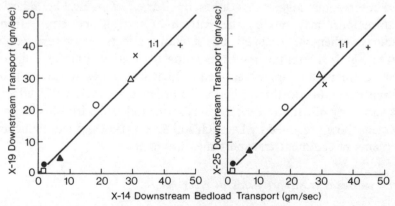

Figure 8.18   Comparison of measured downstream bedload transport rate for 7 sizes of sediment at three sections in bend (see figure 8.21 for explanation of symbols)

cross-stream components of sediment transport. Furthermore, because ultimately the paths which individual grains take through the bend are of great importance, it is useful to compare transport rates for individual size classes at successive sections. Figure 8.18 shows such a comparison for three sections in the Muddy Creek bend.

Bedforms and sediment transport processes in a sand-bedded meander

Figure 8.19 (a–f) shows a downstream sequence of photographs of the Muddy Creek stream bed taken with a camera suspended about 7 m over the channel during the same period as the bedload and flow measurement. Flow is towards the bottom of the figure. Specific locations and scales are given in the figure caption. The photographs are representative of the dune geometry, because for a given reach of the bend, the dunes tend to have a roughly constant orientation, amplitude and crest speed. The dunes are strongly three dimensional across the channel, with sinuous, often oblique crests. In the deep water in the upstream part of the bend where the sediment is fine sand, ripples predominate, but ripples and ripple-like low crested bedforms also occur throughout the bed. Ripples are superimposed on upstream strongly oblique limbs (figure 8.19a) in the lee of the upstream point bar. Three crest lines of these limbs are clearly visible. Sequential photographs (which were taken at ten minute intervals for several hours at each location through the bend) showed that as the dunes propagated into the bend, their outer limbs slowly merged onto the new stagnant outermost limb visible in the photograph.

Further downstream, the limb is abandoned, the dunes skew under the cross-stream gradient of boundary shear stress (highest near the inside bank), and develop spurs which tend to migrate inward (figure 8.19b–d). Two dune fields start to develop in this reach (b to d) on either side of the centreline, approximately where the shoaling effect of near-bed outward flow ends and inward secondary flow is strong (figure 8.8). Near-bed velocity on the stoss side of the dune in figure 8.19 is convergent toward the centreline in this reach. Average dune crest height was greatest (6 to 17 cm) close to the centreline throughout the bend. In many places, but particularly in association with the highest-crested dunes, the separation cell in the trough of dunes would break, rotate and generate a boil-like structure, sometimes capable of suspending even the coarsest sand on the bed. Distinct local clouds of suspended sediment can be seen in the centre of figures 8.19b and d. Because of favourable sun angle, the distorted water surface due to a boil is clearly visible in two places in figure 8.19b.

The break-up of the bed into two dune fields ends between section 19 and 20 (figures 8.19e and 8.20a, b) where the shoaling-induced outward flow terminates and the boundary shear stress and bedload transport maxima have

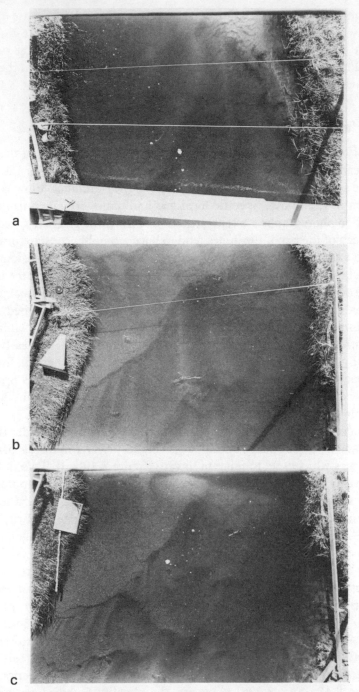

Figure 8.19 Photographs of streambed taken from camera suspended approximately 7 m above the bed. Scale differs somewhat in each picture. (a) bed between cross-sections 10 and

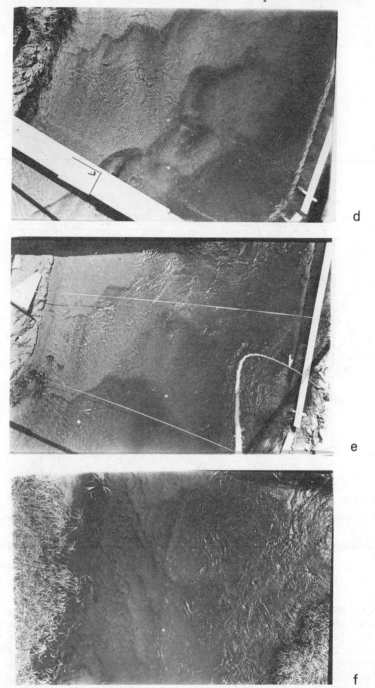

12; (b) tape is stretched across section 14; (c) bed between sections 14 and 18; (d) bed between sections 18 and 19; (e) bed between sections 19 and 20; (f) bed upstream of section 24

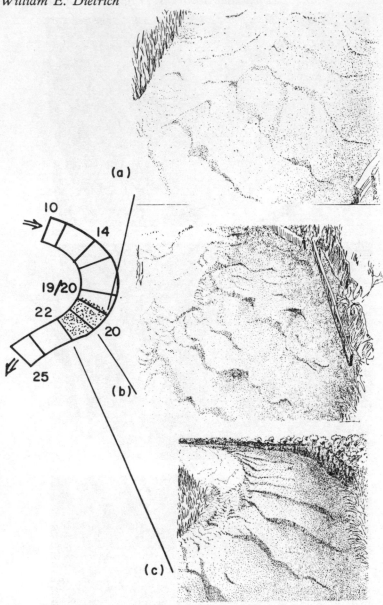

Figure 8.20   Sketches of stream channel and bed looking from outer bank upstream. The map gives locations of viewer. The channel bed at section 19/20, corresponding to E in figure 8.19, is shown in (a). In (b) the left bank at section 20 is at the downstream end of the closest railing. Section 19/20 is near the intersection of the two railings. In (c) the railing has been deleted to simplify the drawing. The sketch is from the left bank at section 22. Note that in all three drawings greatest dune height is at the transition from the shallow point-bar surface to the steep side-slope of the point bar near the channel centreline, not in the deepest water. This is also where significant local suspension of sediment occurred due to boils. Sketches are by Lenora Wilson (from Dietrich and Smith, 1984a)

shifted towards the pool. In figure 8.19e, three almost evenly spaced, large-amplitude dunes are visible on the point-bar slope and two spurs extend downstream from the middle crest. Further downstream towards section 24 (figure 8.19f and 8.20c), sun reflection off the turbulent eddies shed from the bank obscure the well developed dunes developed in the deeper water. As seen in figure 8.19a, ripple-covered limbs of major dunes swing into the shallow flow, merge and stagnate.

The suspended-sediment transport field appears to be strongly controlled by the ejection of bed material by boil-like features from the large-crested dunes near the centre of the channel. The maximum suspended sediment load (two to three times cross-sectional average) stayed slightly towards the outside of the centreline (see Dietrich and Smith, 1984a) throughout the meander. On the other hand, median settling velocity of the vertically averaged suspended-sediment load varied across the channel in proportion to the local boundary shear stress, and the cross-stream variation of the median settling velocity paralleled that of the bedload, although the values were much lower. Strong suspension of bed material should tend to counteract the inward secondary current effects, preferentially carrying smaller particles higher in the flow toward the pool and larger ones near the bed towards the inside bank. In Muddy Creek, this effect is small because of the small loads involved. In streams with high concentrations this may be an important process in sorting sediment and adjusting the bed topography. Regrettably there appear to be no other detailed field data with which to examine this hypothesis, although Ikeda (1985) has made an important theoretical investigation of this problem.

In order to describe briefly the cross-stream transport and sorting of sediment in the bend, figures 8.21 and 8.22 are included to show the observed downstream bedload transport rates for seven settling-velocity classes of sediment, and the cross-stream structure of the median grain size through the bend. Figure 8.14 shows that in the bend depicted in figure 8.19, net inward transport occurred in the upstream region (from photographs a to c), a reach where the channel width increases from about 4.6 to 6.0 m. Relative to the channel centreline, the width to the base of the outside bank stayed essentially constant; most of the increase of the width of active sediment transport was along the inner bank. Hence, net inward cross-stream transport developed. The dunes appear to have contributed significantly to generating inward transport. As Dietrich and Smith (1984a) described, the large-crested dunes and corresponding deep scour hole near the channel centreline (figure 8.19b) allowed inward cross-channel flow near the bed to develop completely to the down-stream crest. Also the dune obliquity generated strong inward troughwise transport.

Through this reach (sections 12–18A, figure 8.21 and 8.22) the downstream transport fields for different sediment sizes varied little. The maximum flux

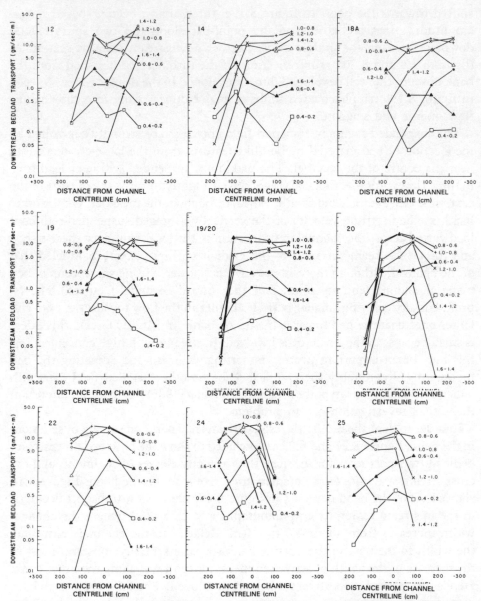

Figure 8.21   Downstream bedload transport fields of seven size classes of settling velocity at nine sections through bend. Vertical axis is bedload transport in gm/sec-100 cm. Symbols used correspond to logarithmic settling-velocity intervals and represent the same interval at each section. Conversion from settling velocity to grain size is given in figure 8.22. Values shown in that graph, 0.2 and 1.6, correspond to 0.12 mm and 8.6 mm, respectively. Note that the logarithmic vertical scale, used in order to show transport in all size classes, reduces the cross-stream slope of the transport fields.

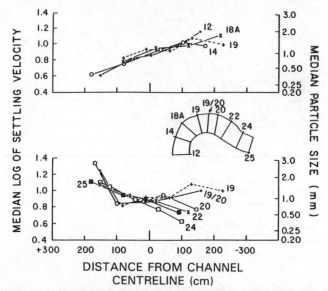

Figure 8.22 Variation of median $\log_{10}$ settling velocity and particle size across the channel at successive sections. The map shows the section locations
(from Dietrich and Smith, 1984a)

rate for particles coarser than about 0.7 mm was near the inside bank, for particles finer than about 0.5 mm the flux rate was systematically greater toward the outer bank. Note that the bulk median grain size for Muddy Creek is 0.7 mm (or 0.94 logarithmic settling velocity). In this reach most of the sediment would follow a zig-zag path; outward or weakly inward over the stoss side of the dune and strongly inward along the trough.

From sections 18 through 24, the zone of maximum boundary shear stress shifted outwards and net cross-stream transport of sediment towards the pool was about 10 per cent of the downstream sediment flux rate (figure 8.14). This small cross-stream component shifted the centre of mass of the bedload transport field from 75 cm towards the inner bank to 75 cm towards the outer bank – that is, through about 150 cm or close to 40 per cent of the channel width occupied by a mobile bed. Although the median particle size (or settling velocity) quickly increases near the pool (figure 8.22) the position of the maximum flux rate for each size (or settling velocity) class shifts progressively outwards, only moving close to the outer bank at the exit of the bend. Hence, figure 8.21 and 8.22 do not show the same patterns, and shifting median grain size through the bend does not accurately portray the outward shift of bedload sediment.

The effect of dunes on the cross-stream transport and sorting is extensively discussed elsewhere (Dietrich and Smith, 1984a). The principal findings are illustrated in figure 8.23. The shoaling-induced outward flow near the bed is

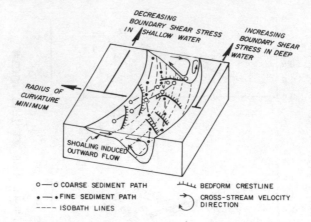

Figure 8.23   Processes controlling bed morphology and particle sorting in a river meander. Flow is from lower to upper end of figure
(from Dietrich and Smith, 1984b)

effective on the shallow point-bar surface (figure 19d and e, figure 8.20a and b) in causing net transport of the bulk of the sediment to the edge of the point-bar top at the break in slope. In the troughs of the thin, oblique dunes on the bar top, weak troughwise currents can carry just the fine sediment brought up the point-bar slope by the inward near-bed flow there. The troughs, then, create a low velocity region on the gently sloping point-bar surface where large and small particles can cross paths (figure 8.23). On the bar slope the large particles will tend to roll outward against the inward near-bed flow and finer particles will tend to roll less far or be carried inwards. Rolling is enhanced in the troughs oriented normal to the flow direction (figure 8.19e). On dunes that extend across the bar slope, grain avalanching during dune migration will also produce an outward transport component. Further downstream in the bend strong dune obliquity generates a troughwise current in a direction opposite to the near-bed flow on the stoss side of dunes which is capable of transporting large amounts of sediment across the channel. Although clearly influencing local sediment flux rate and direction, the net effects of dunes on sorting, sediment transport processes and channel morphology are not easily defined. In the upstream part of the bend, oblique dunes prevent particles from rolling into the pool, and as Dietrich et al. (1979) proposed this may cause the upstream end of the pool to deepen and reduce the local boundary shear stress to critical. An opposite effect may occur in the downstream end of the bend where rolling in dune troughs and troughwise transport towards the pool may reduce the cross-stream slope needed to generate sufficient outward transport to match the outward shifting boundary shear-stress maximum. Overall, the effects of dunes on sorting may be to increase the strength of the cross-stream variation in sediment size. These effects will only be identified once theory has advanced to the point of being sufficiently physically-based so that failure to include dune influences can be shown to give an inaccurate result.

CONCLUSION: PROBLEMS REMAINING

Although considerable progress has been made in recent years in understanding the mechanics of flow and sediment transport in bends, many questions remain. Most of these questions derive from an almost complete lack of detailed field measurements. Channel-bed morphology appears to be strongly influenced by the width–depth ratio; with increasing width relative to depth, the point-bar surface flattens and extends well across the channel. No detailed measurements of the kind needed to investigate mechanics and test theory have been collected in bends of high width–depth ratio. Many large amplitude bends tend to become non-symmetric and develop multiple bars within a single major bend. There are very few field data on flow and sediment transport processes in such bends; consequently the mechanisms responsible for planform deformation and multiple bar formation are not well understood. The role of intermittent suspension of bed material in the sorting and bar development of fine sand-bedded streams is virtually unexplored in the field. Similarly, detailed field investigations of flow and sediment-transport processes in gravel-bedded river bends have not been reported. Here grain-size adjustments may play a major role in accommodating shifting boundary shear-stress fields.

Until thorough data on sediment transport and boundary shear-stress fields are generated during geomorphologically significant stages, theoretical investigations cannot be properly tested. Theories are becoming progressively more physically based and are employing fewer imposed, mathematically convenient assumptions. This makes such investigations complex and dependent on computer-based numerical analysis. In parallel with these advances, engineers are improving their analytical solutions using a blend of empiricism and theory such that fairly accurate predictions can be made of flow, boundary shear-stress fields and bed topography.

This chapter has focused on processes in a bend of a given planform. As in this case, theoretical investigations of meander evolution are more advanced than the available field data. There remains the fundamental problem of making definitive field measurements that link the fluid mechanics of the flow through a bend with the erosion rate and sediment transport processes on and at the base of the bank.

ACKNOWLEDGEMENTS

The field data from Muddy Creek were collected in collaboration with J. Dungan Smith, Thomas Dunne and several of their graduate students. Support was in part provided through National Science Foundation grant ENG78-16977 and CEE-8307142. Ron Shreve provided valuable comments on a draft of the chapter. Discussions with J. Nelson, J. Dungan Smith and Peter Whiting were particularly helpful. Eileen Hughes assisted in the final preparation of the manuscript.

REFERENCES

Allen, J. R. L. 1970: *Physical Processes in Sedimentation.* London: Allen and Unwin.

Brice, J. C. 1984: Planform properties of meandering rivers. In C. M. Elliott (ed.), *River Meandering: Proceedings of the Conference Rivers '83*, Am. Soc. Civ. Eng., 1–14.

Bridge, J. S. 1977: Flow, bed topography, grain size and sedimentary structure in bends: a three dimensional model. *Earth Surface Processes*, 2, 401–16.

Bridge, J. S. 1984: Flow and sedimentary processes in river bends: comparisons of field observations and theory. In C. M. Elliott (ed.), *River Meandering: Proceedings of the Conference Rivers '83*, Am. Soc. Civ. Eng., 857–72.

Bridge, J. S. and Jarvis, J. 1976: Flow and sedimentary processes in the meandering river South Esk, Glen Cova, Scotland. *Earth Surface Processes*, 1, 303–36.

Bridge, J. S. and Jarvis, J. 1982: The dynamics of a river bend: a study in flow and sedimentary processes. *Sedimentology*, 29, 499–541.

Chitale, S. R. 1970: River channel patterns. *J. Hydraulic Div., Am. Soc. Civ. Eng.*, 96, 201–21.

Church, M. and Jones, D. 1982: Channel bars in gravel-bed rivers. In R. D. Hey, J. C. Bathurst and C. R. Thorne (eds), *Gravel-bed Rivers* Chichester: Wiley, 291–338.

DeVriend, H. J. and Geldof, H. J. 1983: Main flow velocity in alternating river bends. *J. Hydraulic Engineering, Am. Soc. Civ. Eng.*, 109, 991–1011.

Dietrich, W. E. 1982: Flow, boundary shear stress and sediment transport in a river meander. Unpublished PhD dissertation, Seattle: University of Washington.

Dietrich, W. E. and Smith, J. Dungan, 1983: Influence of the point bar on flow through curved channels. *Water Resources Research*, 19, 1173–92.

Dietrich, W. E. and Smith, J. Dungan, 1984a: Bedload transport in a river meander. *Water Resources Research*, 20, 1355–80.

Dietrich, W. E. and Smith, J. Dungan, 1984b: Processes controlling the equilibrium bed morphology in river meanders. In C. M. Elliott (ed.) *River Meandering: Proceedings of the Conference Rivers '83*, Am. Soc. Civ. Eng., 759–69.

Dietrich, W. E., Smith, J. Dungan and Dunne T. 1979: Flow and sediment transport in a sand-bedded meander. *J. Geol.*, 87, 305–15.

Dietrich, W. E., Smith, J. Dungan and Dunne, T. 1984: Boundary shear stress, sediment transport and bed morphology in a sand-bedded river meander during high and low flow. In C. M. Elliott (ed.), *River Meandering: Proceedings of the Conference Rivers '83*, Am. Soc. Civ. Eng., 632–9.

Elliott, C. M. (ed.) 1984: *River Meandering: Proceedings of the Conference Rivers '83*, Am. Soc. Civ. Eng.

Engelund, F. 1974: Flow and bed topography in channel bends. *J. Hydraulic Div., Am. Soc. Civ. Eng.*, 100, 1631–48.

Ferguson, R. I. and Werritty, A. 1983: Bar development and channel changes in the gravelly River Feshie, Scotland. *Spec. Pub. Int. Ass. Sediment*, 6, 181-93.

Forbes, D. L. 1983: Morphology and sedimentology of a sinuous gravel-bed channel system: lower Babbage River, Yukon coastal plain. *Spec. Publs. Int. Ass. Sediment*, 6, 195-206.

Friedkin, J. F. 1945: *A Laboratory Study of the Meandering of Alluvial Rivers*. Vicksburg, Mississippi: US Waterways Experimental Station.

Fujita, Y. 1982: On the formation of stream channel pattern. In *Proceeding of Third Congress of the Asian and Pacific Regional Division of the International Association for Hydraulic Research*, 276-87.

Hasegawa, K. 1983: *A study on flows and bed topographies and planforms of alluvial meanders*. Unpublished PhD dissertation, Hokkaido University.

Hasegawa, K. and Yamaoka, I. 1984: Phase shifts of pools and their depths in meander bends. In C. M. Elliott (ed.), *River Meandering: Proceedings of the Conference Rivers '83*, Am. Soc. Civ. Eng., 885-94.

Hey, R. D. and Thorne, C. R. 1975: Secondary flows in river channels. *Area*, 7, 191-5.

Hooke, J. M. 1984: Changes in river meanders: a review of techniques and results of analyses. *Progress in Physical Geography*, 8, 473-508.

Hooke, J. M. and Harvey, A. M. 1983: Meander changes in relation to bend morphology and secondary flows. In J. D. Collison and J. Lewin (eds), *Modern and Ancient Fluvial Systems*. Oxford: Basil Blackwell, 121-32.

Hooke, R. L. 1974: Distribution of sediment transport and shear stress in a meander bend. *Uppsala Univ. Naturgeografiska Inst. Rapport*, 30.

Hooke, R. L. 1975: Distribution of sediment transport and shear stress in a meander bend. *J. Geol.*, 83, 543-65.

Hubble, D. W., Stevens, H. H., Skinner, J. V. and Beverage, J. P. 1985: New approach to calibrating bedload samples. *J. Hydraulic Engineering, Am. Soc. Civ. Eng.*, 111, 677-94.

Ikeda, S. 1982: Incipient motion of sand particles on side slopes. *J. Hydraulic Engineering*, 108, 95-114.

Ikeda, S. 1984: Flow and bed topography in channels with alternate bars. In C. M. Elliott (ed.), *River Meandering: Proceedings of the Conference Rivers '83*, Am. Soc. Civ. Eng., 733-46.

Ikeda, S. 1985: Bed topography in bends of sand-silt rivers. *J. Hydraulic Engineering, Am. Soc. Civ. Eng.*, 111, 1397-411.

Jackson, R. G. 1976: Depositional model of point bars in the Lower Wabash River. *Journ. Sed. Pet*, 46, 579-94.

Kalkwijk, J. P. Th. and DeVriend, H. J. 1980: Computations of the flow in shallow river bends. *J. Hydraulic Research*, 18, 327-42.

Keller, E. A. 1972: Development of alluvial stream channels: a five-stage model. *Geol. Society of America Bulletin*, 83, 1531-40.

Keller, E. A. and Melhorn W. 1973: Bedforms and fluvial processes in alluvial stream channels: selected observations. In M. Morisawa (ed.), *Fluvial Geomorphology*, SUNY Binghamton: Publication in Geomorphology, 253-83.

Kikkawa, H., Ikeda, S. and Kitagawa, A. 1976: Flow and bed topography in curved open channels. *J. Hydraulics Div., Am. Soc. Civ. Eng.*, 102, 1327–42.

Kinoshita, R. 1961: *An investigation of channel deformation of the Ishikari River*. Natural Resources Div. Ministry of Science and Technology of Japan Publication no. 36 (in Japanese).

Knighton, D. 1984: *Fluvial forms and processes*. London: Edward Arnold.

Leopold, L. B. 1982: Water surface topography in river channels and implication for meander development. In R. D. Hey, J. C. Bathurst, and C. R. Thorne (eds), *Gravel-bed Rivers* Chichester: Wiley, 359–88.

Lewin, J. 1976: Initiation of bedforms and meanders in coarse grained sediment. *Bulletin of the Geological Society of America*, 87, 281–5.

Lisle, T. E. 1979: A sorting mechanism for a riffle pool sequence. *Bulletin of the Geological Society of America*, 90, 1142–57.

Lisle, T. E. 1986: Stabilization of a gravel channel by large streamside obstructions and bedrock banks, Jacoby Creek, Northwestern California. *Bulletin of the Geological Society of America*, 97, 999–1011.

Nanson, G. C. and Hickin, E. J. 1983: Channel migration and incision on the Beatton River. *J. Hydraulic Engineering, Am. Soc. Civ. Eng.*, 109, 327–36.

Nelson, J. and Smith, J. Dungan, 1985: Numerical prediction of meander evolution. *EOS*, 66, 910.

Odgaard, A. J. 1981: Transverse bedslope in alluvial channel bends. *J. Hydraulic Div., Am. Soc. Civ. Eng.*, 107, 1677–94.

Odgaard, A. J. 1986: Meander flow model. I. Development; II. Applications. *J. Hydraulic Engineering, Am. Soc. Civ. Eng*, 112, 1117–36 and 1137–50

Onishi, Y. 1972: *Effects of meandering on sediment discharges and friction factors of alluvial streams*. Unpublished PhD dissertation, University of Iowa.

Parker, G. 1976: On the cause and characteristic scale of meandering and braiding in rivers. *J. Fluid Mechanics*, 76, 459–80.

Parker, G. and Andrews, E. D. 1985: Sorting of bedload sediments by flow in meander bends. *Water Resources Research*, 21, 1361–73.

Reid, J. B. 1984: Artificially induced concave bank deposition as a means of flood plain erosion control. In C. M. Elliott (ed.), *River Meandering: Proceedings of the Conference Rivers '83*, Am. Soc. Civ. Eng., 295–305.

Richards, K. 1982: *Rivers: Form and Process in Alluvial Channels*. London: Methuen.

Rozovskii, I. L. 1957: *Flow of water in bends of open channels* (in Russian), Kiev: Academy of Sciences of the Ukranian SSR (English translation, Israel Program for Scientific Translation, Jerusalem, 1961).

Schumm, S. A. 1963: Sinuosity of alluvial rivers on the Great Plains. *Bulletin of the Geological Society of America*, 74, 1089–100.

Sigenthaler, M. C. and Shen, H. W. 1984: Shear stress uncertainties in bends from equations. In C. M. Elliott (ed.), *River Meandering: Proceedings of the Conference Rivers '83*, Am. Soc. Civ. Eng. 662–74.

Smith, J. Dungan, and McLean, S. R. 1984: A model for flow in meandering streams. *Water Resources Research*, 20, 1301–15.

Struiksma, N., Olesen, K. W., Flokstra, C. and DeVriend, H. J. 1985: Bed deformation in curved alluvial channels. *J. Hydraulic Research*, 23, 57–79.

Thorne, C. R. and Rais, S. 1984: Secondary currents in a meandering river. In C. M. Elliott (ed.), *River Meandering: Proceedings of the Conference Rivers '83*, Am. Soc. Civ. Eng., 675–86.

Thorne, C. R., Zevenbergen, L. W. Bradley, J. and Pitlick, J. C. 1985a: *Measurements of bend flow hydraulics on the Fall River at bankfull stage*. Fort Collins, Colorado: Water Resources Field Support Laboratory Report.

Thorne, C. R., Zevenbergen, L. W., Pitlick, J. C., Rais, S., Bradley, J. B. and Julian, P. Y. 1985b: Direct measurement of secondary currents in a meandering sand-bed river. *Nature*, 316, 746–7.

Van Alphen, J. S. L. J., Bloks, P. M. and Hoekstra, P. 1984: Flow and grainsize patterns in a sharply curved river bend. *Earth Surface Processes*, 9, 513–22.

Whiting, P. J., Dietrich, W. E., Leopold, L. P. and Collins, L. 1985: *The variability of sediment transport in a fine-gravel stream (abstract)*. Ft. Collins, CO: Publication of the Third International Fluvial Sedimentology Conference.

Yamaoka, I. and Hasegawa, K. 1984: Effects of bends and alternate bars on meander evolution. In C. M. Elliott (ed.), *River Meandering: Proceedings of the Conference Rivers '83*, Am. Soc. Civ. Eng., 783–93.

Yen, B. C., 1965: *Characteristics of subcritical flow in a meandering channel*. Unpublished PhD dissertation, Iowa City: University of Iowa.

Yen, C. and Yen, B. C. 1971: Water surface configurations in channel bends. *J. Hydraulic Div., Am. Soc. Civ. Eng.*, 97, 303–21.

9
Channel Boundary Shape–Evolution and Equilibrium

T. R. H. Davies

INTRODUCTION

The problem of understanding and predicting the behaviour of rivers and alluvial canals has perplexed scientists and engineers for many years. Because river floodplains have favourable soils and topography for human use they are often densely settled, and in order for mankind to live in close proximity to a river it is necessary to be able to control or restrain the river's natural behaviour. The practical requirements of society thus demand successful methods for designing river control works, which in turn require some degree of understanding of river behaviour. In addition, the strikingly consistent shapes of flow boundaries such as meanders, ripples and river (and desert) dunes have focused the attention of many natural scientists on these phenomena. There is a huge volume of literature which discusses river behaviour, as a brief scrutiny of recent texts will show (e.g. ASCE, 1976; Richards, 1982).

It can be seen, in turn, that river 'behaviour', in the context of mankind's need to coexist with and use rivers, is simply the time-varying boundary shape (geometric characteristics) and location of the channel. If the shape of the channel can be predicted, then the other hydraulic parameters such as sediment transport capacity, bed and bank shear stresses and erosion or deposition rates are accessible; it is then reasonable to view the prediction of channel boundary shape as being fundamental to the development of rational methods for river management.

Although modern technology allows the best possible use to be made of current (mainly empirical) knowledge of river shape characteristics, it is the writer's opinion that our degree of fundamental understanding is disappointing in view of the many studies which have been reported. In particular, in recent years much attention has been paid to predictive methods which are based on extremal hypotheses (for example, that a river achieves equilibrium when it is dissipating potential energy at the minimum possible rate per unit time), and sophisticated computer-based design procedures are now available; as long as the physical reasons for the empirical successes of these procedures remain unknown, however, the methods cannot be used with much confidence in new situations.

This chapter is an attempt to make some progress by seeking an explanation for the river behaviour implied by these extremal hypotheses, and hence perhaps easing the controversy which has accompanied their appearance. The scene is first set by a brief discussion of channel boundary shapes and their significance, following which a review of the various approaches to predicting these shapes leads to a summary of the extremal hypotheses and the context of their development. A simple rational explanation for certain boundary shapes implied by the hypotheses is then presented, and the vital significance of constraints due to boundary material properties, hydraulics and functional relationships is shown by a study and explanation of the development of lower flow regime bedforms. The wider possibilities of this technique are then briefly explored in the context of meanders, and finally the philosophical implications of the suggested explanation are outlined.

CHANNEL BOUNDARY SHAPE

The basic components of channel boundary shape are the mean dimensions (width and depth) of the cross-section, the deviations from these mean values as functions of distance along the channel, and the location of the channel centreline. In order to study the various components of channel shape, however, one usually concentrates on the form of a particular flow boundary (bed or banks) and attempts to explain the (consistent or random) deviations from linearity that it displays. Thus it is the boundary shape rather than the flow shape which is studied, and while this may seem illogical since it is the flow which deforms the boundary, it will become apparent that the increase in convenience resulting from this approach is justified as long as its nature is borne in mind (is a 'ripple' bedform, for instance, a basic unit of boundary shape, or is it simply the solid boundary remaining between two adjacent scour-holes?).

Although channel boundaries can have an infinite variety of shapes, it has been shown by, for example, Ferguson (1976) and Davies and Tinker (1984) that these often complex shapes result from random environmental influences modifying a deterministic tendency to achieve a consistent geometry character-istic of the flow. In many natural rivers the random influences are strong enough to swamp the characteristic shape, giving a geometry which on analysis is shown to be random (Ghosh and Scheidegger, 1971); in others, a more or less consistent geometry is detectable (Carson and Lapointe, 1983), while under ideal laboratory conditions random influences can be excluded and very consistent shapes result (Davies, 1980; Davies and Tinker, 1984).

Even where random influences are minor, however, several factors can give rise to complex combinations of basic shapes; for example, bedforms in sand channels can exist at three different scales (Davies, 1982a) and superposition of bedforms of different sizes is possible. It is quite common for bedforms of the same scale, but different stages of development, to coexist, as in the so-called 'ripple-on-dune' bed configuration (Davies, 1982a; 1982b). When the flow rate which deforms the channel boundary varies, as it does in most natural flows, the boundary shape which exists at a given instant will in general not be in equilibrium with the instantaneous flow, but will be evolving towards equilibrium with it; the boundary will thus be in a state of continuous evolution towards an ever-changing equilibrium (Allen, 1978). While all these factors have been researched in the case of bedforms (essentially two-dimensional vertical deformations of the channel bed), the introduction of lateral variations in flow direction or properties will allow the bed configuration to vary laterally, and the channel banks might also deform, giving rise to characteristic planform shapes such as alternate bars, meandering or braiding. Even without the influence of random factors such as variations in bed and bank material properties (erodibility), vegetation and artificial structures, channel boundary shapes can be a complicated combination of small, medium and large, young and old, time-varying forms all interacting in three dimensions. It is clear that analysis of such a combination would be extremely difficult; it is also clear, however, that until we can explain the basic boundary shapes individually (e.g. ripples, or meanders) there is no hope for a fundamental explanation of river behaviour in general. 'Explanation', in this context, means the ability to understand and predict:

1 the flow and boundary conditions at which a boundary will begin to evolve towards a particular basic shape;
2 the way in which the evolution of the boundary will progress, how it will affect the flow past it, and how such effects will in turn further affect the boundary evolution;
3 the flow and boundary conditions at which a given type of boundary deformation will cease to change its characteristic geometry (although it might experience variations in details of shape, and slow translation of shape elements up- or down-stream); this is the so-called 'equilibrium' condition.

The basic process of channel shape change is that of bed and bank material motion, which is in turn determined by the fluid shear stresses acting at the boundary and the ability of the boundary material to resist these stresses. This suggests that any explanation of the observed consistency of channel shapes should be sought in the spatial and temporal variations of boundary shear stresses in turbulent flow, and in the constraints exerted on the action of these stresses by flow and material properties. It will be seen later that this line of reasoning leads directly to a plausible explanation for certain equilibrium boundary shapes.

Depending on the scale of the boundary deformation, channel shape is of practical significance in various ways. For example, deformations of a size (amplitude) much less than flow depth or width can be considered as roughness elements which do not give rise to large-scale flow disturbances; their main effect is then to change the roughness coefficient or friction factor of the flow, which is the empirical factor used in calculating channel capacity, or the flow velocity corresponding to a given depth and slope. This effect is significant in predicting the stage-discharge curve of a river or the capacity of a canal. Larger-scale deformation of the boundary can cause consequent bed and bank erosion and hence changes in the course and character of the river, and might give rise to severe difficulties for bankside developments or protection works. In many cases, for example, a change in the basic geometry or position of meanders in a river could cause the location of the river within its floodplain to change and lead to the abandonment of facilities such as bridges, water offtakes and jetties.

In order to make good long-term use of the resources of a river, we must be able to predict the way in which it will behave if the present uses and hydrological regime remain unchanged, and also the way in which it would respond to future developments. Unless such prediction of flood stages and channel changes is possible, the costs of development (in terms of damage, maintenance and river control works) cannot be assessed and hence development proposals cannot be evaluated properly.

EXPLANATIONS OF BOUNDARY SHAPE

In this section some of the more significant methods which have been used to explain and predict channel shape are considered, in terms of the principles involved rather than of the detail of their practical application. The purpose of this summary is to clarify the context of the modern extremal methods and of the subsequent suggested basis for their success.

Empirical regime methods

As a result of difficulties experienced by engineers on the Indian sub-continent in the late nineteenth and early twentieth centuries in the operation of irrigation canals fed by alluvial rivers, a series of data was collected from those canals which *did* operate satisfactorily, i.e. in which channel dimensions, slope, flow rate and sediment input were in long-term equilibrium. Such canals were said to be 'in regime'. The data were fitted with a series of empirical equations which were then used to guide the design of new canal cross-sections. Dimensional analysis was used to establish the form of the equations, especially in later formulations and extensions of the method (Blench, 1967), and the regional limitation to the application of regime equations was relaxed to some extent by the introduction of factors describing the character of the bed and bank sediments. While largely successful for the design of straight canals with little variation in flow rate, regime methods are much less satisfactory for use with natural rivers due to the greater variability of planform, flow rate and boundary materials; Griffiths (1983) describes a method for predicting the mean equilibrium dimensions (cross-section) of a river channel based on measurement of (assumed) equilibrium sections elsewhere on the same river, but again the planform and boundary shape of the river seem to be inaccessible.

Being essentially empirical there seems to be little prospect of applying regime equations beyond the conditions from which they were derived. Appreciation of this point led Brebner and Wilson (1967) to try to explain the forms of regime equations using principles of thermodynamics; the attempt was similar in nature to early formulations of extremal hypotheses (e.g. Yang, 1971) and was not wholly convincing (Davy and Davies; 1979, 1980) because of the assumption that the principle of minimum entropy production (Nicolis and Prigogine, 1977), known to be valid in linear systems, was also valid in non-linear turbulent streamflow.

Model studies

Hydraulic models have long been used to solve specific problems of river behaviour, including that of predicting the shape which will be assumed by a particular river if it is modified in a particular way. Such studies are, however, purely empirical, their only advantage over field studies being the ease with which flow conditions can be controlled and the rapidity with which the channel boundary shape changes. More general studies of channels having small discharges provide a testing-ground for hypotheses of river behaviour, and can often be carried out in hydraulic modelling basins. Of particular value is the ease with which unwanted environmental influences can be excluded. In a philosophical sense a model or flume study is simply asking nature a question in a particular way; the answer will always be true, but it might be different from the answer which will be received in response to a similar question posed in a different context – for example, that of a large river in a natural environment. It is clear that the same basic principles underlie each situation, and that they might be more easily discovered by studying easily controlled and rapidly responding 'model' rivers than by inconvenient field studies of large ones.

Stability analyses

There have been many attempts to predict the flow and sediment conditions under which an initially plane flow boundary (bed or bank) will respond to the introduction of a small-amplitude displacement by increasing the amplitude of the displacement. Such methods have been quite successful in predicting the onset and initial period of, for example, antidunes (Kennedy, 1963), meanders (Callander, 1969) and braiding (Parker, 1976) and have in recent years become rather sophisticated. All, however, apply only to very small amplitude disturbances; once the boundary shape evolves to a larger amplitude the process equations become non-linear and the linear stability solutions fail. The practical utility of predicting the initial behaviour of a plane boundary seems to be small, since such boundaries are rarely found in rivers, and there is never any lack of sizeable disturbances which can initiate boundary development. It is of much greater importance to predict the conditions and geometry at which a boundary deformation ceases to increase in amplitude, since this is the equilibrium condition, but to do this would need a stability analysis capable of handling the strongly non-linear processes which occur at high amplitudes (Nicolis and Prigogine, 1977; Davy and Davies, 1979). A start in this direction has been made by Parker et al. (1982), whose non-linear analysis predicts the asymmetry of high-sinuosity meanders found in natural (Carson and Lapointe, 1983) and laboratory (Davies and Tinker, 1984) streams, but the equations do not seem capable of predicting the conditions at which meander geometry will stabilize.

Analytical methods

In principle, prediction of the depth, width, slope and planform shape of a river channel fed with water and sediment at predetermined rates (i.e. when flow rate Q_w and sediment transport Q_s are independent variables) requires four independent equations. From the many studies of water flow and sediment transport in channels, there is available a wealth of semi-empirical equations for sediment transport (Q_s related to Q_w, slope s, depth d and width w) and resistance to flow (Q_w related to s, d and w) for sediment of known grain sizes and density; the continuity relationship

$$Q_w = w \, d \, \bar{v} \tag{9.1}$$

where $\bar{v}$ = mean velocity, is also available. A fourth equation is needed for a complete solution, and in recent years a number of studies have assumed such an equation in the form of an *extremal hypothesis*, in which a channel is assumed to achieve equilibrium when a particular parameter achieves an extreme value (maximum or minimum). Thus, for example, the hypothesis of minimum energy dissipation rate (MEDR) assumes that when the rate at which the river dissipates potential energy ($Q_w s$) cannot become any lower, the river ceases to change its shape. Other such hypotheses involve minimum unit stream power (MUSP) in which the product $\bar{v}s$ is minimized, maximum sediment transport rate (MTR) in which Q_s is maximized, and maximum friction factor (MFF) in which the Darcy-Weisbach friction factor f, given by

$$f = \frac{8gw^2 d^3 s}{Q_w^2} \tag{9.2}$$

is maximized. These hypotheses are explained and compared in Davies and Sutherland (1983) and the references therein, leading to the conclusion that the hypotheses are equivalent in many situations, but that MFF is more widely applicable and in some cases more correct than the others.

Using modern computer methods, iterative solutions to the four equations can be developed which have been shown in many cases to be in reasonable agreement with observed river and canal behaviour (e.g. Chang, 1980; 1985; Yang et al., 1981). This method thus shows considerable promise in the useful prediction of river behaviour, despite the warning of Bettess and White (1985) that care is needed in choosing the particular combination of resistance, sediment and extremal equations, and the opinion of Griffiths (1984) that the progress offered by extremal methods is illusory. The writer's opinion is that the successes of the extremal methods are deeply significant, and indicate the possibility of fundamental understanding of river behaviour; but that *until the reasons for the successes are known*, the basis of the methods will remain as so much guesswork and the methods themselves will be unattractive because the limits to their applicability remain unknown. There have been many attempts to explain the various hypotheses from physical reasoning, but as described by Davy and Davies (1979) and Davies and Sutherland (1983; 1984 and references therein) these attempts have all been unconvincing for one reason or another; some are based on unjustified analogies, others on extension of laminar flow properties to turbulent flows, still others on conditions being 'close to static equilibrium' and so on. It is now clear that the best justification for the use of extremal methods lies in their many empirical successes, and that the search for a rational explanation of these successes should continue (C. T. Yang, personal communication, 1985).

In the following section an explanation is given for extremal behaviour under one set of independent variables, and it is believed that because all the extremal hypotheses are closely related, this one instance also supports the credibility of the hypotheses in other situations.

AN EXPLANATION OF EXTREMAL BEHAVIOUR

Implications of extremal hypotheses

In a comparison of the various hypotheses, Davies and Sutherland (1983) showed that to a large extent they are similar in effect in that they each predict that a river will achieve equilibrium under the same conditions; that is, a river will achieve minimum unit stream power under the same conditions of depth, slope, width etc. at which it achieves maximum friction factor, and so on. Sometimes a particular hypothesis cannot be applied. For example when Q_w and s are independent variables MEDR cannot be used because Q_ws cannot then be minimized, but in many cases, and certainly when in a laboratory flume or in the short-term adjustment of a natural river Q_w and s are independent, those hypotheses (MUSP, MFF, MTR) which can be used are equivalent.

In maximizing the friction factor f with Q_w and s independently determined, it is sufficient to maximize the product w^2d^3 since g is also constant; in a laboratory flume w might be constant, and even where a channel chooses its own width it is known that w is a close function of Q_w for a given stream, so that w is in effect fixed by Q_w (Leopold, Wolman and Miller, 1964). Thus maximizing f is equivalent to maximizing d^3 or d, and the extremal hypotheses indicate that equilibrium will occur when d is a maximum. Since in steady uniform flow the mean bed shear stress $\bar{\tau}$ is given by

$$\bar{\tau} = \varrho gdS \tag{9.3}$$

(where ϱ = fluid density) then a further possible hypothesis, maximum shear stress (MSS), is suggested. This supports the earlier proposition that since bed shape is changed by the action of shear stress, an explanation for equilibrium bed shape might be found by considering shear-stress behaviour. We now have the situation in which a stream is thought to achieve equilibrium, i.e. unchanging shape, when f or $\bar{\tau}$ are maxima. Figure 9.1 illustrates this behaviour; since the bed configuration C_m corresponds to the maximum possible mean shear stress $\bar{\tau}_m$, the bed does not change shape any more once it has achieved C_m. Davies (1980) showed that this behaviour does indeed occur for the particular case of lower flow regime bedforms.

The occurrence of equilibrium at maximum shear stress can actually be explained by a simpler, but still sufficient, hypothesis, namely that *the shape of a channel boundary changes under the influence of fluid flow so as to cause $\bar{\tau}$ to increase*. Thus equilibrium can only occur at $C = C_m$ (figure 9.1) because with any other value of C it is still possible for $\bar{\tau}$ to increase; only when $C = C_m$ can $\bar{\tau}$ no longer increase and so channel shape will cease to change. If this

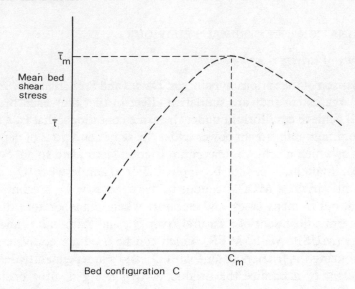

Figure 9.1   Variation of mean bed shear stress $\bar{\tau}$ with bed configuration C
(after Davies, 1980)

hypothesized tendency for $\bar{\tau}$ to increase could be shown to occur in channels, then, an explanation for the successes of the extremal hypotheses would be at hand.

The tendency for bed shear stress to increase

By considering the forces acting on the fluid in a wide, straight open channel, it can be shown that in order for the downslope component of the gravity force to be balanced by the upslope boundary shear force, the mean shear stress exerted on the bed by the flow is given by equation (9.3). Then, there being no net force on the fluid, the flow is steady, i.e. non-accelerating.

When flow in such a channel is turbulent, the instantaneous bed shear stress $\tau(t)$, which acts on an area of bed so small that spatial variation of τ is negligible, varies with time (t) due to the passage of turbulent eddies. Grass (1970) and Blinco and Simons (1974) show that the probability distribution of this instantaneous stress is lognormal in shape, both for a fixed bed and for a moveable bed of fine sand. Figure 9.2 illustrates such a distribution; note that the mean value of shear stress $\bar{\tau}$ is at the centre of area of the distribution and must also fulfil equation (9.3).

The extent to which a given steady bed shear stress is capable of deforming the area on which it acts depends on the value of the stress and on the time for which it acts. Thus the effectiveness of a stress τ in figure 9.2 can be written as

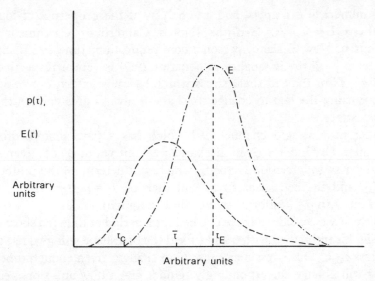

Figure 9.2 Probability of occurrence p(τ) and effectiveness E(τ) of instantaneous bed shear stress τ

$$E(\tau) = \phi(\tau)\,p(\tau) \tag{9.4}$$

where $\phi(\tau)$ is the rate per unit time at which τ can deform the bed and p(τ) is the proportion of total time for which τ is present, this latter quantity being also the probability that τ will occur as in figure 9.2. It is well known that the rate at which a given shear stress can erode material from a boundary is of the form:

$$\phi(\tau) = k(\tau - \tau_c)^m \tag{9.5}$$

where k and m are constants, and τ_c is the critical bed shear stress below which no material moves. The value of m has been found empirically to be close to 1.5 (Bagnold, 1940; Richards, 1982). From equations (9.4) and (9.5)

$$E(\tau) = k(\tau - \tau_c)^{1.5}\,p(\tau) \tag{9.6}$$

The form of E(τ) for the probability distribution of figure 9.2 is shown on that figure, using a realistic value of τ_c and assuming arbitrarily that k = 1 (this assumption does not affect the eventual result). It is seen that the peak value of the E(τ) curve occurs at a value τ_E of τ such that

$$\tau_E > \bar{\tau} \tag{9.7}$$

Further numerical examples, and an analysis of the properties of lognormal distributions by G. A. Griffiths (North Canterbury Catchment Board, Christchurch, New Zealand, personal communication, June 1985) show that so long as $m = 1.5$ the inequality in equation (9.7) is valid irrespective of the value of τ_c. Thus the bed shear stress which has most effect, over a period of time, in causing the bed to change its shape is always greater than the mean bed shear stress.

Consider now a rigid channel bed which has a particular (bedformlike) configuration C. Under a given discharge per unit width q at a given slope s, C will give rise to a friction factor f_C which will determine the uniform flow depth d_C, and the bed shear stress will then be $\bar{\tau}_C = \varrho g d_C s$. Hence C is in equilibrium with $\bar{\tau}_C$ (uniform, steady flow assumed).

Similarly, if we consider a moveable bed for a period of time too short for C to change significantly, then with q and s fixed the bed shape will give rise to a bed shear stress $\bar{\tau}_{Cm}$. This stress may cause C to change, given enough time; if this occurs, $\bar{\tau}$ will change correspondingly. Under given flow and slope, each bed configuration C has a corresponding uniform flow shear stress τ_C. Conversely, it seems reasonable to assume that, given q and s, a mobile bed which is acted on by a given (momentarily steady) shear stress $\bar{\tau}_C$ will evolve towards the bed configuration which would cause $\bar{\tau}_C$ to occur under these conditions, namely C.

Suppose that we have a mobile bed of configuration C_A which because of turbulence experiences a time-varying shear stress such as that in figure 9.2. The mean bed shear stress $\bar{\tau}_A$ corresponds to C_A, and flow is uniform. Each small area of the bed experiences from moment to moment a succession of different shear stresses τ_i, and while each of them is present the shape of a bed area will evolve towards C_i. Over a period of time, however, the shear stress most effective in reshaping the bed is τ_E, and each bed area will thus evolve farther towards C_E than towards any other shape. It may then be expected that the bed as a whole begins to evolve from the configuration C_A towards C_E, and as it does so it will pass through a series of intermediate configurations $C_{A+\delta A}$, $C_{A+2\delta A}$ . . . which will give rise to shear stresses $\tau_{A+\delta A}$, $\tau_{A+2\delta A}$ . . . Assuming that the relationship between τ_C and C is well-behaved, as indeed the experiments of Davies (1980) and references therein show it to be, then since $\tau_E > \bar{\tau}$, $\tau_{A+\delta A} > \tau_A$. Hence the mean shear stress caused by flow over the changing shape of each small bed area will increase, and the mean shear stress experienced by the whole bed will increase. Because $\bar{\tau}$ must always lie at the centre of area of the probability distribution curve (figure 9.2), this distribution must change as $\bar{\tau}$ increases, by changing shape, or translating to the right, or both; in any case it is likely that the value of τ_E will also increase as $\bar{\tau}$ increases, hence there is no obvious reason for expecting that equation (9.7) will cease to be valid, provided that $p(\tau)$ remains lognormal.

It might be objected, at this stage, that the traditional division of total shear stress τ into a part τ_g balanced by grain roughness (and responsible for bed grain motion) and a part τ_f balanced by the much larger bed form roughness, means that bed configuration C is caused by grain motion resulting from τ_g and is not necessarily related to τ as required by the assumption that shear stress and friction factor behave similarly. However, the commonly observed fact that bedload motion (caused by τ_g) increases monotonically with τ despite variations in bedform (and τ_f) implies that τ and τ_g have simultaneous maxima with respect to, for example, bed configuration C, and the objection is therefore invalid. There is thus a plausible explanation for the tendency of a flow boundary to change its shape in a manner such that $\bar{\tau}$ increases with time. To complete the explanation we need some way of halting this change of shape so that equilibrium is attained, and since there is no obvious intrinsic mechanism, we shall consider the nature and operation of the constraints that might affect the increase of shear stress.

Constraints on bed evolution

One type of constraint is that already shown in figure 9.1; if the bed shear stress shows a maximum as the bed shape changes, then a tendency to increase $\bar{\tau}$ causes the shape of the bed to cease changing when the shear stress achieves this maximum value. This is a *functional* constraint, and is known to control, for example, the length : height ratio of lower flow regime bedforms (Davies, 1980), the spatial density of large grains in an armoured bed, and possibly the wavelength : radius of curvature ratio of meanders (Davies and Sutherland, 1980).

A second type of constraint will occur if the bed shear stress becomes so great that any further increase will cause bed forms to change their basic shape because the bed material cannot resist the applied stress where it is highest. Thus, for example, sharp-crested bedforms become flat-crested when the crestal shear stress exceeds the shear resistance of the material at the crest (Davies, 1982a). It is then impossible for the bed to change shape so as to cause any further increase in shear stress since the bed material is insufficiently resistant to support such an increase. This is a *material* constraint which controls bed shape and hence shear stress.

A *flow* constraint comes into effect when the bed achieves such a shape that a flow process previously responsible for bed shape changes can no longer operate; for example, local scour behind ripple crests causing troughs to deepen. There is a limit to the depth to which a trough can be scoured with given flow and sediment inputs, and when this limit is reached the bedform must cease growing because no further material is available to build up the crest downstream. In order to continue the bedform growth more energy is needed, i.e. an increase of flow, to allow trough scouring to continue.

In summary, then, we have a mechanism which, in combination with a variety of types of constraint, explains the observed behaviour of rivers under certain circumstances. Since the extremal hypotheses operate consistently under a range of circumstances, a rational explanation for one of them in one case strengthens the credibility of all of them in all cases. The present explanation is not restricted to laminar, or static, or linear situations; indeed, some form of fluctuating behaviour, such as that shown by Nicolis and Prigogine (1977) to be characteristic of strongly non-linear behaviour, is vital so that the shear stress is suitably distributed in time. Any correspondence between river equilibrium and minima of stream power or energy dissipation rate now seems to be coincidental, which is in line with Nicolis and Prigogine's (1977) finding that the equilibrium state of non-linear systems is not characterized by any particular rate of entropy production. The present explanation is purely mechanical and results from the form of the probability distribution of shear stress, which in turn results from the nature of turbulence (in the case of bedforms) or of hydrological time-series (in the case of meanders discussed below). The shape of natural probability distributions has been examined by, for example, Chow (1954), Wolman and Miller (1960) and Bagnold and Barndorff-Neilson (1980), and the latter have suggested a physical explanation for their proposed log-hyperbolic distribution (which is, however, difficult to manipulate).

The condition $\tau_E > \bar{\tau}$ does not depend on having $\tau_c > 0$; the mechanism outlined above can thus be applied to any type of flow boundary, and is a candidate for explaining, for example, ripples on the ice cover of rivers, solution meanders in limestone, and meandering of ocean and density currents, in all of which $\tau_c = 0$. To illustrate the ability of the proposed mechanism to clarify processes of fluvial evolution, the development of lower flow regime bedforms is discussed more fully below.

RIPPLES AND DUNES

Consider the evolution of an initially plane bed of medium sand under the influence of free surface flow. If the flow is strong enough to move sand grains, it is known that the bed will deform into a series of wave-like forms (Williams and Kemp, 1971). At first these are of very low amplitude, and have an initial wavelength controlled by near-bed flow conditions (Davies, 1977; Yalin, 1977). The forms evolve rapidly in shape to achieve their final dimensionless geometry (length: height ratio, Yalin, 1977); Davies (1980) has shown that this geometry is exactly that which gives rise to the maximum value of bed shear stress or friction factor achievable by variations in length : height ratio. Having achieved a constant dimensionless shape, the bedforms then evolve so as to increase $\bar{\tau}$

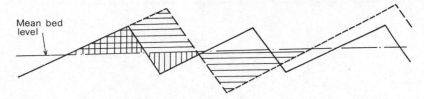

Mean bed
level

Figure 9.3 Small bedforms (vertical hatching) require a smaller scour-hole depth than similarly shaped large bedforms (horizontal hatching)

by growing in size; Vittal et al. (1977) show that friction factor increases monotonically as the ratio of bedform height : flow depth increases. Thus far, bedform evolution clearly matches the concept of increasing shear stress, and eventually one of two constraints comes into play to stop the increase in bedform size.

Firstly, while the ratio of bedform height : flow depth is small (~ 0.1), the shape of the bedforms is not changed by the proximity of crests to the free surface. In this case the forms can only increase in size if their troughs can be scoured more deeply by the eddies behind the crests, and the scoured material deposited on the crest downstream, since the volume of material above the mean bed level must always equal the volume of scour holes below mean bed level (figure 9.3). If the eddies can no longer increase the depth of scour holes because the limit of scour corresponding to the given flow and sediment conditions has been reached (ASCE, 1976; Zanke, 1978), then the bedforms must cease to grow. An equilibrium bed configuration results. The realism of this suggestion is enhanced by the similarity between the geometry of a scour-hole behind a negative step (ASCE, 1976) and that of the scour-hole between two adjacent bed-forms (Zanke, 1978); indeed, the scour-hole shape seems to be much more consistent than the shapes of the bedforms it separates, and one suspects that it might be well worth while studying bedforms in general as phenomena dictated by the scouring, rather than the depositional, aspect of their development.

Secondly, if the scour limitation constraint does not come into play before the bedform crest approaches sufficiently close to the water surface, then flow convergence between the crest and the water surface can cause the crestal shear stress to increase markedly (Davies, 1982a). This increased stress may be so great that continued scouring in troughs leads to material being deposited downstream of, rather than at, bedform crests. The crests then become flattened (figure 9.4) and may be quite long in the direction of flow, and the material constraint on bedform height has caused a change in bedform shape. Corresponding to this new shape is a different length : height ratio which causes maximum friction factor or $\bar{\tau}$ and when this is attained no further increase of $\bar{\tau}$ can occur, thus equilibrium is achieved.

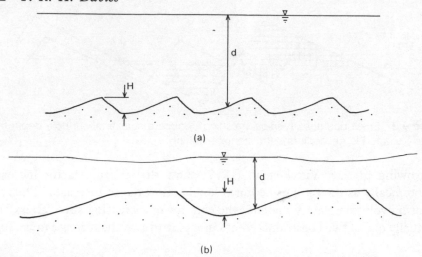

Figure 9.4   (a) Sharp-crested bedforms ('ripples')
(b) Flat-crested bedforms ('dunes')

In this way the equilibrium shape of bedforms can be explained simply in conceptual terms, and the research needed to describe the functional, flow and material constraints in order to quantify this explanation is obvious.

One further aspect of bedform behaviour which has caused some difficulty in the past is the gradual evolution to equilibrium of a bed configuration consisting of sharp-crested ripples following a decrease of flow. As Yang and Song (1984) have pointed out, this process involves a gradual *decrease* of friction factor (and $\bar{\tau}$) as equilibrium is approached, and appears to contradict both the MFF hypothesis and the proposed tendency to increase $\bar{\tau}$. From the perspective of the present approach, however, this behaviour is seen to result from the action of constraints (figure 9.5), as follows.

Under the initial flow rate Q_1 a mean bed shear stress $\bar{\tau}_1$ is achieved at equilibrium, with a bedform height H_1. Q_1 is now quickly reduced to Q_2; in the short term the bedform height remains at H_1 and bed shear stress changes to $\bar{\tau}_{21}$. Since the reduced flow rate Q_2 cannot maintain the bedform height H_1, however, H_1 now gradually reduces to H_2 (and the bed-form length adjusts simultaneously so as to maintain the optimum length : height ratio). This causes the shear stress to *reduce* gradually from $\bar{\tau}_{21}$ to $\bar{\tau}_2$ at equilibrium. It is the *constraint*, namely H, which has caused the reduction in $\bar{\tau}$; the tendency to increase $\bar{\tau}$ has been present all the time, but the maximum achievable $\bar{\tau}$ has gradually reduced because H has decreased. The observed behaviour is thus fully compatible with the proposed tendency to increase $\bar{\tau}$, and emphasizes the importance of appreciating the role of constraints in both progress towards, and achievement of, equilibrium.

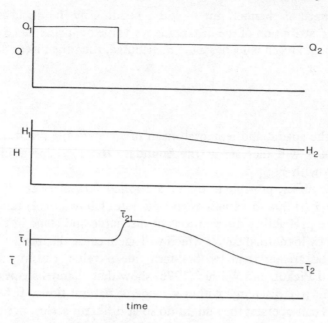

Figure 9.5 Variation of bedform height H and mean bed shear stress $\bar{\tau}$ in response to a sudden decrease of flow Q over a bed of sharp-crested forms

EXTENSION TO MEANDERS

If the suggested tendency to increase $\bar{\tau}$ is indeed of basic significance in explaining river behaviour it should also be capable of application to aspects of river shape other than bedforms. The most widely described characteristic boundary shape (apart from bedforms) is the meandering planform detectable in many rivers.

Meanders are features with a much larger spatial scale than the bedforms discussed above, and are unlikely to be caused by the rapid, small-scale fluctuations of shear stress, due to turbulence, which have been shown to cause the growth of ripples and dunes (Williams and Kemp, 1971). The mechanisms available to cause large-scale lateral deformations of channels are many, however, ranging from lateral instability of flow over bedforms to random and introduced disturbances such as engineering works. The subsequent development and consistent final equilibrium form of meanders may still be susceptible to explanation by the tendency to increase $\bar{\tau}$.

Any bend or introduced disturbance will, if its amplitude is great enough, cause a perturbation to the lateral structure of turbulence on a scale comparable with 2π times the channel width (Yalin, 1977), which might be expected also to cause a temporal variation in the spatial mean bed (or bank) shear stress over a similar length of channel, due to eddy shedding by the disturbance. If the probability distribution of the instantaneous value of spatial mean shear stress $\bar{\tau}_S(t)$ over such a reach is lognormally distributed, then the most effective value of $\bar{\tau}_S(t)$ will be

$$\bar{\tau}_{SE} > \bar{\bar{\tau}} \qquad (9.8)$$

where $\bar{\bar{\tau}}$ is the spatial and temporal mean of $\tau(t)$ over the reach. Again, then, the value of $\bar{\bar{\tau}}$ will increase as the boundary (bank) shape adjusts towards equilibrium with $\bar{\tau}_{SE}$.

A separate effect, possible in the uncontrolled flow of rivers, is the natural variation in $\bar{\tau}_S(t)$ due to variations in flow rate. Chow (1954) refers to works in which the probability distributions of discharge and stage in rivers can be represented by lognormal curves which will again cause the most effective value of $\bar{\tau}_S(t)$ to be greater than its long-term mean value, causing the latter to increase, and Pickup and Warner (1976) show that channel shape responds to the most effective discharge within a range of natural flows. If both of these mechanisms can operate, they might do so at different scales, perhaps causing an effect similar to the superposition of bedforms of different scales. This should be detectable by autocorrelation analysis of meander planforms such as that of Ferguson (1976).

Certainly it seems likely that a functional constraint causes the shape of meander bends to stabilize when the ratio of radius of curvature : channel width has a value of about 3 (Davies and Sutherland, 1980), and Bagnold (1960) suggests that the form of the function may be due to flow separation as the radius of curvature decreases, so that a flow constraint may be involved. It is also very clear that bank strength can be a constraint on the increase of curvature in bends, and it seems likely that such a material constraint causes meanders in steep channels of non-cohesive material to change to a braided form.

In a study of surface-tension meanders, Davies and Tinker (1984) found that in a flow with no obvious fluctuations due to turbulence or flow variation, meanders very similar to those of rivers developed. Obviously no such mechanism as that suggested herein was present, and the channel shape must be explained in some other way. Howard's (1972) subtle commentary on extremal principles gives a clue: he showed that with low Reynolds' numbers (as in laminar flow) a hypothesis of minimum energy dissipation is bound to be correct because there are in fact sufficient equations to predict these flows, and so there is no choice of conditions from which a hypothesis can select one set: 'Any selection principle will be correct when there is no choice' (Howard, 1972, p. 467). When the surface-tension meander experiment is set up, therefore, one could predict the end-state of the stream if one knew enough about the boundary conditions, simply by applying known equations of laminar flow. It is interesting that only where flow variations cause the equations of motion to be difficult to solve can the tendency to increase $\bar{\tau}$ be operative; the very temporal fluctuations which complicate the problem also provide the means for its solution.

GENERAL DISCUSSION

The many different physical situations in which a tendency to maximize the friction factor or drag coefficient is present (Song and Yang, 1982) suggest that a tendency such as that to increase boundary shear stress might be widespread in operation, and that studies to clarify its operation and constraints would be worthwhile. It seems preferable to suggest work of this nature rather than further efforts to justify directly the various extremal hypotheses by transferring principles from other fields and conditions, which has to date been a very time-consuming and unsatisfactory pursuit. In particular, quantification of the nature and operation of the various constraints which dictate the equilibrium forms of flow boundaries needs intensive study so that useful predictions of channel shape can be made. No doubt some of this information can be obtained from existing data in regime formulae and bedform phase diagrams, but more explicit information is needed to widen the applicability and usefulness of predictive methods such as that of Chang (1980; 1985).

The recent attempts to use variational calculus to detect extrema (Griffiths, 1984; Bettess and White, 1985) can be seen in the context of the present approach to be capable of detecting only explicit functional constraints among the flow variables related to the chosen resistance and transport formulae. Material and flow constraints will not be detectable unless they are implicit in these formulae, and Davies and Sutherland (1983) have shown that the variational approach is not capable of detecting a constraint resulting from the form of a bed shape-shear stress (or friction factor) function.

The only conditions under which the present approach will not be applicable seem to be those that result in $\bar{\tau}$ being an independent variable, i.e. with flow depth and slope independent. Such conditions seem unlikely to occur in natural or laboratory streams; if they did, inequality (9.7) could still apply, but it might be necessary to invoke friction factor rather than shear stress as the determining factor. Since f involves three variables at least, it cannot be fixed by any realistic combination of independent variables.

CONCLUSION

In this chapter it has been demonstrated that modern methods of predicting channel boundary shape, based on extremal hypotheses, can be shown to have a rational basis in the tendency for channel shape to change so as to increase boundary shear stress. The value of this demonstration lies in the increased confidence it gives to predictions by the extremal methods, and the emphasis it places on the various constraints which limit the maximum shear stress which can be achieved. It is also useful in distracting attention from the pursuit of wills-of-the-wisp in the form of various mysterious principles of energy dissipation and entropy production previously thought to underlie the successes of the extremal hypotheses; instead, a simple hydraulic process resulting from the empirically known character of turbulence and flow series is shown to be capable of explaining the hypotheses, in combination with the constraints which limit the process. This points the way to a new philosophy for further investigations of river behaviour.

ACKNOWLEDGEMENTS

I am extremely grateful for lengthy and valuable discussions over the past decade with A. J. Sutherland, C. Tinker, D. J. Painter, I. Karcz, M. P. Mosley, G. A. Griffiths, M. A. Carson, H. H. Chang, C. T. Yang, R. Bettess and B. W. Davy, during which the concepts presented here have gradually taken shape. I also acknowledge the value of written advice and opinions from G. Nicolis, G. Parker and many anonymous reviewers.

REFERENCES

Allen, J. R. L. 1978: Computational models for dune time-lag; Stein's rule for dune height. *Sedimentary Geol.*, 20, 165–216.
A.S.C.E. 1976: *Sedimentation Engineering*. ed. V. A. Vanoni, New York: Am. Soc. Civil Eng.
Bagnold, R. A. 1940: *The Physics of Blown Sand and Desert Dunes*, London: Methuen.
Bagnold, R. A. 1960: Some aspects of the shape of river meanders. *US Geological Survey, Prof. Paper* 282-E.
Bagnold, R. A. and Barndorff-Neilson, E. 1980: The pattern of natural size distributions. *Sedimentology*, 27, 199–207.
Bettess, R. and White, W. R. 1985: Extremal hypotheses applied to river regime. In *Proc., 2nd Int. Gravel-Bed Rivers Workshop, Pingree Park, Colo., Aug. 12–17*
Blench, T. 1967: *Mobile-bed Fluviology*. Edmonton, Alberta: Univ. of Alberta Press.
Blinco, P. H. and Simons, D. B. 1974: Characteristics of turbulent boundary shear stress. *J. Eng. Mech. Div., ASCE*, 100, 203–20.
Brebner, A. and Wilson, K. C. 1967: Derivation of regime equations from relationships for pressurised flow. *Proc. Inst. Civil Eng.*, 36, 42–67.
Callander, R. A. 1969: Instability and river channels. *J. Fluid Mech.*, 36, 465–80.

Carson, M. A. and Lapointe, M. F. 1983: The inherent asymmetry of river meander planform. *J. Geol.*, 91, 41–55.

Chang, H. H. 1980: Geometry of gravel streams. *J. Hydraul. Div., ASCE*, 106, 1443–56.

Chang, H. H. 1985: River morphology and thresholds. *J. Hydraul. Eng.*, 111, 503–19.

Chow, V. T. 1954: The log-probability law and its engineering applications. *Proc. Am. Soc. Civil Eng.*, 80.

Davies, T. R. H. 1977: Discussion of 'On the determination of ripple length' by M. S. Yalin. *J. Hydraul. Div., ASCE*, 103, 439

Davies, T. R. H. 1980: Bedform spacing and flow resistance. *J. Hydraul. Div., ASCE*, 106, 423–33.

Davies, T. R. H. 1982a: Lower flow regime bedforms – rational classification. *J. Hydraul. Div., ASCE*, 108, 343–60.

Davies, T. R. H. 1982b: Discussion of 'Bed shear stress over subaqueous dunes, and the transition to upper-stage flat beds' by J. S. Bridge. *Sedimentology*, 29, 740–3.

Davies, T. R. H. and Sutherland, A. J. 1980: Resistance to flow past deformable boundaries. *Earth Surf. Proc.*, 5, 175–9.

Davies, T. R. H. and Sutherland, A. J. 1983: Extremal hypotheses for river behaviour. *Water Resour. Res.*, 19, 141–8.

Davies, T. R. H. and Sutherland, A. J. 1984: Reply to comment. *Water Resour. Res.*, 20, 741–2.

Davies, T. R. H. and Tinker, C. C. 1984: Fundamental characteristics of stream meanders. *Bull. Geol. Soc. Amer.*, 95, 510–2.

Davy, B. W. and Davies, T. R. H. 1979: Entropy concepts in fluvial geomorphology: a re-evaluation. *Water Resour. Res.*, 15, 103–6.

Davy, B. W. and Davies, T. R. H. 1980: Reply to comment. *Water Resour. Res.*, 16, 251.

Ferguson, R. I. 1976: Disturbed periodic model for river meanders. *Earth Surf. Proc.*, 1, 337–47.

Ghosh, A. K. and Scheidegger, A. E. 1971: A study of natural wiggly lines in hydrology. *J. Hydrol.*, 13, 101–26.

Grass, A. J. 1970: Initial instability of fine bed sand. *J. Hydraul. Div., ASCE*, 96, 619–31.

Griffiths, G. A. 1983: Stable channel design in alluvial rivers. *J. Hydrol.*, 65, 259–70.

Griffiths, G. A. 1984: Extremal hypotheses for river regime – an illusion of progress. *Water Resour. Res.*, 20, 113–8.

Howard, L. N. 1972: Bounds on flow quantities. *Ann. Rev. Fluid. Mech.*, 4, 473–94.

Kennedy, J. F. 1963: The mechanics of dunes and antidunes in erodible bed channels. *J. Fluid Mech.*, 16, 521–44.

Leopold, L. B., Wolman, M. G. and Miller, J. P. 1964: *Fluvial Processes in Geomorphology*. San Francisco: W. H. Freeman.

Nicolis, G. and Prigogine, I. 1977: *Self-organisation in Non-equilibrium Systems*. New York: Wiley.

Parker, G. 1976: On the cause and characteristic scales of meandering and braiding rivers. *J. Fluid. Mech.*, 76, 457–80.

Parker, G., Sawai, K. and Ikeda, S. 1982: Bend theory of river meanders; Part 2, nonlinear development of finite amplitude bends. *J. Fluid Mech.*, 115, 303–14.

Pickup, G. and Warner, R. F. 1976: Effects of hydrologic regime on magnitude and frequency of dominant discharge. *J. Hydrol.*, 29, 51–75.

Richards, K. 1982: *Rivers: Form and Process in Alluvial Channels*. London: Methuen.

Song, C. C. S. and Yang, C. T. 1982: Minimum energy and energy dissipation rate. *J. Hydraul. Div., ASCE*, 108, 690–706.

Vittal, N., Ranga Raju, K. G. and Garde, R. J. 1977: Resistance of two dimensional triangular roughness. *J. Hydraul. Res.*, 15, 19–36.

Williams, P. B. and Kemp, P. H. 1971: Initiation of ripples on flat sediment beds. *J. Hydraul. Div., ASCE*, 97, 505–22.

Wolman, M. G. and Miller, J. P. 1960: Magnitude and frequency of forces in geomorphic processes. *J. Geol.*, 68, 54–74.

Yalin, M. S. 1977: *Mechanics of Sediment Transport*, 2nd edition. Oxford: Pergamon.

Yang, C. T. 1971: Potential energy and stream morphology. *Water Resour. Res.*, 7, 312–22.

Yang, C. T. and Song, C. C. S. 1984: Comment on 'Extremal hypotheses for river behaviour', *Water Resour. Res.*, 20, 738–40.

Yang, C. T., Song, C. C. S. and Woldenberg, M. J. 1981: Hydraulic geometry and minimum rate of energy dissipation. *Water Resour. Res.*, 17, 1014–8.

Zanke, U. 1978: Zusammenhänge zwischen Strömung und Sedimenttransport, Teil 2. *Mitt., Franzius-Institut, Univ. Hannover*, 48.

10

Small- and Medium-scale Bedforms in Gravel-bed Rivers

Pamela S. Naden and Andrew C. Brayshaw

INTRODUCTION

Gravel bedforms, other than large-scale channel bars, have received relatively little attention in the literature on gravel-bed rivers. This would seem to stem from the problems of recognition and definition of distinct bedform features in highly variable sediments of large size. Here, bedforms are often of the same order of magnitude as individual grains and the detailed surveys required to identify them are lacking. Experimental data are also limited in so far as few flume channels are capable of transporting particles greater than 30 mm in diameter. However, increased awareness of the relation between bed topography and sediment transport and of the important influence of the protrusion of individual grains on transport thresholds (Fenton and Abbott, 1977) has focused attention on a number of small- and medium-scale features.

The smaller bedforms, or microtopography, can be conveniently classed as cluster bedforms. These consist of groups of interlocking clasts formed around exceptionally large bed particles and standing slightly above an otherwise planar gravel bed. The principle components of clusters have been shown to be an *obstacle clast*, around which is developed an upstream *stoss* deposit and a downstream *wake* deposit (figure 10.1). Such bedforms have been widely recognized in poorly sorted gravel-bed channels with differing clast lithologies (Dal Cin, 1968; Teisseyre, 1977; Brayshaw, 1983) and include imbricate clusters (Rust, 1972; Martini, 1977), boulder shadows (Laronne and Carson, 1976) and current shadows (Gustavson, 1974). The obstacle particle forms the nucleus of a cluster and stoss-side clasts are often tightly interlocked against the obstacle and so prevented from movement. Grains which comprise wake accumulations are shielded from the flow by being trapped in the separation zone downstream from the obstacle (figure 10.2). Typical dimensions of clusters are given in

Figure 10.1 Cluster bedforms showing upstream stoss deposits and downstream wake deposits. Flow direction is from left to right

table 10.1. Their wavelengths fall between 8 and 11 times the median grain size and are closely related to the size of the obstacle clast (figure 10.3). They may occupy as much as ten per cent of the channel floor and seriously limit the availability and mobility of particles during phases of transportation.

In addition to these cluster bedforms, recent experiments on coarse-grained sediment (Whittaker and Jaeggi, 1982; Bathurst et al., 1982) have highlighted a second set of bedforms associated with steep upland channels in which flow depths are of the same order as the grain size. These bedforms include antidunes

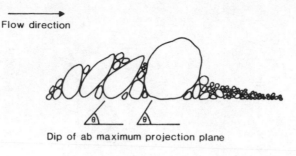

a

Flow direction

Dip of ab maximum projection plane

b

Direction of depositing current

Orientation of bedform

Figure 10.2 Diagrammatic representation of cluster bedforms (a) in section; (b) in plan

(Shaw and Kellerhals, 1977; Bathurst et al., 1982), transverse ribs (Koster, 1978; McDonald and Day, 1978) and step-pool systems (Whittaker and Jaeggi, 1982); and others are discussed by Bluck in chapter 7, this volume. These larger-scale features are typified by the measurements reported in table 10.2. The roughness elements reported by Thompson and Campbell (1979) are included to show the comparison with small-scale bedforms. The bedforms observed are strongly related to the intensity of sediment transport (Bathurst et al., 1982; Ikeda, 1983) and show a greater consistency in the relation of wavelength to flow depth rather than to grain size. Froude number criteria (Kennedy, 1963; Reynolds, 1965; Parker, 1976) provide some basis for the identification of such bedforms but not for their sediment transport associations.

Table 10.1 Typical dimensions of cluster bedforms

	Wye (mm)	Widdale Beck (mm)	Turkey Brook (mm)
Median grain diameter	22.6	52.0	14.9
B axis of obstacle clast	103.1	114.0	56.7
Bedform length	245.4	480.8	132.5
Wake length	170.9	231.3	91.9
Stoss length	145.7	153.4	35.3

Mean values given in mm

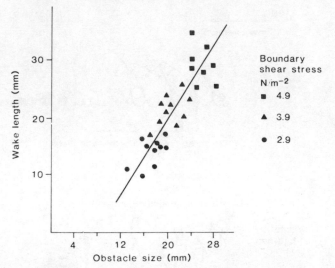

Figure 10.3   Data from flume experiments showing the relation of wake length to size of obstacle clast

This chapter presents two contrasting aspects of gravel bedforms. First, it discusses the formation of bedforms in gravel and describes an extension of Langbein and Leopold's (1968) kinematic wave model as applied to small- and medium-scale bedforms. Second, it looks in more detail at the category of cluster bedforms, with particular emphasis on their effect on initial sediment movement as shown by a comparison of field measurements with calculations based on existing threshold formulae.

FORMATION OF GRAVEL BEDFORMS

In the case of both the cluster bedforms and meso-scale forms described above, two observations stand out – first, that bedforms are generated by the sediment transport process, and second, that the arrangement of individual grains on the bed is of fundamental importance. One way of investigating the formation of such bedforms is by means of a simple queueing model. This idea was first introduced by Langbein and Leopold (1968) in the context of gravel bars and sand dunes but was never followed up. In essence, queueing theory states that the length of a queue is related to the traffic intensity or ratio of the probabilities of arrival at and departure from the queue. In Langbein and Leopold's original model, the probability of arrival was the same as the probability of departure and traffic intensity was therefore equal to one. In this case, infinitely long queues are possible but no equilibrium solution. With traffic intensities of less

Table 10.2 Typical dimensions of medium-scale bedforms

	Median grain size (mm)	Bedform length (mm)	$\frac{\lambda}{D_{50}}$	$\frac{\lambda}{Y}$	Froude no.	$\frac{Y}{D_{50}}$
Roughness elements[1]	486	3183	7.0	2.67	0.72	2.2
Reach No. 5[1]	270	4900	18.2	4.50	0.97	4.0
Antidunes[2]	8	403	50.4	7.14	1.08	7.4
Antidunes[3]	15	406	27.1	5.17	1.30	5.7
Step-pool systems[3]	15	233	15.8	4.16	0.56	4.7

λ Is bedform wavelength, D_{50} is median grain diameter, Y is total flow depth
Sources 1 Thompson and Campbell (1969), 2 Shaw & Kellerhals (1977), 3 Whittaker and Jaeggi (1982).

than one, Wilson and Kirkby (1980) show that the probabilities of different queue lengths are given by

$$p(n) = (1 - \alpha)\alpha^n \qquad (10.1)$$

where p(n) is the probability of a queue of length n, and α is the traffic intensity. Mean queue lengths for different values of traffic intensity are given together with the probability distributions in figure 10.4.

Now, if a bedform is seen as a queue of particles within the sediment transport process, then it is clear that the size of bedforms is related to the ratio of the probabilities of deposition and erosion of particles. Furthermore, if these probabilities could be generated by physically-based criteria of erosion, particle movement and deposition, as related to river flow and grain geometry, then some progress could be made towards formulating an explicit link between sediment transport and bedform generation.

Simulation model

One method of setting up such a queueing model is by using computer simulation techniques. A particular implementation, described in detail in Naden (1985), is outlined below and compared with recently published flume data. Two major simplifications have been assumed – the model operates in only two dimensions (vertical and downstream), and just two sizes of spherical grain, one twice the diameter of the other, have been used to represent the range of grain sizes. These grains are arranged in a two-dimensional grid as shown in figure 10.5. Although the grid and the grain sizes limit the variety of geometrical arrangements of the grains, there are some 36 different mobile combinations of grains and this range is thought adequate to represent bed microtopography. It can be illustrated

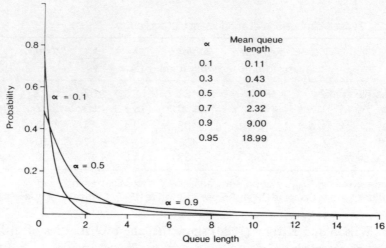

Figure 10.4 Queue length probabilities and mean queue lengths for different levels of traffic intensity

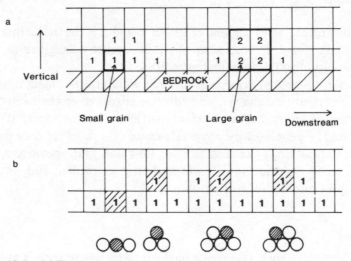

Figure 10.5 (a) Representation of grains in a two-dimensional computer simulation model; (b) The four basic geometries for a single grain size and their grid representations (shading indicates the grain under consideration)

in the single-grain case by the four basic geometries and their grid representations shown in figure 10.5b. In addition, grains below the average level of the bed and those whose tangents to adjacent grains intersect above the bed are considered to be immobile.

Sediment movement is envisaged as a grain-by-grain process of grain jumps, with sliding or rolling movements, which are relatively rare except at extremely low transport stages (Francis, 1973), being represented by the lowest saltation trajectories (height less than one grain diameter). In terms of the queueing nomenclature used above, the probability of arrival of grains at a bedform will depend on the sediment supply from upstream – that is, in the absence of extraneous sources of sediment, on the probability of erosion upstream, the length of the grain trajectory and the number of intervening opportunities for deposition prior to arrival. This effectively puts a limit on the spacing of bedforms. The probability of deposition (i.e. joining the queue on arrival) will depend on the grain diameter, the local bed shear velocity and the contact which the grain makes with the bed. In turn, the probability of erosion is a function of the local bed shear velocity, grain diameter, average bed slope and the protrusion of the grain from the bed. So long as the rate at which grains arrive at a bedform is less than the rate at which they leave, equilibrium bedform sizes in line with the flow conditions will be generated.

Table 10.3 summarizes the relationships which have been used to derive the relevant probabilities and generate the bedforms. Use of a water-surface profile-fitting technique such as that described by Richards (1978), which adjusts the flow according to the bed topography but not for a frictional effect over and above that of the grains, and the assumption of a simple logarithmic velocity profile, allow the model to be run using just four parameters – discharge per unit width, average bed slope, median grain size and percentage of small grains. The stochastic element of the model is incorporated by considering the turbulent fluctuations in near-bed velocity as derived from an analysis of McQuivey's (1973) data. This is considered in detail by Naden (1987). A simplified flow diagram outlining the sequence of calculations performed in the model is given in figure 10.6.

Table 10.3 Summary of grain movement equations used in model

Description	Equation	Derivation
Particle trajectories	$H_{max}/D = 0.43u_*^2D[(\varrho_s - \varrho)/\varrho] + 0.663$ $L/D = 10H/D - 3.5 + 0.01m\bar{U}/D$	Abbott and Francis (1977)
Grain speed	$\bar{U}/V_g = 11.8u_*/V_g - 0.44$	Francis (1973)
Deposition criterion	$\bar{U} < \sqrt{[(\varrho_s - \varrho)gD/\varrho_s]}\ \sin\theta/\sin(\theta - \epsilon)$	Gordon et al. (1972)
Erosion threshold	$F_D + G\sin\beta = (G\cos\beta - F_L)\tan\phi$	Naden (1987)

H_{max} is maximum height of grain trajectory (m), D is grain diameter (m), L is length of grain trajectory (m), u_* is bed shear velocity (ms⁻¹), ϱ_s is density of sediment (kgm⁻³), ϱ is density of water (kgm⁻³), m is number of uplifts experienced by grain in flight, $\bar{U}$ is mean grain speed (ms⁻¹), θ is angle of impact of grain (degrees), ϵ is angle of descent of grain (degrees), V_g is settling velocity of grain (ms⁻¹), F_D is drag force on grain (N), F_L is lift force on grain (N), G is gravity force on grain (N), β is average bed slope, ϕ is friction angle of grain as modified by position in the bed (degrees).

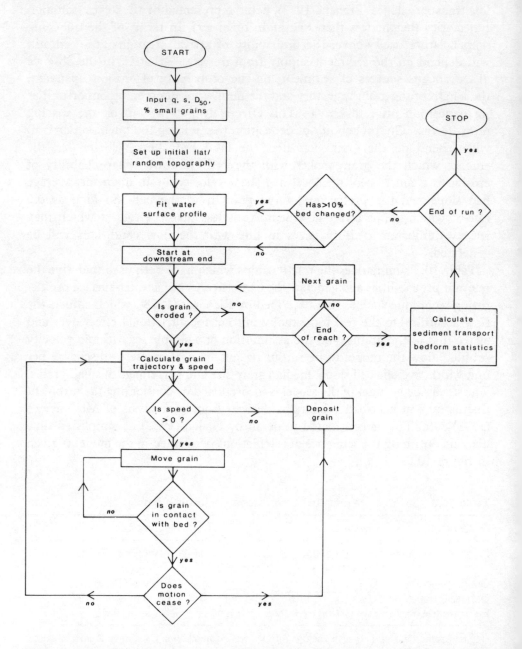

Figure 10.6 Simplified flow diagram of calculations performed in simulation of sediment transport.

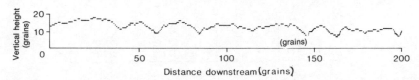

Figure 10.7 Typical model results showing various scales of bed topography

Model results

As shown in figure 10.7, the simulation produces an extremely variable bed topography in which at least two scales of bedform may be identified, with features of 5–10 grain wavelengths superimposed on other forms whose wavelength is up to 30–40 grains.

Simple geometry (figure 10.8a) may be used to pick out the frequency distribution of cluster bedforms which give fairly constant wavelength to grain size ratios of between 7 and 12 (figure 10.8b). This is in line with the field data quoted in table 10.1. The formation of cluster bedforms limits the availability of particles for transport by reducing the number of potentially mobile grains as shown in figure 10.9. With more intense sediment movement, expressed by the product of discharge per unit width and average bed slope, some of the clusters begin to be destroyed and the number of potentially mobile grains again increases although it is still less than that found in the initial random allocation. This change in the availability of grains is in agreement with the field observations from Turkey Brook reported below. Looking at the distribution of grain geometries (figure 10.10), it is also apparent that with the development of clusters there is a tendency for the more mobile grain geometries to be eliminated. Those that remain relate to larger obstacle grains or small grains in stoss or infilled (Laronne and Carson, 1976) positions. In this particular model, grains in wake positions are classed as immobile and are only released when the obstacle grain moves. The net effect of this is for the overall probability of grain movement to be reduced and the onset of incipient motion, as described below, to be delayed.

In order to pick out the larger scales of bedform, the more sophisticated techniques of spatial autocorrelation and spectral analysis (Richards, 1976) are required. To illustrate the model results with respect to medium-scale bedforms a comparison is made between the model performance and the flume data presented by Whittaker and Jaeggi (1982). Running the model with the discharges, slopes and grain size used by Whittaker and Jaeggi, two types of periodogram are generated by the spectral analysis (figure 10.11). The first is an extremely long, low, multi-peaked periodogram in which there is no one

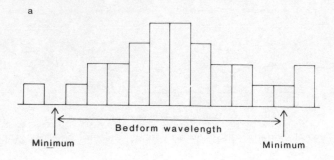

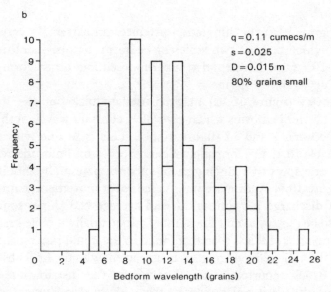

Figure 10.8   (a) Series of bed height elevations generated in the model showing the geometrical definition of cluster bedforms; (b) Distribution of cluster bedform wavelengths from a typical model run

wavelength which explains more than about two per cent of the variance in the series of bed elevations. These correspond to the cases described by Whittaker and Jaeggi as step-pool systems and presumably, also to the irregular antidunes described by Bathurst et al. (1982). The second type of periodogram reveals a much more rapid cut-off in significant frequencies and a single dominant peak which explains over 11 per cent of the variance in bed heights. This corresponds to the more regular features described as antidunes. Although there are a large number of significant frequencies in the series of bed heights (142 and 94 respectively), the frequency which explains the most variance in the data was selected and plotted, in terms of wavelength, against the mean wavelength measured in Whittaker and Jaeggi's flume experiments (figure 10.12a). This

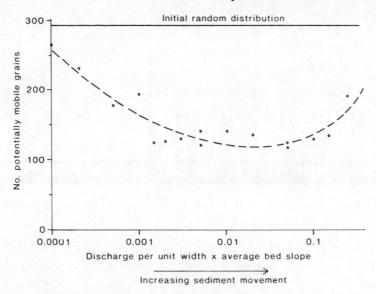

Figure 10.9 Number of potentially mobile grains following the development of cluster bedforms at increasing levels of sediment transport. Dashed line shows the trend of the relationship (fitted by eye); solid line is the number of potentially mobile grains in the initial random allocation to the grid

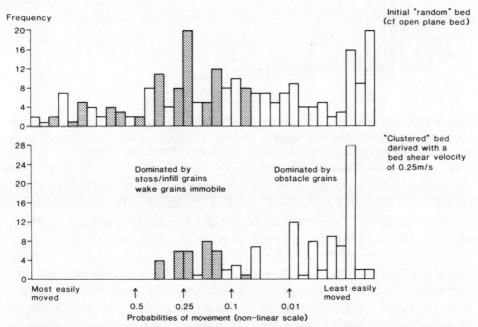

Figure 10.10 Distribution of grains between the 36 mobile geometries represented in the model for the initial allocation of grains and following the development of cluster bedforms. Shading indicates the smaller of the two grain sizes.

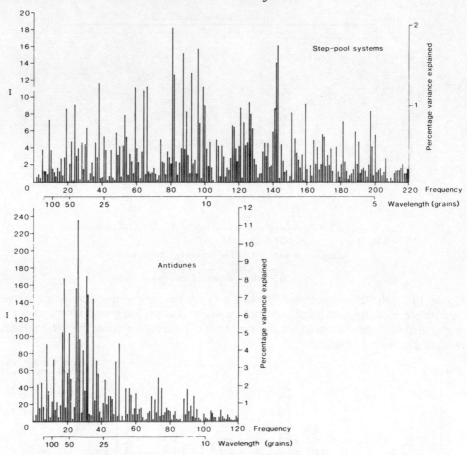

Figure 10.11 The two types of periodogram found in the analysis of bed height series. $I_k = (n/2)(a_k^2 + b_k^2)$ where a_k and b_k are cosine and sine coefficients expressing amplitude, and phase angle, of individual waves of frequency k, and n is the number of observations (1000)

shows reasonable agreement between the model and flume results with model wavelengths all falling within one standard deviation of the measured mean values. Agreement is also seen in the initial flow depth conditions as shown in figure 10.12b. These are the conditions under which most of the sediment movement occurs and the bedforms are formed. The correspondence between model results and flume data, however, breaks down in the case of final flow depths over step-pool systems (figure 10.12c) probably due to the fact that the feedback between the bedforms and the flow, via the effect of form roughness generated by the bed structure itself, is not built into the model.

While this model for generating bedforms from individual particle movements remains speculative, detailed experiments on cluster bedforms lend support

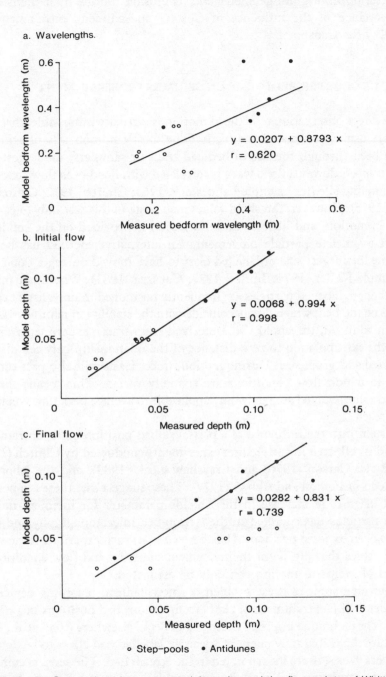

Figure 10.12 Comparison between model results and the flume data of Whittaker and Jaeggi (1982): (a) bedform wavelengths; (b) initial flow depths; (c) final flow depths

to its description of grain geometry and its erosion routine by demonstrating the importance of the influence of clusters on sediment entrainment and availability for transport.

EFFECT OF CLUSTER BEDFORMS ON SEDIMENT ENTRAINMENT

Because direct observation of bedload motion is virtually impossible, threshold values are usually estimated indirectly. The most common way of achieving this has been through the use of bedload traps or samplers; the largest-sized particle trapped during a flood wave is correlated with flood-peak flow conditions at the sampling site (for example Fahnestock, 1963; Church, 1972; Church and Gilbert, 1975). However, threshold values may relate in this case only to particles already in motion, and little or no information is provided on the conditions required to initiate particle movement. An alternative method has been to determine the largest size of labelled clast to have moved during a flood wave (for example Keller, 1970; Butler, 1977; Cavazza, 1981). Where not marked *in situ*, though, labelled particles are frequently positioned in unrealistic exposed locations on the bed, which do not coincide with the stability of naturally existing clasts. In addition, threshold values derived from tracer experiments usually rely on the extrapolation to zero distance of the relationship between distance transported and grain size. During motion, tracer clasts will also pass through a reach in which flow conditions are spatially varied. This means that the threshold values quoted are really only applicable to average peak flow conditions for the reach.

An insight into the influence of a particle's bed position on its entrainment threshold is reflected in the seeding experiments conducted by Church (1972), Laronne and Carson (1976) and Brayshaw et al. (1983), and the laboratory experiments of Fenton and Abbott (1977). These suggest that there is a possible order of magnitude increase in the Shields parameter for incipient motion, between particles incorporated in the stream-bed microtopography and those seeded in open exposed positions. Data derived from such experiments, however, yield no values that pin-point the movement of clasts, and flow conditions at the onset of incipient motion can only be estimated.

To overcome some of these problems, a new bedload recording device was used to detect the entrainment of clasts from various bed positions in a natural channel. The technique has been described in detail elsewhere (Reid et al., 1984) and enables the initial movement of specially labelled bed clasts to be detected as they pass over sensors incorporated in the stream bed. The sensors comprise balanced transmitting and receiving coils which generate an electromagnetic field. The clasts, labelled with ferruginous material, distort this field when they pass through it, producing a signal which can be recorded on a potentiometric chart recorder.

Experimental design

Two bedload sensors were installed 11 m apart in a straight, uniform reach of Turkey Brook, a flint gravel-bed stream in Enfield Chase, England. Stream width is 2.45 m, mean channel slope varies from 0.006 to 0.008, and water depth at bankfull flow is 0.8 m.

One sensor was used to investigate the displacement of particles from differing bed positions within cluster bedforms: 50 particles were seeded in the wake of obstacle clasts, on the stoss side of obstacles and in loosely clustered configurations. The movement of these particles was compared with the movement of 50 control particles from *open plane-bed* positions seeded above the second sensor. Grains in open plane-bed positions conform to particles that make up Church's (1972) 'normally loose boundary'; they can easily be removed from the bed without dislodging neighbouring grains. Care was taken when seeding labelled particles within clusters that neighbouring clasts were preserved as in the original cluster bedform. In an attempt to eliminate as many variables as possible, all seeded particles were of similar size and shape (D = 28 mm; $\psi = (c^2/ab)^{0.33} = 0.71$, where ψ is sphericity and a b and c are the long, intermediate and short axes of the grains respectively).

In acknowledging the principle aim of the experimentation – to determine the pattern of initial movement of particles as a function of the position which they occupy on the bed – tagged clasts had to be seeded as close to the sensor head as possible; signals generated by tagged particles would then indicate, as nearly as possible, first displacement. Given the need to find appropriate niches for all 50 labelled clasts, they were seeded within one metre of the sensor. Because there can be no claim that registered signals implicitly represent the precise initial movement of tagged clasts, the moment of registration must be considered to be very close to the time at which particles are first dislodged. Furthermore, in as much as visual contact with the bed was precluded by increasing turbidity at flood flow, the results provide the best estimate of incipient motion that could be achieved. In the treatment of the results, the time of registration of particles by the sensors is taken as the time at which initial motion occurred.

Critical flow velocity at the bed was calculated for all tagged particles crossing the sensors in each bedload transport event, from both control and clustered positions. Since the centroid of drag force acting on a bed clast is approximately 0.6 diameters up from the bottom of the particle (Einstein and El Samni, 1949; Egiazaroff, 1967; Helley, 1969), bed velocity was determined for 0.6 c where c is the mean length of the c axis of labelled clasts. Velocity profiles were measured for a range of water depths varying from 0.2 to 0.8 m. The data from these were used to produce a single dimensionless average velocity profile by regression:

$$\log\,(y/y_{max}) = \log\,0.00542 + (u/\bar{u})\,\log\,77.868$$

(10.2)

$$(N = 42;\ r = 0.89)$$

where y is the height above the bed (m); u is the point velocity measured at y (ms^{-1}); $\bar{u}$ is the mean velocity measured at 0.6 of the total water depth (ms^{-1}); y_{max} is the total water depth (m); N is the total number of data points; r is the Pearson product-moment correlation coefficient.

This equation was used to derive bed velocity from a single depth and velocity measurement during flood flows when velocity profile measurements were unobtainable.

Results

Examples of histograms of the shear stress at which particles from clustered and plane-bed seeding positions are registered by the sensors are shown in figure 10.13. In each flood, the mean bed velocity required to initiate the movement of particles from cluster positions is higher than for control plane-bed seeded clasts; for example, for the flood wave on 20/10/81, clustered clasts were entrained at a mean bed velocity of 0.43 ms^{-1} compared with 0.38 ms^{-1} for plane-bed seeded clasts; with ranges of 0.32–0.56 ms^{-1} and 0.30–0.47 ms^{-1} respectively.

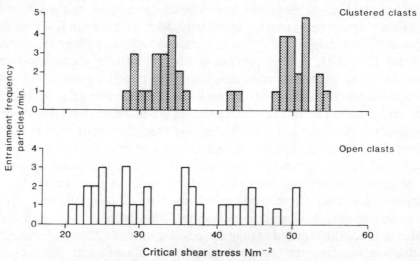

Figure 10.13 Entrainment frequency of particles from clustered and open positions, Turkey Brook, England

Where particles occur in loosely clustered groups on the bed – even if there is no direct particle-to-particle contact – their congregation ensures a corporate threshold value above that for particles of similar size and shape in open positions. The results for particles seeded in wake and stoss positions are even more convincing: entrainment of clustered clasts is delayed well beyond the entrainment of their counterparts from plane-bed positions. However, an important finding for all flood events is the substantially lower proportion of particles entrained from microtopographical bed positions compared with the control particles. These results are in line with the queueing model described above, and the reduction in potentially mobile grains with the development of cluster bedforms as shown in figure 10.9.

EVALUATION OF FORMULAE FOR THE PREDICTION OF THRESHOLD CONDITIONS

The measurements of incipient motion obtained for the experiments conducted at Turkey Brook were used to appraise a number of existing incipient motion equations. However, attention was first given to Helley's (1969) analysis of initial particle motion, since it exists in bedload transport studies as one of the few formulae which attempts to deal explicitly with the problems of coarse clast motion. Unlike many previous studies, Helley (1969) uses both laboratory and field measurements to derive an expression for predicting critical bottom velocity. The formula is particularly suited to coarse-grained sediments since, although being similar to Rubey's (1938) sixth power law, it considers both the geometry of the particle and the position which it happens to occupy on the bed. The formula takes the form:

$$u_{(0.6c)} = 1.81 \sqrt{\frac{(\gamma_s - 1) \, a \, (b+c)^2 \, MR_L}{C'_D \, ca \, MR_D + C_L \, ba \, MR_L}} \qquad (10.3)$$

where a, b, c are the long, intermediate and short axes of the particle (m); γ_s is the specific gravity of the particle; MR_L and MR_D are the lift and drag force turning arms (m); C_L is a lift coefficient; C'_D is an adjusted drag coefficient.

The computed theoretical threshold velocity for tagged clasts from open plane-bed positions is $0.24 \, ms^{-1}$. This underestimates the mean threshold velocity recorded for particles in Turkey Brook. The discrepancy can be explained by reference to the method by which Helley derived the lift and drag coefficients and the orientation angle, which affects the turning arms, of an idealized particle resting in an interstice on the bed: these are determined, like many foregoing formulae, for a particle resting in a fully exposed position on top of the bed – considerably more exposed than the position in which tagged particles were seeded or, indeed, particles are found naturally.

For particles on a natural river bed, considerable modifications to Helley's C_D, C_L and orientation angle are necessary so as to depict more accurately how individual particles are seated in the highly complex floor of gravel-bed rivers. If we consider, for example, the parameter C_D, Helley determines this for a free-falling body of similar shape to a bed particle. Yet the resulting magnitude of drag coefficients predicted for particles incorporated within the microtopography of natural stream beds has been shown to vary with the position of the particle. Thus, for example, a solitary hemisphere on the bed has a drag coefficient of 0.42 whereas a similar hemisphere located one particle diameter downstream, and therefore in the wake, has a drag coefficient of only 0.08; and a hemisphere located two particle diameters downstream still has a reduced drag coefficient of 0.29 (Brayshaw et al., 1983). The variation in Helley's theoretical threshold with the drag coefficient is shown in figure 10.14. This graph suggests that the critical bed velocity needed to move a particle may be as much as ten per cent greater than that predicted by Helley due to the position of the particle in the bed.

It is clear that greater bottom velocities will be required in order to entrain particles with lower drag coefficients, such as those occupying wake positions in which they hide behind neighbouring clasts. Even where particles are more exposed to the flow and benefit from higher drag coefficients, interlock with a downstream juxtaposed grain may hinder their incipient motion. The net effect of mutual interference between neighbouring particles in gravel-bed rivers is, therefore, to delay incipient motion.

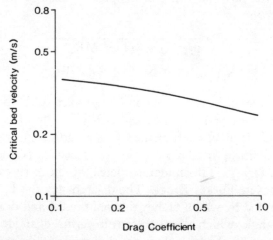

Figure 10.14   Effect of drag coefficient on Helley's (1969) theoretical threshold bed velocity (logarithmic scales)

Table 10.4 Computed critical velocity and critical shear stress of particle entrainment against mean measured values for open and clustered particles in Turkey Brook

Source	Formula	Computed u_{cr} (ms^{-1})	Computed τ_{cr} (Nm^{-2})
Forchheimer (1914)	$u_{cr} = 4\sqrt{D}$	0.72	
Schoklitsch (1934)	$\tau_{cr} = 0.076\,(\varrho_s - \varrho)Dg$		39.6
Mavis et al. (1937)	$u_{cr} = 3.28\,D^{0.44}\,\sqrt{(\varrho_s - \varrho)/\varrho}$	0.92	
Leliavsky (1955)	$\tau_{cr} = 166\,Dg$		52.4
Helley (1969)	$u_{cr} = 1.81\,\sqrt{\dfrac{(\gamma_s - 1)a(b+c)^2 MR_L}{C'_D caMR_D + C_L baMR_L}}$	0.24	
This study			
Open plane-bed seeded		0.38	20.2
Cluster seeded		0.43	22.5

u_{cr} is critical bed velocity (ms^{-1}), τ_{cr} is critical bed shear stress (Nm^{-2}), D is grain diameter (m), g is acceleration due to gravity (ms^{-2}), ϱ_s is particle density (kgm^{-3}), ϱ is water density (kgm^{-3}), a,b,c are the long, medium and short axes of the particle (m), γ_s is the specific gravity of the particle, MR_L and MR_D are the lift and drag force turning arms (m), C_L is a lift coefficient, C'_D is an adjusted drag coefficient
Equations are converted into SI units

The recorded threshold conditions at which particles were moved from cluster and plane-bed positions were also compared with a number of additional critical velocity and tractive force formulae (table 10.4). An interesting finding is that in contrast to Helley's predicted value, formulae developed by Forchheimer (1914), and Mavis et al. (1937), using near-bed, time-averaged velocities, both predict critical threshold conditions greater than those recorded for tagged particles in Turkey Brook. Similarly, formulae suggested by Schoklitsch (1934) and Leliavsky (1955) predict an average critical tractive force for initial motion greater than that measured for tagged particles. This is thought to be due to the fact that, in addition to the bed conditions, the magnitude of velocity, pressure and turbulent eddy fluctuations (Brayshaw et al., 1983) also vary considerably in coarse-grained channels. Micro-relief features, such as particle clusters protruding into the flow, control the shedding of wake eddies and hence influence the critical tractive force for surrounding stream-bed particles. Thus, it is apparent that whilst threshold equations can make reasonable estimates of the critical condition for particles of like size and shape on experimental beds, their applicability for coarse-grained particles on natural stream beds still remains very limited.

CONCLUSION

This chapter has discussed the range of bedforms of small and medium scale found in gravel-bed rivers. Whereas the overall emphasis is on the intimate association between bedforms and sediment transport, two contrasting approaches to this topic have been presented.

A simple queueing model, based on individual particle movements, has been used to investigate the formation of gravel bedforms. In a computer simulation, both cluster bedforms and medium-scale features such as step-pool systems and antidunes found in steep, shallow channels, are generated. The effect of cluster bedforms in limiting the availability and mobility of sediment is also demonstrated.

In agreement with this, the field example has highlighted the importance of the position of a particle on the bed in determining its exposure to the flow and the fluid forces it experiences. The entrainment threshold of particles has been shown to vary according to their position relative to neighbouring grains. As in similar comparative studies (for example Chien, 1954), little agreement is found between formulae aimed at predicting threshold conditions for incipient motion.

ACKNOWLEDGEMENTS

The work by PSN was begun while financed by a Leeds University Scholarship; while the work by ACB was carried out under the tenure of a NERC research studentship at Birkbeck College, University of London, under the supervision of Ian Reid and Lynne Frostick.

REFERENCES

Abbott, J. E. and Francis, J. R. D. 1977: Saltation and suspension trajectories of solid grains in a water stream. *Philosophical Transactions of the Royal Society of London*, 284A, 225-54.
Bathurst, J. C., Graf, W. H. and Cao, H. H. 1982: Bedforms and flow resistance in steep gravel-bed channels. In B. Mutlu Sumer and A. Muller, (eds), *Mechanics of Sediment Transport*, Rotterdam: A. A. Balkema, 215-21.

Brayshaw, A. C. 1983: *Bed Microtopography and Bedload Transport in Coarse-grained Alluvial Channels*. Unpublished PhD thesis, University of London.

Brayshaw, A. C., Frostick, L. E. and Reid, I. 1983: The hydrodynamics of particle clusters and sediment entrainment in coarse alluvial channels. *Sedimentology*, 30, 137–43.

Butler, P. R. 1977: Movement of cobbles in a gravel-bed stream during a flood season, *Bulletin of the Geological Society of America*, 88, 1072–4.

Cavazza, S. 1981: Experimental investigations on the initiation of bedload transport in gravel rivers. In *Erosion and sediment transport measurement, Proceedings of the Florence Symposium, June 1981*, International Association of Hydrological Sciences Publication, 33, 53–61.

Chien, N. 1954: The present status of research on sediment transport. *Journal of the Hydraulics Division, American Society of Civil Engineers*, 80.

Church, M. 1972: Baffin Island Sandurs. *Bulletin of the Geological Survey of Canada*, 216.

Church, M. and Gilbert, R. 1975: Proglacial fluvial and lacustrine environments. In A. V. Jopling and B. C. McDonald (eds), *Glaciofluvial and Glaciolacustrine Sedimentation*, Society of Economic Paleontologists and Mineralogists Special Publication, 23, 22–100.

Dal Cin, R. 1968: Pebble clusters: their origin and utilization in the study of paleocurrents. *Sedimentary Geology*, 2, 233–41.

Egiazaroff, I. V. 1967: Sediment transportation mechanics – initiation of motion. *Journal of the Hydraulics Division, American Society of Civil Engineers*, 93, 281–7.

Einstein, H. A. and El-Samni, E. A. 1949: Hydrodynamic forces on a rough wall. *Reviews of Modern Physics*, 21, 520–4.

Fahnestock, R. K. 1963: Morphology and hydrology of a glacial stream – White River, Mount Rainier, Washington, *US Geological Survey Professional Paper*, 422-A.

Fenton, J. D. and Abbott, J. E. 1977: Initial movement of grains on a stream bed: the effect of relative protrusion. *Proceedings of the Royal Society of London*, 352A, 523–37.

Forchheimer, P. 1914: *Hydraulick*. Leipzig: Teuber.

Francis, J. R. D. 1973: Experiments on the motion of solitary grains along the bed of a water stream. *Proceedings of the Royal Society of London*, 332A, 443–71.

Gordon, R., Carmichael, J. B. and Isackson, F. J. 1972: Saltation of plastic balls in a 'one-dimensional' flume. *Water Resources Research*, 8, 444–59.

Gustavson, T. C. 1974: Sedimentation on gravel outwash fans, Malaspina Glacier Foreland, Alaska. *Journal of Sedimentary Petrology*, 44, 374–89.

Helley, E. J. 1969: Field measurement of the initiation of large bed particle motion in Blue Creek, near Klamath, California. *US Geological Survey Professional Paper*, 562-G.

Ikeda, H. 1983: Experiments on bedload transport, bed forms, and sedimentary structures using fine gravel in the 4-meter-wide flume. *Environmental Research Centre Paper, University of Tsukuba, Iboraki, Japan*, 2.

Keller, E. A. 1970: Bedload movement experiments: Dry Creek, California. *Journal of Sedimentary Petrology*, 40, 1339–44.

Kennedy, J. F. 1963: The mechanics of dunes and antidunes in erodible-bed channels. *Journal of Fluid Mechanics*, 16, 521–44.

Koster, E. H. 1978: Transverse ribs: their characteristics, origin and paleohydraulic significance. In A. D. Miall (ed.), *Fluvial Sedimentology*, Canadian Society of Petroleum Geologists Memoir, 5, 161–86.

Langbein, W. B. and Leopold, L. B. 1968: River channel bars and dunes – theory of kinematic waves. *US Geological Survey Professional Paper*, 422-L.

Laronne, J. B. and Carson, M. A. 1976: Inter-relationships between bed morphology and bed material transport for a small gravel-bed channel. *Sedimentology*, 23, 67–86.

Leliavsky, S. 1955: *An Introduction to Fluvial Hydraulics*. London: Constable.

Martini, I. P. 1977: Gravelly flood deposits of Irvine Creek, Ontario, Canada. *Sedimentology*, 24, 603–23.

Mavis, F. T., Liu, T. and Soucek, E. 1937: The transportation of detritus by flowing water II. *Studies in Engineering, University of Iowa*, 341.

McDonald, B. C. and Day, T. J. 1978: An experimental flume study on the formation of transverse ribs. *Geological Survey of Canada Paper*, 78-1A, 441–51.

McQuivey, R. S. 1973: Summary of turbulence data from rivers, conveyance channels and laboratory flumes. *US Geological Survey Professional Paper*, 802-B.

Naden, P. S. 1985: *Gravel bedforms – the development of a sediment transport model*. Unpublished PhD thesis, University of Leeds.

Naden, P. S. 1987: An erosion criterion for gravel-bed rivers. *Earth Surface Processes and Landforms*, 12, 83–93.

Neill, C. R. 1967: Mean velocity criterion for scour of coarse uniform bed material. In *International Association of Hydraulics Research, 12th Congress*, Fort Collins, Co.

Parker, G. 1976: On the cause and characteristic scales of meandering and braiding in rivers. *Journal of Fluid Mechanics*, 76, 457–80.

Reid, I., Brayshaw, A. C. and Frostick, L. E. 1984: An electromagnetic device for automatic detection of bedload motion and its field applications. *Sedimentology*, 31, 269–76.

Reynolds, A. J. 1965: Waves on the erodible bed of an open channel. *Journal of Fluid Mechanics*, 22, 113–33.

Richards, K. S. 1976: The morphology of riffle-pool sequences. *Earth Surface Processes*, 1, 71–88.

Richards, K. S. 1978: Simulation of flow geometry in a riffle-pool stream, *Earth Surface Processes*,3, 345–54.

Rubey, W. W. 1938: The flow required to move particles on a stream bed, *US Geological Survey Professional Paper*, 189-E.

Rust, B. 1972: Pebble orientation in fluvial sediments. *Journal of Sedimentary Petrology*, 42, 384–8.

Schoklitsch, A. 1934: Geschiebetrieb und die Geschiebefracht. *Wasserkraft und Wasserwirtsch*, 39.

Shaw, J. and Kellerhals, R. 1977: Paleohydraulic interpretation of antidune bedforms with applications to antidunes in gravel. *Journal of Sedimentary Petrology*, 47, 257–66.

Teisseyre, A. K. 1977: Pebble clusters as a directional structure in fluvial gravels: modern and ancient examples. *Geologia Sudetica*, 12, 79–92.

Thompson, S. M. and Campbell, P. L. 1979: Hydraulics of a large channel paved with boulders. *Journal of Hydraulics Research*, 17, 341–54.

Whittaker, J. G. and Jaeggi, M. N. R. 1982: Origin of step-pool systems in mountain streams. *Journal of Hydraulics Division, American Society of Civil Engineers*, 108, 758–73.

Wilson, A. G. and Kirkby, M. J. 1980: *Mathematics for Geographers and Planners*. Oxford: Clarendon Press.

11

Measuring and Modelling Bedload Transport in Channels with Coarse Bed Materials

James C. Bathurst

INTRODUCTION

Historically, most research into sediment transport processes has concentrated on the sand- and silt-bed rivers typical of lowland areas. Only relatively recently, in response to development pressures throughout the world's mountain regions, has a comparable degree of interest been shown in the gravel- and boulder-bed rivers of more upland areas. As this interest has developed, though, it has become clear that standard techniques for modelling and measuring bedload transport in sand-bed channels are not always directly applicable to channels with coarse bed materials. Two extra factors in particular have to be considered.

1 *The wide range of sediment sizes.* Whereas a sand sediment encompasses a size range of only a few millimetres, coarse bed materials may include a range from sand to gravels, cobbles and boulders up to a metre or more in diameter. Sediment transport is then influenced by bed armouring and packing effects which may normally be neglected in sand-bed channels. Partial bedload transport may also occur, with some of the sizes in motion and others stationary. Unlike the case for sand-bed rivers there may be long periods of insignificant bedload transport, especially in the seasonal, snowmelt regimes typical of many mountain environments. Mathematical prediction of bedload transport must therefore take into account the size distribution of sediment to a greater degree than is necessary with sand-bed channels.

2 *Temporally- and spatially-variable sediment sources.* The upland areas in which gravel- and boulder-bed channels are found are also the source areas for supply

of sediment to the channels. Since the supply events (such as landslides and bank collapses) are non-uniform and episodic, the in-channel sediment transport also tends to be non-uniform, unsteady and characterized by hysteresis loops. Bedload transport calculations must therefore allow for both hydraulic and geomorphological factors, whereas equations developed for sand-bed rivers generally consider only hydraulic factors.

This review examines the effects of size distribution and supply on bedload transport and the consequences for modelling of transport rates. Discussion is limited to channels with a high proportion of coarse bed material (gravel, cobbles and boulders). However, sediment size distributions in such channels are often bimodal and allowance is therefore made for the significant contribution which sand and fine gravel can make to the bedload. Some of the points are illustrated with data collected from the Roaring River, a boulder-bed river with a snowmelt regime in the Rocky Mountains, Colorado, USA. Further details of this study are reported by Bathurst et al. (1986). The chapter begins with a brief summary of some of the more commonly used methods for collecting field data.

MEASURING TECHNIQUES

Bedload transport studies tend to be empirically based and therefore require field data on transport and bed-material characteristics. Available measuring techniques, though, tend to be designed for either the coarse (gravel) or the fine (sand) end of the sediment size range and not for mixtures. There are particular difficulties, therefore, in sampling bed materials and bedloads which are composed of constantly varying proportions of sand, gravel and boulders. Further, while the sand fraction may move as bedload under some flow conditions, it can move as suspended load under others. No standard measuring techniques have yet been agreed upon for gravel- and boulder-bed channels but both fixed structures and portable equipment are used.

Fixed structures for bedload transport

The simplest bedload trap consists of a pit excavated in the channel bed. This collects the total volume of bedload moved during a given period, such as a storm, and provides gross yields rather than instantaneous transport rates (e.g. Newson, 1980). The similar monitoring of bedload yields in mountain rivers through the operation of sediment diversion structures is described by Lauffer and Sommer (1982).

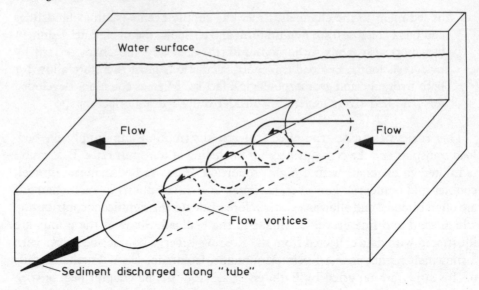

Figure 11.1 Design of a vortex tube bedload sampler
(adapted from Hayward and Sutherland, 1974)

A more sophisticated device, the vortex tube sampler, provides instantaneous transport rates. A circular tube, open at the top, is set into the bed and angled diagonally across the channel (figure 11.1). The bedload falls into this and is carried along the tube by a vortex action induced by the flow of water across the top of the tube. It is then discharged into an adjacent work area for sampling. Examples are described by Hayward and Sutherland (1974), O'Leary and Beschta (1981), Klingeman and Emmett (1982) and Tacconi and Billi (1987).

Movement of individual gravel clasts can be monitored with an electromagnetic bedload sensor. The sensor, laid across the bed of the channel, acts in the same way as a conventional metal detector. It thus registers the passage of clasts which are susceptible to magnetism. Such susceptibility may be natural (Ergenzinger and Custer, 1983), enhanced by heat treatment (Arkell et al., 1983) or introduced artificially (Reid et al., 1984). The sensor is particularly useful for studying the critical conditions for initiation of bedload transport (Reid and Frostick, 1984).

Portable equipment for bedload transport

Increasing attention is being paid to the pressure difference sampler designed by Helley and Smith (1971) for sampling instantaneous transport rates (figure 11.2). It can be operated from bridges and cableways in much the same way as a current meter, although practical difficulties may impede its operation at high flow. Field calibrations for sand-bed rivers are published by Emmett (1980) and tests with gravel are reported by, among others, Johnson et al. (1977), O'Leary and Beschta (1981) and Hubbell et al. (1985). With an increased bag mesh and size, the sampler can also be used satisfactorily in flows carrying particulate organic material which might otherwise clog the bag (Beschta, 1981). However, there is still no standard approach to sampling in boulder-bed channels (Bathurst et al., 1986). Not only does the unevenness of the bed prevent easy placement of the sampler on the bed but also the transport consists typically of sand and gravel moving in threads between the cobbles and boulders. This laterally non-uniform pattern complicates conversion of the measurements into an overall transport rate.

The movement of individual clasts can be monitored by marking or painting them, replacing them on the bed and then recovering them following a period of bedload transport. Again, an electromagnetic sensor, in the form of a metal detector, can be used to trace clasts with magnetic properties (Arkell et al., 1983) and by this means, clasts can be found even when buried. However, it may be necessary to allow for the variation in hydraulic conditions along the path travelled. In other words, the distance travelled by a clast is a function of changing hydraulic conditions, not just those at the starting point. Clast tracing is especially convenient for studying the interaction of the bedload with channel features, such as bends and pool/riffle systems, and storage features, such as bars. Further information on in-channel storage, as well as the amount of material supplied to the channel by bank and cliff collapses, can be obtained from surveying and photogrammetric techniques (Leeks, 1984; Bathurst, et al. 1986). Carling (chapter 13, this volume) adopts an alternative approach to the estimation of bedload transport, based on consideration of scour depth and clast velocity.

Comparison of techniques for bedload transport

Most of the above techniques are still experimental and have their own advantages and disadvantages. They may also have different sampling efficiencies for the different fractions of the bed material size distribution; for example, Hayward and Sutherland (1974) found the vortex tube to be practically 100 per cent efficient for sizes greater than about 10 mm. In a comparison of a vortex tube and a Helley-Smith sampler, O'Leary and Beschta (1981) found much the same, but for finer particles, the vortex tube was much less efficient than was the Helley-Smith sampler. On the other hand the efficiency of the latter sampler can be reduced if the bag mesh becomes clogged with fine sediment or organic matter. In addition, the maximum size which can be caught is, of course, limited by the size of the sampler's aperture. Consequently the analysis of data should consider carefully the characteristics of the field technique used in collecting

a

b

those data. This is especially true if data obtained by two different methods are to be compared. A related problem is that the existing understanding of bedload transport processes is accumulated mainly from small, single-thread rivers, because these can be sampled relatively easily. It is uncertain whether this understanding is directly applicable to the different flow conditions of large rivers, especially if they are braided, since it cannot easily be checked by sampling.

Bed material size distribution

For coarse sediments it is impracticable to apply the standard technique used for sand sediments, that of collecting and sieving large bulk samples. Very large weights of sample (of the order of hundreds or even thousands of kilograms) would be required to be representative of the bed (e.g. de Vries, 1970; Church et al., 1987). In addition, the subsurface material is usually less coarse than the surface or armour material, although both may contain the same overall range of sizes. It is therefore necessary to collect separate surface and subsurface samples.

The surface material is usually sampled on a grid basis (Wolman, 1954), although this technique may not accurately represent the finer sizes, especially for bimodal sediments. The size distribution is then analysed according to the number, rather than the weight, of clasts in each size class. Kellerhals and Bray (1971) show that this technique, applied to a surface layer one particle thick, is equivalent to bulk sieve analysis. A means of calculating the sample size required to produce a prescribed level of precision for grid sampling is presented by Hey and Thorne (1983), and Mosley and Tindale (1985) have shown that very large samples may be necessary to characterize the particle size of a cross-section with an acceptable precision, because of spatial variation with depositional environment within the section.

Sampling of the subsurface layers has not yet been standardized and a variety of techniques is available (e.g. Klingeman and Emmett, 1982). However, a method which is proving to be increasingly popular is the freeze-core technique (e.g. Everest et al., 1981; Carling and Reader, 1982).

The difficulties of sampling channel beds composed of a wide range of materials (sand, gravel and boulders), which vary spatially and with depth according to the depositional environment, and of sampling underwater, mean that different techniques are used at different sites and even at one site. Quantitative comparison

---

Figure 11.2 *(Opposite)* Examples of Helley-Smith bedload samplers: (a) cable-suspended sampler with a tail fin; (b) rod-held sampler with a box-kite tail, manufactured by Mr Andrew Smart (Llanidloes, Wales, UK) according to a design by Dr Malcolm Newson (Institute of Hydrology, UK)

of different sets of size-distribution data should therefore be made with care (Kellerhals and Bray, 1971; Church et al., 1987).

APPROACH TO MODELLING BEDLOAD TRANSPORT

Many of the existing bedload transport equations are based on studies carried out with approximately uniformly-sized sediments. In such cases it can be assumed that all the available sizes begin to move at the same critical flow conditions, and that below this critical flow, there is negligible bedload movement. Most transport equations then calculate the transport as a function of the excess of some flow quantity, such as shear stress or discharge, above the critical value (e.g. Simons and Şentürk, 1977, pp. 509–16).

Natural sediments, on the other hand, have non-uniform size distributions. Particle sizes typically lie in the ranges 1–100 mm in gravel-bed rivers and 1–1000 mm in boulder-bed rivers. The forces required to set the different size fractions of a given sediment into motion may then differ to the extent that, at a given flow, some sizes can be in motion while others are stationary. It may not therefore be possible to define a single critical flow for the initiation of movement for all the sizes. The mobility of each size fraction may have to be considered separately and the total calculated bedload transport rate be obtained by summing the individual rates calculated for each size fraction. The changing availability of different size fractions as a result of armour layer break-up and of sediment supply events from the catchment further complicates the picture. In the following, the factors affecting bedload transport and the available concepts and models for accounting for them are discussed, under the headings of initiation of transport, and transport rates.

INITIATION OF BEDLOAD TRANSPORT

The most familiar approach to the prediction of the critical conditions for bedload movement is the Shields (1936) equation

$$\frac{\tau_c}{(\varrho_s - \varrho)\, gD} = \tau_{*c} \tag{11.1}$$

where τ_c = critical shear stress; ϱ_s = sediment density; ϱ = water density; g = acceleration due to gravity; D = sediment particle median diameter; and τ_{*c} = the Shields parameter or critical dimensionless shear stress. Typically the parameter is assigned a value of 0.04–0.06 for flows with high particle Reynolds numbers, $u_{*c} \, D/v \geqslant 500$, where u_{*c}=critical shear velocity $(\tau_c/\varrho)^{1/2}$ and v=kinematic viscosity (e.g. Simons and Şentürk, 1977, p. 412). However, while this equation has achieved considerable success with uniform and fine sediments, its application to non-uniform gravels has proved more difficult. Variations in the measured value of the parameter have also been noted for steep channels where water depth is of the same order of magnitude as the sediment size.

Effect of non-uniform size distribution

Several studies have shown that for non-uniform sediments, the smaller particles are sheltered behind the larger particles and require a stronger flow to set them in motion than would be necessary for uniform sediments of the same size. Similarly, the larger particles project into the flow and can be moved by flows weaker than would be necessary for uniform sediments of the same size (White and Day, 1982; Andrews, 1983; Proffitt and Sutherland, 1983). These studies have also found that the stability of a particle depends on the position of its size within the overall size distribution, relative to a critical diameter (Egiazaroff, 1965; White and Day, 1982). Typically this critical diameter is of the order of D_{50}, that size for which 50 per cent of the particles are finer.

Andrews (1983) has quantified the effect empirically with field data, giving, for the range $0.3 < D_i/D_{50} < 4.2$

$$\tau_{*ci} = 0.0834 \left[\frac{D_i}{D_{50}} \right]^{-0.872} \tag{11.2}$$

where τ_{*ci}=the average critical Shields parameter for particles of size D_i in the surface or armour layer; i=the size fraction; and D_{50} refers to the subsurface or parent material. Typically D_{50} for the surface layer is 1.5 to 3 times D_{50} for the subsurface layer (Parker et al., 1982; Thorne and Hey, 1983). Since τ_{*ci} thus varies almost inversely with particle size, the effect of particle exposure or sheltering nearly compensates for the effect of particle size or weight on particle mobility. In other words, substitution of equation (11.2) into equation (11.1) yields approximately the same critical shear stress τ_c for all size fractions. Thus, while the smaller particles in the distribution can still be entrained by flows weaker than the flows necessary for the larger particles, the range of critical flows is relatively small.

This conclusion may not apply to boulder-bed rivers where the range of sediment sizes is very large. Data collected from the Roaring River with a Helley-Smith sampler show that there is a range of critical flows in which the maximum size in motion retains a definite dependency on the water discharge. This dependency is significant because the range of critical discharges (about 2 to

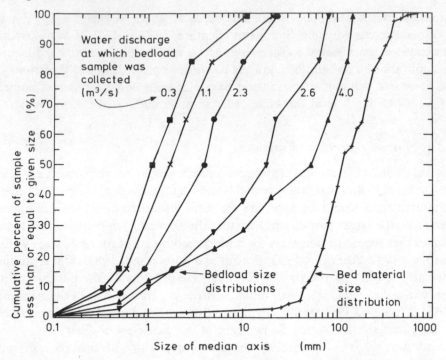

Figure 11.3 Variation of bedload size distribution with water discharge for the Roaring River, Colorado, USA, July 1984. The samples were collected with a Helley-Smith sampler and their frequency analysis was by weight. Also shown is the bed material size distribution for the same site, obtained by grid sampling with frequency analysis by number

$5 \, \text{m}^3/\text{s}$ or, in terms of discharge per unit width, about 0.33 to 0.83 m^2/s) is relatively wide compared with the total range of discharges observed in the river (typically 0.5 to 5 m^3/s or about 0.08 to 0.83 m^2/s). Only at the highest flows does the size distribution of the bedload approach that of the bed material, i.e. with all available size fractions in motion (figure 11.3). (For the bedload data in figure 11.3, it should be noted that the maximum size of particle that could be caught was 150 mm, this being the aperture of the sampler.)

The foregoing discussion of the exposure effect has most relevance to loose or unconsolidated sediments. In many cases, though, the variety of clast sizes and shapes allows the clasts to consolidate into a tightly interlocking structure during periods of negligible bedload transport (Laronne and Carson, 1976). The value of the critical Shields parameter may then be increased by a factor of three or more (Reid and Frostick, 1984; Reid et al., 1985). Conversely, on the falling stage of a flood, transport may continue to a value of the Shields parameter up to six times lower than that corresponding to initiation of motion on the rising stage. As a result of both this and of the supply of sediment during storm events, bedload transport can continue at relatively high rates for several days after a storm (e.g. Tacconi and Billi, 1987). There may also be an aftermath of relatively high transport rates in subsequent storms (Newson, 1980).

Effect of slope and large-scale roughness

Several studies have shown that the critical Shields parameter increases to values of 0.1 and higher as slope increases above about 1 per cent and the ratio of depth to sediment size decreases below about ten (Ashida and Bayazit, 1973; Bathurst et al., 1987). This may possibly arise from the effect of the larger clasts in changing the characteristic shape of the flow velocity profile. However, attempts to develop a relationship linking the Shields parameter with the ratio of depth to sediment size have so far met with only partial success (Ashida and Bayazit, 1973; Bettess, 1984).

As an alternative, the critical conditions can be calculated in terms of unit water discharge q, instead of shear stress (Schoklitsch, 1962). Using data from flumes and rivers with gravel or boulder beds and slopes in the range 0.1 to 10 per cent, Bathurst et al. (1987) found empirically that, for the bed as a whole,

$$q_{*c} = \frac{q_c}{g^{1/2} D_{16}^{3/2}} = 0.21 \ s^{-1.12} \tag{11.3}$$

where q_{*c} = dimensionless critical water discharge per unit width, defined mathematically as shown; q_c = unit critical water discharge for initiation of motion; s = slope; and D_{16} applies to the surface or armour layer of the bed. (These variables may be evaluated using any consistent set of units). This equation does not necessarily apply to all fractions of the size distribution where the distribution is wide. In other words it predicts the first movement of bedload but this may consist of the smaller particles (sand and fine gravel) while the larger material (coarse gravel, cobbles and boulders) is still stationary.

BEDLOAD TRANSPORT

General characteristics

The coarser the bed material, the greater tends to be the proportion of the total sediment load which is represented by bedload rather than suspended load. For sand-bed rivers the proportion is typically 5 to 20 per cent (Simons and Şentürk, 1977, p. 509) and similar percentages may be measured in gravel-bed rivers.

However, the proportion may rise to 10 to 50 per cent for boulder-bed mountain streams (e.g. Lauffer and Sommer, 1982; Ergenzinger and Custer, 1983; Bathurst et al., 1986). On the other hand the bedload transport is not continuous, as for sand, but is episodic. The coarser the material, the more apparent this becomes and Miller (1958) observed that, in mountain rivers, a large fraction of the bed material is immobile even at bankfull flows. Thus, for lengthy periods, bedload transport is either negligible or restricted to the finer size fractions. For bimodal sediments, such transport may consist of sand

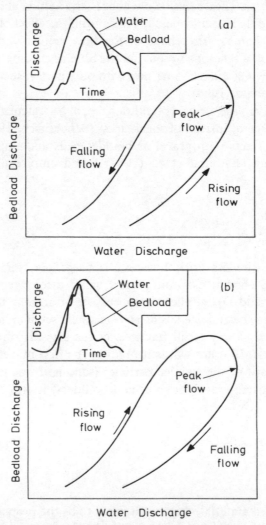

Figure 11.4 Variation of bedload transport with water discharge through a flood hydrograph: (a) where sediment becomes available during the falling limb; (b) where sediment supplies are depleted during the rising limb. Water and bedload discharge hydrographs are inset

and fine gravel moving in threads between the cobbles and boulders. This is the case for the two lowest flow discharges shown in figure 11.3.

When more general transport does occur, it is characteristically non-uniform and unsteady, as illustrated in the following examples.

1 *Variations through a flood hydrograph.* During the rising limb, transport may be inhibited by the presence of an armour layer or tightly packed surface layer. Break-up of this layer near the peak flow releases material from below the layer and allows greater transport during the falling limb of the hydrograph (e.g. Klingeman and Emmett, 1982; Reid et al., 1985). This produces the hysteresis loop shown in figure 11.4a. The opposite may occur if, instead, the rising limb is able to tap supplies of sediment which have been accumulating along the channel since the previous flood. Rapid depletion of these supplies means that transport during the falling limb is relatively low, as in figure 11.4b (VanSickle and Beschta, 1983).

2 *Seasonal and interstorm variations.* Rivers dominated by snowmelt regimes often carry relatively high bedloads in the early meltwater flows, fuelled by sediment accumulated during the winter. Depletion of the supply during the summer, though, means that the same flow in the autumn may carry rather less bedload (e.g. Østrem et al., 1971). On the other hand a snowmelt flood is likely to carry less sediment than will a rainfall flood of the same magnitude, since the latter is more heavily supplied by the erosion products of overland flow. A two-orders-of-magnitude difference in transport rates has been noted for the Roaring River, where the rain is able to erode material from cliffs of glacial moraine (figure 11.5). In general the influence of sediment supply is history-dependent and involves a complex sequence of supply, storage and transport processes (e.g. Newson, 1980; Moore and Newson, 1986).

3 *Unsteady transport.* Most sediment transport takes place under unsteady flow conditions and is therefore itself likely to be unsteady. Graf and Suszka (1985) indicate that bedload transport rates may then be increased beyond those expected for the equivalent steady flow conditions. However, even at a constant water discharge, both bedload and suspended load can fluctuate considerably, often over time intervals of a few minutes (e.g. Hayward and Sutherland, 1974; Jackson and Beschta, 1982; Klingeman and Emmett, 1982; Tacconi and Billi, 1987). Figure 11.6 shows an example for the Roaring River. The fluctuations are not caused by bedforms, such as dunes, since these are absent from gravel- and boulder-bed channels. Nor do they seem to be related to variations in the size distribution of the bedload. They may result from local armour-layer disruptions and scour and fill connected with pool/riffle systems (Jackson and Beschta, 1982) and from

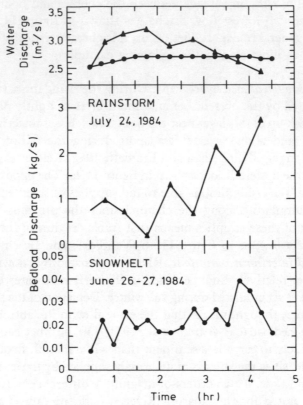

Figure 11.5 Comparison of bedload transport rates arising from rainstorm and snowmelt events with similar water discharges for the Roaring River, Colorado, USA, June–July 1984

the sporadic break-up of clusters of sediment particles (Reid and Frostick, 1984; Reid et al., 1985).

4 *In-channel storage.* Swanson et al. (1982) note that the volume of material temporarily stored in bars and along the channel is commonly more than ten times the average annual export of total particulate sediment. Thus moderate changes in storage, perhaps arising from increased channel flows caused by an altered catchment runoff response, could result in major changes in sediment yield, even if there is no change in external supply. On the other hand, in-channel storage of sediment can also delay and attenuate the movement of sediment waves resulting from external supply events.

The foregoing indicates that a given flow can carry widely-varying bedloads. The corollary to this is that the full carrying capacity of the flow is not always being satisfied. Under these conditions the prediction of bedload transport cannot

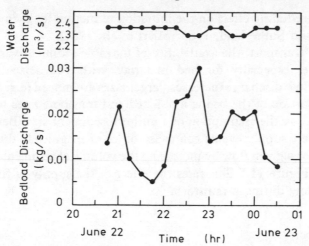

Figure 11.6 Fluctuations in the bedload transport rate for the Roaring River, Colorado, USA, June 1984

rest on the assumption that there is an unlimited supply of movable sediment but must instead take account of the availability of movable size fractions. A conceptual approach which may be appropriate to rivers with coarse bed materials is the two-phase model of transport advanced in several recent studies (Jackson and Beschta, 1982; Klingeman and Emmett, 1982; Beschta, 1987).

Phase 1 transport

Flow discharge is below the threshold for break-up of the coarse surface or armour layer and the bedload consists of the finer size fractions of the bed material (sand and fine gravel) passing over the coarser size fractions (e.g. Gomez, 1983; Lauffer and Sommer, 1982). Under these conditions the observed transport rate for the moving size fractions is not directly comparable with the rate for a uniform sediment of the same mean diameter as those size fractions moving under the same conditions. The former is always smaller than the latter because it is determined by the limited availability or proportion of those size fractions within the bed material (Çeçen and Bayazit, 1973; White and Day, 1982). Consequently, bedload transport predictions based on the assumption of a uniform sediment size will overpredict the observed rate since they assume that once any transport begins, all size fractions are in motion. For boulder-bed rivers, in which bedload transport is mostly of the phase 1 type, this overprediction can be of several orders of magnitude (Haddock, 1978; Gomez, 1983; Bathurst et al., 1987). Transport predictions must therefore involve sediment routing by size fraction (e.g. Bennett and Nordin, 1977; Borah et al., 1982), with allowance for the exposure/hiding effect on the initiation of motion for each size fraction (e.g. Proffitt and Sutherland, 1983; Misri et al., 1984).

For phase 1 transport, the availability of movable sediment varies with the flow discharge, especially for bed materials with wide size-distributions. Generally, as flow discharge increases, larger sizes are moved (e.g. figure 11.3), a greater proportion of the bed is mobilized and transport rates tend towards those predicted on the assumption of a uniform sediment size (Bathurst et al., 1987). However, supply events can cause order of magnitude fluctuations in the transport for a given flow by increasing the volume of sediment fine enough to be moved. Figure 11.5 illustrates the effect of the supply of fine sediment by overland flow during a rainstorm.

Phase 2 transport

Flow discharge exceeds the critical value for movement of the coarse surface or armour material. It is possible for all size fractions to be moved, so availability of movable sediment is theoretically unlimited. However, not necessarily all particles are actually moved and a coarse surface layer may therefore be maintained (Andrews and Parker, 1987). As a result of a subtle balance derived from the presence of the coarse surface material and from the exposure/hiding effect, there is also approximately equal mobility of all size fractions. The size distribution of the bedload is therefore similar to that of the parent or subsurface material, while still remaining finer than that of the surface layer (Çeçen and Bayazit, 1973; Parker et al., 1982; Andrews and Parker, 1987). The effect of the non-uniform size distribution is then minimal and predictions of bedload transport can be based on just one particle diameter (e.g. the D_{50} size of the parent material) rather than involve sediment routing by size fraction. Phase 2 transport is most likely to occur in rivers with a relatively restricted range of bed material sizes (1–100 mm), in which typical sediment-moving events involve flow discharges significantly in excess of the threshold discharges for initiation of bedload transport. Such rivers are generally likely to be gravel-bed, rather than boulder-bed, and to have slopes less than about 1 per cent (Bathurst et al., 1987).

Infiltration of fine sediment into the bed

As mentioned earlier, the bed material size distribution is often bimodal, with a matrix of sand and fine gravel filling the pores of the coarser gravel, cobble and boulder framework. Discussion of bedload transport would therefore not be complete without some reference to the infiltration of this finer material into the bed.

A bedload of sand and fine gravel moving over coarser material (phase 1 transport) is an obvious source of infiltrating material, although suspended material may also be important. Flume studies by Beschta and Jackson (1979) and Carling (1984), and a field study by Frostick et al. (1984), have indicated the principal mechanisms affecting the infiltration of sand into a gravel bed to be as follows:

1 transport and deposition of sand particles in the surface voids of the bed. This is determined by the relationship between the particle size and shape and the void size and by the local water turbulence.
2 settling of the particles into the deeper gravel voids, primarily under gravitational influence but assisted also by turbulent pulses. Again, the relationship between particle size and void size is important.

The upper layer of the gravel is kept relatively free of sand by the action of the main flow turbulence. Winnowing or flushing of the deeper fines can also occur as the turbulence increases at higher flows. However, this is generally limited to the near surface region (i.e. the armour layer) unless the framework gravels are set in motion. Away from the surface, therefore, clogging can occur as the fines block the voids. Frostick et al. (1984) found that rates of accumulation of the fines are higher for periods with higher peak discharges and that major floods also generate much of the sand-sized infiltrating sediment. However, prolonged or frequent periods of high flow are likely to deplete the reservoir of fines.

Milhous (1982) presents a conceptual model of the role of the gravel framework, and the surface or armour layer in particular, in controlling the release of the fine, matrix sediments to the flow. This indicates how the reservoir of fines can act as a source of material for sediment transport as the surface layer is broken up by a rising flow. Reformation of the surface layer during a falling flow, though, transforms the bed into a sediment sink.

Modelling bedload transport

The preceding sections have shown that bedload transport is non-uniform and unsteady and can fluctuate by an order of magnitude or more for given flow conditions as well as over a variety of time-scales. Most bedload transport occurs during relatively short periods of high flow and hysteresis loops characterize the pattern of transport over the rise and fall of flow discharge, both seasonally and for single events. No single rating curve relating bedload transport and flow discharge can be applied to all events (Klingeman and Emmett, 1982) and a full understanding of the relationship between flow discharge and bedload transport through time is often achieved only when day-to-day changes are studied in chronological order (Østrem et al., 1971). Such conditions pose severe difficulties for the mathematical modelling of bedload transport. Several different approaches are therefore being studied.

A deterministic approach (in which no uncertainties in prediction are admitted) is particularly suitable for modelling the effects of the non-uniform sediment size distribution on armour layer development and on bedload transport. In this approach the water and sediment are both routed along the channel according to the relevant partial differential equations of mass and momentum. Bennett and Nordin (1977) note that such models must contain three basic components:

1 *Component for routing the flow of water.* This is generally based on the St Venant equations for the conservation of mass and momentum
2 *Component for routing the flow of sediment.* This is generally based on the equation for the conservation of sediment mass.
3 *Component for keeping an account of the local channel-bed elevation and sediment size composition.* This allows for erosion, deposition, armouring and availability of different size fractions on the bed.

Techniques for solving the equations are presented by Chen (1979) and Borah et al. (1982) among others.

An important aspect of this approach is the choice of bedload transport equation. Since all available equations have an empirical element they should not be applied to flow conditions and sediments atypical of those used in their calibration. In this case it is therefore necessary to use equations which have been designed specifically for gravel- and boulder-bed rivers or have otherwise been tested with data from such rivers. The various contenders include the Ackers and White (1973) total load equation; the bedload equations of Meyer-Peter and Müller (1948), Schoklitsch (1962), Mizuyama (1977), Bagnold (1980), Smart (1984) and Parker et al. (1982) and the total load equation of Yang (1984). A test of all but the last two by Bathurst et al. (1987), for flume flows with unlimited availability of gravel sediment, found that the most accurate was the Schoklitsch equation originally tested for relatively large gravel-bed rivers in central Europe:

$$q_s = \frac{2.5}{\varrho_s / \varrho} \, s^{3/2} \, (q - q_c) \tag{11.4}$$

where q_s = unit bedload discharge; q = unit water discharge; q_c = unit critical water discharge for initiation of motion (given by equation (11.3)); and the units are SI. Where sediment size distribution effects are important, equation (11.4) would have to be solved separately for each size fraction.

Most sediment transport models consider only the hydraulic interaction of flow and bed material and few attempt to simulate the variability derived from sediment supply processes. Deterministic models can be used in this context, for example in simulating the erosion of soil particles by raindrop impact and surface runoff (e.g. Li, 1979). Other models, developed for suspended load transport, allow for the build-up of supplies during inter-storm periods and their removal during storm events as a function of the amount of sediment in storage and the details of the river flow (VanSickle and Beschta, 1983; Moore, 1984). More simply, an empirical relationship can be sought between the bedload transport and those factors thought to influence or represent the supply, such as drainage density and valley-side slope (Haddock, 1978). Generally, though, the extremely complex nature of sediment supply processes provides a considerable obstacle to the development of such models. Attempts have therefore also been made to construct stochastic models of sediment yield. The basis of these is that the sediment yield is considered to be a random variable which can be described by a probability distribution function. The processes of sediment erosion, entrainment, transport and deposition can then be described as stochastic processes, occurring through time in a manner controlled by probabilistic laws (e.g. Griffiths, 1980; Woolhiser and Renard, 1980; VanSickle, 1982).

CONCLUSIONS

Bedload transport in channels with coarse bed materials is an extremely complex process and this review has therefore highlighted only the most significant aspects. Two factors in particular are responsible for the complexity, these being the wide size-distributions of the bed materials and the supply of material from outside the channel.

Because of the wide range of particle sizes, initiation of bed material motion may not occur simultaneously for all the available size fractions. To some extent this is counterbalanced by the exposure/hiding effect in which larger sizes become easier, and smaller sizes more difficult, to move. However, prediction of initiation of motion may still have to be carried out for each size fraction in turn. Similarly, for phase 1 bedload transport, only some of the available size fractions are in motion and sediment routing must be carried out by size fraction. These conditions are typical of boulder-bed rivers with bimodal sediment size distributions, where the finer fractions (sand and fine gravel) are carried over a stationary bed of coarse gravel, cobbles and boulders. Only for phase 2 conditions, when all sizes are in motion, is it possible to predict bedload transport on the basis of a single representative percentile of the size distribution.

Supply of sediment to the channel is episodic and non-uniform and the resulting bedload transport is non-uniform, unsteady and characterized by hysteresis loops. Geomorphological as well as hydraulic processes are important and simulation of the overall supply effect may be more susceptible to the stochastic rather than the deterministic approach. Considerably more research is required into the processes of supply, storage and transport and the means of describing them mathematically.

Finally, further bedload transport data are needed to test existing equations and models and to provide information on the processes of initiation and cessation of motion and of weak transport under phase 1 conditions. This is especially so for large rivers because of their great practical significance. However, the wide variations in bed materials and bedload transport characteristics have given rise to a range of sampling techniques. These are not always compatible and care should be taken in comparing data obtained by different techniques.

ACKNOWLEDGEMENTS

The author is most grateful to Dr Robert Beschta (Oregon State University, USA), Dr Malcolm Newson and Mr Graham Leeks (Institute of Hydrology, UK) and Dr Colin Thorne (Colorado State University, USA) for their very helpful comments on this paper. The basis for the paper was provided by a literature review written by the author for the United States Department of Agriculture Tucannon River Pilot Study. He therefore acknowledges the arrangements made in this context by Dr Fred Theurer (Soil Conservation Service) and Dr Donn DeCoursey (Agricultural Research Service). The Roaring River study was supported by NATO Collaborative Research Grant 092/84 and by the United States National Park Service. The field data for July 1984 were kindly provided by Dr Colin Thorne (Colorado State University).

REFERENCES

Ackers, P. and White, W. R. 1973: Sediment transport: new approach and analysis. *J. Hydraul. Div., Am. Soc. Civ. Engrs.*, 99, 2041-60.
Andrews, E. D. 1983: Entrainment of gravel from naturally sorted riverbed material. *Geol. Soc. Am. Bull.*, 94, 1225-31.
Andrews, E. D. and Parker, G. 1987: The coarse surface layer as a response to gravel mobility. In C. R. Thorne, J. C. Bathurst and R. D. Hey (eds), *Sediment Transport in Gravel-bed Rivers*, Chichester: Wiley.
Arkell, B., Leeks, G., Newson, M. and Oldfield, F. 1983: Trapping and tracing: some recent observations of supply and transport of coarse sediment from upland Wales. *Spec. Publs. Intl. Ass. Sedimentology*, 6, 107-19.
Ashida, K. and Bayazit, M. 1973: Initiation of motion and roughness of flows in steep channels. In *Proc. 15th Congress Intl. Ass. Hydraul. Res., Istanbul, Turkey, 1*, 475-84.
Bagnold, R. A. 1980: An empirical correlation of bedload transport rates in flumes and natural rivers. *Proc. Roy. Soc. London*, A372, 453-73.

Bathurst, J. C., Graf, W. H. and Cao, H. H. 1987: Bed load discharge equations for steep mountain streams. In C. R. Thorne, J. C. Bathurst and R. D. Hey (eds), *Sediment Transport in Gravel-bed Rivers,* Chichester: Wiley.

Bathurst, J. C., Leeks, G. J. L. and Newson, M. D. 1986: Field measurements for hydraulic and geomorphological studies of sediment transport - the special problems of mountain streams. In A. C. E. Wessels (ed.), *Measuring Techniques in Hydraulic Research,* Rotterdam: A. A. Balkema 137-51.

Bennett, J. P. and Nordin, C. F. 1977: Simulation of sediment transport and armouring. *Hydrol. Sci. Bull., Intl. Ass. Hydrol. Sci.,* 22, 555-69.

Beschta, R. L. 1981: Increased bag size improves Helley-Smith bed load sampler for use in streams with high sand and organic matter transport. In *Proc. Intl. Ass. Hydrol. Sci. Symposium on Erosion and Sediment Transport Measurement, Florence, Italy,* IAHS Publ. 133, 17-25.

Beschta, R. L. 1987: Conceptual model of sediment transport in streams. In C. R. Thorne, J. C. Bathurst and R. D. Hey (eds), *Sediment Transport in Gravel-bed Rivers,* Chichester: Wiley.

Beschta, R. L. and Jackson, W. L. 1979: The intrusion of fine sediments into a stable gravel bed. *J. Fish. Res. Board. Can.,* 36, 204-10.

Bettess, R. 1984: Initiation of sediment transport in gravel streams. *Proc. Instn. Civ. Engrs.,* 77, 79-88.

Borah, D. K., Alonso, C. V. and Prasad, S. N. 1982: Routing graded sediments in streams: formulations. *J. Hydraul. Div., Am. Soc. Civ. Engrs.,* 108, 1486-503.

Carling, P. A. 1984: Deposition of fine and coarse sand in an open-work gravel bed. *Can. J. Fish. Aquat. Sci.,* 41, 263-70.

Carling, P. A. and Reader, N. A. 1982: Structure, composition and bulk properties of upland stream gravels. *Earth Surf. Processes & Landforms,* 7, 349-65.

Çeçen, K. and Bayazit, M. 1973: Critical shear stress of armored beds. In *Proc. 15th Congress Intl. Ass. Hydraul. Res., Istanbul, Turkey,* 1, 493-500.

Chen, Y. H. 1979: Water and sediment routing in rivers. In H. W. Shen (ed.), *Modeling of Rivers,* New York: Wiley, 10.1-10.97.

Church, M., McLean, D. G. and Wolcott, J. F. 1987: River bed gravels: sampling and analysis. In C. R. Thorne, J. C. Bathurst and R. D. Hey (eds), *Sediment Transport in Gravel-bed Rivers,* Chichester: Wiley.

Egiazaroff, I. V. 1965: Calculation of nonuniform sediment concentrations. *J. Hydraul. Div., Am. Soc. Civ. Engrs.,* 91, 225-47.

Emmett, W. W. 1980: A field calibration of the sediment trapping characteristics of the Helley-Smith bedload sampler. *US Geol. Survey Prof. Paper* 1139.

Ergenzinger, P. and Custer, S. 1983: First experiences measuring coarse material bedload transport with a magnetic device. In B. M. Sumer and A. Müller (eds), *Mechanics of Sediment Transport,* Rotterdam: A. A. Balkema, 223-7.

Everest, F. H., Lotspeich, F. B. and Meehan, W. R. 1981: New perspectives on sampling, analysis and interpretation of spawning gravel quality. In *Proc. American Fisheries Society Symposium on Acquisition and Utilization of Aquatic Habitat Inventory Information, Portland, Oregon,* 325-33.

Frostick, L. E., Lucas, P. M. and Reid, I. 1984: The infiltration of fine matrices into coarse-grained alluvial sediments and its implications for stratigraphical interpretation. *J. Geol. Soc. London*, 141, 955–65.

Gomez, B. 1983: Temporal variations in bedload transport rates: the effect of progressive bed armouring. *Earth Surf. Processes & Landforms*, 8, 41–54.

Graf, W. H. and Suszka, L. 1985: Unsteady flow and its effect on sediment transport. In *Proc. 21st Congress Intl. Ass. Hydraul. Res., Melbourne, Australia*.

Griffiths, G. A. 1980: Stochastic estimation of bed load yield in pool-and-riffle mountain streams. *Wat. Resour. Res.*, 16, 931–7.

Haddock, D. R. 1978: *Modeling Bedload Transport in Mountain Streams of the Colorado Front Range*. Unpublished MS thesis. Fort Collins: Colorado State University.

Hayward, J. A. and Sutherland, A. J. 1974: The Torlesse Stream vortex-tube sediment trap. *NZ. J. Hydrol.*, 13, 41–53.

Helley, E. J. and Smith, W. 1971: Development and Calibration of a Pressure-difference Bedload Sampler. Open-file Rep., US Geol. Survey, Menlo Park, California.

Hey, R. D. and Thorne, C. R. 1983: Accuracy of surface samples from gravel bed material. *J. Hydraul. Engrg., Am. Soc. Civ. Engrs.*, 109, 842–51.

Hubbell, D. W., Stevens, H. H., Skinner, J. V. and Beverage, J. P. 1985: New approach to calibrating bedload samplers. *J. Hydraul. Engrg., Am. Soc. Civ. Engrs.*, 111, 677–94.

Jackson, W. L. and Beschta, R. L. 1982: A model of two-phase bedload transport in an Oregon Coast Range stream. *Earth Surf. Process. & Landf.*, 7, 517–27.

Johnson, C. W., Engleman, R. L., Smith, J. P. and Hanson, C. L. 1977: Helley-Smith bed load samplers. *J. Hydraul. Div., Am. Soc. Civ. Engrs.*, 103, 1217–21.

Kellerhals, R. and Bray, D. I. 1971: Sampling procedures for coarse fluvial sediments. *J. Hydraul. Div., Am. Soc. Civ. Engrs.*, 97, 1165–80.

Klingeman, P. C. and Emmett, W. W. 1982: Gravel bedload transport processes. In R. D. Hey, J. C. Bathurst and C. R. Thorne (eds), *Gravel-bed Rivers*, Chichester: Wiley, 141–69.

Laronne, J. B. and Carson, M. A. 1976: Interrelationships between bed morphology and bed material transport for a small, gravel-bed channel. *Sedimentology*, 23, 67–85.

Lauffer, H. and Sommer, N. 1982: Studies on sediment transport in mountain streams of the eastern Alps. In *Proc. 14th Congress Intl. Commission on Large Dams, Rio de Janeiro, Brazil*, 431–53.

Leeks, G. J. 1984: Development of field techniques for assessment of river erosion and deposition in mid-Wales, UK. In T. P. Burt and D. E. Walling (eds), *Catchment Experiments in Fluvial Geomorphology*, Norwich: Geo Books, 299–309.

Li, R. M. 1979: Water and sediment routing from watersheds. In H. W. Shen (ed.), *Modeling of Rivers*, New York: Wiley, 9.1–9.88.

Meyer-Peter, E. and Müller, R. 1948: Formulas for bed-load transport. In *Proc. 2nd Meeting Intl. Ass. Hydraul. Structures Res., Stockholm, Sweden*, Appendix 2, 39–64.

Milhous, R. T. 1982: Effect of sediment transport and flow regulation on the ecology of gravel-bed rivers. In R. D. Hey, J. C. Bathurst and C. R. Thorne (eds), *Gravel-bed Rivers*, Chichester: Wiley, 819–42.

Miller, J. P. 1958: High mountain streams: effects of geology on channel characteristics and bed material. *State Bureau of Mines and Mineral Resources, New Mexico Institute of Mining and Technology, Socorro, New Mexico, Memoir* 4.

Misri, R. L., Garde, R. J. and Ranga Raju, K. G. 1984: Bed load transport of coarse nonuniform sediment. *J. Hydraul. Engrg., Am. Soc. Civ. Engrs.*, 110, 312–28.

Mizuyama, T. 1977: *Bedload Transport in Steep Channels*. Unpublished Doctoral thesis, Kyoto, Japan: Kyoto University.

Moore, R. J. 1984: A dynamic model of basin sediment yield. *Wat. Resour. Res.*, 20, 89–103.

Moore, R. J. and Newson, M. D. 1986: Production, storage and output of coarse upland sediments: natural and artificial influences as revealed by research catchment studies. *J. Geol. Soc. London*, 143, 921–6.

Mosley, M. P. and Tindale, D. S. 1985: Sediment variability and bed material sampling in gravel-bed rivers. *Earth Surf. Processes & Landforms*, 10, 465–82.

Newson, M. 1980: The erosion of drainage ditches and its effect on bedload yields in mid-Wales: reconnaissance case studies. *Earth Surf. Process.*, 5, 275–90.

O'Leary, S. J. and Beschta, R. L. 1981: Bedload transport in an Oregon Coast Range stream. *Wat. Resour. Bull., Am. Wat. Resour. Ass.*, 17, 886–94.

Østrem, G., Ziegler, T., Ekman, S. R., Olsen, H. C., Andersson, J. E. and Lunden, B. 1971: Slamtransportstudier i Norska glaciärälver 1970. *Forskningsrap. 12*, Naturgeografiska Institutionen, Stockholms Universitet, Stockholm, Sweden (in Swedish with English summary).

Parker, G., Klingeman, P. C. and McLean, D. G. 1982: Bedload and size distribution in paved gravel-bed streams. *J. Hydraul. Div., Am. Soc. Civ. Engrs.*, 108, 544–71.

Proffitt, G. T. and Sutherland, A. J. 1983: Transport of non-uniform sediments. *J. Hydraul. Res.*, 21, 33–43.

Reid, I. and Frostick, L. E. 1984: Particle interaction and its effect on the thresholds of initial and final bedload motion in coarse alluvial channels. In E. H. Koster and R. J. Steel (eds), *Sedimentology of Gravels and Conglomerates*, Canadian Soc. Petroleum Geologists, Memoir 10, 61–8.

Reid, I., Brayshaw, A. C. and Frostick, L. E. 1984: An electromagnetic device for automatic detection of bedload motion and its field applications. *Sedimentology*, 31, 269–76.

Reid, I., Frostick, L. E. and Layman, J. T. 1985: The incidence and nature of bedload transport during flood flows in coarse-grained alluvial channels. *Earth Surf. Processes & Landforms*, 10, 33–44.

Schoklitsch, A. 1962: *Handbuch des Wasserbaues*, 3rd edition. Vienna: Springer-Verlag.

Shields, A. 1936: Anwendung der Ähnlichkeitsmechanik und Turbulenzforschung auf die Geschiebebewegung. *Rep. 26*, Mitteil. Preuss. Versuchsanst. Wasserbau und Schiffsbau, Berlin.

Simons, D. B. and Şentürk, F. 1977: *Sediment Transport Technology*. Fort Collins, Colorado: Water Resources Publications.

Smart, G. M. 1984: Sediment transport formula for steep channels. *J. Hydraul. Engrg., Am. Soc. Civ. Engrs.*, 110, 267–76.

Swanson, F. J., Janda, R. J. and Dunne, T. 1982: Summary: sediment budget and routing studies. In F. J. Swanson, R. J. Janda, T. Dunne and D. N. Swanston (eds), *Sediment Budgets and Routing in Forested Drainage Basins*, Rep. PNW-141, US Dept. Agric., Forest Service, Pacific Northwest Forest and Range Experiment Station, 157-65.

Tacconi, P. and Billi, P. 1987: Bedload transport measurements by the vortex trap on Virginio Creek, Italy. In C. R. Thorne, J. C. Bathurst and R. D. Hey (eds), *Sediment Transport in Gravel-bed Rivers*, Chichester: Wiley.

Thorne, C. R. and Hey, R. D. 1983: Discussion of 'Bedload and size distribution in paved gravel-bed streams' by G. Parker, P. C. Klingeman and D. G. McLean. *J. Hydraul. Engrg., Am. Soc. Civ. Engrs.*, 109, 791-3.

VanSickle, J. 1982: Stochastic predictions of sediment yields from small coastal watersheds in Oregon, USA. *J. Hydrol.*, 56, 309-23.

VanSickle, J. and Beschta, R. L. 1983: Supply-based models of suspended sediment transport in streams. *Wat. Resour. Res.*, 19, 768-78.

deVries, M. 1970: On the accuracy of bed-material sampling. *J. Hydraul. Res.*, 8, 523-34.

White, W. R. and Day, T. J. 1982: Transport of graded gravel bed material. In R. D. Hey, J. C. Bathurst and C. R. Thorne (eds), *Gravel-bed Rivers*, Chichester: Wiley, 181-213.

Wolman, M. G. 1954: A method of sampling coarse river-bed material. *Trans. Am. Geophys. Union*, 35, 951-6.

Woolhiser, D. A. and Renard, K. G. 1980: Stochastic aspects of watershed sediment yield. In H. W. Shen and H. Kikkawa (eds), *Application of Stochastic Processes in Sediment Transport*, Colorado: Water Resources Publications, 3.1-3.28.

Yang, C. T. 1984: Unit stream power equation for gravel. *J. Hydraul. Engrg., Am. Soc. Civ. Engrs.*, 110, 1783-97.

12

The Classification and Characterization of Rivers

M. P. Mosley

INTRODUCTION

Classification, the process of ordering or arranging objects into groups or sets on the basis of their characteristics or relationships, is a tool which has been used in virtually all sciences, particularly in their early stages of development. It is part of the process of 'cognitive description' (Harvey, 1969, p. 78-82), which includes collection, ordering and classification of data and which provides a simple, weak form of explanation, in its broadest sense. Classification has long been a mainstay of geomorphologists (cf. Fairbridge, 1968); the process of classifying landforms implies the existence of some theory or hypothesis for their formation, which may provide a basis for more detailed work.

Rivers in particular have been a frequent subject for classification, by practitioners from a wide range of disciplines in addition to geomorphologists. Motivations for identifying different types or classes of river have varied widely, from the desire of the scientist to enhance his understanding of river behaviour and morphology by highlighting common characteristics of a given river type, to the need of an engineer or freshwater fishery manager to extrapolate experience and knowledge of a given river to rivers which behave in a similar fashion. The primarily scientific motivation for river classification is typified by the genetic classification introduced by Powell (1875); to enhance understanding of the structure and historical geology of an area by elucidating the history of its rivers is a prime objective of this classification. Other classifications may have an immediate practical application - for example, Nevins (1965) and Simons (1978), both river engineers, divided New Zealand rivers into several classes, each with common characteristics and management problems, and for each of which certain control techniques are appropriate. Nevins used two main criteria as his basis for classification, the lithology of the catchment and position along the longitudinal profile, which is in turn associated with channel gradient and sediment character. He divided New Zealand into four types of rock, each with different erodibilities and producing different types of detritus – namely the greywacke and granite mountains of the mountain backbone, the softer schists which give rise to lower mountains, soft shales and mudstones on which is formed the hill country so characteristic of New Zealand, and the volcanic rocks and sediments of the central North Island. Nevins divided the rivers themselves into the *mountain or torrent phase*, the *shingle* (i.e. gravel) *phase*, the *silt phase*, and the *tidal phase*, each having their distinctive characteristics and problems. Simon's classification had very similar elements; for example, he identified steep, 'shingle'-carrying rivers rising in the greywacke ranges, management problems in which relate to heavy bedload and unstable channels, and for which an appropriate management tool is either reduction of erosion in the mountains (a forlorn hope) or extraction of gravel in problem reaches. At the other end of the scale, he identified a class of sluggish, low gradient rivers in which the main problems tend to be siltation and reduction of flood capacity, and the most appropriate solutions are dredging, clearance of trees from the channel, and construction of stopbanks (levees or floodbanks).

Biologists too have classified rivers, although for very different purposes and using different criteria. The classification of running-water sites in Britain presented by Wright et al. (1984), based upon macroinvertebrate communities and the physical and chemical characteristics of the sites, has application in conservation, biological surveillance, pollution control and other aspects of water management (Furse et al., 1984). Thus, for example, for a polluted river, a classification based upon physical and chemical criteria can be used to predict the type of community that would exist if there were no pollution, and hence may be used as a baseline against which to assess attempts to improve water quality. Hawkes (1975) noted that 'with the increasing need for water conservation, both quantitatively and qualitatively, a system of river-zone classification is invaluable in predicting the likely effect on the ecology of the river of projected management policies such as water abstraction and flow regulation'. Organisms in different types of river vary markedly, and so also do the responses of river types to human activity; for example, a thermal discharge into an upland stream which raises its temperature only a few degrees could have a severe impact on the relatively intolerant salmonid fish found there, whereas a larger induced rise in temperature in a lowland river may be relatively unimportant ecologically, because the species present have different temperature requirements and tolerances. Platts (1980) entered a 'plea' for fisheries habitat classification, as a means of organizing fishery information so that it can be integrated into planning and management (Lotspeich and Platts, 1982). He suggested a hierarchical framework for handling information, which could describe the fishery by quantifying the variables that control the system (temperature, discharge, etc.) and the response of the system to changes in those variables.

It will be apparent that the characteristics of rivers emphasized in the various classificatory approaches may vary widely, depending on the purpose of the classifier. They include the relationship of the river to its geologic environment, the characteristics of the sediment of which the channel is composed, the chemical composition of the water conveyed, and the species of fish and other life forms which inhabit the river. Before considering in more detail the characteristics which various students of rivers deem significant, it is desirable to review the principles of classification. Grigg (1965, 1967) has outlined some fundamentals of classification in a geographical context. They may be summarized as follows (Mosley, 1981a):

1 classification should be designed for a specific purpose;
2 objects which differ in kind will not easily fit into the same classification;
3 classifications are not absolute but may change as more information becomes available;
4 differentiating characteristics should be properties of the objects classified, rather than factors assumed to affect or determine the objects;
5 classification should be exhaustive (include all objects in a class) and the classes should be exclusive (each object should be assigned to only one class);
6 classification should proceed at every stage of classification as far as possible on a single characteristic;
7 differentiating characteristics must be important or relevant to the purpose of classification; and finally
8 properties used to classify at the broader-scale levels must be more important for the purpose of classification than those at the finer-scale (more detailed) levels.

There are probably few classifications that conform to all these principles, and many students have concluded that the problems of applying a rigorous classification procedure to rivers, which may differ so subtly one from another, necessitate a different approach which emphasizes the continuum of rivers rather than their division. This view will be considered later.

RIVER CLASSIFICATIONS

Geomorphological classifications

The criteria or characteristics used for grouping rivers into classes have varied remarkably, depending on the perspective of the classifier, or the body of theory

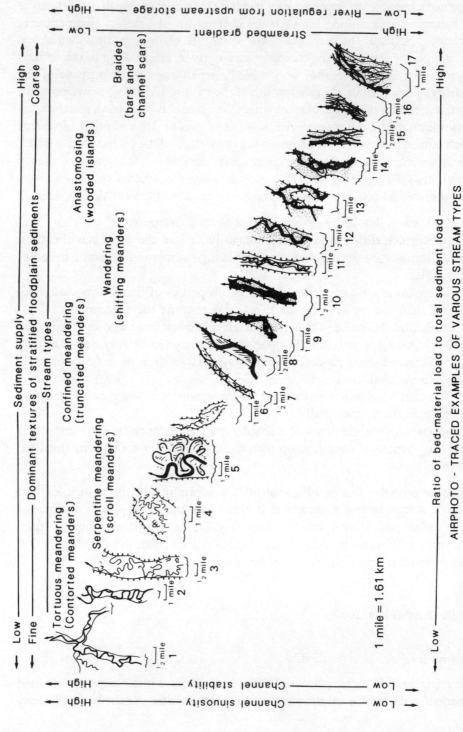

Figure 12.1   Classification by planform of river types, and their relationship to controlling variables (from Mollard, 1973)

and knowledge on which his work is based. The dominant classificatory system taught and used for many years by geographers was developed by geologists, and placed greatest emphasis on the genesis, history and structural geologic relationships of rivers. It recognized rivers such as the *consequent* river, whose course was determined by the original slope of the land surface; the *subsequent* river, whose course was controlled by structure and lithologic variations; or the *superimposed* river which was superimposed from overlying rocks onto rocks with which it has no simple, clear relationship (Cotton, 1922).

A simple morphological classification of river channels, with particular reference to the plan form of reaches, is that of Popov (1964), who recognized non-meandering channels with transverse dunes, non-meandering with alternate bars, limited meandering in which there is downstream migration of low-amplitude bends, free meandering, incomplete meandering, and braided. This classification is a development of the more widely known division into straight, meandering and braided channels popularized by Leopold and Wolman (1957), and a simpler alternative to that of Brice (1984), which emphasizes the character and degree of sinuosity, braiding and anabranching. These three related classifications of rivers use planimetric form as the criterion for classification, with rather limited consideration of the mechanisms which cause the morphological differences. Closely related classifications were proposed by Schumm (1963), Mollard (1973) and Schumm (1981), which also use planimetric form as the primary classificatory criterion, but explicitly recognize the inter-relationships between planimetric form, sediment load and type, channel gradient, and channel stability (figure 12.1). Warner (chapter 2, this volume) employs a classification based on bed characteristics and channel stability. Such classifications clearly have a powerful (if qualitative) explanatory capability, and firmly relate the river type to the factors supposed to dominate the morphology of the channel, and to its dynamics. They also tend to recognize that rivers form a continuum, rather than a series of exclusive classes.

Whole river system classifications

Biologists have, perhaps appropriately, developed a rich diversity of river classifications (Illies and Botosaneanu, 1963; Hawkes, 1975). There have been a number of attempts to classify whole river systems, using as criteria such factors as nature of source (e.g. from hills or mountains, springs and land drains, marsh or fenland – Butcher, 1933); physiography (e.g in South Africa, coastal-belt rivers with mountain sources; coastal-belt rivers with non-mountain sources; rivers of the elevated central plateau – Allanson, 1965); or chemical characteristics such as calcium concentration (Ohle, 1937) or pH (Townsend et al., 1983). However, most workers accept that classification of a whole river system is of little value

Table 12.1 Classification of Ontario streams by Ricker (1934)

A. CREEKS Flow on 1 June < 0.28 m^3s^{-1} Width < 3.0 m		*B. RIVERS* Flow on 1 June > 0.28 m^3s^{-1} Width > 3.0 m	
Spring creeks: permanent, usually spring-fed. Max. summer temp. < 20°C a Stony bottom Moderate-rapid current Aquatic mosses on bottom b Sandy bottom Moderate-rapid current No vegetation c Mud bottom Slow current Watercress or no vegetation d Dead leaves and other vegetation debris Slow current Moss or no vegetation	Drainage creeks not spring-fed or far from springs. Max. temp. > 20°C - usually much higher - often dry up	1 Trout streams max. temp. < temp. < 24°C principal piscivorous fish: *Salvelinus fontinalis* a Slow trout streams Slow current Mud bottom Vegetation: *Nymphaea*, *Potamogeton* ai Slow/hard waters Bicarbonate > 100 mg.l^{-1} (as $CaCO_3$) Hardness > 150 mg.1^{-1} Vegetation: *Chara* not *Brasonia*, *Castalia* Flow (1 June) < 2.8 m^3s^{-1} aii Slow/soft waters Bicarbonate < 25 mg.1^{-1} Hardness < 50 mg.1^{-1} Vegetation: *Brasonia* not *Chara* Flow (1 June) (< 14 m^3s^{-1}) b Swift trout streams Moderate-rapid current Stony bottom Vegetation: *Cladophora*, moss Typical invertebrates: Hydropsychidae Heptageniidae Simuliidae bi Swift/hard waters Bicarbonate > 100 mgl^{-1} Hardness > 150 mgl^{-1} Flow (1 June) > 4.2 m^3s^{-1} *Simulium*: merely 'frequent' bii Swift/soft waters Bicarbonates < 25 mgl^{-1} Hardness < 50 mgl^{-1} Flow (1 June) < 14 m^3s^{-1} *Simulium*: abundant	2 Warm rivers max. temp. not < 24°C principal piscivorous fish of the families: Centrarchidae Esocidae a Stony bottom Moderate-swift current Association: *Cladophora* Hydropsychidae Etheostominae b Mud bottom Slow current Association: *Nymphaea* Unionidae Catostomidae Cyprinidae

except in the case of such distinctive (and restricted) types as 'chalk streams'; variation along a river requires that homogeneous stretches be identified and individually classified.

Pennack (1979) identified eight distinctive types of waterway segment in the conterminous USA: springbrooks, montane tundra streams, mountain trout streams, sandy streams, rivers of the Great Plains, medium to large silty rivers, river segments polluted by sewage, and irrigation ditches. Such segments he considered remarkably similar from one part of the country to another, but he concluded that in addition there is a vast range of less distinctive types which differ from each other in a hopelessly intergrading and haphazard fashion and in terms of a wide range of variables.

Longitudinal zonation

A common procedure has been to divide a river system longitudinally into classes, on the basis of a variety of factors, particularly temperature and the fauna present. Such a classification was proposed by Ricker (1934) for Ontario streams, but is widely applicable to North America (table 12.1). The primary variables used in classification are summer flow and channel width, but other variables used for identifying sub-groups are bed sediment, water temperature, current velocity, water quality, vegetation and invertebrates. A similar classification for British streams, which used flow regime, channel size and shape, bed sediment character and water quality, had earlier been offered by Carpenter (1928) (table 12.2).

Fishery biologists may identify the same river segments described by Carpenter or Ricker, in terms of the dominant fish species present. Examples are the classification of North American streams by Pennack (1971) (table 12.2), or the four-fold division of European rivers by Huet (1949; 1954):

Trout zone: steep, fast-flowing stream with variable width and depth, a rocky, bouldery or cobble bed, and cool, well aerated water;

Grayling zone: larger stream with a riffle and pool form and gravel bed;

Barbel zone: moderate gradient and current with alternating rapids and quiet stretches, the latter being more extensive;

Bream zone: slow flowing, often deep channel (river, canal or ditch), with warm, turbid, oxygen-depleted water.

The fullest development of this 'longitudinal zonation' approach has been advanced by Illies (1961) and Illies and Botosaneanu (1963):

Zone 1: sources;
Zone 2: rills and rivulets;

Table 12.2 Comparison of longitudinal river zones

Strahler order	Illies and Botosaneanu (1963)	Illies (1961)	Ricker (1934)	Huet (1954)	Carpenter (1928)	Pennack (1971)	Nevins (1969)
0	Source	Eucrenon			Head stream		
1	Rill and rivulet	Hypocrenon	Spring creek			Dace trickle	
2	Small stream, fed by 2 + rills	Epirhithron	Swift trout stream		Trout zone	Trout feeder	Mountain or torrent phase
3	Brook or stream, fed by 2 + small streams	Metarhithron	Slow trout stream	Trout zone		Trout stream	
4–6	Montane or piedmont river	Hyporhithron		Grayling zone	Minnow reach	Bass or pickerel stream	Shingle phase
6–8	Middle course of a river	Epipotamon	Warm river	Barbel zone	Upper reach	Catfish or carp stream	Silt phase
>7	Lower plains course	Metapotamon		Bream zone	Lower reach		
		Hypopotamon			Brackish estuary	Tidal stream	Tidal phase

(Highland brooks — Lowland course)

Zone 3: small stream resulting from the confluence of two or more rills and rivulets;

Zone 4: brook or stream, resulting from the confluence of two or more zone 3 streams;

Zone 5: montane or piedmont rivers;

Zone 6: middle course of a river, downstream from zone 5;

Zone 7: lower, plains course (including estuary).

The similarity of this scheme to the stream-ordering system developed by Horton (1945) and Strahler (1957) is striking; its correspondence to several other classificatory schemes is made clearer in table 12.2. Platts (1979), Barila et al. (1981) and Cushing et al. (1983) demonstrated relationships between stream order, ecologically significant variables (gradient, channel width and depth, and bed sediment character), and fish species present. However, although the reality of this longitudinal variation in river character and ecology has been demonstrated by many studies, there is an increasingly strong view that it has the nature more of a continuum than of a series of distinctive zones or river types.

THE RIVER AS A CONTINUUM

Although there may be morphological and ecological discontinuities along a river system, particularly when tributaries introduce water with a distinctive chemical character or a distinctive sediment load (Miller, 1958; Wright et al., 1984, p. 251), the variables which may be used to characterize a river system generally change in a progressive fashion downstream, and the characteristics of the river ecosystem similarly change in harmony. This river continuum concept (Vannote et al. 1980) is explicitly based on geomorphic principles, particularly those expressed in hydraulic geometry and dynamic equilibrium relationships. The environmental variables considered significant by Vannote et al. include both physical factors like channel size, morphology and temperature regime, and biotic factors such as the relative importance of riparian vegetation as a food source, the characteristics of particulate organic matter in the flow, the character of the plant life in the waterway, and the ratio of photosynthesis to respiration. As these change down-channel, the structural and functional attributes of the stream communities, indicated by the relative numbers of different groups of invertebrates, also change.

This concept is basically consistent both with earlier work on the longitudinal distribution of fish and invertebrates, and with attempts to identify river zones which have distinctive communities. Thus, for example, Illies (1953) used data on benthic invertebrate communities along the River Fulda to identify groups (indicative of zones along the river) of observation sites having similar communities. Five groups were identified which were broadly consistent with the fish zones; nevertheless, a progressive downstream change underlies the zonation, and is not inconsistent with the river continuum concept. More recently, Culp and Davies (1982) found that the river continuum concept generally predicted longitudinal trends in macroinvertebrate feeding groups in the Oldman and south Saskatchewan Rivers, the trends being attributable primarily to downstream increases in periphyton biomass, nutrient concentrations, and water temperatures. They nevertheless recommended that the concept should be combined with a watershed classification scheme such as that proposed by Lotspeich and Platts (1982). Although within a given river system macroinvertebrate communities change longitudinally in response to the physical and biotic characteristics of the river, these characteristics are in turn a function of the environment of the river basin – its landforms, rock and soil types, vegetation, etc.

Objective classification by multivariate analysis

In the light of all the evidence that stream biota respond in a quantifiable and predictable fashion to variations in the physical and chemical characteristics, many biologists have established classifications of stream segments in terms of defined ranges of selected variables. Pennack (1971; 1979), for example, proposed that 13 criteria could be used to classify any stream segment, and suggested 4 to 6 classes for each (table 12.3). This approach is very similar to the geomorphological-hydrological classification approach used by Kellerhals et al. (1972), Kellerhals et al. (1976) and Mosley (1982a), which results not so much in a *classification* as in a *characterization* of rivers. The term 'characterization' is used here to denote the process of describing a river in terms of a specified set of characteristics or attributes. These may be variables that are measurable on a continuous scale (e.g. water surface width), an ordinal scale (e.g. the commonly accepted six class scale of difficulty for canoeists and rafters), or a nominal scale (Mosley (1985b) assigned rivers to one of eight classes of water colour). The key requirement is that the set of attributes and the procedures and scales of measurement are defined so that objective, reproducible results can be obtained as far as possible.

Perhaps the most sophisticated and complete application of this multivariate classificatory approach has been by Wright et al. (1984) and Furse et al. (1984). For each of 268 sites on 41 British river systems, macroinvertebrate species lists and information on 28 characteristics of the river environment were collected. Two-way indicator species analysis (TWINSPAN) was used to classify the sites into 16 groups, and multiple discriminant analysis (MDA) was used to explore the relationship between the site groupings and the environmental data. The first two discriminant functions generated by the MDA were respectively most highly correlated with:

1 mean bed sediment size, alkalinity, and total oxidized nitrogen;
2 discharge, width, depth, slope and distance from source.

Wright et al. suggested that these axes account respectively for differences between rivers, and for position along the length of a river (cf. the similar conclusion of Culp and Davies (1982), referred to above). The MDA had a 76 per cent success rate in assigning the 268 sites to the correct TWINSPAN (biological) group, using environmental data. The analysis was repeated using only 228 sites, and classification was attempted for the remaining 40 sites using environmental data; the rate of successful classification to the correct biological group was only 50 per cent but even when the prediction was incorrect the similarity between the fauna of the group predicted and the actual fauna was often high enough for the prediction to be of value. Wright et al. concluded that 'in view of the lack of natural discontinuities between sites, any classification is bound to be arbitrary. It can, however, still be of value, so long as it is appropriate to the needs of the user'.

Cushing et al. (1980) also adopted multivariate analysis in an attempt to classify stream sites, using measurements of 15 physical and chemical variables on 34 rivers. Five groups were identified by cluster analysis; the clusters were located in a three-dimensional space defined by three axes which were respectively most highly correlated with:

1 watershed area, phosphate concentration, total dissolved solids, solar radiation, annual precipitation, the ratio of stream length to watershed area, and terrestrial litter input;
2 temperature fluctuation and nitrate concentrations; and
3 summer base flow.

The three axes respectively accounted for 83.5, 9.8 and 4.8 per cent of among-group variability, although their physical meanings are not entirely clear. However, in a later study, the same authors (Cushing et al., 1983) concluded that 'streams are best viewed as gradients, or continua, and classification systems which separate discrete reaches are of little ecological value'. This was on the basis of a multivariate analysis which showed that biological variables (indices of the structure of the stream invertebrate community, such as the ratio of the numbers of shredders to grazers) changed in a predictable progression from small to large streams, and that annual precipitation, stream gradient and the ratio of stream length to watershed area were effective predictors of biological character. They suggested that there is 'an array of differences structured around the

Table 12.3 Pennack's (1971) proposed criteria for classifying lotic habitats

Mean width (m) during 10 months	<1	1–5	5–20	20–50	50–200	>200
Flow	temporary	permanent				
Mean current (km h^{-1}) during 10 lowest months	<0.5	0.5–2.5	2.5–5.0	5–10	>10	
Dominant substrate	rubble and boulders	gravel	sand	organic or inorganic silt	coarse inorganic debris	hardpan
Summer maximum temperature (°C)	>30	20–30	10–20	5–10	<5	
Winter minimum temperature (°C)	<20	10–20	5–10	0–5		
Mean turbidity for 10 clearest months (ppm Fuller's earth)	exceptionally clear (<10)	clear (10–50)	slightly turbid (50–100)	turbid (100–500)	highly turbid (>500)	
Total dissolved inorganic content (mg l^{-1})	very small (<30)	small (30–100)	medium (100–300)	large (>300)		
Total dissolved organic content (mg l^{-1})	very small (<30)	small (30–100)	medium (100–300)	large (>300)		
Water hardness (ppm bound CO_2)	soft (0–10)	medium (10–40)	hard (40–100)	very hard (>100)		
Organic pollution (mean annual day-time dissolved O_2, % saturation)	absent (>95%)	slight (80–95%)	moderate (50–80%)	heavy (10–50%)	severe (<10%)	
Maximum rooted aquatic cover	absent or negligible	restricted (<10%)	moderate (10–50%)	dense (>50%)		
Dominant stream-side vegetation	absent or negligible	herbs and grasses	brush with some herbs and grasses	woodland; more or less forested, with ground cover		

geomorphic processes and also incorporating thermo-chemical features which suggest an intergrading gradient (continuum) not only along, but also among streams'.

INCREMENTAL ANALYSIS OF THE STREAM ENVIRONMENT

There is now a vast body of literature which demonstrates the intimate and detailed relationship between stream biota and the physical characteristics of watercourses. Some of this work has been at the scale of habitats such as riffles and pools (already familiar to geomorphologists – O'Neill and Abrahams (1984)), runs, glides and backwaters (Mosley, 1982a; Platts et al., 1983). Lewis (1969), for example, found that in a Montana stream, the physical characteristics of pools were a major determinant of the standing crop of trout, while many studies have compared the biota of riffles, pools and runs, which have markedly different characteristics (Scullion et al., 1982; Pridmore and Roper, 1985), or have focused data collection on one or other of these habitats (Lewis, 1969; Mosley, 1982b; Glova et al., 1985).

At an even more detailed level, biologists have considered the influence of microhabitat characteristics on stream communities, recognizing that freshwater biota respond to conditions at a point – particularly water depth and velocity, the character of the bed sediment, and the type of concealment or cover available – as well as to more general conditions such as water temperature and chemistry (Smith, 1979). Examples are the detailed work of Edington (1968), Binns and Eisermann (1979), Gore and Judy (1981) and Shirvell and Dungey (1983). Earlier work of this type is summarized by Stalnaker and Arnette (1976) and Church et al. (1979).

Although some methods of stream channel inventory therefore deal with the characteristics of watercourses at the scale of habitats like riffles and pools, which cover areas of tens or hundreds of square metres (Herrington and Dunham, 1967; Platts et al., 1983; Mosley, 1985a), inventory work has increasingly focused upon point measurements of habitat conditions. This has given rise to an approach to the analysis of the stream environment and aquatic habitats which is generally known as incremental analysis (Bovee, 1978; Milhous and Grenney, 1980; Jowett, 1982; Orth and Maughan, 1982; Mosley, 1985a). It is assumed that the requirements of organisms (including man) that use a watercourse can be defined in terms of a number of physical attributes which may (but need not) be related in a predictable fashion to water discharge. Thus, for example, the habitat requirements of a spawning brown trout may be defined in terms of water depth, velocity, temperature, chemistry, cover, and stream bed sediment. These factors are in turn related to flow regime and watershed condition. If suitable ranges of these variables have been defined by direct observation of the conditions under which trout actually spawn, then the suitability for spawning of any location in a stream may be assessed. The effect on suitability for spawning of changes in discharge, commonly by flow manipulation or abstraction or watershed management, may then be estimated.

The incremental approach, which is now widely used in North America and New Zealand for watershed and river management purposes, focuses on the characteristics of the river environment at a point, and it is implicit that the suitability of a river as habitat for a given organism is controlled not by average conditions, such as mean depth, mean velocity or width at a cross-section, but by the joint frequency distributions of several variables at all points in the river. By aggregating measurements made at a large number of points, which are normally arranged along several closely spaced cross-sections at a site which is considered to be representative of a river segment, an index of the suitability of the segment as a whole for the organism may be derived (e.g. Mosley, 1982c; 1983; Mosley and Jowett, 1985). This index is known as weighted usable area, and its variation with discharge is commonly analysed in order to identify optimum or minimum acceptable flows for a variety of instream uses.

Incremental analysis is thus a special form of hydraulic geometry, which, because it uses distributions of stream-channel attributes rather than simply measures of central tendency, discriminates between channels in a much more subtle way (Mosley, 1983). For practical purposes, such as assessing areas of water suitable for the rearing of juvenile trout (which requires generally slow, shallow water) or for children to swim (which requires slow moving water with a depth of about 1 m), such data are of more value than measurements of average conditions.

SIGNIFICANT RIVER CHARACTERISTICS

The preceding sections have drawn deliberately from non-geographical literature, to indicate both the centrality of geographical and geomorphological factors to applications and research in other disciplines, the wide variety of factors used for characterizing rivers in addition to those that are commonly used by geomorphologists, and the need to deal with distributions of variables rather than simply measures of central tendency.

The types of analysis which have been commonly carried out by geomorphologists have perhaps been conditioned by the close links between geomorphology, hydrology and river engineering, and by the goal of developing general models. Thus, a major need of river engineers, which led to the development of regime theory (Blench, 1957), has been to predict channel width, permissible velocities, cross-sectional area, slope, sinuosity, meander wavelength, and bend radius, given information on flow regime, sediment load and floodplain slope (Nevins, 1969). The geomorphological equivalent, hydraulic geometry (Leopold and Maddock, 1953), has similarly had as a major goal to elucidate the relationships between controlling variables – some index of discharge such as mean annual flood, floodplain slope, and sediment load – and the morphological response variables – mean width, depth and velocity, channel slope, meander wavelength, and other less commonly considered variables such as roughness factor, suspended sediment concentration and radius of curvature. This type of work is reviewed by Leopold et al. (1964) and Richards (1982) and by other chapters in the present volume; it is typified, on the New Zealand scene, by the engineering-oriented studies of Griffiths (1981; 1983) and the hydraulic geometry studies of Griffiths (1980) and Mosley (1981b).

Models of river form

The goal of developing general models of river form and behaviour is implicit in a vast body of geomorphological and hydraulic research; the need to limit consideration to a small range of variables to make the goal at all achievable is evident by the distance still to go. The 'state of the art' has progressed little beyond the deductive models of channel development proposed by Schumm (1969), Hey (1978; 1979) and Pickup and Rieger (1979), and the inductive model developed by Mosley (1981b), using data for 72 rivers in New Zealand. Mosley used 11 morphometric variables to describe bankfull channel morphology, 11 to describe the hydrologic regime, and 5 to describe the character of the sediment. Canonical correlation analysis indicated that nearly 70 per cent of the variation in average channel morphology of the 72 rivers could be described by three canonical vectors which reflected cross-sectional area, cross-section shape and channel slope; nearly 50 per cent could be 'explained' by three canonical vectors which reflect discharge magnitude, sediment character, bank erodibility and discharge variability.

Multiple regression analysis demonstrated, however, that 65–90 per cent of the variance of some aspects of channel morphology is explained by the hydrological and sediment variables used, whereas other properties appear to be completely independent of the supposed controlling variables. Thus, the best-fit stepwise regression equations for slope s, cross-sectional area A, aspect ratio WP/R and relative depth R/D_{75} (where WP is wetted perimeter, R is hydraulic radius and D_{75} is the size of bed sediment, sampled by the Wolman (1954) method, at which 75 per cent is finer) had R^2 values of 0.75, 0.88, 0.66 and 0.78 respectively. On the other hand, equations for sinuosity P, braiding index B (number of subchannels at a cross-section) and shape factor d_{max}/R (where d_{max} is maximum depth) had R^2 values less than 0.34.

Mosley concluded that, apart from statistical problems such as the non-normal distributions of sinuosity and braiding index and the narrow range of values of d_{max}/R, much unexplained variability could be a result of random variations in channel morphology. He showed (Mosley, 1985a) that estimation to ± 10 per cent of their true value of even easily measured morphometric variables such as channel width requires several tens of measurements in even relatively uniform channels; a smaller sample would inevitably increase lack of fit in a statistical model. Furthermore there are many factors in addition to those included in the analysis which undoubtedly influence channel morphology, although in a fashion that is not readily quantified. He pointed particularly to variability in bank erodibility due to variation in sediment and vegetation characteristics, and to the effect of bedrock outcrops. The crucial influence of bank erodibility on channel morphology is of course the basis for river control work which relies on tree planting, placement of riprap, and construction of groynes and retards (Acheson, 1968; Winkley, 1972; Mosley, 1984).

A geomorphological classification of New Zealand rivers

A need was discerned by New Zealand fishery and water resource managers in the 1970s to develop a classification system which would permit extrapolation of knowledge about the freshwater ecosystem. Rivers which have similar physical characteristics – that is, which are of the same type or class – may have similar flora and fauna which react to management practices in common, predictable ways. The probable impacts of management on a given river about which little is known may thus be predicted by reference to another river of the same type, for which more data are available.

Because none of the many existing subjectively defined, special-purpose classifications appeared to be suitable for New Zealand rivers, it was decided to develop an objective classification, using multivariate statistical methods. This approach had already been used to examine hydrologic regions (an areal classification) in New Zealand (Mosley, 1981a). A sample of 190 rivers was selected which had at least a ten year hydrologic record, and a survey reach established near each gauging station. The sample was not restricted to alluvial rivers, since a large proportion of New Zealand's rivers is to a greater or lesser extent bedrock controlled.

Five cross-sections were surveyed in each reach to define the average bankfull channel parameters used by Mosley (1981b); sinuosity, floodplain slope, braiding index and median bed material size (D_{50}) were measured for the reach, and a number of other factors characteristic of the river environment (type of bank vegetation, percentage of banks and bed composed of bedrock, etc.) were also surveyed (Mosley, 1982a). Hydrologic regime was characterized by a number of parameters derived from the instantaneous flow record and the sequence of annual maximum and minimum flows.

Canonical correlation broadly confirmed the results of the earlier analysis; cluster analysis was then used to investigate the existence of distinctive groups or classes of rivers (SAS Institute Inc., 1982). There are no satisfactory methods for determining the optimum number of clusters, but the SAS CLUSTER program provides a plot of a 'cubic clustering criterion' (CCC), based on minimizing the within-cluster sum of squares, which is of assistance.

A series of cluster analyses using different combinations of variables was carried out. In no case did the CCC plot indicate the existence of a clearly defined set of clusters (river classes). When the variables cross-section area A, slope s, shape factor d_{max}/d, aspect ratio w/d, and relative depth d/D_{50} (where w is water surface width and d is mean depth) were included in the analysis, inspection of the clusters did, however, reveal some apparently real groupings. Within the ten major clusters, four appeared to have physical reality (figure 12.2). Most distinctive were:

a braided rivers, with large values of w/d;
b the 'lowland' course of large rivers, with large values of A and small values of s;
c small headwater streams, with large values of s; and
d a group of entrenched channels with low values of w/d, commonly located in mudstone catchments.

However, the other clusters appeared to have little or no physical reality; while they could be objectively defined by discriminant functions they included watercourses which to the geomorphologist or biologist appear quite different.

As the number of variables used in the clustering process was increased the composition of the clusters changed, often quite dramatically, except for the four groups noted above, which were highly stable. The addition of variables made discernment of 'real' clusters if anything more difficult, although in principle the process was including more of the information which one intuitively uses to discern similarities and differences.

This negative result is consistent with the earlier attempt to define objective hydrologic regions in New Zealand. In that study, a number of hydrologically distinctive groups were identified which in some cases had geographical reality (i.e. they constituted hydrologic regions) and in others were related to lithology, topography or dominant weather systems. However, in most cases, hydrologic behaviour reflected a number of co-dominant factors, which produced a complex mosaic of environments and prevented identification of a meaningful regional pattern. Given the complexity of hydrologic response and the difficulty of identifying meaningful hydrological groups, it is not surprising that river channels – which are, of course, shaped in response to the flows that they convey,

a

Figure 12.2 Representatives of the four most distinctive types of New Zealand river: (a) The Ahuriri River, a braided river in South Canterbury; (b) The Waipaoa River, a low-gradient river with a sand-silt bed and sinuous course near Gisborne; (c) Reynolds Creek, a small headwater stream on Banks Peninsula, Canterbury; (d) The Hoteo River near Auckland, an entrenched channel in a mudstone catchment

b

c

d

as well as to other factors such as sediment type, bedrock outcrops, etc – should be at least as difficult to classify.

The result is also consistent with Pennack's (1979) conclusion that, although some classes of watercourse can be distinguished, most channels show such complex, intergrading variations in character that classification is not feasible. The multivariate approach to characterizing – rather than classifying – channels recommended by Pennack (1979) and Cushing et al. (1983) therefore appears to be the most practicable approach to prediction of stream communities, management impacts and so on.

DISCUSSION

Although this volume mainly views rivers from a geomorphological perspective, this particular chapter attempts to provide a broader context. Rivers have been studied in quantitative fashion by engineers for 80 years and more, and by geomorphologists for 40 years. Regime theory and hydraulic geometry have dealt, particularly in their earlier years, with average values of fairly gross indices of channel form, discharge and sediment characteristics, such as meander wavelength, mean depth, width, and mean annual flood, and have dealt primarily with alluvial channels. Good progress has been made towards an understanding of river morphology at this level, as is shown by the review by Richards (1982).

However, water resource and river management is undergoing a rapid evolution, and increasing attention is being paid to the biological and social aspects of the river environment, rather than to the purely physical aspects which are considered for design of flood control and bank protection schemes. The physical scientist is being called upon to look at rivers with new eyes – almost literally, with the eyes of the fish or the invertebrates which live in the rivers, or of the people who use them for recreation. Thus, it is no longer sufficient, for example, to evaluate the relationship between mean depth and bankfull discharge; a migrating quinnat salmon is more concerned with the minimum depths available at the riffles it must pass, while a child on holiday is more interested in the area of a channel which is about one metre deep, flowing at less than $0.1 \, \mathrm{ms}^{-1}$, and which has a sandy bed. In other words, it is increasingly necessary, for practical purposes, to examine the spatial and frequency distributions of variables, rather than their average values. Moreover, because rivers are used for different activities at different times of year, the variation of the salient river characteristics with time, as flows vary, must also be considered. Again, frequencies and durations of occurrence, the precise sequence of conditions, and extreme conditions associated with low or high flows are of practical significance, because it is these rather than average conditions which are the greatest constraints on instream river users.

An increasing range of variables must also be considered. Included are morphometric characteristics such as the dimensions of pools (Platts et al., 1983), the quantity and disposition of channel obstructions like log jams (Swanson et al., 1976), and the character of the channel perimeter and water surface (Mosley, 1982a). However, the river manager is concerned with many factors which are less familiar to the geomorphologist. In particular, these include indices of water quality – temperature, dissolved oxygen, pH, turbidity, and concentrations of various solutes – and characteristics of the aquatic and riparian vegetation. In addition, of course, there are the characteristics of the animal communities themselves – the species of fish and invertebrates present, their densities, and details of inter-specific competition, habitat requirements, food supply and so on. Consideration of a river as a recreational or scenic resource widens the field still further. Chubb and Baumann (1977) listed a large number of factors considered to influence river recreation potential; they included characteristics of the river itself, its immediate environment, the surrounding landscape, and socio-economic factors. In a recent analysis of the preference of the New Zealand public for river scenery, Mosley (1985b) concluded that the scenic beauty of a riverscape was primarily influenced by the characteristics of the surrounding landscape – the amounts of forest and alpine land visible, local relief, the confinement of the view, and the angle of view up to the most prominent landscape feature. Characteristics of the river itself – the area of water visible, its colour, and channel straightness – were apparently relatively unimportant. Variables which had been expected to be important, such as channel slope, channel dimensions, or water velocity, were shown by the statistical analysis to be of less importance.

It is not, of course, suggested that fluvial geomorphologists should transform themselves into freshwater biologists or recreation researchers, or should abandon areas of endeavour which they have traditionally pursued. However, geomorphologists and geographers are well qualified to work with and guide the other disciplines, both because they deal with the basic 'raw material' (the physical environment, which provides the basic constraint for river users), and because they are commonly more familiar with quantitative techniques. As geomorphologists become increasingly involved in applied studies, familiarity with the needs of other disciplines and with the characteristics of rivers which are of immediate practical significance will be a growing asset.

REFERENCES

Acheson, A. R. 1968: *River Control and Drainage in New Zealand*. Wellington, New Zealand: Ministry of Works.

Allanson, B. R. 1965: Introduction to Symposium, Biology of South African rivers. *Archive für Hydrobiologie*, 61, 378-9.

Barila, T. W., Williams, R. D. and Stauffer, J. R. 1981: The influence of stream order and selected stream bed parameters on fish diversity in Raystown Branch, Susquehanna River drainage, Pennsylvania. *Journal of Applied Ecology*, 18, 125-31.

Binns, N. A. and Eiserman, F. M. 1979: Quantification of fluvial trout habitat in Wyoming. *Transactions of the American Fisheries Society*, 108, 215-28.

Blench, T. 1957: *Regime Behaviour of Rivers and Canals*. London: Butterworth Scientific.

Bovee, K. D. 1978: The incremental method of assessing habitat potential for coolwater species, with management implications. *American Fisheries Society Special Publication*, 11, 340-6.

Brice, J. C. 1984: Planform properties of meandering rivers. In C. M. Elliott (ed.), *River meandering, Proceedings of Conference Rivers '83*, New York: American Society of Civil Engineers, 1-15.

Butcher, R. W. 1933: Studies on the ecology of rivers - I. On the distribution of macrophytic vegetation in the rivers of Britain. *Journal of Ecology*, 21, 58-91.

Carpenter, K. E. 1928: *Life in Inland Waters with Especial reference to Animals*. London: Sidgwick and Jackson.

Chubb, M. and Baumann, E. H. 1977: *The RIVERS Method: a Pilot Study of River Recreation Potential Assessment*. East Lansing, USA: Department of Geography, Michigan State University.

Church, D. F., Davies, S. F. and Taylor, M. E. U. 1979: A review of the habitat requirements of fish in New Zealand rivers. *Water and Soil Technical Publication, Ministry of Works and Development, New Zealand*, 12.

Cotton, C. A. 1922: *Geomorphology*. Christchurch: Whitcombe and Tombs.

Culp, J. M. and Davies, R. W. 1982: Analysis of longitudinal zonation and the river continuum concept in the Oldman-South Saskatchewan River system. *Canadian Journal of Fisheries and Aquatic Science*, 39, 1258-66.

Cushing, C. E. and six others 1980: Comparative study of physical-chemical variables of streams using multivariate analyses. *Archive für Hydrobiologie*, 89, 343-52.

Cushing, C. E. and six others 1983: Relationships among chemical, physical and biological indices along river continua based on multivariate analyses. *Archive für Hydrobiologie*, 98, 317-26.

Edington, J. M. 1968: Habitat preferences in net-spinning caddis larvae with special reference to the influence of water velocity. *Journal of Animal Ecology*, 37, 675-92.

Fairbridge, R. W. 1968: *Encyclopedia of Geomorphology*, New York: Reinhold Book Co.

Furse, M. T., Moss, D., Wright, J. F. and Armitage, P. D. 1984: The influence of seasonal and taxonomic factors on the ordination and classification of running-water sites in Great Britain and on the prediction of their macro-invertebrate communities. *Freshwater Biology*, 14, 257-80.

Glova, G. J., Bonnett, M. L. and Docherty, C. R. 1985: Comparison of fish populations in riffles of three braided rivers of Canterbury, New Zealand. *New Zealand Journal of Marine and Freshwater Research*, 19, 157-65.

Gore, J. A. and Judy, R. D. 1981: Predictive models of benthic macroinvertebrate density for use in instream flow studies and regulated flow management. *Canadian Journal of Fisheries and Aquatic Sciences*, 38, 1363-70.

Griffiths, G. A. 1980: Hydraulic geometry relationships of some New Zealand gravel bed rivers. *Journal of Hydrology (NZ)*, 19, 106-18.

Griffiths, G. A. 1981: Stable channel design in gravel bed rivers. *Journal of Hydrology*, 52, 291-305.

Griffiths, G. A. 1983: Stable channel design in alluvial rivers. *Journal of Hydrology*, 65, 259-70.

Grigg, D. B. 1965: The logic of regional systems. *Annals of the Association of American Geographers*, 55, 465-91.

Grigg, D. B. 1967: Regions, models and classes. In R. J. Chorley and P. Haggett (eds), *Models in Geography*, London: Methuen, 461-509.

Harvey, D. 1969: *Explanation in Geography*. London: Edward Arnold.

Hawkes, H. A. 1975: River zonation and classification. In B. A. Whitton (ed.) *River Ecology*, University of California Press, 312-74.

Herrington, R. B. and Dunham, D. K. 1967: A technique for sampling general fish habitat characteristics of streams. *US Forest Service Research Paper* INT-41.

Hey, R. D. 1978: Determinate hydraulic geometry of river channels. *Journal of the Hydraulics Division, American Society of Civil Engineers*, 104, 869-85.

Hey, R. D. 1979: Dynamic process-response model of river channel development. *Earth Surface Processes*, 4, 59-72.

Horton, R. E. 1945: Erosional development of streams and their drainage basins: hydrophysical approach to quantitative morphology. *Geological Society of America Bulletin*, 56, 275-370.

Huet, M. 1949: Apercu des relations entre la pente et les populations des eaux courantes. *Schweiz. Z. Hydrol.*, 11, 333-51.

Huet, M. 1954: Biologie, profils en long en travers des eaux covantes. *Bull. Fr. Piscic.*, 175, 41-53.

Illies, J. 1953: Die Besiedlung der Fulda (inskes. Das Benthos der Salmonidenregion) nach dem jetzigen Stand der Untersuchung. *Ber. Limnologie Flußstat. Freudenthal*, 5, 1-28.

Illies, J. 1961: Versuch einer allgemeinen biozönotischen Gliederung der Fließgewässer. *Internationale Rev. ges. Hydrobiologie*, 46, 205-13.

Illies, J. and Botosaneanu, L. 1963: Problèmes et méthodes de la classification et de la zonation écologique des eaux courantes, considerées surtout du point de vue faunistique. *Internationale Vereinigung fur Theoretische und Angewandte Limnologie*, 12, 1-57.

Jowett, I. G. 1982: The incremental approach to studying stream flows: New Zealand case studies. In R. H. S. McColl (ed.) *River Low Flows: Conflicts of Water Use*, Water and Soil Miscellaneous Publication 47, Ministry of Works and Development, New Zealand.

Kellerhals, R., Church, M. and Bray, D. I. 1976: Classification and analysis of river processes. *American Society of Civil Engineers*, 102, 813-29.

Kellerhals, R., Neill, C. R. and Bray, D. I. 1972: Hydraulic and geomorphic characteristics of rivers in Alberta. *River Engineering and Surface Hydrology Report, Research Council of Alberta, Edmonton*, 72.1.

Leopold, L. B. and Maddock, T. 1953: The hydraulic geometry of stream channels and some physiographic implications. *US Geological Survey Professional Paper* 252.

Leopold, L. B. and Wolman, M. G. 1957: River channel patterns: braided, meandering and straight. *US Geological Survey Professional Paper* 282-B.

Leopold, L. B., Wolman, M. G. and Miller, J. P. 1964: *Fluvial Processes in Geomorphology*. San Francisco: Freeman.

Lewis, S. L. 1969: Physical factors influencing fish populations in pools of a trout stream. *Transactions of the American Fisheries Society*, 98, 14–19.

Lotspeich, F. B. and Platts, W. S. 1982: An integrated land-aquatic classification system. *North American Journal of Fisheries Management*, 2, 138–49.

Milhous, R. T. and Grenney, W. J. 1980: The quantification and reservation of instream flows. *Progress in Water Technology*, 13, 129–54.

Miller, J. P. 1958: High mountain streams: effects of geology on channel characteristics and bed material. *New Mexico Institute of Mining and Technology, Socorro, New Mexico, Memoir*, 4.

Mollard, J. D. 1973: Airphoto interpretation of fluvial features. Fluvial processes and sedimentation. In *Proceedings of Hydrology Symposium, University of Alberta*, Department of the Environment, Canada, 341–80.

Mosley, M. P. 1981a: Delimitation of New Zealand hydrologic regions. *Journal of Hydrology*, 49, 173–92.

Mosley, M. P. 1981b: Semi-determinate hydraulic geometry of river channels, South Island, New Zealand. *Earth Surface Processes and Landforms*, 6, 127–37.

Mosley, M. P. 1982a: A procedure for characterising river channels. *Water and Soil Miscellaneous Publication, Ministry of Works and Development, New Zealand*, 32.

Mosley, M. P. 1982b: Critical depths for passage in braided rivers, Canterbury, New Zealand. *New Zealand Journal of Marine and Freshwater Research*, 16, 351–7.

Mosley, M. P. 1982c: Analysis of the effects of changing discharge on channel morphology and instream uses in a braided river, Ohau River, New Zealand. *Water Resources Research*, 18, 800–12.

Mosley, M. P. 1983: Response of braided rivers to changing discharge. *Journal of Hydrology (NZ)*, 22, 18–67.

Mosley, M. P. 1984: Channelisation and bank stabilisation. In C. W. Finckl (ed.), *Encyclopedia of Applied Geology*, New York: Van Nostrand Reinhold Co., 40–5.

Mosley, M. P. 1985a: River channel inventory, habitat and instream flow assessment. *Progress in Physical Geography*, 9, 494–523.

Mosley, M. P. 1985b: Scenic beauty. *Streamland (Ministry of Works and Development, New Zealand)*, 40.

Mosley, M. P. and Jowett, I. G. 1985: Fish habitat analysis using river flow simulation. *New Zealand Journal of Marine and Freshwater Research*, 19, 293–309.

Nevins, T. H. F. 1965: River classification with particular reference to New Zealand. In *Proceedings, 4th New Zealand Geography Conference*, Dunedin, 83–90.

Nevins, T. H. F. 1969: River training – the single thread channel. *New Zealand Engineering*, 24, 367–73.

Ohle, W. 1937: Kalksystematik unserer Binnengwässer und der Kalkgehalt Rügener Bäche. *Geol. Meere un Binnengew*, 1, 291–316.

O'Neill, M. P. and Abrahams, A. D. 1984: Objective identification of pools and riffles. *Water Resources Research*, 20, 921–6.

Orth, D. J. and Maughan, O. E. 1982: Evaluation of the incremental methodology for recommending instream flows for fishes. *Transactions of the American Fisheries Society*, 11, 413–45.

Pennack, R. W. 1971: Toward a classification of lotic habitats. *Hydrobiologia*, 38, 321–34.

Pennack, R. W. 1979: The dilemma of stream classification. In *Classification, Inventory and Analysis of Fish and Wildlife Habitat*, US Fish and Wildlife Service, Biological Services Program FWS/OBS-78/76, 59–66.

Pickup, G. and Rieger, W. A. 1979: A conceptual model of the relationship between channel characteristics and discharge. *Earth Surface Processes*, 4, 37–42.

Platts, W. S. 1979: Relationships among stream order, fish populations and aquatic geomorphology in an Idaho River drainage. *Fisheries*, 4, 5–9.

Platts, W. S. 1980: A plea for fishery habitat classification. *Fisheries*, 5, 2–6.

Platts, W. S., Megahan, W. F. and Minshall, G. W. 1983: Methods for evaluating stream, riparian and biotic conditions. *US Forest Service General Technical Report*, INT-138.

Popov, I. V. 1964: Hydromorphological principles of the theory of channel processes and their use in hydrotechnical planning. *Soviet Hydrology*, 2, 188–95.

Powell, J. W. 1875: *Exploration of the Colorado River and its Tributaries*. Washington, DC: Smithsonian Institution.

Pridmore, R. D. and Roper, D. S. 1985: Comparison of the macroinvertebrate faunas of runs and riffles in three New Zealand streams. *New Zealand Journal of Marine and Freshwater Research*, 19, 283–91.

Richards, K. S. 1982: *Rivers: Form and Process in Alluvial Channels*. London: Methuen.

Ricker, W. E. 1934: An ecological classification of certain Ontario streams. *Ontario Fisheries Research Laboratory Publication*, 49, 1–114.

SAS Institute Inc. 1982: *SAS User's Guide: Statistics*. Cary, North Carolina: SAS Institute Inc.

Schumm, S. A. 1963: A tentative classification of alluvial river channels. *US Geological Survey Circular*, 477.

Schumm, S. A. 1969: River metamorphosis. *Journal of the Hydraulics Division, American Society of Civil Engineers*, 95, 255–73.

Schumm, S. A. 1981: Evolution and response of the fluvial system, sedimentologic implications. *SEPM Special Publication*, 31, 19–29.

Scullion, J., Parish, C. A., Morgan, W. and Edwards, R. W. 1982: Comparison of benthic macroinvertebrate fauna and substratum composition in riffles and pools in the impounded River Elan and the unregulated River Wye, mid Wales. *Freshwater Biology*, 12, 579–95.

Shirvell, C. D. and Dungey, R. G. 1983: Microhabitats chosen by brown trout for feeding and spawning in rivers. *Transactions of the American Fisheries Society*, 112, 355-67.

Simons, P. K. 1978: Comments on North Island Rivers. In *Proceedings of the Conference on Erosion Assessment and Control in New Zealand*, New Zealand Association of Soil Conservators, 156-8.

Smith, G. L. (ed.), 1979: Proceedings, workshop on instream flow habitat criteria and modelling. *Colorado Water Resources Research Institute Information Series, Fort Collins*, 40.

Stalnaker, C. B. and Arnette, J. L. (eds), 1976: *Methodologies for the Determination of Stream Resource Flow Requirements: an Assessment*. Office of Biological Services, US Fish and Wildlife Service, FWS/OBS-76/03.

Strahler, A. N. 1957: Quantitative analysis of watershed geomorphology. *American Geophysical Union Transactions*, 38, 913-20.

Swanson, F. J., Lienkaemper, G. W. and Sedell, J. R. 1976: History, physical effects, and management implications of large organic debris in western Oregon streams. *US Forest Service General Technical Report*, PNW-56.

Townsend, C. R., Hildrew, A. G. and Francis, J. 1983: Community structure in some southern English streams: the influence of physicochemical factors. *Freshwater Biology*, 13, 521-44.

Vannote, R. L., Minshall, G. W., Cummins, K. W., Sedell, J. R. and Cushing, C. E. 1980: The river continuum concept. *Canadian Journal of Fisheries and Aquatic Science*, 37, 130-7.

Winkley, B. R. 1972: Practical aspects of river regulation and control. In H. W. Shen (ed.), *River Mechanics*, Fort Collins: H. W. Shen.

Wolman, M. G. 1954: A method of sampling coarse river bed material. *American Geophysical Union Transactions* 35, 951-6.

Wright, J. F., Moss, D., Armitage, P. D. and Furse, M. T. 1984: A preliminary classification of running water sites in Great Britain based on macro-invertebrate species and the prediction of community type using environmental data. *Freshwater Biology*, 14, 221-56.

13

Bed Stability in Gravel Streams, with Reference to Stream Regulation and Ecology

P. A. Carling

INTRODUCTION

In recent years there has been an increasing interest in the management of the salmonid fish stocks of UK gravel-bed rivers (Milner et al., 1981). These fish are valuable as a recreational fishery but the nursery areas in headwater streams are also important for recruitment to the commercial salmon fisheries in the North Atlantic. Such attention, as well as being ecologically desirable, is also increasingly necessary as enhanced use of the environment by man has resulted in detrimental effects to both river quality and biota (Mosley, 1985).

Activities such as agricultural and forestry drainage, mining or heavy construction work may result in high suspended solids loads in rivers which under undisturbed conditions carry small loads. These sediments may settle into gravel spawning-beds infilling the interstitial spaces. Alternatively, regulation of flows, in relation to impoundments and water transfer schemes, usually results in prescribed minimum discharges and the elimination of high discharges. Management practices in this respect may result in either silting, or localized scour of non-renewable spawning gravels below impoundments.

Impact of bed sediment movement on salmonid eggs,
alevins and invertebrates

Salmonid fishes such as salmon and trout bury their eggs within stream-bed gravels to a depth of typically 8–30 cm below the bed surface (Milner et al., 1981). Once laid they are subject to mortality owing to a variety of causes (Neave, 1953). Flood flows capable of reworking the gravel stream-bed have often been

(a)

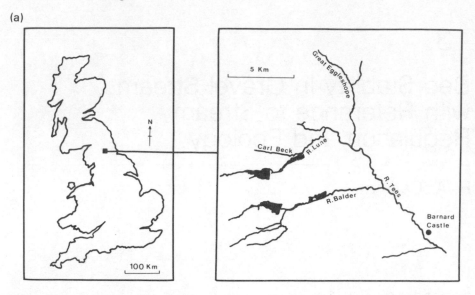

Figure 13.1   (a) Location map showing streams investigated in relation to the River Tees and its main tributaries; (b) View of the study reach in Great Eggleshope Beck with near bankfull discharge conditions (flow direction top to bottom of picture); (c) A similar view to (b) during low flow; (d) Example of gravel bed material in Great Eggleshope Beck. Typical particle size data are given in table 13.1

(b)

c

d

cited as injurious to the recruitment of the young stages of salmonids. Usually evidence for disturbance of eggs and alevins and subsequent physical damage is indirect (Hobbs, 1937; McNeill, 1966), although Elliott (1976) observed a correlation between the number of salmonid eggs drifting downstream and the current velocity.

Invertebrates are similarly affected by scouring flows. Specific composition and numerical density may be altered by displacement (Maitland, 1964) and also by crushing of individuals (Harker, 1953), and these impacts will vary both across the stream width and downstream, depending upon the spatial intensity of the scouring process (Hynes, 1970).

More moderate flows will winnow fine silts from the surface gravel layers although this process will not extend to any depth until the gravel framework particles are mobilized (Beschta and Jackson, 1979; Carling, 1984). Framework gravels free of the fine silts, which commonly fill the void spaces within the coarser population, are preferable for salmonid propagation as water content and permeability are increased. More rapid intra-gravel flow and consequent enhanced oxygen transfer rates to the developing fish embryos generally result in lower egg mortalities (Wickett, 1975). However, silting on a permanent basis may occur once scouring discharges are precluded by regulation (Petts, 1984), and as well as affecting the recruitment of young salmonids, may alter the fish's food source by affecting the invertebrate diversity and biomass (Luedthe and Brusven, 1976).

Consequently, from a biological standpoint, bedload movements may prove beneficial or deleterious, depending on magnitude and timing of events and the nature of the processes involved. Some biological consequences of the specific scouring process reported here will be considered by a separate publication. The purpose of this chapter, however, is to quantify the relevant process rates and to draw attention to those areas of research which require considerably more detailed investigation.

Research area

Despite the evident increased interest in the dynamics of fluvial gravel beds in recent years (e.g. Hey et al., 1982) there is still little information concerning sediment movement in steep upland streams in the UK. Consequently to augment the meagre data base, a series of observations was made between 1978 and 1984 to investigate the dynamics of sand to boulder-size material in two small upland streams in northern England (figure 13.1a). Catchment and stream characteristics are outlined in figure 13.1 and table 13.1; aspects of the sediments and criteria for their initial motion have been reported elsewhere (Carling and Reader, 1982; Carling, 1983) and only brief sedimentological details are given here.

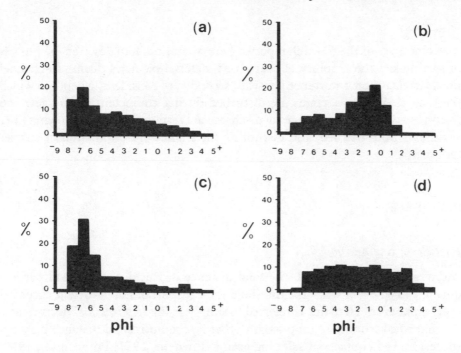

Figure 13.2   (a) Particle size distribution of bed sediments in Great Eggleshope Beck. Histogram is the average of 35 bulk freeze-core samples; (b) Particle size distribution of bedload sediments in Great Eggleshope Beck. Histogram is the average of 78 samples representative of individual floods over six years; (c) Particle size distribution of bed sediments in Carl Beck. Histogram is the average of 22 bulk freeze-core samples; (d) Particle size distribution of bedload sediments in Carl Beck. Histogram is the average of 83 samples representative of individual floods over six years

The stream beds consist predominantly of pebble and cobble-size sandstone and limestone clasts which form a self-supporting and interlocking framework (figure 13.1d). Infilling the interstices between these elements is a finer population of sands and granules, generally in the sand-size grades (figures 13.2a and 13.2c).

Although finer sediments may be winnowed from the surface layers during moderate discharges, the largest framework particles are only entrained under high flow conditions which approach or exceed bankfull discharge. These large particles (>4 mm) control the local bed morphology having a relatively high threshold of motion and consequently a long residence time in the system. In contrast, the finer sand-size bed material may pass through the system more rapidly in suspension. These materials may be stored temporarily in the void space of the gravels to be released during scouring discharges. Within the study reaches there were no bed-forms other than various cluster assemblages (Brayshaw et al., 1983).

Objectives

The objectives of the research reported here were, firstly, to describe the process of sorting and the mobility of coarse bed-material particles during in-channel floods having short recurrence intervals; secondly, to consider the depth to which these coarse-bedded streams are disturbed during competent discharges; and thirdly, to consider what ranges of discharge are responsible for winnowing finer sediments from the bed, and disrupting the framework population of coarser sediments.

RATIONALE

Particle sorting and mobility

Although little investigated, the total distance of travel of a bedload particle during a flood event when the threshold for transport of the particle is exceeded is of importance. Here this is referred to simply as the *step-length*. This is clearly distinguished from the 'jump-length', that is, the horizontal distance between successive bed contacts of saltating grains (Einstein, 1937; Poreh et al., 1970; Murphy and Amin, 1979).

The distance travelled by a particle of given size is relevant to bedload transport modelling, defining the residence time of sediment in the system, and describing the selective transportation of size fractions. The data may also be applied to dynamic considerations of the geometry of gravel bed forms, because the dimensions and spacing of bed features, for example pool-riffle sequences, may be related to the step-length (Naden, 1981; Naden and Brayshaw, chapter 10, this volume).

Active-layer dynamics

The thickness of the bed-layer disturbed by scouring discharges is relevant to bedload–transport modelling and channel–stability studies. As well as a vertical dimension to the problem there is also a further spatial perspective in that the degree of disturbance is likely to vary across the section.

Magnitude of winnowing or scouring discharges

Bedload transport in gravel-bedded rivers at any given section may be divided conceptually into two phases. During a range of lower competent flows the framework gravels may be winnowed at the surface leaving an open-work surface layer; the fine sediments are transported over a basically stable coarser bed (Carling and Reader, 1982). This phase has been variously described as 'throughput load', 'under-capacity load' or 'phase 1 transport' by a number of authors (e.g. Bathurst, chapter 11, this volume). For a range of higher flows the framework of the bed becomes disrupted with increasingly larger particles being entrained until eventually the D_{50} of the bedload becomes approximately equivalent to the D_{50} of the bed-material population. This latter phase has been variously referred to as 'bed-material load', 'capacity load' or 'phase 2 transport', when the bed is approaching a fully active state and significant changes in channel section morphology are possible.

In terms of channel stability and the cleansing of heavily silted gravels it is useful to identify two suites of flows based on the above definition. For convenience we can term the two phases (phase 1 and phase 2) 'winnowing flows' and 'scouring flows' and seek a sedimentological distinction in terms of the bedload granulometry, although clearly in some streams the two suites of discharges may represent end-members of a continuum of variation in granulometry.

METHODS

Particle sorting and mobility

Tracers used to study particle motion consisted mainly of a large number of painted and numbered particles. Gravel was collected in bulk from the streambed surface and the fraction less than 4 mm in size was discarded. The tracer sample for Great Eggleshope Beck consisted of 80% pebbles and 20% cobbles, whilst that for Carl Beck was 87% pebbles and 13% cobbles (nomenclature after Wentworth-Lane – see Pettijohn, 1975). Several boulders were also used as tracers. The weight and the lengths of three major axes of each particle were recorded. Particles were split into three batches, painted a distinctive colour and a reference number was painted on each clast. In Great Eggleshope Beck a total of 647 particles were painted and in Carl Beck, 279 painted particles were used.

In each stream three straight reaches, free from pool-riffle sequences, were selected. This ensured that the distances particles moved would reflect particle mobility rather than local changes in the gross hydraulic environment. Particles were placed on the bed in rows across the stream during low flows in August 1978. Each particle was approximately eight diameters from its nearest neighbour to minimize particle wake interaction (Langbein and Leopold, 1968). No attempt was made to replace existing particles embedded in the sediment body as the mobility of entrained particles was of interest rather than the threshold conditions for motion of grains.

Table 13.1   Physical characteristics of sites investigated

Variables	Great Eggleshope Beck	Carl Beck
Catchment area (km^2)	11.68	2.18
Max. altitude (m)	653	513
Min. altitude (m)	343	122
Channel gradient	0.01	0.04
Max. stream width (m)	9	2.5
Max. stream depth (m)	1	0.72
Sinuosity	1.08	1.11
Mean annual discharge (m^{3}s^{-1})	0.20	0.05
Mean annual flood[a] (m^{3}s^{-1})	6.38	3.00
Bankfull discharge (m^{3}s^{-1})	5.60	2.35
Base flow index[b]	0.33	0.23
D_{90} (mm)	110	135
D_{50} (mm)	20	50
Percentage < 4 mm	29	16

[a] Estimated from partial duration series, return period 1.76 years (NERC, 1975).
[b] Ratio of base flows to total flow in a hydrograph. Ranging between theoretical limits of 0 and 1.0, it may be interpreted as a general index of stream 'flashiness' with 'flashy' streams having low index values. See Anon. (1978).

In each reach 'bankfull' was defined using the minimum width–depth ratio (e.g. Wolman, 1955; Pickup and Warner, 1976) which conformed generally to the intersection of the plane of the floodplain surface with the bank profile. The discharge with a return period of 0.9 yr on the partial duration series was found to most closely match gauged discharges at bankfull (table 13.1). For the purposes of this chapter other gauged discharges have usually been expressed as percentages of the bankfull value.

In Carl Beck, small floods which exceeded the transport threshold defined by the Shields parameter (Simons and Şentürk, 1977) for all the particle sizes, occurred on the 2 (ungauged) and 15 November 1978 (51% bankfull) and 8 December 1978 (17% bankfull). In Great Eggleshope Beck a 97% bankfull flood occurred on the 8 December 1978. During these floods thresholds were exceeded for about 40–48 hrs. Subsequent to these dates material was too dispersed for further investigation. After each flood the distance each particle had moved downstream was measured. In Carl Beck the step length of 222 particles was measured but unfortunately in Great Eggleshope Beck the passage of a further flood occurred before field survey was complete and only 26 particle distances had been measured.

Active-layer dynamics

Grids of scour chains across the full stream width and 1 m apart were installed in straight single-channel reaches in Carl Beck and Great Eggleshope Beck. A record was made of net scour or deposition over the grid sites for each of a total of 12 and 21 floods in Great Eggleshope Beck and Carl Beck respectively for the water years 1980 and 1981. Scour and deposition data were analysed separately to yield mean depth of scour, maximum depth of scour, mean and maximum depth of deposition and the percentage of the bed area affected.

The method allows reasonable estimates of scour or deposition at a section to be made, but unfortunately it is not possible to relate these processes to the rising or falling stages of a hydrograph. Instead results were correlated with the instantaneous (five-minute integral) peak discharge preceding each scour survey, obtained from continuously recorded discharge data at gauging sites adjacent to the scour/fill sections. No bedforms developed in the coarse gravels, so it was considered reasonable to seek a first-order correlation of discharge with scour or fill.

Magnitude of winnowing and scouring discharges

In order to characterize the granulometry of bed material moved by flood events, bedload was trapped in pit-type traps (see Carling, 1983; Carling and Hurley, 1987). Representative grain-size histograms were drawn for 160 bulk samples of bedload. Each sample represented a single flood event, the discharge characteristics of which were known precisely.

RESULTS

Particle sorting and mobility

In the Great Eggleshope study reaches between 45 and 82% of tagged material moved during the flood. Of the total material, on average, 18% of material was unmoved, 60% was recovered and the remaining 22% was presumed to be buried in the stream. In Carl Beck 72% of material was moved and only 2% was buried, as in the latter stream the bed tends to be more compacted. Whether or not material was entrained appeared to depend not on the grain size but on the local orientation of the particle in relation to other bed material, although this was not examined in detail.

Plotting the grain-size distributions of the original tracer material and the recovered material indicated a progressive skewing of the data to coarse sizes

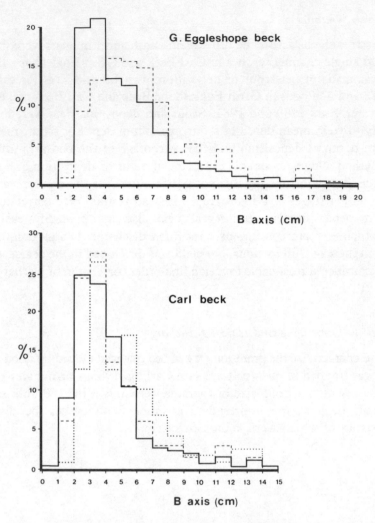

Figure 13.3 Histograms of the length of the tracer particle intermediate axes. Solid curve is the original tracer. The pecked and dotted lines represent the recovered tracer after one and two floods respectively

as finer pebble material was selectively incorporated into the stream-bed (figure 13.3). In each stream a little material was recovered chipped or broken, indicative of abrasion.

In Great Eggleshope Beck for the bankfull flood the maximum distance travelled was 63 m, averaging 12.65 m (standard error (SE), 3.64 m). In Carl Beck, for the series of smaller floods, the maximum distance was 14 m, averaging 1.14 m (SE 0.076 m). Given a typical flood duration of 48 hours average particle

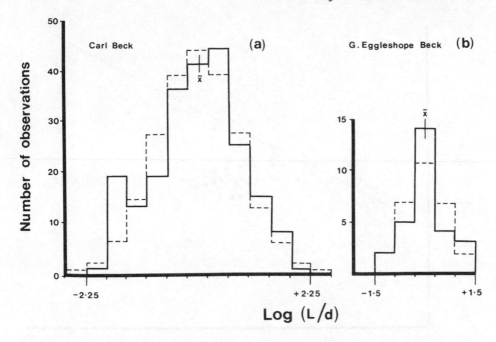

Figure 13.4 Distribution of logarithms of the non-dimensional particle step-lengths (solid line) compared with the theoretical log-normal distribution (pecked line). Histogram intervals represent ± one half or one standard deviation about a zero mean

'velocities' *including periods of rest,* varied between $2\,\mathrm{cm\,h^{-1}}$ for intermediate flows and $26\,\mathrm{cm\,h^{-1}}$ at bankfull, depending on the site and the individual event. There was no evidence of consistent differences between sites, and an increase in distance travelled with the higher magnitude event is as might be expected (Church, 1972; Stelczer, 1981). In addition, there was no relationship between particle diameter, weight or shape (the latter expressed by the Zingg classification; Pettijohn, 1975) and distance travelled. However when comparing the Zingg classification of recovered particles with the original tracer, a propensity for slightly more rod-like particles to have been moved was apparent at some sites.

The non-dimensional step-length is defined as the ratio between the distance travelled (L) and the particle intermediate diameter (d), i.e. L/d. The distance travelled and the particle step-length distributions are not significantly different from log-normal (2.5% level, chi-squared test) (figure 13.4). The value at the cumulative fifty percentile represents the central tendency of the distribution. In the case of Carl Beck L/d at 50% is 12.4 and the 95% and 5% values are 0.2 and 129.4 respectively. For Great Eggleshope Beck the values are 50.5, 3.6 and 717.5 respectively.

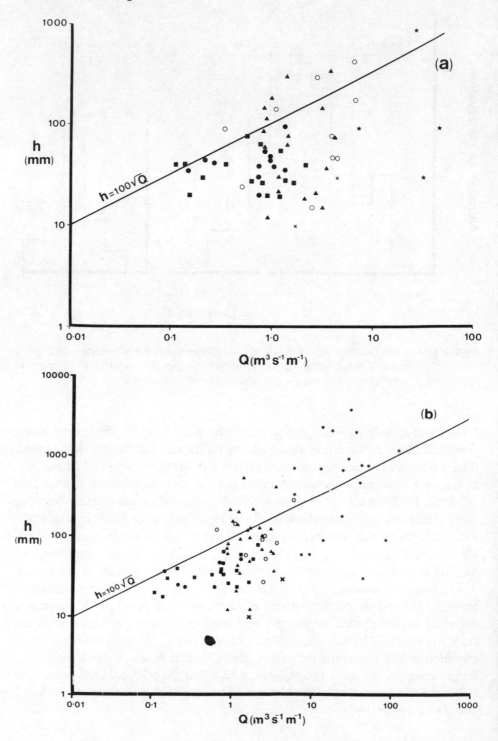

Active-layer dynamics

Scour and fill. No significant correlation could be obtained between the reach averaged mean scour or maximum scour and the peak discharge per metre of bed-width in either stream. Although the chains were checked during a range of low discharges, no movement at all was measured for discharges less than about $0.113 \, \mathrm{m^3 \, s^{-1} \, m^{-1}}$ ($0.07 \, \mathrm{m^3 \, s^{-1} \, km^{-2}}$).

Emmett and Leopold (1965) found a relationship between the mean scour depth (h) and discharge per unit bed-width (Q) for an ephemeral coarse sand-bedded stream using scour chain data,

$$h = a\sqrt{Q} \tag{13.1}$$

where $a = 100$ with Q measured in $\mathrm{m^3 \, s^{-1} \, m^{-1}}$ and h measured in mm. This relationship is shown in figure 13.5. The Carl Beck and Great Eggleshope Beck data have a mean value for scour of 37.8 mm (SE 3.1 mm) and a mean discharge of $0.83 \, \mathrm{m^3 \, s^{-1} \, m^{-1}}$. A discharge of this value substituted into equation (13.1) gives a predicted scour depth of 91.3 mm in sand. The ratio $37.8/91.3 = 0.4$ indicates that mean scour depth in the coarse gravel is about two-fifths of the predicted scour depth in the sand-bedded stream.

Maximum scour depth had a mean value of 65.0 mm (SE 7.7 mm; $N = 32$). The ratio $65.0/91.3 = 0.7$ indicates that the mean value of the maximum scour depth in gravel is less than three-quarters of the mean scour depth in sand as predicted from equation (13.1).

Combining data for both streams, the depth of deposition expressed as the mean or maximum depth was correlated with the peak discharge per metre bed width.

Mean deposition	$= 42.06 \, Q^{0.34}$	$r^2 = 0.45$	$p < 0.001$	(13.2)
Maximum deposition	$= 81.14 \, Q^{0.54}$	$r^2 = 0.58$	$p < 0.001$	(13.3)

The 95% confidence limits (Draper and Smith, 1966) on β, are ± 0.15 in equation (13.2) and ± 0.18 in equation (13.3). The similarity of equations (13.2) and (13.3) to equation (13.1) should be noted.

Figure 13.5 *(opposite)* (a) Depth of scour in study streams (together with additional published data) as a function of discharge per unit channel width. The curve is the relationship proposed by Emmett and Leopold (1965) (see text). ● = Great Eggleshope Beck; ■ = Carl Beck; ○ = sandy gravels; ▲ = sands, source - Culbertson and Dawdy (1964); * = cobbles, source - Hickey (1969); x = gravel, source - Slaymaker (1972). (b) Depth of deposition in study streams (together with additional published data) as a function of discharge per unit channel width. Other details as for figure 13.5a

To ascertain whether the Teesdale data are representative of other gravel-bedded rivers additional data for large rivers are also included in figure 13.5. Scour and fill data from Culbertson and Dawdy (1964) are for stream beds of mixed sand and gravel. Additional data for sand-bedded streams are also included for comparison. Discharge values are not necessarily peak values but are the largest recorded on each survey date during periods of high flow and rapid scour or fill. Data for cobble-bedded streams are taken from Hickey (1969) and Slaymaker (1972 . In the former case discharge is the peak value of a flood which had an estimated recurrence interval of 400 yr (Brown and Ritter, 1971).

There is no consistent trend from limited scour in coarse gravel to deep scour in sand. Culbertson and Dawdy's deposition data overlap the Teesdale data, but exhibit a greater range, with most high deposition values associated with sand-bedded streams. Hickey's data are interesting in that discharges were high; deposition of cobble-material was greater than an extrapolation of the regression line through the Teesdale data would indicate.

An equation describing the trend of the 46 data points for scour in gravel-bed streams in figure 13.5a is;

$$\text{Mean scour} \qquad = 43.20 \, Q^{0.27} \qquad r^2 = 0.19 \qquad p < 0.01 \qquad\qquad (13.4)$$

Similarly an equation for the 62 points for deposition (Fig. 5b) is;

$$\text{Mean deposition} = 54.23 \, Q^{0.58} \qquad r^2 = 0.54 \qquad p < 0.001 \qquad\qquad (13.5)$$

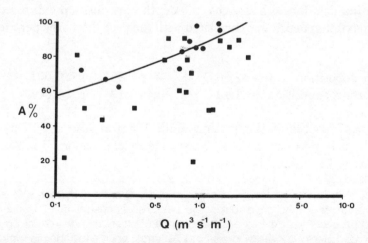

Figure 13.6   Relationship between the area of the active bed in the study reach and the discharge of the stream per unit bed width. ● = Great Eggleshope Beck; ■ = Carl Beck. Curve represents equation (13.6) in the text

Area of bed scoured or filled. In the study reaches, stream width (W) increases with discharge (Q) approximately to the power of 1/6 or 1/7. It is reasonable therefore to anticipate a similar result when considering the area of bed which scoured *or* filled. The exponent for percentage change in the active bed area (A) varied little, typically between 1/5 and 1/7 depending on stream reach. The Eggleshope data for example,

$$A = 88.55 \, Q^{0.175}, \qquad r^2 = 0.70 \qquad p < 0.001 \tag{13.6}$$

describes an approximate trend for the area of bed affected for a given discharge (figure 13.6). At the threshold for scour, $Q = 0.113 \, m^3 \, s^{-1} \, m^{-1}$, some 60% of the bed width may be expected to be active, rising to 100% at a discharge of $2.0 \, m^3 \, s^{-1} \, m^{-1}$ which is in excess of the mean annual flood.

Relationship between maximum scour and mean scour. Colby (1964) believed that the maximum depth of scour recorded using scour chains is not always indicative of a change in mean bed elevation in the cross-section. This observation is not applicable to the present investigation, because it relates to sand-bed streams with significant local variations in bed elevation related to dune bedform migration.

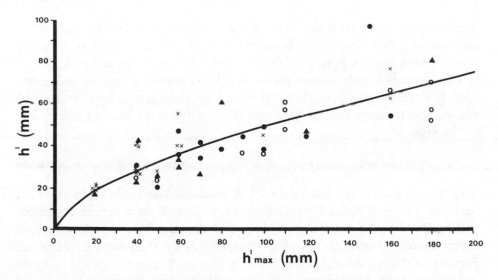

Figure 13.7 Relationship between mean depth of the active layer ($\bar{h}$) for each flood event and the corresponding maximum depth of the layer (h_{max}). The curve is equation (13.7) in the text. Great Eggleshope Beck: $\circ$ = deposition; $\bullet$ = scour; Carl Beck: $\blacktriangle$ = deposition; x = scour

Preliminary data analysis indicated that mean scour and maximum scour, and mean disposition and maximum disposition each display a power function relationship with little variation in the regression coefficient between both Carl Beck and Great Eggleshope Beck. Consequently a single relationship was derived for all the data (figure 13.7) using the least squares procedure;

$$\bar{h} = 3.17\,h_{max}^{0.5962} \qquad (13.7)$$

where $N = 64$ and with an r^2 value of 0.81 the relationship is statistically significant at the $p < 0.001$ level.

Thickness of active bed-layer.   For high flows capable of moving the bed material, the mean scour depth may be regarded as indicative of the thickness of the active bed-layer (h), which may be related to a *potential* bedload transport rate per metre bed width (I_b');

$$I_b' = \bar{h}\,U_b\,\varrho_s\,(1-\lambda) \qquad (13.8)$$

where U_b is the transport velocity of the bed-layer for fully established particle motion, ϱ_s is the density of the sediment grains and λ is the bed porosity.

In the present investigation,

$$\bar{h} \approx 0.55\bar{d} \qquad (13.9)$$

where $\bar{d}$ is the mean grain size of the bed material. Equation (13.9) implies that lage sediment particles are not in motion or very few are in motion at a given time. Consequently a process of selective winnowing of the surface bed-layer can be envisaged with coarser grains remaining stable or settling to a lower equilibrium level. However, scatter about the mean value of scour together with the maximum values recorded indicate that locally, scour may be greater and of the order of

$$\bar{h}_{max} = 0.94\,\bar{d} \simeq \bar{d} \qquad (13.10)$$

To solve equation (13.8) a value for U_b is required. Many investigations of the relative velocities of bedload particles and the fluid medium have been conducted (Allen, 1984, p. 95) which demonstrate that particle velocity at low bedload concentrations increases rapidly once fully established particle motion is achieved. Particles, although moving at less than the average stream velocity (e.g. Ippen and Verma, 1955; Steidtmann, 1982) have velocities not dissimilar to the near-bed velocity (e.g. Einstein, 1950; Ippen and Verma 1955; Abbott and Francis, 1977). Here, complications introduced owing to particle shape and size differences with respect to the bed material have of necessity been ignored and particle velocities equated to the near-bed velocities. The latter were obtained from detailed velocity profiles extrapolated to a reference height above the bed equal to $0.5\,\bar{h}$.

The term $\bar{h}\,U_b\,\varrho_s\,(1-\lambda)$ was solved for the field data in Great Eggleshope Beck to yield a maximum potential transport rate. Similarly the mean sediment transport rate (I_b) associated with each flood was calculated from an unpublished well-defined streampower (ω) - sediment transport function derived from field data obtained during the period of the scour survey.

The relationship between I_b and $\bar{h}\,U_b\,\varrho_s\,(1-\lambda)$ is shown in figure 13.8. If all the bedlayer which is disturbed contributed to the bedload, I_b would equal $\bar{h}\,U_b\,\varrho_s\,(1-\lambda)$. This is evidently not the case.

Magnitude of winnowing and scouring discharges

The bed materials in both streams generally have unimodal size distributions (figure 13.2). The lack of distinct bimodality in distributions however does not mean that deposits cannot be viewed as bi- or multi-component mixtures (Harding, 1949; Pettijohn, 1975). Carling and Reader (1982) noted that in distinctly bimodal deposits the frequency minima between the two modes fell in the 2–3 mm size range.

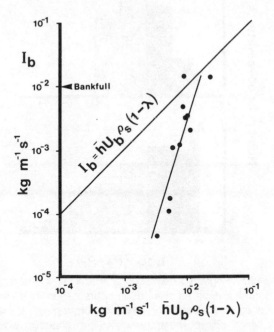

Figure 13.8 Relationship between the measured bedload transport rate, I_b, and the 'active-layer' transport rate, $\bar{h}U_b\,\varrho_s\,(1-\lambda)$ (see text for details)

Although processes such as clast to mineral-grain disintegration may account for bimodality in some deposits (Dreimanis and Vagners, 1971), in the present deposits experimental investigations (Carling and McCahon, in press) have shown that this division can be described as a two-component mixture whereby mobile grains finer than 4 mm have a high probability of entering the interstices of a static coarse-pebble mixture, whilst coarser sediments are only incorporated into the framework population when the bed is disrupted by high flows. The frequency minimum is also in general accord with the findings of Carling and Hurley (1987) that material coarser than 2 mm only moves as bedload whilst finer sediments, as well as moving as a bedload, may frequently occur in suspension. It therefore seems justifiable to expect a division between 'winnowed bedload' and 'framework bedload' in this grain-size region (i.e. 2–4 mm). Although a few bedload grain-size distributions had the mode centred in the region 2–4 mm or were distinctly bimodal, with modes either side of this range, the greater majority of histograms were either fine- or coarse-skewed. The separation point between 'winnowed bedload' and 'framework bedload' was identified as that frequency interval in the average histogram for

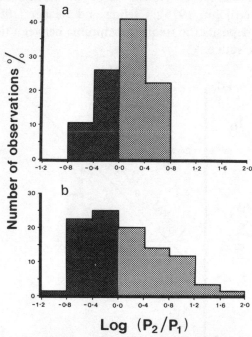

Figure 13.9 Frequency histogram of framework to matrix ratios of bedload size distributions P_2 represents the percentage of the distribution coarser than 4 mm whilst P_1 represents the percentage finer than 4 mm. Log $(P_2/P_1) > 0$ therefore represents predominantly phase 2 transport events which disrupt the framework (light shading) whilst Log $(P_2/P_1) < 0$ represent phase 1 transport events which winnow the bed sediments (dense shading). (a) Carl Beck; (b) Great Eggleshope Beck

all flood data (figures 13.2b and 13.2d) which had the smallest standard error whilst the errors increased on either side of this point. For Carl Beck the interval was 2–4 mm and in Eggleshope it was 4–16 mm. Closer definition is not possible but it confirmed that conceptually the two populations (coarse- and fine-skewed) grade into one another at about 4 mm.

Turning to a consideration of winnowing or scouring discharges, scouring events can now be defined as having the bulk by weight of the load coarser than 4 mm whilst winnowing events have predominately finer material. Consequently the D_{50} should also be greater than 4 mm or less than 4 mm depending upon the category so that flood events can be classified on the basis of the bedload D_{50} value. The lack of a distinct separation in the streams between winnowing and scouring flows is shown in figure 13.9 wherein the distributions of ratios of coarse to fine sediments are unimodal. In Carl Beck 50% of floods significantly modified the framework population but in no case did the D_{50} of the bedload become equal to the D_{50} of the framework although some material of equivalent and larger size was transported in most 'phase 2' floods. Associated discharges averaged 75% bankfull (SE 6.8%) whilst competent flows for phase 1 averaged 23% bankfull (SE 7%) indicating a roughly normal distribution of flood flows. In Great Eggleshope Beck some 27% of floods modified the framework population. These discharges averaged 94% of bankfull (SE 4.6%). For phase 1 floods, discharges averaged 36% of bankfull (SE 3.91%) indicating a non-normal distribution of flood magnitudes for Great Eggleshope Beck (see Carling and Hurley, 1987).

DISCUSSION

Particle sorting and mobility

Although the theoretical threshold of motion for an exposed grain on a planar bed was exceeded for all particles during each flood, not all particles were entrained. Clearly the attitude of an exposed particle in relation to surrounding embedded particles is important when considering the entrainment of natural mixtures (Brayshaw el al., 1983), although the position of the particle in the channel cross-section has also been regarded as important (Butler, 1977).

The lack of a relationship between particle diameter or mass and the distance travelled has been reported from other investigations (Butler, 1977; Brayshaw et al., 1983). Although from theoretical reasoning, one might expect particles of small mass to have greater transport velocities and hence to travel greater distances, larger particles (despite their mass) present a greater surface area to the flow and are consequently subject to a greater drag force. The latter argument was used by Meland and Norrman (1966) to advocate greater mobility for larger particles although field data have often indicated that the reverse actually occurs (e.g. Leopold et al., 1966; Laronne and Carson, 1976). This discrepancy between theory and field observation has been discussed briefly by Frostick and Reid (1980). The relationship between the size distribution of the mobile particles and the size distribution and packing of the bed material is clearly important. In a natural stream, small particles can readily become entrapped in the interstices of an immobile surface layer of cobble bed-material even during high flows when the mobility of small particles might be expected to be maximized. In contrast, particles larger than the average grain size of the bed material are less likely to find a niche in which to settle, can easily roll over the underlying bed material, but owing to their mass are unlikely to be transported very far.

The residence time of particles stored in the bed is unknown. However, although the experiments were terminated in the autumn of 1978, tagged particles were still occasionally being exhumed by flood flows in the experimental reaches in 1983–4. These particles may have been exposed and reburied on a number of occasions, but evidently some material can essentially remain in store for several years, being transported only a few metres downstream.

The step-lengths are not great and lay emphasis on Church's (1972) general observation that 'individual cobbles do not appear to move very far at any one time'. In Church's investigation transport distances were less than the riffle spacing and therefore more than one flood event was required to move cobbles through the intervening pools. Although in this investigation the reaches chosen were free from pool-riffle sequences the average step-length is also much less than the spacing or riffles in upland streams (i.e. 3–10 stream widths – Ferguson, 1981). However the average step-lengths and the range of values are very similar to theoretical calculations of characteristic gravel bedform lengths reported by Naden (1981). Naden also reported observed bedform lengths in gravel-bedded streams including Great Eggleshope Beck but no explanation was given as to how characteristic bedforms and lengths were defined in the field. Nevertheless, the similarity between the dimensions of observed step-lengths in the present investigation and Naden's theoretical bedform dimensions may indicate a causal link and should be examined further (Naden and Brayshaw, chapter 10, this volume).

Active-layer dynamics

The data presented are by no means conclusive. There is a limited range of discharge values (only two orders of magnitude) in the Teesdale streams coupled with a large inherent variance in the data from the scour chains. Nevertheless the values of the exponents in equations (13.2) and (13.3) suggest that scour and deposition of gravels have a functional relationship with discharge very similar to that of scour of sand.

Additional evidence is however available to verify that the scour-chain data are reasonably representative of the thickness of the active bed-layer. Ottaway (unpublished report) recorded scour by repeated levelling in the same reach as the scour-chain grids in Great Eggleshope Beck. A maximum depth of scour of 200 mm and of deposition of 170 mm were recorded. In Carl Beck, Ottaway buried artificial colour-coded fish eggs at various depths up to 130 mm below the gravel surface. After a season of spates, eggs were relocated by digging the gravel over. Recovery of eggs buried at 120 mm and over was close to 100% whilst recovery of eggs buried at 60 mm depth was very low at 2%. These data compare favourably with the average value of maximum scour depth obtained from scour chains – 65.0 mm.

Better correlation with discharge was obtained for deposition than was obtained for scour. This may be because measured deposition probably occurs primarily during the waning hydrograph (e.g. Colby, 1964); deposits consequently are undisturbed when chains were relocated. In contrast, chains recording scour may have been subject to a degree of infilling during the falling stage of the hydrograph so that the record is less clear. Nevertheless perceptible bedload movement was not recorded at discharges less than $0.113 \, \text{m}^3 \, \text{m}^{-1} \text{s}^{-1}$, which represents a general threshold for scour or fill in these two streams.

The percentage of the bed area scoured or filled during the passage of a hydrograph is approximately defined (figure 13.6). Notwithstanding the scatter in the data it is clear that in these simple trapezoidal channels over half of the bed area exhibits a degree of mobility once the threshold discharge is exceeded. However, reflecting their essentially stable nature, the whole bed-width does not become active until discharges in excess of bankfull are attained.

The sediment transport rate as indicated by the depth of the active layer is much greater than the measured transport rates (figure 13.8). Even allowing for the assumptions explicit in deriving a solution for equation (13.8), the discrepancy suggests that many sediment grains disturbed by the flow are not actively transported but remain as an unstable bedlayer (Emmett and Leopold, 1965). Grains close to the threshold of motion may be envisaged as vibrating and bouncing in scour hollows in the bed (e.g. Urbonas, quoted in Simons and Şentürk, 1976, p. 675), whilst slightly larger grains may remain virtually stationary in an activated bed-layer (Milhous and Klingeman, 1973). The data plotted in figure 13.8 only become coincident with equation (13.8) at a sediment transport rate associated with bankfull discharge when the disturbed bed-layer is fully activated and all grain sizes present in the bed material have been recorded moving as bedload.

Magnitude of winnowing and scouring discharges

It is useful to review the magnitudes of the winnowing and scouring discharges in the context of the concept of a 'dominant' or 'effective' discharge. The dominant discharge concept at its simplest specifies that a critical discharge can be isolated which is responsible for the channel capacity. Alternatively this discharge can in fact represent a suite of channel-forming discharges but in itself may be regarded as a standard conceptual reference point (Pickup and Rieger, 1979) with a presumed morphogenic function. Although the concept originally was related to the development of regime theory for the engineering design of canals, numerous investigators have applied the concept to natural alluvial rivers. The consensus appears to indicate that the dominant discharge may not be constant through time but generally it tends to equal the bankfull discharge (Thomas, 1976). Intuitively this seems reasonable as the capacity of a channel must be adjusted to a discharge which fills it. In practice the definition may vary to some degree depending on which morphological or hydraulic geometry parameter is of immediate interest (Ackers and Charlton, 1970).

An alternative viewpoint, which may be more appropriate, is to consider as dominant or effective that discharge which moves most bedload (Prins and de Vries, 1971) or disrupts the boundary, as channel shape must be adjusted to bedload throughput (Pickup, 1976). This approach has the advantage of being complementary to the classical Wolman and Miller (1960) view on the significance of the magnitude and frequency of channel-forming processes and effective discharges may be equivalent to the bankfull value in many instances (Hey, 1975). The procedure is not without its problems. Many coarse gravel-bedded streams may have a large bedload transport of finer sediments passing over an essentially stable channel perimeter; this is the case of 'phase 1 transport'. Consequently there is a need to consider both winnowing and scouring discharges. Winnowing discharges are unlikely to promote large-scale channel changes although the local deposition of fine sediments as bars may effect channel roughness and capacity and hence through hydraulic adjustments induce morphological change. Scouring discharges on the other hand must be viewed as morphologically significant. As has been demonstrated above, a wide range of flows may move framework particles and the overall depth of disturbance is small. Nevertheless a range of scouring discharges was identified based on the granulometry of the bedload and was used to define closely a 'dominant' or 'effective' discharge representative of the range of effective discharges.

In the case of Carl Beck this value, i.e. 75% bankfull, is considerably less than the bankfull value and has an estimated return period of about six months on the partial duration series. In Great Eggleshope Beck the value, 94% bankfull, is not significantly different from bankfull and has an estimated return period of about ten months (see Carling and Hurley, 1987). It is important to consider these values in relation to the bankfull discharge noting also that the full bed-width in Great Eggleshope Beck is probably not active until discharges in excess of bankfull occur (figure 13.6).

Great Eggleshope Beck is an alluvial stream running through a valley-fill deposited by the stream. Bedrock constraints on the channel shape are absent in the study reaches. The channel is free to adjust its shape so that concordance of the dominant discharge (in terms of that mean discharge effective in scouring the framework bed material) with the bankfull value may reasonably be expected.

Although all bed material grain sizes may be mobile at bankfull discharge the full width does not necessarily become activated until discharges in excess of bankfull occur. In this respect the channel may be adjusted to the bankfull flow and over short time-spans may be viewed as close to steady-state in that it displays a degree of insensitivity to floods of the order of the bankfull discharge. High flows, it should be noted, are sustained only briefly and downcutting and lateral expansion of bed activity may be curtailed as high bedload transport rates probably induce negative feedback and a tendency to renewed bed stabilization. This is as might be anticipated from the evidence of a small active layer thickness and short particle step-lengths. Consequently, with minimal bed level changes one might expect any adjustments to channel geometry to occur in the stream width. Comparison of cross-sections throughout the study period demonstrates that stream response to overbank floods is indeed largely by lateral migration induced by erosion of the gravel and silt banks.

By contrast, the channel of Carl Beck is entrenched largely in till, with a coarser and more compact bed than Great Eggleshope Beck. Large boulders provide frequent control on channel size and shape. Therefore it is not truly alluvial. The present channel capacity appears to be over-adjusted to the present discharge regime, in that the effective discharge is substantially less than the bankfull value. Nevertheless the bankfull discharge has a return period comparable to that in Great Eggleshope Beck, being slightly less than one year. In this respect the return periods for bankfull discharge in both streams are in accordance with observations of Nixon (1959) and others that upland streams in the UK have bankfull return periods somewhat less or equivalent to the commonly quoted value of 0.9 yr (1.5 yr on the annual series) for larger gravel-bedded rivers (Hey, 1975).

CONCLUSIONS

Problems of channel stability or alluviation associated with river regulation will only be better understood when more attention has been given to process mechanics, rates and magnitudes. The present investigation also highlights the need to consider whether streams under investigation may be regarded either as truly alluvial and free to adjust their hydraulic geometry, or as having a geometry (as in the case of Carl Beck) which is partially constrained or inherited from previous discharge regimes. The results for the alluvial stream, Great Eggleshope Beck, tend to confirm the generalization that bankfull discharge may be regarded as the effective, or dominant, discharge in these small upland gravel bedded streams. The recurrence interval on the partial duration series for this discharge is slightly less than one year. The discharge is effective in that it is representative of a suite of discharges which promote channel bed scour, although it should be noted that even at bankfull the full stream width was not active. Discharges in excess of bankfull are required for extensive channel change and at bankfull the channel is essentially in a steady-state condition with negative feedback rapidly promoting bed stability.

In the management context and with regard to regulation of similar streams or rivers, the imposition of an altered discharge regime may lead to channels adjusting their overall dimensions through scour or deposition. From an ecological perspective the proportion of fines in the stream bed material is also of consequence, although this topic has not been addressed in detail in this chapter. The present results indicate that for discharge less than bankfull, winnowing of the surface layers in a gravel-bed channel may consist of the selective removal of matrix sediments by 'phase-1 flows' or by partial movement of the framework by 'phase-2 flows'. However only the surface layer, which is about one mean grain-diameter in thickness is effectively winnowed and this process will be most effective in the channel centre. At depth in the gravel of a regulated stream bed, an increase in the percentage of fine matrix sediments will occur as the regulated-stream bed will be less active. Fines cannot be flushed out except by flows which exceed bankfull and grossly disrupt the framework sediments; and such events are less frequent under flow regulation. Consequently, even over a wide range of in-channel discharges, surface deposits of fines might be expected to persist at the lateral margins of a regulated stream channel.

ACKNOWLEDGEMENTS

The project was funded by the Department of the Environment, the Natural Environment Research Council, the Northumbrian Water Authority, the Water Research Centre and the Ministry of Agriculture, Fisheries and Food. Mr N. A. Reader is thanked for assistance in field work and Mr M. S. Glaister drafted the figures.

REFERENCES

Abbott, J. E. and Francis, J. R. D. 1977: Saltation and suspension trajectories of solid grains in a water stream. *Phil. Trans. Roy. Soc. London*, 284A, 225-54.

Ackers, P. and Charlton, F. G. 1970: The slope and resistance of small meandering channels. *Proc. Inst. Civ. Engr. Suppl.*, XV, 349-70.

Allen, J. R. L. 1984: *Sedimentary Structures: Their Character and Physical Basis*. Amsterdam: Elsevier.

Anon. 1978: *Low Flow Study Report, No. 1 April*. Wallingford, England: Institute of Hydrology.

Beschta, R. L. and Jackson, W. L. 1979: The intrusion of fine sediments into a stable gravel bed. *J. Fish. Res. Board Can.*, 36, 204-10.

Brayshaw, A. C., Frostick, L. E. and Reid, I. 1983: The hydrodynamics of particle clusters and sediment entrainment in coarse alluvial channels. *Sedimentology*, 30, 137-43.

Brown, W. M. and Ritter, J. R. 1971: Sediment transport and turbidity in the Eel River basin, California. *US Geol. Surv. Water Suppl. Paper*, 1986.

Butler, P. R. 1977: Movement of cobbles in a gravel-bed stream during a flood season. *Geol. Soc. Am. Bull.*, 88, 1072-4.

Carling, P. A. 1983: Threshold of coarse sediment transport in broad and narrow natural streams. *Earth Surf. Processes & Landforms*, 8, 1-18.

Carling, P. A. 1984: Deposition of fine and coarse sand in an open-work gravel bed. *Can. J. Fish. Aq. Sci.*, 41, 263-70.

Carling, P. A. and Hurley, M. A. 1987: A time-varying stochastic model of the magnitude and frequency of bedload transport events in small trout streams. In C. R. Thorne, J. C. Bathurst and R. D. Hey (eds) *Sediment Transport in Gravel-bed Rivers*, Chichester: Wiley.

Carling, P. A. and Reader, N. A. 1982: Structure, composition and bulk properties of upland stream gravels. *Earth Surf. Processes & Landforms*, 7, 349-65.

Carling, P. A. and McCahon, C. P. In press: Natural siltation of brown trout (*Salmo trutta* L.) spawning gravels during low flow conditions. In J. F. Craig and J. B. Kemper (eds), *Regulated Streams: Advances in Ecology*, New York: Plenum Press, 229-44.

Charlton, F. G. 1977: An appraisal of available data on gravel rivers. *Report, Hydraulics Research Station, Wallingford, England*, INT 151.

Church, M. 1972: Baffin Island sandurs: a study of Arctic fluvial processes. *Geol. Surv. Canada Bull.*, 216, 93-7.

Colby, B. R. 1964: Scour and fill in sand-bed streams. *US Geol. Surv. Prof. Paper*, 462-D.

Culbertson, J. K. and Dawdy, D. R. 1964: A study of fluvial characteristics and hydraulic variables, Middle Rio Grande New Mexico. *US Geol. Surv. Water Suppl. Paper*, 1498-F.

Draper, N. R. and Smith, H. 1966: *Applied Regression Analysis*. New York: John Wiley.

Dreimanis, A. and Vagners, U. J. 1971: Bimodal distribution of rock and mineral fragments in basal tills. In R. P. Goldthwait (ed.), *Till – a Symposium*, Ohio State University Press, 237-50.

Einstein, H. A. 1937: Der Geschiebebetrieb als Wahrscheinlichkeits-problem. *Mitteilung der Versuchanstalt für Wasserbau*, Hochschule in Zürich.

Einstein, H. A. 1950: The bed-load function for sediment transportation in open channel flows. *US Dept Agric. Tech. Bull.*, 1026, 1–71.

Elliott, J. M. 1976: The downstream drifting of eggs of brown trout, *Salmo trutta* L. *J. Fish Biol.*, 9, 45–50.

Emmett, W. W. and Leopold, L. B. 1965: Downstream pattern of riverbed scour and fill. *US Dept Agric. Misc. Publ.*, 970, 399–409.

Ferguson, R. 1981: Channel forms and channel changes. In J. Lewin (ed.), *British Rivers*, London: Allen & Unwin, 90–125.

Frostick, L. E. and Reid, I. 1980: Sorting mechanisms in coarse-grained alluvial sediments: fresh evidence from a basalt plateau gravel, Kenya. *J. Geol. Soc. London*, 137, 431–41.

Harding, J. P. 1949: The use of probability paper for the graphical analysis of polymodal frequency distributions. *J. Mar. Biol. Assoc.*, 28, 141–53.

Harker, J. E. 1953: An investigation of the distribution of the mayfly fauna of a Lancashire stream. *J. Anim. Ecol.*, 2, 1–13.

Hey, R. D. 1975: Response of alluvial channels to river regulation. In *Proc. 2nd World Congress of Inter. Water Resources Assoc.*, 183–8.

Hey, R. D., Bathurst, J. C. & Thorne, C. R. (eds) 1982: *Gravel-bed Rivers: Fluvial Processes, Engineering and Management*. Chichester: Wiley.

Hickey, J. J. 1969: Variation in low-water streambed elevations at selected stream-gauging stations in north western California. *US Geol. Surv. Water Suppl. Paper*, 1879-E.

Hobbs, D. F. 1937: Natural reproduction of quinnat salmon, brown and rainbow trout in certain New Zealand waters. *New Zealand Mar. Dep. Fish Bull.*, 6, 1–104.

Hynes, H. B. N 1970: *The Ecology of Running Waters*. Liverpool: Liverpool Univ. Press.

Ippen, A. T. and Verma, R. P. 1955: Motion of particles on bed of a turbulent stream. *Trans Am. Soc. Civ. Engrs.*, 120, 921–38.

Langbein, W. B. and Leopold, L. B. 1968: River channel bars and dunes – theory of kinematic waves. *US Geol. Surv. Prof. Paper*, 422-L.

Laronne, J. B. and Carson, M. A. 1976: Interrelationships between bed morphology and bed-material transport for a small, gravel-bed channel. *Sedimentology*, 23, 67–85.

Leopold, L. B., Emmett, W. W. and Myrick, R. M. 1966: Channel and hillslope processes in a semi-arid area, New Mexico. *US Geol. Surv. Prof. Paper*, 352-9.

Luedthe, R. J. and Brusven, M. A. 1976: Effects of sand sedimentation on colonization of stream insects. *J. Fish Res. Bd. Can.*, 33, 1881–6.

Maitland, P. S. 1964: Quantitative studies on the invertebrate fauna of sandy and stony substrates in the River Endrick, Scotland. *Proc. R. Soc. Edin.*, B68, 288–301.

McNeill, W. J. 1966: Effect of the spawning bed environment on reproduction of pink and chum salmon. *Bull. US Fish Wildl. Serv. Fish*, 65, 495–523.

Meland, N. and Norrman, J. O. 1966: Transport velocities of individual size fractions in heterogeneous bed load. *Geografiska Annaler*, 51 (A), 127–44.

Milhous, R. T. and Klingeman, P. C. 1973: Sediment transport system in a gravel-bottomed stream. In *Hydraulic Engineering & the Environment. Proc. 21st Annual Hydraulics Div. Speciality Conf. Montana State Univ., Bozeman, Montana*, New York: ASCE, 293–303.

Milner, N. J., Scullion, J., Carling, P. A. and Crisp, D. T. 1981: The effects of discharge on sediment dynamics and consequent effects on invertebrates and salmonids in upland rivers. *Adv. Appl. Biol.*, 6, 153-220.

Mosley, M. P. 1985: River channel inventory, habitat and instream flow assessment. *Prog. Phys. Geogr.*, 9, 494-523.

Murphy, P. J. and Amin, M. I. 1979: Compartmented sediment trap. *J. Hydr. Div.*, *ASCE*, 105, 489-500.

Naden, P. S. 1981: Gravel bedforms: deductions from sediment movement. *Working Paper, Univ. Leeds, School of Geogr.*, 314.

Neave, F. 1953: Principles affecting the size of pink and chum salmon populations in British Columbia. *J. Fish. Res. Bd Can.*, 9, 450-91.

NERC 1975: *Flood Studies Report. Vol. 1. Hydrological Studies*. London: HMSO.

Nixon, M. 1959: A study of bankfull discharges of the rivers of England and Wales. *Proc. Inst. Civ. Engrs.*, 12, 157-74.

Pettijohn, E. J. 1975: *Sedimentary Rocks, 3rd Edition*. New York: Harper International.

Petts, G. E. 1984: Sedimentation within a regulated river. *Earth Surf. Proc. & Landforms*, 9, 125-34.

Pickup, G. 1976: Adjustment of stream channel shape to hydrologic regime. *J. Hydrol.*, 30, 365-73.

Pickup, G. and Rieger, W. A. 1979: A conceptual model of the relationship between channel characteristics and discharge. *Earth Surf. Processes*, 4, 37-42.

Pickup, G. and Warner, R. F. 1976: Effects of hydrological regime on magnitude and frequency of dominant discharge. *J. Hydrol.*, 29, 51-75.

Poreh, M., Sagiv, A. and Seginer, I. 1970: Sediment sampling efficiency of slots. *J. Hydr. Div.*, *ASCE*, 96, 561.

Prins, A. and de Vries, M. 1971: On dominant discharge concepts for rivers. In *Proc. XIV Congress IAHR, 3, C20*, 160-70.

Simons, D. B. and Şentürk, F. 1977: *Sediment Transport Technology*. Fort Collins: Water Resources Publ.

Slaymaker, H. O. 1972: Patterns of present sub-aerial erosion and landforms in mid-Wales. *Trans. Inst. Brit. Geogr.*, 55, 47-68.

Steidtmann, J. R. 1982: Size-density sorting of sand-size spheres during deposition from bedload transport and implications concerning hydraulic equivalence. *Sedimentology*, 29, 877-83.

Stelczer, K. 1981: *Bed-load Transport: Theory & Practice*. Littleton, Colorado: Water Resources Publ.

Thomas, A. R. 1976: Discussion of 'Non-equilibrium river form'. *J. Hydr. Div.*, *ASCE*, 102, 532-4.

Wickett, W. P. 1975: Mass transfer theory and the culture of fish eggs. In W. A. Adams (ed.), *Chemistry and Physics of Aqueous Gas Solutions*, Princeton: Electrochemical Soc., 417-34.

Wolman, M. G. 1955: The natural channel of Brandywine Creek Pennsylvania. *US Geol. Surv. Prof. Paper*, 271.

Wolman, M. G. and Miller, J. P. 1960: Magnitude and frequency of forces in geological processes. *J. Geol.*, 68, 54-74.

14

Applied Fluvial Geomorphology: River Engineering Project Appraisal in its Geomorphological Context

K. S. Richards with D. Brunsden,
D. K. C. Jones and M. McCaig

INTRODUCTION

The management of natural river systems and the design of artificial channels for water conveyance have given the study of fluvial processes a strong applied context for thousands of years, since the riparian civilizations of Mesopotamia, Egypt, China and India (Biswas, 1970). Responsibility for this management and design has traditionally lain with hydraulic engineers. There are, of course, several additional contexts for the *application* of fluvial geomorphology; for example, in the mapping of fluvial sedimentary facies and the analysis of the relationships between alluvial landform dynamics and the distribution of sediment types, the fluvial geomorphologist can contribute to the search for aggregates (Chester, 1980) and placer deposits (Best and Brayshaw, 1985). Furthermore, direct analysis of channel and flow characteristics plays a crucial role in assessment of the suitability of river reaches for various in-stream recreational uses, such as fishing, boating, and swimming, and identifies the conflicts that can arise between these and other uses such as power generation (Mosley, 1983; 1985).

However, some issues recently emphasized in geomorphology have an important bearing on fluvial geomorphology particularly in relation to engineering project appraisal and design. These are:

1 a concern with more explicit linkage of the results of investigation of geomorphological processes in the short term (on what are conventionally engineering time-scales) with evaluation of longer-term landform development. Douglas (1982) has noted that . . . 'much of the work on geomorphic

processes was begun with the notion of improving understanding of landform evolution' but refers to this as an 'unfulfilled promise'; and

2 a concern with geologically recent (Late Quaternary) palaeohydrology. This has been given considerable impetus by the International Geological Correlation Programme Project 158 on 'Palaeohydrological changes in the Temperate Zone in the last 15 000 years', and involves the development and application of techniques of hydraulic and hydrologic reconstruction using morphological, sedimentological and stratigraphic evidence (cf. Gregory, 1983). It is therefore an area of inquiry aimed directly at the solution of the first issue noted above.

This chapter therefore considers some geomorphological contributions to engineering project appraisal in the context provided by these concerns.

Applied fluvial process studies can develop significantly in one of two directions. On the one hand, they can emphasize fluid dynamics and sediment transport, with particular reference to mobile channel beds, erodible banks, and the migratory characteristics of natural alluvial streams. The analysis of sedimentological constraints on bed material transport and deposition in gravel-bed streams has received much recent attention (Bathurst, chapter 11, this volume) and understanding of this unsteady, non-stationary and non-linear process is essential for successful management of freshwater fisheries in rivers subjected to various forms of flow regulation (Carling, chapter 13, this volume). Two prerequisites for a rigorous deterministic model of channel morphology, presently precluded by the discrepancy between the numbers of physical relationships and degrees of freedom (Hey, 1978), are sub-models for, firstly, bank erosion and cross-section form, of the type developed by Parker (1978) and tested by Pizzuto (1984); and secondly, meander planform morphology and development, such as that of Howard (1984). These are critical areas of study to which important geomorphological contributions can be made; consider, for example, some of the river management problems arising from interaction between a de-stabilized river bed, accelerated bank erosion, and meander migration. However, it would be naive for a fluvial geomorphologist to assume that concern with mobile bed conditions and migratory channels represents a *distinctively* geomorphological contribution; Leliavsky (1955), Raudkivi (1967) and Blench (1969) testify to a long engineering tradition in this field.

A second direction, therefore, in which the applied role of the fluvial geomorphologist is distinctive, involves the development, evaluation and application of palaeohydrological techniques to the analysis of stability and change in fluvial landscapes over time-scales that have been hitherto relatively neglected by geomorphologists – 10 to 1000 years – but which bracket the engineer's project time-scale. This simultaneously would address issues central to the function of geomorphology as a discipline concerned with explaining the processes of landform development. It is ironic that, as Hickin (1983) notes, precisely when fluvial sedimentologists and geomorphologists have increasingly used engineering frameworks of analysis, so engineers have increasingly demanded information on the historical and future contexts of adjustment and adjustability in the natural fluvial systems they seek to manage over what are geomorphological time-scales. A close analogy exists in the study of hillslopes. Geomorphologists adopted stability analysis, particularly the infinite-slope method (Skempton and De Lory, 1957; Carson, 1969), as a framework for the interpretation of general slope evolution. In such a context, these methods are essentially overdetermined (Anderson et al., 1980), and except in the interpretation of the evolution of single slopes, of little value. While this was being realized, engineers were themselves adopting the frameworks of Quaternary studies and denudation chronology to establish the evolutionary characteristics of slopes as a background to site investigation (cf. Skempton, 1976).

At least four areas can be identified in which geomorphological concepts can be brought to bear directly on engineering problems, especially at the feasibility and design stages of project formulation (Jones, 1983). These are:

1 *Evaluation of the sensitivity to change of landforms inherited from the Pleistocene.* In many drainage basins there is a Pleistocene legacy of stored glacial, fluvioglacial and periglacial sedimentary landforms which are now being reworked and excavated from these basins by river erosion (Kirkby, 1967; Slaymaker, 1972). Engineers require information on the potential for destabilization and accelerated erosion of these materials following a project development. This implies a need for information on background sediment yields over time-scales greater than those for which directly monitored data are usually available, but of the type which is becoming available as a result of studies of lake sediments (Foster et al., 1985) and sediment storage in engineering structures (Richards and McCaig, 1985; Newson and Leeks, 1985).

2 *Evaluation of rates of landform change in relation to both secular trends and extreme events.* The context of engineering project development is a landscape which is changing in relation to both (systematic) long-term climatic and environmental shifts and to the (random) extreme meteorological and hydrological events generated within the present climatic regime. It is necessary to establish whether landforms are at a critical point in their secular development, and what morphological responses are therefore likely to occur during extreme events before and after engineering intervention. Schumm (1979) also suggests that it may be possible to engineer conditions in which a river

maintains a stable state, for example by restricting the sediment supply that threatens to encourage an unstable, braided channel pattern.

3 *Assessment of the magnitude-frequency relationships between river form and process.* It is now recognized that different aspects of river process reflect different event frequencies. Suspended sediment transport is dominantly effected by flows well below 1–2 year return period (Andrews, 1980), bank erosion by events of 3–10 year return period (Pickup and Warner, 1976), and point-bar construction by events of 15–30 year return period (Hickin and Nanson, 1975). However, the morphological and sedimentological roles of different event magnitudes remain to be researched, so that their relationships can be used in 'palaeo'hydrological analysis which bridges the gap between Quaternary and engineering time-scales.

4 *Evaluation of linkages between geomorphological systems.* River management cannot occur independently of management of contiguous systems, particularly those connected by sediment transport/transfer processes. Hillslopes deliver water and sediment to river channels, rivers supply littoral environments, and surface and subsurface drainage systems interact. These linkages are ignored at the peril of environmental engineering projects. Perhaps the clearest and classic illustration of this is Gilbert's (1917) study of the impact of hydraulic mining debris in the Sierra Nevada on fluvial, estuarine, and coastal processes.

These general issues are illustrated below with reference to three case studies in which fluvial geomorphological information has been sought in the early, feasibility-study stages of engineering project development.

THREE CASE STUDIES; PROJECT BACKGROUND

The three case studies cover a wide range of spatial scales and regional environments, with catchment areas from 2.35 km^2 to 7550 km^2, and climatic conditions varying from cool temperate to arid subtropical. The engineering contexts for the fluvial investigations also range widely between sedimentation problems, irrigation water supply, and flood control, and involve management in the 'source' (Scotland), 'armoured' and 'sand' (Saudi Arabia) and 'backwater' channel zones as defined by Warner (chapter 2, this volume).

Aonach Mor, Ben Nevis, Scotland

The 2.35 km^2 catchment of Allt an t'Sneachda drains the north-facing slope of Aonach Mor, one of the subsidiary peaks of the Ben Nevis massif in the Western Grampians of Scotland. It ranges from 240 m to 1200 m, and although

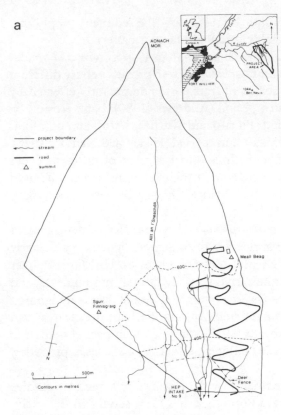

a

AONACH
MOR

project boundary
stream
road
△   summit

Allt an t'Sneachda

600

△ Meall Beag

Sgurr
Finnisg-aig
△

400

N

0   500m

Contours in metres

HEP
INTAKE
No 9

Deer
Fence

Figure 14.1   (a) The catchment of Allt and t'Sneachda draining the slopes of Aonach Mor, Ben Nevis, in the western Highlands of Scotland, illustrating the proposed road development; (b) General view of Aonach Mor from the north-west; project area is the snow-filled depression on the left-hand peak

b

about 1800 m across at an elevation of 650 m, it tapers both unslope and downslope where it forms a plan concavity (figure 14.1). The stream in this headwater catchment has a gradient comparable to that of the slope it drains, and slope processes act along lines roughly parallel to the stream but converging downslope. The relative relief (m m^{-1}) is 0.30, and the drainage density from 1:25 000 maps is 3.08 km km^{-2}. The mean annual rainfall is about 1900 mm, with on average 240 rain days per annum; the mean annual daily maximum rainfall is 54 mm, and the 10-year daily maximum is 100 mm. Above 800 m microclimatic zonation classifies the catchment as Oroarctic (Birse, 1976), and by 1000 m the ground is bare granitic rock debris, block-field, and marginally-active periglacially-sorted and solifluucted sediment.

A proposed ski development in the Allt an t'Sneachda catchment above 600 m, with an access road, building, car park and ski lifts presented a potential hazard for an intake to the water tunnel supplying a hydro-electric power station. The Allt an t'Sneachda drains into this intake, and accelerated sediment yield was anticipated during both the construction and operational phases of the development.

Wadi Dhamad, south-west Saudi Arabia

The Tehama coastal plain along the eastern Red Sea shore consists of a series of coalesced telescopic alluvial fans of widely varied sedimentology (cobbles to silt) fronting the fault-scarp of the Asir Mountains, which have been tectonically active during the Quaternary and which range up to over 2500 m. The mountains are deeply-dissected with steep, bare slopes exposing impermeable bedrock of schist and granite. The 50 km-wide plain experiences daytime temperatures in excess of 25°C all year, and annual rainfalls of less than 400 mm. Conditions are rendered less arid by the flood flows arriving on the plain following orographically intensified rainfalls of up to 1000 mm in the mountains, where runoff is extremely rapid. Wadi Dhamad (figure 14.2) is one of the intermittent rivers carrying these floods; it drains a catchment of about 1000 km^2, and on average about 40 floods a year reach the head of its alluvial plain. The wadi is incised into late Tertiary or early Quaternary volcanic rocks at its head, where a lava flow flanks its left bank. It is here about 100 m wide and cobble-floored. About 10 km downstream it is wider (200 m) with cobbles outcropping in its bed and banks. Further downstream still it is up to 1000 m wide with near-vertical silty banks up to 10 m high, and at about 25 km downstream it has a wide, shallow, indistinct sandy channel with marginal sand dunes.

A long tradition of spate irrigation exists in the Tehama wadis, with artificial bunds across their beds (figure 14.2b) ponding floodwater until it spills into the fields on the wadi banks via earth-banked canals. When an upstream

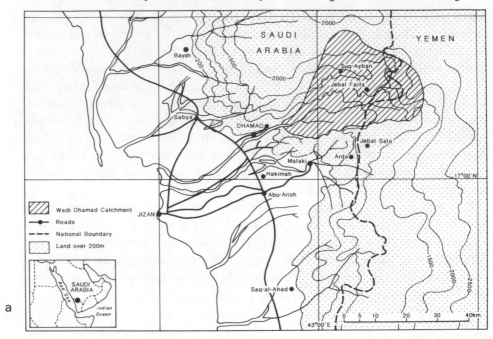

Figure 14.2   (a) The location of Wadi Dhamad, south-west Saudi Arabia; (b) A typical transverse bund on the wadi floor, breached after passage of the last flood wave

agricultural area has received sufficient irrigation water, the wadi bund is breached and the floodwater is released towards the next bund downstream. In recent years population growth and technological development have encouraged increasing use of the floodwaters, and larger bunds are created by bulldozer. As a result, spate flows of given size are transmitted increasingly less far downstream, and the traditional balance of water use has been threatened. Experience with a reservoir impoundment in the neighbouring wadi (Jizan) has demonstrated that its evaporation losses and high sedimentation rate render it an inefficient means of replacing the traditional schemes, and a planned development for Wadi Dhamad therefore involved formalization of the traditional method of water use by the construction of five diversion weirs leading to properly designed and maintained irrigation canal networks. This raised the question of wadi stability, since a capital-intensive diversion structure would be a dangerous investment if faced with possible abandonment after wadi avulsion (an expectable process on an alluvial fan surface). Furthermore, the absence of any reliable gauging systems in this extremely flashy runoff environment placed a premium on indirect methods of flood estimation for design purposes.

Rio Aguan, Honduras, Central America

The Rio Aguan drains a catchment of about 7550 km^2 to the Caribbean coast of Honduras, and forms a broad alluvial plain 10–15 km wide in its lower reaches between the parallel mountain ranges of the Cordillera Nombre de Dios and the Sierra la Esperanza Paya (figure 14.3). These are predominantly of Pre-Cambrian metamorphics (phyllites, gneisses and quartzites), reach elevations of 1800–2400 m, and are deeply dissected with drainage densities of up to 6 km km^{-2} (mapped from 1:20 000 air photographs) and sharp-crested hillslopes. Although subtropical temperatures are experienced throughout, rainfall conditions vary markedly with distance from the coast, where mean annual rainfalls of 2200–2500 mm are normal with monthly totals ranging seasonally from 350 mm in October to 80 mm in March, and frequent tropical cyclonic storms in the period June to November. A typical example, Hurricane Fifi, generated a 20-year event in which 500 mm of rainfall occurred locally between 16–20 September 1974. More generally, a daily rainfall of 10-year return period would produce about 250 mm. Inland the climate is significantly drier because the higher parts of the Cordillera exclude marine influences; total annual rainfalls decline to about 1200 mm, and 10-year and other extreme daily falls are more than halved. This is reflected in the natural vegetation, which is tropical hardwood forest on the coastal mountains (although mostly cleared by shifting cultivation), xerophytic vegetation on the sandy valley-floor terraces around Olanchito, and pine savannah in the hills at the head of the basin.

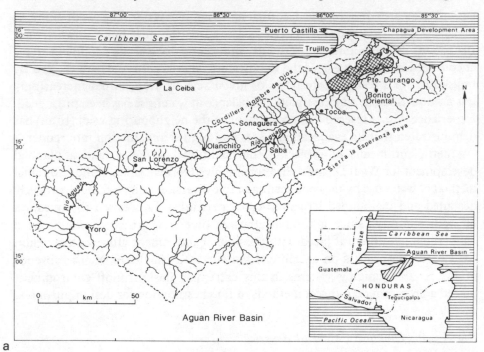

Aguan River Basin

a

b

A major agricultural development project was proposed for the lower Aguan valley especially in the vicinity of its left bank 'distributary', the Chapagua. Its objective was to select crops (oil palm) appropriate to the wetland environment, the country's needs, and the agricultural experience and technology of the landless poor, who were to be encouraged to abandon their shifting cultivation practices in the hills. Parallel with this was an engineering scheme of flood control by deliberate flood-flow diversion and flood dyke construction. Major geomorphological questions concerned the potential for unexpected channel avulsion, channel migration by bank erosion that would endanger the proposed dykes, and accelerated overbank sedimentation between the dykes that could limit their flood-control effectiveness.

SENSITIVITY TO CHANGE OF INHERITED
QUATERNARY SEDIMENTS AND LANDFORMS

A key to the interpretation of landform response to both systematic environmental changes and random environmental events is an appreciation of landform sensitivity (Brunsden and Thornes, 1979), which in turn reflects the magnitude of the external influences and the capacity of the system to resist change. Greater sensitivity characterizes both semi-arid climatic regimes lacking the protective effect of vegetation, and smaller-scale landform assemblages or components (Wolman and Gerson, 1978). It is also characteristic of the unconsolidated sedimentary features forming the legacy of Pleistocene processes; however, sediment mobility also varies spatially – see chapters 2 and 4, this volume. Furthermore some landforms may be sensitive to change by virtue of their proximity to an intrinsic threshold (Schumm, 1979); for example, increased discharge in a meandering stream may or may not result in a pattern change to a braided state, depending on the initial discharge conditions and the relevant threshold slope-discharge combination (Ferguson, chapter 6, this volume). Assessment of sensitivity to change is clearly of importance when an engineering project alters the hydrological processes in a catchment or the hydraulic processes in a channel, but it is necessary to evaluate this against the normal background conditions.

At Aonach Mor, the proposed development could potentially destabilize Quaternary deposits adjacent to the streams. These include the lodgement till at 550–600 m and fragmentary kame terraces at 350–400 m. This disturbance could follow increased runoff during and after construction, causing accelerated sediment yield likely to damage the HEP intakes and pipe runs.

Figure 14.3 *(opposite)* (a) The catchment of the Rio Aguan, Honduras, indicating the location of proposed agricultural development in the lower valley in the Rio Chapagua area; (b) Oblique aerial view of the Aguan valley in the Olanchito area

The intermittent background geomorphological processes in British uplands such as the Scottish Highlands must be evaluated initially. Sediment yield is discontinuous and occurs as a non-stationary response to meteorological events. Similar storms can generate dissimilar yields depending on pre-existing supply and storage conditions. Newson (1980) has illustrated this tendency for storms in mid-Wales; some are associated with slope erosion and other, similar events cause channel erosion. In the Scottish Highlands high magnitude storms are not uncommon as a result of stagnating occluded depressions and thunderstorms, and have been observed to cause intensive debris-flow activity (Common, 1954; Baird and Lewis, 1957). The Ben Nevis area, for example, experienced such slope failure after a 39 mm rainfall in two hours in 1953. However, a 120-year event on 19 September 1981 in Wester Ross generated runoff of $4-5\,m^3s^{-1}km^{-2}$ in a $13\,km^2$ catchment, causing few slope failures but major channel erosion (Acreman, 1984), probably because low antecedent moisture status in slope regoliths placed them sufficiently far below the threshold pore water pressure condition for failure.

This inherent discontinuity of sediment yield presents problems for assessment of natural sediment yield, which must be integrated over long enough periods to average the variability, and generally over longer periods than those for which monitored data are available. Fortunately, boulder traps exist to protect engineering works on the neighbouring streams, Allt a'Mhuillin and Allt Daim, and the volume of sediment stored since their construction gives a medium-term (12-year) average of $26t\,km^{-2}\,yr^{-1}$ (Richards and McCaig, 1985). These catchments are respectively 6.2 and $5.8\,km^2$ in area, with similar drainage densities to Allt an t'Sneachda, but a trough-shaped valley delivering slope sediments directly to the stream along transport paths perpendicular to the general stream alignment. Although further research is required into the delivery ratio of coarse bedload (Walling, 1983), its yield probably diminishes with increasing area faster than does that of suspended load. Thus this estimated yield is probably a minimum for Allt an t'Sneachda, although the area effect may be offset by the different catchment topographies.

The availability of sediment in the Allt an t'Sneachda catchment can only be assessed by a detailed field inventory of sediment storage within and immediately adjacent to the channel and its tributaries. Storages occur in the forms of alternating bars in steep but sinuous reaches where the streams are incised deeply through till, and in boulder jams forming the risers in step-pool reaches. The former average about $20\,m^3$ and the latter are more variable, ranging from 5 to $30\,m^3$. At a larger scale are fan deposits formed where the stream gradients slacken as they flow onto the treads of kame terrace fragments. Together the total stored sediment immediately adjacent to the stream constitutes about $600-800\,m^3$ and therefore represents about 15–30 years of sediment yield at the rates estimated from the boulder traps on the adjacent streams.

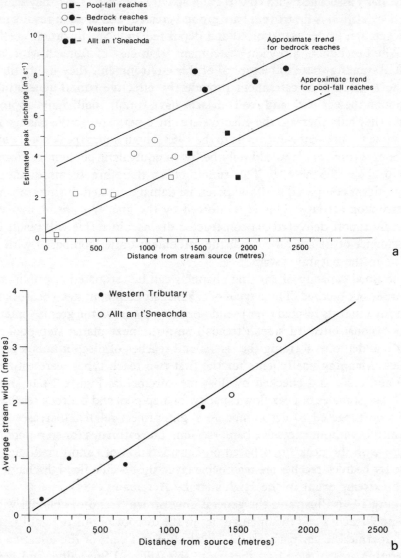

Figure 14.4 (a) Estimates of peak (bankfull) flow capacity for sections in bedrock and step-pool reaches of the Allt an t'Sneachda; (b) Downstream increase in width of channel sections in step-pool reaches, and in the open gully sections of discontinuous pipe-gully systems

The activation of temporarily stored sediment along the Allt an t'Sneachda will depend on direct disturbance by both construction and increased post-construction activity on the slopes, as well as on increased runoff from impermeable surfaces created by the proposed development (car park, roads). At other Scottish ski centres (e.g. Cairn Gorm) there is evidence that erosion is particularly associated with construction activity (Watson, 1967; Bayfield, 1974), when vegetation is destroyed, bare ground created, and erosion results in burial of vegetation under transported and deposited soil. Storm runoff coefficients for Allt Leachdach, a 6.9 km^2 catchment 9 km east of Aonach Mor, average 0.40. Assuming these to be typical of this environment, they imply that 94 ha of the Aonach Mor catchment provide the effective runoff-generating area. Although the car park and road surfaces have runoff coefficients approaching unity, they only increase the effective area by 5 per cent, so the change in peak discharge for an event comparable to the 1953 2-hour storm (peak hourly intensity of about 20 mm hr^{-1}) would only be by an equivalent percentage from about 5.2 to about 5.5 m^3 s^{-1}. The runoff effect therefore seems quantitatively insignificant compared with the potential damage created during uncontrolled construction activity. This is reinforced by the greater transmission velocity of storm runoff delivered via constructed drains, since this will result in non-coincidence of its arrival time at the catchment outlet compared with that of runoff in the natural system.

The flood capacity of existing channels can be estimated approximately by the area-slope method. Three types of channel are common: steep bedrock reaches with smooth beds formed over pseudo-bedding planes in the granite, interrupted by occasional outward steps ('treads') onto the next plane; step-pool reaches with boulder jams forming the risers; and reaches of discontinuous pipes and gullies. Manning coefficients for the first two reach types were estimated as 0.10 and 0.20, and checked by float measurements. Figure 14.4a shows the resulting estimates of peak flow capacity for step-pool and bedrock reaches. Both could be expected to accommodate slight project-related increases in flood magnitude without excessive bank erosion. The estimates for step-pool reaches accord with the peak flows based on consideration of runoff coefficients, and those for bedrock reaches are reasonable given the specific flood discharges noted in an extreme event in the Highlands by Acreman (1984).

Figure 14.4b illustrates the general downstream trend of channel width for step-pool reaches and the open gullies in the discontinuous pipe-gully reaches. An impermeable car park would constitute 9 per cent of the effective run-off generating area of a 35 ha tributary to the Allt an t'Sneacdha, and would be equivalent to increasing the basin area by an amount commensurate with an additional 200 m of channel length. Discontinuous pipe-gully reaches give way to step-pool reaches once the runoff is sufficient to maintain a width greater than 1–1.5 m. Thus beyond a stream length of about 600 m it is likely that the increased runoff would lead to permanent opening of pipes, resulting in a feedback which causes increased runoff efficiency in the channel system. Notwithstanding this evidence, it appears likely that construction phase erosion and destabilization of steep slopes by increased pressure by walkers in summer will be more damaging in terms of reactivating sediments stored in and near the channel, than will increased runoff from impermeable surfaces created by the development. Management of both construction and non-skiing use of the slope appears to be the key to avoidance of sediment problems.

LANDFORM CHANGE: SYSTEMATIC TRENDS AND RANDOM EVENTS

Tendency for morphological change reflects in part the erodibility of the materials comprising a landform. However, the agency of change is normally the imposed hydrological regime. Some fluvial landforms or landform components adjust progressively in response to secular change in the average flood magnitudes generated by their catchments. This is particularly characteristic of stable environments in which the ratio of the magnitudes of rare and common events is relatively small. In other areas, fluvial landforms undergo step-function changes, either because this is the nature of external hydrological change (Warner, chapter 2, this volume), or because their internal resistance to change delays their response to continuous external variation until threshold conditions are reached. Others still respond violently to individual extreme events which cause a sudden impact, after which a damped oscillation occurs in the landform as it hunts, often unsuccessfully, for a new equilibrium. This characterizes environments where rare events are also extreme events. In addition to these varied responses to external influence, a combination of gradual evolution and sudden change is characteristic of landforms which involve slow depositional and weathering processes coupled to more rapid processes of sediment transfer which require an initial preparatory period of material accumulation. Alluvial fans represent an example of such landforms. The conditions in which gradual morphological evolution can give way to rapid alteration of surface form clearly must be understood before a capital-intensive engineering project is initiated, for example in an alluvial-fan environment prone to channel avulsion.

Alluvial fans, such as that traversed and constructed by Wadi Dhamad, accumulate as roughly conical, low-angle depositional forms with their apices at the points where rivers leave their mountain catchments at abrupt, especially fault-guided, mountain fronts. The fan depositional process is favoured in arid environments where reduction in flow by evaporation and by transmission loss into the coarse, permeable fan sediments are added to the effect of the abrupt loss of confinement of the flow. Empirical data from a spatial sample of fans indicate general adjustments of fan area and slope to catchment area, rock erodibility in the source area, and sediment calibre (Bull, 1977). However, on a single fan the morphology departs from the form of a regular cone as the depositional locus varies through time; one area experiences aggradation until height differentiation encourages diversion into an adjacent low area (Hooke and Rohrer, 1979). Such diversions are therefore normal in the evolution of a fan, and arise from the combined effect of the systematic secular aggradation process and avulsion during a single random flood event.

Evolution of fan morphology often involves several episodes of successive fan-head trenching and aggradation. These may be the result of internally generated cycles, such as that in which deposition steepens the fan-head gradient until a critical slope triggers incision, which is in turn transmitted headwards to increase sediment yield from the upstream catchment (Schumm, 1977, pp. 255–64). However, major phases of trenching and filling are also caused by external influences such as climatic change and tectonic activity, and result in fans with a depositional structure in which successively younger fan components are inset within the preceding entrenchment in a compound or 'telescopic' form. Thus, for example, if the stream down-cutting rate exceeds the rate of uplift in the mountain catchment, the fan-head is entrenched, the stream emerges onto the fan surface at a mid-fan location, and the depositional locus shifts down-fan (Bull, 1964).

Several phases of fan development are evident in the cross-section and long-profile characteristics of Wadi Dhamad, and examination of the wadi morphology and the distribution of sedimentary facies establishes the broad framework of its Quaternary history. Figure 14.5 maps the landforms and sediments of the wadi and its fan, while figure 14.6 presents schematic sections at points downstream from the gauging station (G on figure 14.5). An early fan whose gravels are now desert-varnished appears to have been associated with a wadi

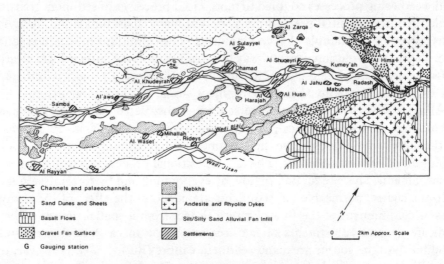

Figure 14.5 Landforms and surface sediments of Wadi Dhamad, mapped in the field and from 1:10 000 orthophotomaps

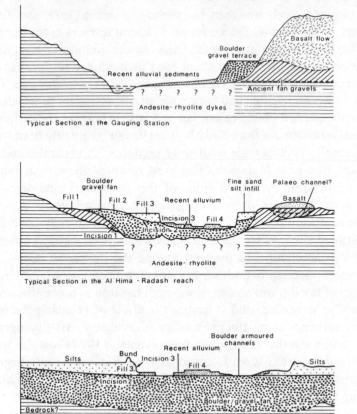

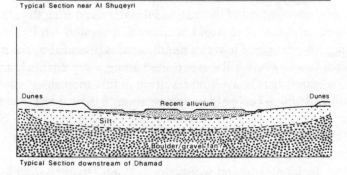

Figure 14.6 Schematic sections of Wadi Dhamad indicating suggested stratigraphic relationships between wadi and fan sedimentation units

alignment just south of the present line; its gravels are seen as a splayed deposit heading at Radash in figure 14.5. The upstream reaches of the wadi palaeochannel appear to have been occupied by a linear basaltic lava flow from the site of Radash village to the head of what is now known as Wadi Blaj. The wadi subsequently incised on a new alignment slightly to the west-north-west. A bouldery fan of coarse torrent gravels was then inset into the incised early fan deposits, and remnants of this boulder fan are found as lateral terraces at the gauging station and as basal sediments in the wadi banks in the vicinity of Khumey'ah. This disposition suggests a steep gradient for this bouldery fill, perhaps indicative of wetter conditions during its deposition, and of active tectonism. The boulder fan was, however, itself incised to provide an entrenchment in which a silty/silty-sand fan then accumulated to overlap and largely blanket the earlier forms and sediments downstream from Radash. This has subsequently been incised again to produce the 1000 m-wide wadi cross-section with vertical silty banks up to 10 m high seen near Mabubah. The most recently phase of activity has been aeolian aggradation by nebkha dunes of grey micaceous sand derived from the wadi bed, and by larger, older and slightly reddened whaleback dunes migrating from the south-south-west and encroaching on the wadi right bank downstream from Dhamad town, where the wadi appears to have changed its general direction leaving a palaeochannel to the west among the dunes.

This recent aeolian deposition has possibly been encouraged by a reduced frequency of flood transmission down-wadi because of more efficient upstream diversion for irrigation, and is having the effect of reducing the freeboard in the wadi and increasing the probability of avulsion. Air photographs of the impoundment and diversion of two flood events in 1974 show that a continuous overflow existed from Wadi Dhamad to Wadi Blaj via a route beginning near Al Harajah, where freeboard in Wadi Dhamad is only 2.7 m. Thus mapping and topographic surveys identify the locations at which potential for avulsion exists, and suggest the scale of protective measures likely to be needed. Furthermore, management of the traditional water use during the planned project development is essential to avoid accidental diversion while construction is proceeding. An example of how this might occur is provided by the neighbouring fan of Wadi Jizan, where villages are sited along a dry channel, and historical evidence indicates that the avulsion resulting in this anomalous pattern occurred in a 1942 flood which probably generated about $3 \, m^3 \, s^{-1} \, km^{-2}$ in a catchment of similar size to that of Wadi Dhamad. The avulsion may have been assisted by injudicious bund construction which encouraged overspill into a pre-existing low palaeochannel whose route then became dominant.

Mapping the landforms and sediments in Wadi Dhamad therefore identifies the existence of palaeochannel alignments, and establishes the latest stages in the migratory Quaternary history of the wadi. More detailed subsurface investigation and improved dating control would be necessary to define more clearly the sequence and chronology of events inferred from the pattern of surface sedimentary facies and landforms. The probability of avulsion during an extreme flood event can be ascertained by combining topographic data on the wadi freeboard, synthetic stage-discharge relationships for the critical wadi sections (derived by the methods outlined in the following section), and a flood frequency analysis.

MAGNITUDE-FREQUENCY ANALYSIS AND FLUVIAL LANDFORMS

The two basic approaches to palaeohydrology involve, firstly, the application to palaeochannel form properties of empirical relationships between contemporary discharge and channel-form variables such as cross-section area or meander wavelength; and secondly, estimation of former flood depths and velocities from theoretical hydraulic relationships between these parameters and the grain sizes in a fluvial deposit. The former method reconstructs discharges of a relatively narrow frequency range, but relies on empirical relationships that may be inapplicable to the palaeochannel fluvial style. The latter method cannot identify the frequency of the reconstructed discharge. Furthermore, it predicts local depths and velocities, and although this may cause few problems when the methods are applied to flash-floods in rock channels (Costa, 1983), the means of extrapolating from point estimates to averages for a wide, shallow cross-section are uncertain in many applications to braided rivers (Maizels, 1983).

Nevertheless, these quantitative palaeohydrological methods provide a basis for bridging the gap between Quaternary and engineering time-scales. They can be used to identify the frequency of events which relate to particular morphological attributes or which may cause sudden morphological change, and they provide an important supplement to the meagre hydrological database in remote, undeveloped and extreme hydrological environments. Measurement of flood flows in Wadi Dhamad has, for example, proved extremely difficult in floods having discharges of up to $2000\ \mathrm{m^3\ s^{-1}}$ and velocities of $4{-}5\ \mathrm{m\ s^{-1}}$, which have destroyed successive installations at a gauging station established at Mushawwaf at the wadi head (G in figure 14.5).

Indirect estimation of discharge is also difficult in a channel which is up to 1000 m wide, and across which there are marked variations of morphology and sedimentology. The method developed to estimate flows therefore began by mapping the form-sediment associations on the wadi bed, and with the identification of units within each cross-section for which dominant roughness influences could be identified (figure 14.7). Arbitrary water surfaces were then drawn across the section, sometimes requiring assessment of the elevations of upstream entry points to low-flow channels in order to justify continuity. For each unit and water surface, the friction factor was estimated and mean flow velocity was calculated, assuming negligible energy losses between adjacent units. It was then possible to calculate from the mean depth, mean velocity and width, the component discharge passing through a unit, at each arbitrary water surface

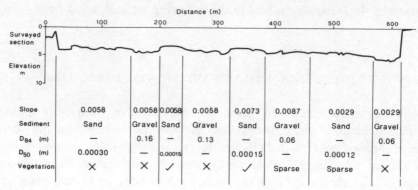

Figure 14.7 Sample cross-section of Wadi Dhamad illustrating definition of units within the section in which particular roughness influences are dominant

elevation (stage). Synthetic stage-discharge relationships could thus be defined by summing the component discharges.

The friction factor estimates were obtained by defining three main roughness controls; pebbles, sand bedforms, and vegetation. In units where gravel, pebbles and boulders controlled the flow resistance, the Darcy-Weisbach friction factor (f) was estimated from

$$1/\sqrt{f} = 2 \log(d/D_{84}) + 1.16 \tag{14.1}$$

where d is depth and D_{84} is the 84th percentile particle intermediate axis (Limerinos, 1969). Where a combination of sand grain roughness and bedform resistance appeared likely to be dominant, total friction was regarded as the sum of a skin friction factor f' and a form friction factor f'', so that

$$f = f' + f'' \tag{14.2}$$

The methods used to estimate f' and f'' were those of Lovera and Kennedy (1969) and Alam and Kennedy (1969). The former present a diagram in which f' is a function of relative smoothness (d/D_{50}) and Reynolds number, and the latter a diagram in which f'' is a function of relative smoothness and a grain Froude number (figure 14.8). Since the Reynolds and Froude numbers incorporate the velocity which is to be estimated, these diagrams must be used iteratively by assuming a reasonable velocity, defining separate grain and form friction factors, summing these and estimating velocity, and repeating this procedure until convergence occurs between initial and final estimates. Velocity itself was calculated from the friction equation

$$v = \sqrt{8gds/f} \tag{14.3}$$

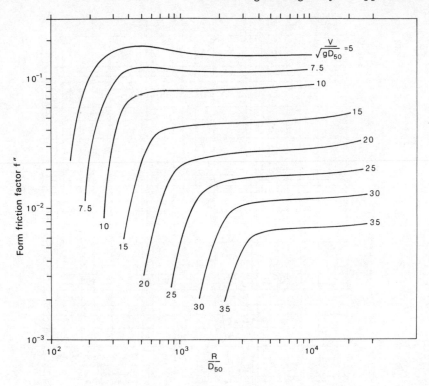

Figure 14.8 Form friction factor f″ as a function of relative smoothness (R/D_{50}) and a grain Froude number ($v/\sqrt{gD_{50}}$). R is hydraulic radius (= depth), D_{50} is median grain diameter, and v is mean velocity (after Alam and Kennedy, 1969)

where $g = 9.81$ m s^{-2} and s is channel slope, used as an approximation for the energy gradient. The method frequently predicted low form friction factors such as might occur under plane-bed conditions, and confirmation in the field was provided by parallel laminations exposed in cut banks through sand bars. A similar iterative method was used to obtain approximate estimates of vegetation roughness where this was dominant on high bar surfaces and lateral terraces. For various densities and heights of grass cover, curves exist defining Manning's n as a function of the velocity-depth product (Chow, 1959). For bushes and trees, alternative methods developed by Petryk (1975) were used, these being based on the upstream projected area of plants.

These methods clearly have their limitations. It is necessary to assume negligible bed scour; to approximate additional large-scale roughness effects rather arbitrarily in the absence of appropriate theoretical methods; to ignore hysteretic effects; and to ignore the effects of the heavy suspended load on flow resistance. However, some check on their consistency was possible.

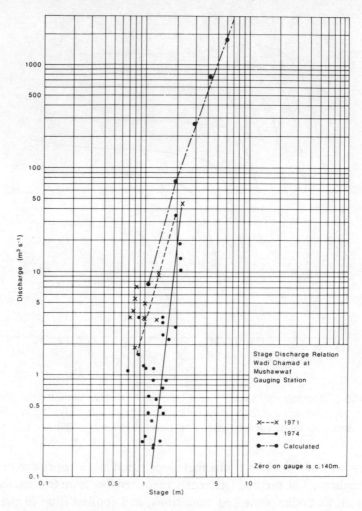

Figure 14.9   Predicted stage-discharge relationship for the gauging station at Wadi Dhamad at Mushawwaf, together with observed stage and discharge data for smaller flood events monitored in 1971 and 1974

Figure 14.9 shows the predicted stage-discharge relationship for the Mushawwaf gauging station, and its extrapolation from manually recorded stage data for floods in 1971 and 1974. These data suggest that some scour and fill occurs in the section, an observation confirmed by comparing 1976 and 1982 surveys (figure 14.10). The gauge reader had noted the surface velocity measured by float at the peak of one flood; this was $4.3 \, \text{m} \, \text{s}^{-1}$, which matches that predicted for discharges of $1500 \, \text{m}^3 \, \text{s}^{-1}$. He had also marked with cairns the water level on both banks in the highest flood in his memory. Since the gauging

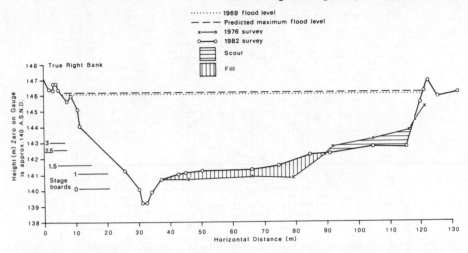

Figure 14.10 The Mushawwaf cross-section illustrating evidence of scour and fill between 1976 and 1982, the left bank boulder terrace formed in the lee of a bend in the rock-cut channel, and the 1969 and maximum predicted water levels, the latter based on prediction from bed material size

station was on a bend, the superelevation could be used to estimate velocity, from

$$\Delta h = v^2 w / g r_c \qquad (14.4)$$

where Δh is the water-surface superelevation between outer and inner banks, v is velocity, w is channel width, and r_c is the bend radius of curvature. This predicts a mean velocity of 4.64 m s^{-1}. Finally, the 1969 flood maximum was estimated by the above methods as 1860 m^3 s^{-1}, which accords with the available flood records which place the 1969 maximum flood at a discharge of 2000 m^3 s^{-1}. Figure 14.11 shows the synthesized hydraulic geometry of the Mushawwaf section, illustrating that the velocity estimated for the 1969 discharge is close to that obtained from the superelevation data.

The maximum flood depths experienced in a section can be estimated by predicting peak bed shear stress from the largest bed material particles showing signs of fluvial transport through imbrication, or upstream dips of their maximum projection planes. Baker and Ritter (1975) developed a simple method which can be used for rivers with particles coarser than 10 mm, where the flow is hydrodynamically rough and bedform roughness is largely absent. It represents a variant on the Shields criterion and involves an empirical relationship between the largest sizes of grain considered mobile (D_{max} in mm, approximated by the mean intermediate axis length of the five largest boulders) and the bed shear

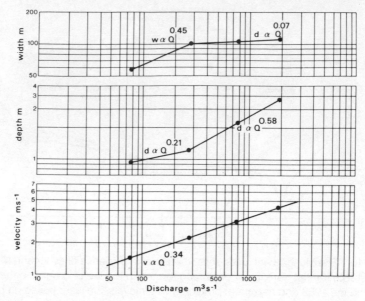

Figure 14.11   The synthesized hydraulic geometry of the Mushawwaf section

stress (τ_0, in kg m^{-2}). This can be used to estimate the shear stress required to transport the particles;

$$\tau_0 = 0.00044 \; D_{max}^{1.85} \tag{14.5}$$

Use of this relationship assumes that there is an adequate supply of particles as coarse as the competence of the flow, and requires that care is taken to ignore immobile, residual grains. Given the channel bedslope and assuming further that it approximates to the energy gradient at the time of entrainment, it is simple to obtain the peak flow depth associated with the predicted shear stress, since the shear stress is the product of slope, depth, and the unit weight of water.

In Wadi Dhamad the channel is always wide relative to peak flow depths, and the complicating influence of bank effects (Carling, 1983) can be ignored. In fact, it is possible to predict peak depths at several points across one section to define the best-fit maximum flood water surface profile. Predictions of local depth are invariably more realistic for cobble/boulder deposits in mid-wadi low-flow channels than for isolated cobbles on sandy bar tops, either because these may be residual grains too large for the flow, or because the supply of coarse grains has been deficient and the grains are smaller than the largest that could be moved by the flow. Table 14.1 lists, for a series of sections in the 10 km downstream from the gauging station, the maximum flood discharges predicted using the peak mean water surface elevation and synthetic stage-discharge

Table 14.1 Peak discharges at sections in Wadi Dhamad downstream from the Mushawwaf gauging station

Distance (km) downstream	Discharge (m³ s⁻¹)	Water level details
0	1950	Reaches top of steep riser of left-bank boulder terrace
2.23	1900	Correlates with minor right-bank terrace and lower limit of varnished pebbles on left bank
2.71	2600	Reaches clear break of slope on left bank
3.74	2000	Just inundates minor bench on right bank
6.04	2050	Would inundate left and right bank terraces to shallow depth in the absence of protective bunds at bank tops
8.23	1700	Reaches front edge of left-bank terrace
9.43	2100	Reaches top of left bank where terrace edge is protected by bund
10.58	1800	Just inundates right-bank terrace

Discharges estimated from the maximum sizes of mobile bed material and synthetic stage-discharge relationships.

relationships defined by the method discussed above. These discharges average $2012 \, m^3 \, s^{-1}$. There is a tendency for the maximum discharge to diminish slightly downstream by about 10 per cent from $2140 \, m^3 \, s^{-1}$ at the gauging station (predicted from a weak regression relationship of maximum discharge on downstream distance). This trend is to be expected given the various locations in the 10 km reach at which overspill of the wadi banks and diversion via lateral canals can occur. A further aspect of the discharge estimates which lends support to the consistency of the method is that the water levels associated with maximum discharges commonly accord with a break of slope on one or both banks of the wadi, where inundation of a terrace causes large increases of width and prevents further significant increase of shear stress (see figure 14.10 for an example). Maximum shear stress is therefore provided by the deepest within-channel flows, and when overbank flow occurs the additional discharge does not contribute significantly to increased shear stress and consequently to an increased maximum mobile grain size.

Flood frequency analysis is plagued by lack of rigorous data in environments such as the Asir Mountains and the Tehama, but could be effected using the stratigraphic methods discussed by Costa (1978) and applied to slackwater deposits in bedrock channels by Patton et al. (1979). Historical evidence suggests that an event in 1942 was the largest in living memory, being associated with a stage of about 7.5 m at Mushawwaf and probably contemporaneous with the flood that caused channel migration in Wadi Jizan. The 1969 event, with a stage of 6.2 m and a discharge of 1860 m³ s⁻¹, appears to have been the second largest since 1942 and therefore to have a return period of about 20 years. It is an event which is capable of overtopping lateral terraces where they are unprotected by bunds, indicating that the potential for channel avulsion clearly exists.

EVALUATION OF LINKS BETWEEN GEOMORPHIC SYSTEMS

Piecemeal environmental management which fails to consider spatial linkages between continuous sediment systems is liable to be unsuccessful. The continuity of sediment transport along coastlines illustrates this. Clayton (1980) demonstrates the problems generated when local beach protection by groyne construction increases cliff erosion downdrift, thereby highlighting the mismatch between

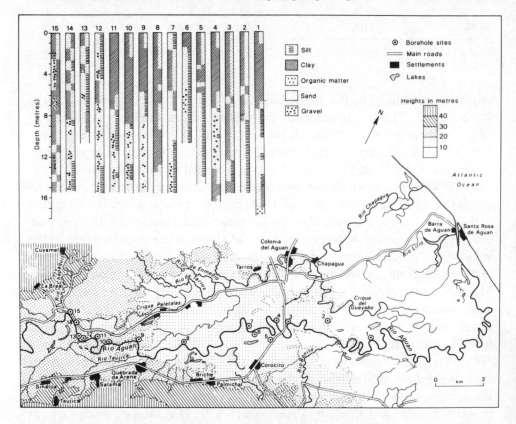

Figure 14.12   The lower Aguan and Chapagua Rivers and other distributary channels, with sedimentological information for 16 borehole sites

the areal units of the relevant administrative authorities and the spatial extent of a natural process. Furthermore, management of and interference within one system can affect another; for example, Hutchinson et al. (1980) have reviewed the history of landslide activity in the Folkestone Warren complex, and show that although failure events have specific meteorological triggers, extensions to Folkestone harbour have also been influential in causing progressive starvation of sediment supply to the beach at the cliff foot.

River and water resource management are commonly effected by catchment-scale strategies which should therefore permit appropriate consideration of the continuity of sediment transport processes. Reservoir impoundment itself demonstrates the consequences of disruption of this continuity, with common problems being sedimentation within the reservoir and river-bed erosion downstream from the dam. However, rivers are themselves influenced by changes in the sediment supply from their catchment hillslopes, and also ultimately

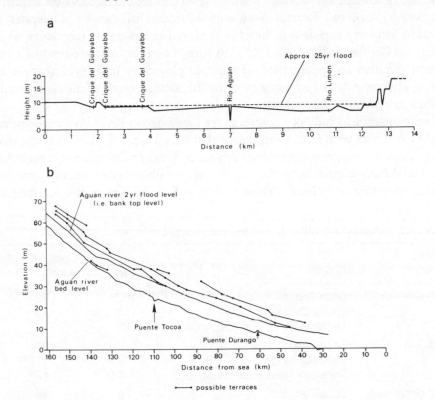

Figure 14.13 (a) Valley floor cross-section of the lower Aguan River valley illustrating the perched nature of the channel; (b) Evidence suggesting that river terraces grade to a sea-level below that of the present day, and are buried by aggradation of fine sediments backfilled from the river mouth

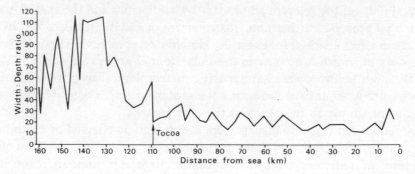

Figure 14.14 Downstream trend of width-depth ratio in the lower Rio Aguan below Tocoa

interact with coastal processes both throughout the supply of sediment to the littoral environment and through the base-level control of channel development exercised by sea-level. Coastal erosion of soft-rock cliffs can be accelerated if sediment formerly supplied to beaches is stored in upstream reservoirs, as is evident in California (Walker, 1978). In turn, however, management of river systems requires an appreciation of the role played by base-level changes in causing Holocene fluvial adjustment in the 'backwater' reach of the river profile (Warner, chapter 2, this volume).

River management and flood control in the lower Aguan River involves exploitation of a complex pattern of distributary channels. Figure 14.12 illustrates that these channels have probably evolved as a succession of palaeochannels occupied by a Rio Aguan migrating to the south-east, possibly under tectonic control. Former alignments include Crique Paletalas-Rio de Tarros-Rio Chapagua,

Table 14.2 Channel morphology in three reaches of the lower Aguan River

Channel property	Reach	Mean	Coefficient of variation (%)
Width (m)	Saba-Tocoa	166	22
	Tocoa-Durango	104	20
	Durango-Santa Rosa de Aguan	75	12
Depth (m)	Saba-Tocoa	2.7	30
	Tocoa-Durango	4.3	11
	Durango-Santa Rosa de Aguan	4.0	12
Width-depth ratio	Saba-Tocoa	70	41
	Tocoa-Durango	24	25
	Durango-Santa Rosa de Aguan	20	28

Based on 21 (Saba-Tocoa), 18 (Tocoa-Durango), and 17 (Durango-Santa Rosa de Aguan) sampled cross-sections.

Rio Lirio, and Crique del Guayabo-Crique Palo Atraversado. All of these have meander bends of greater amplitude and wavelength than their current discharges would suggest; the abandoned bend at Colonia del Aguan is an example. The channels have been maintained through flushing by overbank flood discharges from the Aguan, particularly that entering the Rio Chapagua system at the head of Crique Paletalas. In consequence the Rio Chapagua has been scoured to 2 m below sea-level by bedload-free overflows from the Aguan. The frequency and significance of these overbank flows arise because of the combined effect of Holocene sea-level rise and a strong coastal longshore drift current to the north-west. The latter process has lengthened the lower course of the Aguan by 8–10 km (figure 14.12), resulting in aggradation of the order of 2.5–3 m to create the gradient of $0.35 \, \text{m} \, \text{km}^{-1}$ required to transport bedload with a diminishing discharge as increasing overflow has occurred. As a result the Aguan is perched above the lateral drainage systems of the Rios Chapagua and Limon (figure 14.13), having created a fan- or delta-shaped accumulation of silty-sand fill in its lower valley. The sedimentary logs of a series of boreholes shown in figure 14.12 illustrate that sand and gravel is generally overlain by silt and clay along the course of the Aguan, except in the upstream four cores which may lie near the upstream limit of backfilling. Supportive evidence is provided by river terraces which have bluffs of 3–4 m upstream near Olanchito, but which converge downstream towards the present floodplain, then disappear beneath it. Their gradient reflects steeper Pleistocene rivers transporting sand and gravel to a lower sea-level. Figure 14.13b illustrates these features mapped on 1:10 000 field-survey maps with a 2 m contour interval.

The sedimentology of the lower Aguan strongly influences the present channel morphology and river behaviour. Figure 14.14 shows that the channel width-depth is sharply reduced downstream from Tocoa, and table 14.2 summarizes channel-form data for three reaches of the lower Aguan. Below Durango bridge, where the banks are silty, the river is stable, relatively narrow and deep, and has a high sinuosity meander pattern. The upper reach, with sandy bedload derived from erosion of terrace bluffs, is an unstable pseudo-braided river with a wide, shallow cross-section. Figure 14.15 illustrates the channel pattern mapped from three sources; a 1932 Trujillo Railroad Company map, and 1954 and 1982 air photographs. From Saba to Tocoa there have been numerous changes in river position between these dates, the river being an actively-migrating braided river of sinuosity of about 1.3. Where meander bends occur they have migrated downstream and increased in amplitude in both periods (1932–54 and 1954–82). This process is encouraged by the erodibility of sandy banks. On one bend below Isletas, for example, bank retreat of $30 \, \text{m} \, \text{yr}^{-1}$ occurred over the 8-year period ending in 1983. Between Tocoa and Durango the three channel traces suggest systematic

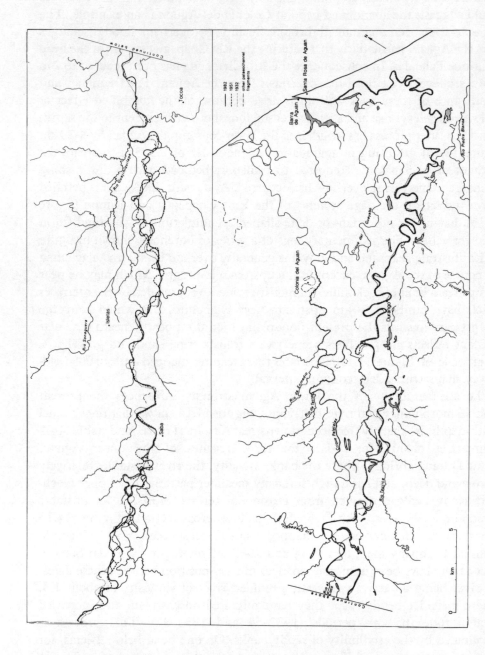

Figure 14.15 Channel traces of the lower Rio Aguan at three dates illustrating the very stable lower course and the more mobile course above Tocoa

downstream meander train migration, somewhat more rapidly from 1932-54 than in the later period. Sinuosities in the reach and at all three dates are in the range 1.5-1.6 and meander wavelengths are all stable at 1600-2000 m. Below Durango bridge the channel traces are virtually identical indicating considerable stability of pattern over 50 years. Sinuosities range from 2.0-2.7 and meander wavelengths are 800-1000 m, consistent with the smaller width and bankfull discharge capacity of this reach. The cross-section, channel pattern and channel stability characteristics are all consistent with a pattern of sedimentology which reflects aggradation caused by the effects of base-level change and lengthening of the lower course by coastal deposition at the mouth.

Channel management for flood control, both past and future, is both necessitated by, and is undertaken within, this natural framework. To minimize flooding of banana plantations at Isletas, channel straightening by artificial cutoff was attempted in the early twentieth century. This increased the channel slope to 0.00084, which is above the threshold slope for braiding given by the Leopold and Wolman (1957) criterion for a bankfull discharge of 730 $m^3 s^{-1}$. The river, probably sensitive to this influence prior to straightening, accordingly widened, shallowed, and has maintained its unstable braided state since. Modern flood control in the lower reaches seeks to utilize the palaeochannel distributary pattern, perhaps with a gated spill structure to the Crique del Guayabo which will also divert some bedload. The implications of such a strategy must be evaluated in the context of the natural fluvial system.

First, the main natural overspill is to Crique Paletalas. To prevent it could encourage aggradation in the Rio de Tarros of sediment from the mountain catchments, since there would be no flushing by overspill floodwater. This could cause soil drainage problems. Second, increasing the overspill to Crique del Guayabo, which drains into the deeply incised Rio Chapagua, could accentuate headcut erosion on this stream and its tributaries (figure 14.16). This could endanger the diversion structure itself. Third, deliberate diversion of Aguan bedload together with the floodwater, when at present the overspill process only leads to loss of water discharge, could initiate bed degradation in the Aguan downstream from the diversion point. This in turn could result in bank destabilization and accelerated meander migration which might endanger flood dykes if they are retired an insufficient distance. Finally, the creation of a floodway between dykes reduces the area on which floodplain sedimentation can take place, and some estimate of accelerated accretion is necessary to ensure that the dyke protection will be maintained over the project lifetime. Estimates based on the frequency, depth and sediment concentration of overbank flows suggest that accretion rates are unlikely to exceed 2 mm yr^{-1}, which indicates that processes of bed aggradation and degradation are more critical.

Figure 14.16 Headcut erosion in silty sediments on a tributary of Crique del Guayabo

It is evident that appreciation of the context of late Quaternary evolution of this fluvial system, coupled with the influence of changing coastal conditions, provides an essential framework for the identification of key questions concerning management options. These may subsequently be answered using appropriate stratigraphic, sedimentological, and river modelling procedures.

CONCLUSION

These case studies illustrate the contributions that fluvial geomorphologists can make to engineering-project appraisal through the evaluation of the spatial and temporal contexts for river management. This conclusion is similar to that reached by Schumm (1977), but distinctive from the concern with channel hydraulics, transport processes and regime equations expressed by Neill and Hey (1982). While these latter concerns are equally appropriate, they constitute problems which are marginal to the central objective of geomorphology, which is to explain landforms. The broader context emphasized in this chapter will hopefully redress the balance somewhat. Certainly experience suggests that engineers are well disposed to accept the kind of information and interpretation outlined above, and that a partnership can exist between the distinctive contributions of geomorphologists and engineers in project plan development. The engineer's appreciation of channel mobility involves a different time-scale from that of the geomorphologist, but the evidence of channel migration; potential avulsion into palaeochannels; flood magnitudes, estimated indirectly, that are liable to endanger almost any structure; and sediment storage and supply as controls of sediment yield, all represent important constraints on the viability of project development. The challenge for geomorphologists is that, while these issues are representative of problems central to the interpretation of form-process relationships, those problems have been neglected in recent years because of the divorce between process and landform investigation. Their solution requires balanced use of stratigraphical, sedimentological, palaeohydrological and historical sources of information on landform adjustment over intermediate time-scales.

ACKNOWLEDGEMENTS

The three projects on which this paper is based were commissioned from Geomorphological Services Ltd by Sir William Halcrow & Partners. We are grateful for the permission to publish the results of the surveys and for the generous support of the staff of these companies.

REFERENCES

Acreman, M. C. 1984: The significance of the flood of September 1981 on the Ardessie Burn, Wester Ross. *Scott. Geogrl. Mag.*, 99, 150-60.

Alam, A. M. Z. and Kennedy, J. F. 1969: Friction factors for flow in sand-bed channels. *Journ. Hydr. Div., Am. Soc. Civ. Eng.*, 95, 1973-92.

Anderson, M. G., Richards, K. S. and Kneale, P. E. 1980: The role of stability analysis in the interpretation of the evolution of threshold slopes. *Trans. Inst. Brit. Geogr., New Ser.*, 5, 100-12.

Andrews, E. D. 1980: Effective and bankfull discharges in the Yampa River basin, Colorado and Wyoming. *Journ. Hydrol.*, 46, 311-30.

Baird, P. D. and Lewis, W. V. 1957: The Cairngorm floods, 1956; summer solifluction and distributary formation. *Scott. Geogrl. Mag.*, 73, 91-100.

Baker, V. R. and Ritter, D. F. 1975: Competence of rivers to transport coarse bedload material. *Geol. Soc. America Bull.*, 86, 975-8.

Bayfield, N. C. 1974: Burial of vegetation by erosion debris near ski lifts on Cairngorm, Scotland. *Biol. Conserv.*, 6, 246-51.

Benson, M. A. and Thomas, D. M. 1966: A definition of dominant discharge. *Bull. Int. Ass. Sci. Hydrol.*, 11, 76–80.

Best, J. L. and Brayshaw, A. C. 1985. Flow separation – a physical process for the concentration of heavy minerals within alluvial channels. *Jour. Geol. Soc.*, 142, 747–55.

Birse, E. L. 1976: The bioclimate of Scotland in relation to a world system of classification and to land use capability. *Trans. Bot. Soc. Edinburgh*, 42, 463–7.

Biswas, A. K. 1970: *History of Hydrology*. Amsterdam: North-Holland.

Blench, T. 1966: *Mobile Bed Fluviology*. Alberta: University of Alberta Press.

Brunsden, D. and Thornes, J. B. 1979: Landscape sensitivity and change. *Trans. Inst. Brit. Geogr., New Ser.*, 4, 463–84.

Bull, W. B. 1964: The geomorphology of segmented alluvial fans in western Fresno County, California. *US Geol. Survey Prof. Paper* 352-E, 89–129.

Bull, W. B. 1977: The alluvial fan environment. *Prog. in Phys. Geog.*, 1, 222–70.

Carling, P. A. 1983: Threshold of coarse sediment transport in broad and narrow natural streams. *Earth Surf. Processes & Landforms*, 8, 1–18.

Carson, M. A. 1969: Models of hillslope development under mass failure. *Geogrl. Analysis*, 1, 76–100.

Chester, D. K. 1980: The evaluation of Scottish sand and gravel resources. *Scott. Geogrl. Mag.*, 96, 51–62.

Chow, V. T. 1959: *Open Channel Hydraulics*. New York: McGraw-Hill.

Clayton, K. M. 1980: Coastal protection along the East Anglian coast. *Zeitschr. fur Geom., Supp.*, 34, 165–72.

Common, R. 1954: A report on the Lochaber, Appin and Benderloch floods, May 1953. *Scott. Geogrl. Mag.*, 70, 6–20.

Costa, J. E. 1978: Holocene stratigraphy in flood-frequency analysis. *Water Resour. Res.*, 14, 626–32.

Costa, J. E. 1983: Palaeohydraulic reconstruction of flash-flood peaks from boulder deposits in the Colorado Front Range. *Geol. Soc. America Bull.*, 94, 986–1004.

Douglas, I. 1982: The unfulfilled promise: earth surface processes as a key to landform evolution. *Earth Surf. Processes & Landforms*, 7, 101.

Foster, I. D. L., Dearing, J. A., Simpson, A., Carter, A. D. and Appleby, P. G. 1985: Lake catchment based studies of erosion and denudation in the Merevale catchment, Warwickshire, UK. *Earth Surf. Processes & Landforms*, 10, 45–68.

Gilbert, G. K. 1917: Hydraulic mining debris in the Sierra Nevada. *US Geol. Survey Prof. Paper* 105.

Gregory, K. J. (ed.) 1983: *Background to Palaeohydrology: a Perspective*. Chichester: Wiley.

Hey, R. D. 1978: Determinate hydraulic geometry of river channels. *Journ. Hydr. Div., Am. Soc. Civ. Eng.*, 104, 869–85.

Hickin, E. D. 1983: River channel changes: retrospect and prospect. In J. D. Collinson and J. Lewin (eds), *Modern and Ancient Fluvial Systems*, Special Publ. No. 6, Int. Ass. Sedim., 61–83.

Hickin, E. D. and Nanson, G. C. 1975: The character of channel migration on the Beatton River, north-east British Columbia, Canada. *Geol. Soc. America Bull.*, 86, 487–94.

Hooke, R. LeB. and Rohrer, W. L. 1979: Geometry of alluvial fans: effect of discharge and sediment size. *Earth Surf. Proc.*, 4, 147–66.

Howard, A. D. 1984: Simulation model of meandering. In C. M. Elliott (ed.), *River Meandering*, New York: Am. Soc. Civ. Eng., 952–63.

Hutchinson, J. N., Bromhead, E. N. and Lupini, J. F. 1980: Additional observations on the Folkestone Warren landslides. *Quart. Journ. Eng. Geol.*, 7, 363–76.

Jones, D. K. C. 1983: Environments of concern. *Trans. Inst. Brit. Geogr., New Ser.*, 8, 429–57.

Kirkby, M. J. 1967: Measurement and theory of soil creep. *Journ. Geol.*, 75, 359–78.

Leliavsky, S. 1955: *An Introduction to Fluvial Hydraulics*. London: Constable.

Leopold, L. B. and Wolman, M. G. 1957: River channel patterns: braided, meandering and straight. *US Geol. Survey Prof. Paper* 282-B.

Limerinos, J. T. 1969: Relation of the Manning coefficient to measured bed roughness in stable natural channels. *US Geol. Survey Prof. Paper* 650-D, 215–21.

Lovera, F. and Kennedy, J. F. 1969: Friction factors for flat bed flows in sand channels. *Journ. Hydr. Div., Am. Soc. Civ. Eng.*, 95, 1227–34.

Maizels, J. K. 1983: Palaeovelocity and palaeodischarge determination for coarse gravel deposits. In K. J. Gregory (ed.) *Background to Palaeohydrology*, Chichester: Wiley, 101–39.

Mosley, M. P. 1983: Flow requirements for recreation and wildlife in New Zealand rivers – a review. *Journ. Hydrol. (NZ)*, 22, 152–74.

Mosley, M. P. 1985: River channel inventory, habitat and instream flow assessment. *Prog. in Phys. Geog.*, 9, 494–523.

Neill, C. R. and Hey, R. D. 1982: Gravel-bed rivers: engineering problems. In R. D. Hey, J. C. Bathurst and C. R. Thorne (eds), *Gravel-bed Rivers: Fluvial Processes, Engineering and Management*, Chichester: Wiley, 15–25.

Newson, M. 1980: The geomorphological effectiveness of floods – a contribution stimulated by two recent events in mid-Wales. *Earth Surf. Processes & Landforms*, 5, 1–16.

Newson, M. and Leeks, G. J. 1985: Mountain bedload yields in the United Kingdom: further information from undisturbed environments. *Earth Surf. Processes & Landforms*, 10, 413–6.

Parker, G. 1978: Self-formed straight rivers with equilibrium banks and mobile bed. Part I: the sand-silt river. *Journ. Fluid Mech.*, 89, 109–25.

Patton, P. C., Baker, V. R. and Kochel, R. C. 1979: Slackwater deposits: a geomorphic technique for the interpretation of fluvial palaeohydrology. In D. D. Rhodes and G. Williams (eds), *Adjustments of the Fluvial System*, Iowa: Kendall-Hunt, 225–53.

Petryk, S. 1975: Analysis of flow through vegetation. *Journ. Hydr. Div., Am. Soc. Civ. Eng.*, 101, 871–84.

Pickup, G. and Warnerm R. F. 1976: Effects of hydrologic regime on magnitude and frequency of dominant discharge. *Journ. Hydrol.* 29, 51–75.

Pizzuto, J. E. 1984: Equilbrium bank geometry and the width of shallow streams. *Earth Surf. Processes & Landforms*, 9, 199–207.

Raudkivi, A. J. 1967: *Loose Boundary Hydraulics*, Oxford: Pergamon.

Richards, K. S. and McCaig, M. 1985: A medium-term estimate of bedload yield in Allt a'Mhuillin, Ben Nevis, Scotland. *Earth Surf. Processes & Landforms*, 10, 407-11.

Schumm, S. A. 1977: *The Fluvial System*. New York: McGraw-Hill.

Schumm, S. A. 1979: Geomorphic thresholds: the concept and its applications. *Trans. Inst. Brit. Geogr., New Ser.*, 4, 485-515.

Skempton, A. W. 1976: Introduction: a Discussion on valley slopes and cliffs in southern England: morphology, mechanics and Quaternary history. *Phil. Trans. Roy. Soc. London*, 283A, 423-6.

Skempton, A. W. and De Lory, F. A. 1957: Stability of natural slopes in London Clay. In *Proc. 4th Int. Conf., Soil Mechs. and Found'n Eng. London*, 2, 378-81.

Slaymaker, O. 1972: Patterns of present subaerial erosion and landforms in mid-Wales. *Trans. Inst. Brit. Geogr.*, 55, 47-67.

Walker, H. J. 1978: Research in coastal geomorphology: basic and applied. In C. Embleton, D. Brunsden, and D. K. C. Jones (eds), *Geomorphology: present problems and future prospects*, Oxford: Oxford University Press, 203-23.

Walling, D. E. 1983: The sediment delivery problem. *Journ. Hydrol.*, 65, 209-37.

Watson, A. 1967: Public pressure on soils, plants and animals near ski lifts in the Cairngorms. In E. Duffy (ed.), *The Biotic Effects of Public Pressures on the Environment*, Monks Wood Exptl. Station, Symp. No. 3, 38-45.

Wolman, M. G. and Gerson, R. 1978: Relative scales of time and the effectiveness of climate in watershed geomorphology. *Earth Surf. Proc.*, 3, 189-208.

The Contributors

JAMES C. BATHURST is a staff member of the Institute of Hydrology, Wallingford, on secondment since 1985 to the Natural Environment Research Council's Water Resource Systems Research Unit, University of Newcastle upon Tyne. His principal fields of interest are sediment transport and flow processes in upland rivers and physically-based distributed catchment modelling, on which he has authored several published papers. Since 1977 he has been involved in research studies in the USA and several European and developing countries.

BRIAN J. BLUCK is Reader in Geology, University of Glasgow. He holds the degrees of B.Sc., and Ph.D (Wales), and D.Sc. (University of Glasgow). He has been Visiting Research Scholar at the University of Illinois (1961) and NATO Research Fellow (1962), and was Elected Fellow of the Royal Society of Edinburgh in 1981. He has received awards from the Royal Society of Edinburgh and the Geological Society of London for his work in fluvial sedimentology, and is Editor of the *Transactions of the Royal Society of Edinburgh*.

ANDREW C. BRAYSHAW graduated from Hull University and received his doctorate from Birbeck College, London, working on sediment transport in gravel-bed rivers. He undertook a Royal Society Post-doctoral Fellowship at the University of Florence, Italy, where he studied the mechanics of fluvial deposition in gravel-bed alluvial channels. He now works for British Petroleum as a sedimentologist.

DENYS BRUNSDEN is Professor of Geography at King's College, London. His academic career there began as an undergraduate, and has only been interrupted by Visiting Lectureships at Canterbury, N.Z. and Louisiana State University. He is a past Chairman of the British Geomorphological Research Group, and is currently Vice-President of the Royal Geographical Society whose Gill Memorial Award he received in 1977 for research on landslides. He has a particular interest in applied geomorphology, and has worked in the Middle East, North Africa, Pakistan, Nepal, North America and New Zealand, and has published numerous papers and several books on slope processes, geomorphological concepts, and applied geomorphology.

PAUL A. CARLING graduated in Geography from Leicester University, then undertook Ph.D research on Intertidal Sedimentation at University College, Swansea. From 1977 he has been employed by the Freshwater Biological Association at Windermere as a hydrologist/sedimentologist to interact in biological programmes. His current basic interests cover river sediment dynamics and freshwater ecology, and current research topics include silting mechanisms in gravel beds, effects of large floods on the landscape, dam-break modelling, bedload transport and mixing processes in large UK rivers.

TIM R. H. DAVIES was born in Devon, England, in 1945 and was educated at the local grammar school and the University of Southampton Civil Engineering Department, where he gained his Ph.D in 1972. He has lectured in civil engineering at Sunderland Polytechnic, England, from 1970 to 1975, and in agricultural engineering at Lincoln College, Canterbury, New Zealand, since 1975. His main interests are the formation, behaviour, use and enjoyment of natural landscape.

WILLIAM E. DIETRICH is an Associate Professor in the Department of Geology and Geophysics, University of California, Berkeley. He joined the Department in 1982 after completing his graduate studies at the University of Washington. In 1985 he was a recipient of the US National Science Foundation Presidential Young Investigator Award, and in 1986 his work on river channel processes was recognized by the British Geomorphological Research Group with the Gordon Warwick Award. His publications have addressed problems in hydrology, weather, hillslope geomorphology, and river form and process.

ROB FERGUSON is a Senior Lecturer in Environmental Science at Stirling University. He obtained his Ph.D at Cambridge University in 1972 for theoretical and statistical research on channel pattern and has published extensively on this and other fluvial topics. His field experience is biased towards active rivers in high-mountain environments in Scotland, Norway, Switzerland, Canada, the US and Pakistan.

DANIEL I. GREGORY received a Master's degree in geology from Colorado State University in 1982. Previously, he was employed by the US Geological Survey as well as several engineering and mining exploration consulting firms. Since 1982 he has been employed as a geomorphologist with Water Engineering and Technology, Inc. in Fort Collins, Colorado.

ALAN D. HOWARD has Geology degrees from Yale (B.A.) and Harvard (M.S.) and a Ph.D in Geography from Johns Hopkins. Since 1968 he has been at the University of Virginia, where he is now Professor in the Department of Environmental Sciences. His research interests include theoretical issues in geomorphology, computer modelling of landform evolution, studies of fluvial morphology and processes, the geomorphology of Mars, and karst processes and landforms.

DAVID K. C. JONES is Reader in Geography at the London School of Economics and Political Science, where he has held appointments since 1967 and after graduating from

King's College, London. His research interests and publications embrace palaeo-geomorphology, landslides and slope development, and applied geomorphology, and he has acted as a consultant geomorphologist in the UK, the Middle East, Nepal and Bangladesh. He has been a member of interdisciplinary research expeditions to the Karakoram Mountains and the Wahiba Sands in Oman.

A. DAVID KNIGHTON is Senior Lecturer in Geography at the University of Sheffield; he has degrees in geography (Cambridge and Manchester Universities) and mathematics (Open University) and research experience in Britain, Norway, Canada, New Zealand and Tasmania. He has been Visiting Lecturer at the University of Ottawa, Research Visitor at the University of Canterbury, New Zealand, and Honorary Visiting Fellow at the University of Tasmania, and is author of several papers as well as *Fluvial Forms and Processes*.

MIKE MCCAIG is a graduate of Hull University and gained a Ph.D from the School of Geography, Leeds University in 1980. His research interests have included headwater hydrogeomorphology and modelling of sediment interactions in small channels. After joining Geomorphological Services Ltd. in 1982 he assisted with geomorphological assessments for engineering projects in the UK, Asia and Central America. He is currently a senior software instructor with the Digital Equipment Corporation.

M. PAUL MOSLEY studied Geography at Cambridge University, under the tutorship of R. J. Chorley, and then Geology and Earth Resources at Colorado State University, under the supervision of S. A. Schumm. Since 1975, he has been involved in research in forest hydrology, river morphology and behaviour, and erosion and sediment transport processes, all in New Zealand. He is now a manager of hydrological research and survey work in the New Zealand Ministry of Works and Development.

PAMELA S. NADEN graduated in 1977 in Geography from Newnham College, Cambridge, and gained a Ph.D from Leeds University in 1985. From 1980 she has been a lecturer in the School of Geography at the University of Leeds. Her research interests include fluvial processes, sediment transport, hydrology and water quality, and she is currently working on a project for the Yorkshire Water Authority to investigate the problem of discoloured runoff from upland catchments.

KEITH S. RICHARDS gained his B.A. and Ph.D (1975) in Geography at Jesus College, Cambridge University, where he was tutored and supervised by B. W. Sparks and R. J. Chorley. He is now a lecturer in the Department of Geography and Fellow of Emmanuel College. His research interests range from fluvial geomorphology to Quaternary studies *via* slopes, but most of his published work, including *Rivers: Form and Process in Alluvial Channels*, deals with fluvial subjects, and is based on field experience in Britain, Norway, Saudi Arabia and Central America. He has been Honorary Secretary of the British Geomorphological Research Group, and now edits *Earth Surface Processes and Landforms*.

S. A. SCHUMM obtained the Ph.D from Columbia University in 1955. He was employed by the US Geological Survey until 1967, when he joined the Department of Earth Resources at Colorado State University. He is also vice-president and principal geomorphologist of Water Engineering and Technology Inc. Among other awards he recently received the G. K. Warren Prize from the US National Academy of Sciences for his contributions to geology.

ROB WARNER gained his B.A. in Geography at the University of Birmingham, then joined the staff at the University of New England, Australia in 1960. While there, he completed a Ph.D on the terraces of the Bellinger River. In 1970 he moved to Sydney where his main interests have been in the environmental geomorphology of temperate and tropical rivers.

Index

Related Titles: List of IBG Special Publications